D1093486

The
PRODUCTION
of
DESIRE

The PRODUCTION of DESIRE

The Integration of Psychoanalysis into Marxist Theory

Richard Lichtman

THE FREE PRESS
A Division of Macmillan Publishing Co., Inc.
NEW YORK
Collier Macmillan Publishers
LONDON

THE FREE PRESS
A Division of Macmillan Publishing Co., Inc.
866 Third Avenue, New York, N. Y. 10022

Collier Macmillan Canada, Inc.

Library of Congress Catalog Card Number: 81-67441

Printed in the United States of America

printing number

1 2 3 4 5 6 7 8 9 10

Library of Congress Cataloging in Publication Data
Lichtman, Richard.
    The production of desire.

    Bibliography: p.
    Includes index.
    1. Psychology—Philosophy. 2. Personality—
Social aspects. 3. Marx, Karl, 1818–1883.
4. Marxian school of sociology. 5. Freud,
Sigmund, 1856–1939. 6. Psychoanalysis.
I. Title.
BF38.L53 1982   150.19′5   81-67441
ISBN 0-02-919010-X   AACR2

Portions of the Introduction and Chapters 1–3 were previously published, in slightly altered form, in *Socialist Revolution:* Number 30 (Vol. 6, No. 4), October–December 1976; Number 33 (Vol. 7, No. 3), May–June 1977; Number 36 (Vol. 7, No. 6), November–December 1977.

Several quotations, cited individually in the text, are taken from *The Collected Papers of Sigmund Freud,* edited by Ernest Jones, M.D.: Volume 2, authorized translation under the supervision of Joan Rivière; Volume 3, authorized translation under the supervision of Alix and James Strachey. Published by Basic Books, Inc., by arrangement with The Hogarth Press and The Institute of Psycho-Analysis, London. Used by permission.

In appreciation of their love and support
this book is dedicated to my mother and father

Contents

Part III.   Social Structure and Therapeutic Practice

Preface and Acknowledgments

I have written this book with several distinct but overlapping interests in mind: first, as a contribution to the growing body of Marx-Freud analysis. Over the past several decades a small but active enterprise has arisen around attempts to synthesize the theories of these seminal thinkers. At its root, the basic contention of this work is that no such synthesis is possible, if that term is used to mean a compromise between the two positions. I argue instead that the systems of Marx and Freud are incompatible and that, consequently, a choice must be made for one and against the other. Once this initial commitment is made, it is possible to integrate the second position into the first. A great deal of the confusion that distinguishes the current Freudian-Marxist literature is engendered precisely by a "tolerant" wish to blend Marx and Freud into a homogenized amalgam. In this era of "the end of ideologies" such a wish is understandable. But, as we shall see, the structure of the two theories makes them ultimate rivals, and so priorities must be established. My own position, for which the following analysis is argument, is that while the doctrines of both Marx and Freud are inadequate as they stand, the Marxist position can be corrected, while Freudian theory is fundamentally unsound. However, working through the limitations of Freud's view makes its very significant insights available for incorporation into an expanded Marxist theory.

Thus, a second interest manifests itself: to move Marxist theory itself further away from its traditional, mechanistic heritage without sacrificing what is profound in its "materialist" conception of human existence. Marxist theory has tended to divide between structuralists and humanists. But both camps have some hold on the truth; for while social structures "act" independently of the professed conscious intentions of human agents, they are nevertheless wholly dependent upon the character of concrete men and women. It is at precisely this juncture that Freudian theory proves so suggestive when restructured through social categories. For the conjunction of individual intention and social structure is embedded dialectically in the alienated institutions of social life *and* in the repressed unconscious of specific social agents. It is therefore not only for such historical reasons as are set forth in chapter 1, nor even for the insight Freud's work provides into the failures of actual and latent social revolutions in this century, that I have undertaken this examination. It is rather for the theoretical-practical consideration that human life cannot be grasped adequately without careful consideration of the mutual interrelation between Freud's understanding of the repressed unconscious and Marx's discovery of the fetishism of social economic structures.

I am well aware that such attempts have been made before. But, in my judgment, they have failed, either through an uncritical reliance on basic Freudian concepts—as in the case of Reich's theory of instinct—or through so attenuated a version of Marx—as in Fromm's avoidance of class analysis—as to prove irrelevant. What has thus far been lacking is a detailed statement of the basic theoretical assertions of Marx and Freud, a comparison of their diverse methodologies and doctrines, and a consideration of the "logic" that accommodates them both. This is a logic, I argue, that affords priority to the social order without losing awareness of the reciprocity of individual and social categories. I know only too well that this book is simply a beginning of such efforts. I am far from satisfied with the completeness or integration that has been achieved here. But I wish to mark off an enterprise devoted to directing Marxist inquiry along lines that can fruitfully explore and absorb the works of non-Marxist writers into a variegated but focused Marxist perspective.

For a third interest consists in setting out the preliminaries of a *Marxist psychology*. This is a more difficult phrase to make intelligible than may appear at first sight. For the term "psychology" has come to stand for so subjective and privatized a notion, corresponding to the real atomism and isolation of contemporary life, that the phrase itself will have to be reconstituted in the process of its realization. And in this regard it is important to insist that Freud is only one figure whose insights need to be critically incorporated into a Marxist perspective. There is as much to be learned from from Mead, Merleau-Ponty, Binswanger, and Piaget as well as from a host of lesser figures. But Freud's doctrine is isomorphic with the social self-reflection of the contemporary world in a way that does not apply to the work of other thinkers, not only for the pervasive sense of determinism and privatized subjectivity that marks his system but also for the obvious significance the practice of psychoanalysis has had for modern life.

This last consideration helps to situate the theoretical level of the present work, which lies between pure theory and empirical social criticism. This is neither a philosophical work dealing with the pure theory of mind nor a practical critique of the changing structure of American life. I hope in later writings to deal with these subjects; the former because it is the ground of this study and the latter because it is the application. My major concern for the present is with the social origins of the self and its relationship to capitalist repression and the technology of psychoanalysis as a therapy. I have not attempted anything like an objective or dispassionate account of these matters, not only for the perfectly adequate reason that such attempts are logically impossible but for the additional reason that the sentiment and conviction that stand behind such efforts seems to me an expression of the alienation of contemporary life, which this work is concerned to critique.

This work has proceded through a lengthly incubation, and many individuals have helped along the way: my students at the Wright Institute, with whom I shared and argued many of these notions in classrooms and corridors; Michael Lerner, who contributed a continual critical commentary and discussed and debated with me all the basic issues contained in this work—always to my enlightenment; Jim O'Connor, who offered an invaluable blend of theoretical and personal reflection and steady support where it was most needed; Michael Bader, who read the greatest part of the manuscript and offered important suggestions; Eli Katz and Kathy Johnson, who read and corrected the most difficult parts of the work and were unfailingly supportive; Ray Barglow, who was an insightful critic and meticulous reader; David Plotke and Harry Chotiner, who cut and edited the early sections to my advantage; Barbara Safran, who provided me with constant interest and careful, devoted participation in the ongoing dialogue that so helped me to clarify my developing thoughts; Ciele Ogren, who nurtured the roots which aided in the present flowering; and Jennifer Church and Karen Mann, who typed my continuing transformations of the original when there were other, more enjoyable, things for them to do.

RICHARD LICHTMAN

The
PRODUCTION
of
DESIRE

Marxist Despondency and the Turn to Freud

Perhaps Marx's most portentous reflection is the following passage from the first volume of *Capital:*

> The advance of capitalist production develops a working class which by *edu-cation, tradition, habit,* looks upon the conditions of that mode of production *as self-evident laws of nature*. The organization of the capitalist mode of pro-duction, once fully developed, breaks down all resistance. The constant gener-ation of a relative surplus population keeps wages in a rut that corresponds with the wants of capital. The dull compulsion of economic relations com-pletes the subjection of the laborer to the capitalist. Direct force, outside economic conditions, is of course still used, *but only exceptionally*. In the ordi-nary run of things, the laborer can be left to the "natural laws of production," i.e., to his dependence on capital, a dependence springing from, and guaran-teed in perpetuity by, the conditions of production themselves.[1]

The grave power of this insight has, to paraphrase Marx, weighed like a nightmare upon the lives of our generation. The feeling that permeates Marx's judgment is more than pessimism; it is despair. So much is evi-dent in the phrase "breaks down all resistance."

Marx himself did not accept the implication of this vision. The tone of the great mass of Marx's commentary is clearly optimistic. Perhaps "ten, twenty, or even fifty years" will need to pass, but finally the working class will rise up against its masters and initiate the movement of human life from the sphere of necessity to "the kingdom of freedom."[2]

But one hundred years have passed without revolution. The apparent stasis of the dialectic and the failure of revolution is the one fundamental problem that Western Marxists face in the twentieth century. Paul Baran put the problem this way:

> While it was thought earlier that people would be incensed by injustice, inequality, and exploitation but would be prevented temporarily from rising against them by fear of divine or civil opprobrium and punishment, under monopoly capitalism they actually do not understand and feel injustice, inequality, and exploitation *as such,* do not *want* to struggle against them but treat them as aspects of the natural order of things. While it used to be thought that bourgeois ideology would guard the existing social order from man's efforts to satisfy basic human needs—decent livelihood, knowledge, solidarity and cooperation with fellow-men, gratification in work and freedom from toil—the actual *wants* of men in the societies of advanced capitalism are determined by aggressive drives, are directed towards the attainment of individual privileges and the exploitation of others, towards frivolous consumption and barren entertainment. With bourgeois taboos and moral injunctions *internalized,* people steeped in the culture of monopoly, capitalism do not want what they need and do not need what they want.[3]

Is it possible, from within Marx's theory itself, to account for this tragic division between want and need? Baran offers two reasons for the failure of Marxist theory to anticipate this catastrophe:

> In the first place, even Marx and Engels, much as they were aware of the plasticity and moldability of human nature, seriously underestimated the extent to which man's wants can be influenced and shaped by the social order within which he is enclosed. And, collaterally, giving capitalism only a relatively short life, they could not possibly anticipate the scope and the depth of *habit* formation resulting from centuries of capitalist development.[4]

In his conclusion, Baran is driven beyond the traditional Marxist vocabulary of productive forces and relations of production, beyond even alienation and ideology, to a distinctly therapeutic mode of discourse:

> If the above considerations are valid, the societies of the advanced capitalist countries are *ill.* Just as protracted *addiction* to alcohol or to narcotics leads sooner or later to disaster, so a prolonged divergence between the needs of men and their wants cannot but result in catastrophe. The failure of an irrationally organized society to generate internal forces pressing towards and resulting in its abolition and replacement by more rational, more human social relations results necessarily in economic stagnation, cultural decay, and a widespread sense of *despondency* [emphasis added].[5]

"Illness," "addiction," and "despondency" are not the vocabulary of Marx and Engels: this is the terminology of mental pathology, of psychic disease. However grave the power of Baran's judgment that "people steeped in the culture of monopoly capitalism do not want what they need and do not need what they want," there is an even more ominous conclusion to be wrung from these reflections: *that people come to want what is destructive of their need.*

Marx grasped ideology as the condition under which men and women could be made to accept as natural, and therefore unalterable, a society in which their human condition was continuously diminished. But he did not consider that people would "willingly" seek out the conditions of their own extinction. Addicts are not only incapable of acting for the sake of their own well-being, they actively pursue the substance that destroys them. Baran is driven to employ the discourse of "illness" and "addiction" because the disaster he is describing has gone beyond passivity to self-destructiveness. He has, almost against his will, been forced onto the terrain of Freudian psychology.

Why did Marxist theory fail to deal with the darker side of social reality? The prevailing thought of the nineteenth century was bound to the theory of the rise and fall of capitalism. Beneath the optimistic façade of progress a countervailing tendency toward stagnation had begun to manifest itself. More perceptive bourgeois writers like Ricardo sensed this growing dissolution. Therefore, while the theory of inevitable progress was the orthodox view of the liberal intelligentsia, a contrary vision of inevitable diminution and final stagnation also haunted bourgeois culture.

Profound transformations racked European life from the end of the eighteenth to the beginning of the twentieth centuries: the French Revolution; the Napoleonic conquests; the uprisings of 1830 and 1848; the unification of Germany, Italy, and the United States; the colonization of Africa and Asia; the continuous growth of industrialization; the expansion of technology; the ruin of artisans and peasants and the breakdown of the previous feudal structures; the mass migration of people from country to city; the development of a world market; the growth of a world socialist movement; and the transformation of the bourgeoisie itself from a progressive to a conservative world historical force. The world was being transformed at an incredible pace. It is hardly surprising that everyday consciousness and social theory reflected this development.

The central intellectual contributions of the nineteenth century were organized into a general cosmic history stretching from physics and chemistry, through biology to the evolution of the animal species and human life. Process supplanted substance as the primary category of reality and thought. Hegel's monumental corpus systematized the transformations that violently remade the fabric of nineteenth-century existence.

If the world view of feudalism was shaped around the conviction of a great chain of being linking the heavens and the most inglorious aspects of matter in a single, continuous and permanent stratification under God's eternal plan, the world view of the nineteenth century was dominated by the conviction that human life was being totally transformed by social forces. This new vision asserted the power of human beings, their ability to transform the universe and even their own nature through their capacity to remake the social world. Agency was relocated. It no longer belonged to forces beyond the human realm, to God and divine law. It belonged, rather, to humanity itself.

However, humanity is too abstract a category. For if humanity were in fact remaking itself, some were certainly more the made than the makers. Few men and women could direct this process of social transformation. Indeed, social forces were recreating human existence, but what precisely were these forces? To some they appeared the prerogative of a minority of powerful men who dominated the new forms of social wealth. To others, the vast majority, they were under no control at all. As Alvin Gouldner has noted:

> The modern concepts of society and of culture arose in a world that, following the French Revolution, men could believe they themselves had made. They could see that it was through their struggles that kings had been overthrown and an ancient religion disestablished. Yet, at the same time men could also see that this was a world out of control, not amenable to men's designs.[6]

The world could be viewed simultaneously as the product of human creativity and as an autonomous, alienated realm, inexorably imposing itself on the raw material of human existence.

In time the two views merged and the split between them broke out in a new way. For as it became less credible to deny the existence of independent social forces, it became more significant how one interpreted their *direction,* that is, their relation to the attainment of human happiness. The autonomy of social forces could be viewed as either benign or malignant. With the ascendancy of the bourgeoisie the doctrine of progress became the official ideology. Yet softly at first, then with increasing intrusiveness, the theme of decline and stagnation appeared, a terror of revolution or of slow coagulation and death.

Adam Smith thought it was advantageous that human beings could not control the social consequences of their separate actions. For then the natural laws of the market could not be flawed by human incompetence, or even by human malice. The "genius" of market exchange was that it flourished on egoism. For though the individual

> intends only his own gain, he is in this, as in many other cases, led by an invisible hand to promote an end which was no part of his intention. Nor is it

worse for the society that it was not part of it. By pursuing his own interest he frequently promotes that of the society more effectually than when he really intends to promote it. I have never known much good done by those who affected to trade for the public good.[7]

At the moment of capitalist ascendancy Smith viewed "alienation"—the separation of intention and consequence—as a decided advantage.

By the time of Ricardo's writings, capitalist optimism had begun to evaporate. The defects of the system were now being revealed as permanent afflictions rather than temporary aberrations. Bourgeois theory could not grasp the root of capitalist dehumanization, but it could feel its effect and respond on rare occasion with a limited but painful honesty. Ricardo's theory was based on the belief that as progressively less fertile lands were available, food prices would rise, pushing up the level of wages and forcing profits into a steady decline. He saw the interests of the landlord as opposed to those of the manufacturer, the consumer, and society as a whole. It is not the factual correctness of Ricardo's view that is here in question, but the previous view of natural harmony and the automatic benevolence of capitalist technological development. In the third edition of the *Principles,* Ricardo stated that "the opinion entertained by the laboring class, that the employment of machinery is frequently detrimental to their interests, is not founded on prejudice and error, but is conformable to the correct principles of political economy."[8]

Smith's view of the benevolence of the invisible hand gradually turned to a conviction of impending chaos. The whole arc of capitalist optimism and despair was captured in Rousseau's prophetic announcement that while human beings were born free they were everywhere in chains. Society came more and more to be viewed as a natural object following quite autonomous laws: when Durkheim advised social theorists to "consider social facts as things," he was articulating a methodology that reflected the reification of bourgeois society. Bourgeois exhaustion reached its nadir in the weariness of Max Weber, its most profound expositor:

> The puritan wanted to work in a calling; we are forced to do so. For when asceticism was carried out of monastic cells into everyday life, and began to dominate wordly morality, it did its part in building the tremendous cosmos of the modern economic order. This order is now bound to the technical and economic conditions of machine production which today determines the lives of all the individuals who are born into this mechanism, not only those directly concerned with economic acquisition, with irresistible force. Perhaps it will so determine them until the last ton of fossilized coal is burnt. In Baxter's view the care for external goods should only lie on the shoulders of the "saint like a light cloak, which can be thrown aside any moment." But fate decreed that the cloak should become an iron cage.

Since asceticism undertook to remodel the world and to work out its ideals in the world, material goods have gained an increasing and finally an inexorable power over the lives of men as at no previous period in history. Today the spirit of religious asceticism—whether finally, who knows?—has escaped the cage. But victorious capitalism, since it rests on mechanical foundations, needs its support no longer. The rosy blush of its laughing heir, the Enlightenment, seems also to be irretrievably fading, and the idea of duty in one's calling prowls about in our lives like the ghost of dead religious beliefs. . . .

No one knows who will live in this cage in the future, or whether at the end of this tremendous development entirely new prophets will arise, or there will be a great rebirth of old ideas and ideals, or, if neither, mechanized petrification, embellished with a sort of convulsive self-importance. For the last stage of this cultural development, it might well be truly said: "Specialists without spirit, sensualists without heart; this nullity imagines that it has attained a level of civilization never before achieved."[9]

What is most significant about Weber's consciousness of degradation is not merely that he records the atrophy of alienation—the cage, the loss of spirit, mechanized petrification, the ascendancy of material goods. What is most significant is the alienated voice in which he speaks. Weber does not merely describe the decay of bourgeois life; he participates in it. The mode of his consciousness is isomorphic with the world process upon which he reflects. For he views social life as proceeding not through the actions of human beings but through the decrees of fate, the undertakings of asceticism, irretrievably, inexorably, irresistibly. The inexorable fate which he records is not merely in the object of his inquiry but in himself, simultaneously, as its subject. The iron cage holds not only social life, but social awareness as well. From the benign independence of the invisible hand to mechanized petrification, the independent forces of social labor turn golem-like against their master.

Marx's theory contains its own version of the bourgeois attitude toward progress and dissolution. But in his view, the stagnation and decline of capitalism are preconditions for the triumph of socialism. And these tendencies are seen as following from independent laws of historical transformation that are autonomous of the wills of individual men and women. In a preface to *Capital*, Marx quotes a Russian reviewer's description of his method:

Consequently, Marx only troubles himself about one thing: to show, by rigid scientific investigation, the necessity of successive determinate orders of social conditions, and to establish, as impartially as possible, the facts that serve him for fundamental starting points. For this it is quite enough if he proves, at the same time, both *the necessity of the present order of things, and the necessity of another order into which the first must inevitably pass over; and this all the same, whether men believe or do not believe it, whether they are conscious or unconscious of it.*

Marx treats the social movement as a process of natural history, governed by laws not only independent of human will, consciousness and intelligence, but rather, on the contrary, determining that will, consciousness and intelligence. [emphasis added].[10]

Marx significantly added the comment that "the writer pictures what he takes to be actually my method, in this striking and (as far as concerns my own application of it) generous way," thereby indicating his approval of the presentation. It is certainly possible to argue that this line of Marx's thought does not express his total position. It is also true that history is "broken," that laws are tendencies, and that men and women are free. Nevertheless, Marx viewed social transformation as "a process of natural history," and it was central to his perspective to maintain that "capitalist production begets, with the inexorability of a law of Nature, its own negation."[11] Marx no more denied the existence of individuals than Freud denied the existence of society. The question for him was the origin and the status of individuality. Individuals make history only insofar as they intersect with historical forces that are fundamentally beyond their personal control. Marx was concerned with individual persons in the mode of their *inter*personal contact and as the manifestations of social forces.

To prevent possible misunderstanding, in a word, I paint the capitalist and the landlord in no sense *couleur de rose*. But here individuals are dealt with only insofar as they are the personifications of economic categories, embodiments of particular class-relations and class-interests. My standpoint, from which the evolution of the economic formation of society is viewed as a process of natural history, can less than any other make the individual responsible for relations whose creature he socially remains, however much he may subjectively raise himself above them.[12]

For Marx, as opposed to Freud, individuals are derivatives of the social system rather than primary elements from which the system is itself constructed.

So far we have painted a portrait of his method that renders it as uncomfortably similar to that of the major bourgeois writers of his time. All seem to have stressed alienation as the primary fact of social life, either as an "invisible hand," "mechanized petrification," or as life "governed by laws not only independent of human will, consciousness and intelligence, but rather, on the contrary, determining that will, consciousness and intelligence."

What totally distinguishes Marx's system from the world view of the bourgeoisie is his insistence that alienation is self-negating. But this contention can be interpreted in very different ways: either (1) that reified human activity comes gradually to suffocate the activity that has produced it, leading to stagnation and eventual death for the system; or (2) that while objectified human labor proceeds through autonomous transformations that produce inevitable crises for capitalism, it is the power of the proletariat, as the subject of history, that finally destroys the system; or (3) that the forces of alienation themselves produce the transformation of society and the passage from capitalism to socialism, either gradually or violently, depending on particular historical circumstances.

Some combination of all these views is to be found in Marx's writings. We began this essay with the pessimism of the first position—applied to the role of the proletariat. In *The Holy Family*, Marx presents the unique form of optimism contained in the third position:

> Since the abstraction of all humanity, even of the semblance of humanity, is practically complete in the full-grown proletariat, since the conditions of life of the proletariat sum up all the conditions of life of society today in all their inhuman acuity, since man has lost himself in the proletariat, yet at the same time has not only gained theoretical consciousness of that loss, but through urgent, no longer disguisable, absolutely imperative need—that practical expression of necessity—is driven directly to revolt against that inhumanity; it follows that the proletariat can and must free itself. But it cannot free itself without abolishing the conditions of its own life. It cannot abolish the conditions of its own life without abolishing all the conditions of life of society today which are summed up in its own condition. . . . The question is not what this or that proletarian, or even the whole of the proletariat at the moment considers as its aim. The question is what the proletariat is and what consequent on that being, it will be compelled to do.[13]

This form of optimism is most relevant to the question of why Marx failed to deal with the darker side of life.

Behind the Marx's apocalyptic optimism lies the logic of a Christianized, Hegelian dialectic. The power of alienation defeats itself through the cunning of material reason. The externalized shell of human labor—reified humanity itself—will proceed through a series of stages which will assure both the demise of alienation and the eventual victory of the proletariat. Through this vision, the victory of the proletariat is inexorable. But the worker becomes as much the personification of external forces as the capitalist and landlord to whom Marx previously referred.

It is precisely this move in the argument that is not convincing. Marx becomes as open to the charge of reification as Weber. For the laws of necessity have been used to account for the realization of freedom. And yet, according to Marx himself, the unfolding of capitalist society follows necessary laws, and is consequently predictable, *for the very reason and to the extent* that these laws are the reflection of institutions over which men and women have no control. The Marxist analysis of the prehistory of human existence is the dissection of human life as lost to its own self-determination.

Men make their history themselves, but not as yet with a collective will according to a collective plan . . . *and for that very reason all such societies are governed by necessity.*[14]

The inexorability of law follows from the alienation of humanity.

But freedom can only grow *from* the life of the subjects of history; it cannot be imposed *upon* them as a fate.

The laws of his own social action . . . will be used with full understanding, and so mastered by [man]. Man's own social organization . . . becomes the result of his own free action. The extraneous objective forces that have hitherto governed history pass under the control of man himself. Only from that time will man himself, with consciousness, make his own history.[15]

Freedom is the victory of the subject, not the manifestation of the object, it cannot be given, it must be taken. That men and women have "an absolutely imperative *need*" to revolt against the conditions of their inhumanity cannot be denied. But as Baran noted, between the need and the want lies the pathos of stagnation. For revolution to become a practical necessity, the requirements of liberation must become as clear and compelling, as deeply initiated, as the process of alienation through which mankind has become lost to itself.

The Relevance of Freud

At this point, Reich's theory marks a real advance over orthodox Marxism.

An effective policy, whose ultimate goal is the achievement of socialism and the establishment of the rule of labor over capital, must not only be based on a recognition of those movements and changes which occur objectively and independently of our will as a result of the development of the productive forces. This policy must also, simultaneously and on the same level, take account of what happens "in people's heads," i.e., in the psychical structures of the human beings who are subjected to these processes and who actually carry them out—people from different countries and cities, people of different occupations, ages and sexes.[16]

If a need for revolution is to be generated throughout capitalist society, it will come neither from the alienation of independent laws (structuralism) nor from the pure freedom of the working class (humanism), but through their dialectic in a manner yet to be invented.

It is necessary to explore "the psychical structures of the human beings who are subjected to these processes and who actually carry them out." It is necessary to create a psychology of alienation, of "pseudo-man," of the human being as commodity. To Reich and the members of the Frankfurt school, Freud seemed a necessary starting point. It was not the "death instinct" that was attractive. The expanding destruction and self-destruction of humanity was clearly a fact, but the introduction of an instinct to explain the phenomenon was merely a hypostatized failure to come to grips with social pathology. No, it was rather the conceptions of repression, unconscious motivation, defense mechanisms, and the superego that promised some understanding of how human beings could come "willingly" to participate in their own dismemberment.

Those educated only in the tradition of Marxist theory came close to the truth but never quite reached the heart of the issue. Korsch is an example:

> In the fateful months after November 1918, when the organized political power of the bourgeoisie was smashed and outwardly there was nothing else in the way of the transition from capitalism to socialism, the great chance was never seized because the *socio-psychological* preconditions for its seizure were lacking. For there was nowhere to be found any decisive *belief* in the immediate realizability of a socialist economic system, which could have swept the masses along with it and provided a clear knowledge of the nature of the first steps to be taken.[17]

The operative phrase is the negative "preconditions were lacking." But more than the mere absence of proper conditions is required. It was not what was absent but what was present that caused the difficulty. Bodies deteriorate not through the absence of health, but through the presence of disease.

Marxism understood the irrationality, wastefulness, violence and self-destruction of the external social system. Freud promised an understanding of how this process had become deeply rooted in the psyche of men and women. His writings are filled with a sense of the perilous, painful nature of childhood under conditions of "normal" family life:

> We have heard how the weak and immature ego of the first phase of childhood is permanently damaged by the strain put upon it in the effort to ward off the dangers that are peculiar to that period of life. Children are protected against the dangers threatening them from the external world by the care of their parents; they pay for this security by a fear of losing their parents' love, which would deliver them over helpless to the dangers of the external world.... From the biological standpoint, then, it may be said that the ego comes to grief over the task of mastering the excitations of the first sexual period, at a time when its immaturity makes it incompetent to do so.[18]

But it is precisely at this stage of development, when the child is immature and dependent upon the love of its parents, that it is forced to make this awesome reality its own.

> A portion of the external world has, at least partially, been given up as an object and instead, by means of identification, taken into the ego—that is, has

become an integral part of the internal world. This new mental agency continues to carry on the functions which have hitherto been performed by the corresponding people in the external world: it observes the ego, gives it orders, corrects it and threatens it with punishments, exactly like the parents whose place it has taken. We call this agency the superego and are aware of it, in its judicial functions, as our conscience. *It is a remarkable thing that the superego often develops a severity for which no example has been provided by the real parents,* and further that it calls the ego to task not only on account of its deeds but just as much on account of its thoughts and unexecuted intentions, of which it seems to have knowledge.[19]

In short, Freud maintained that there was more suffering in the human condition than could be accounted for by the irrationality of external, economic life.

With this clue, it was only a short step for a thinker like Reich, grounded in both the Marxist and Freudian traditions, to draw the conclusion: the purpose of the superstructure is to develop helplessness, accommodation, and self-destruction in the next generations of children. He noted that

social morality which is rooted in all individuals and . . . continually reproduces itself exerts a conservative influence on the socio-economic base: the exploited himself affirms the economic order which guarantees his exploitation; the sexually suppressed affirms himself the sexual order which restricts his gratification . . . and he instinctively wards off any other order which would answer his real needs. . . . Thus, the morality fulfills its socio-economic purpose.[20]

Marx had paid insufficient attention to the mediating institutions through which the mode of economic production and the mode of human production were joined. The family, in particular, was viewed more as a "reflection" of social relations of production than as a training ground in human pathology. Freud focused on this institution as the source of human stultification, and his perspective profoundly shaped the writings of the Frankfurt school and Reich:

In a class society, the ruling class secures its position with the aid of education and the institution of the family, by making its ideologies the ruling ideologies of all members of the society. But it is not merely a matter of imposing ideologies, attitudes, and concepts on members of society. Rather, it is a matter of a deep-reaching process in each new generation of the formation of a psychic structure which corresponds to the existing social order. . . .

Because this order forms the psychic structure of all members of society, it *reproduces itself* in people. . . . The first and most important place of reproduction of the social order is the patriarchal family which creates in children a character structure which makes them amenable to the later influence of an authoritarian order.[21]

Marxist analysis maintained that capitalism, as a class society, was self-constraining. Its social relations prevented the full expansion of its productive forces. The results were stagnation, breakdown, and crisis. What would be "the psychic structure which corresponds to this existing social order"? It would be a self-stultifying psychic structure, a fetter upon the development of human potentiality. Marx saw human beings as the manifestations of social class forces. But if we grasp the external world of capitalism as alienated, brutal, and pathologically weighted with the burden of its own constricted energy, how can we avoid attributing these characteristics to the men and women who are reproduced through this system and who reproduce it in turn? Freud provided the prism through which the destructiveness of the bourgeois world could be viewed in the spectrum of its individual malignancy. Just as Marx and Engels analyzed the dehumanizing effect of the unit of capitalist material production, the factory, so Reich analyzed the destructiveness of the primary institution of the superstructure, the family:

> Its cardinal function is that of serving as a *factory for authoritarian ideologies* and conservative structures. . . . It influences the child in the sense of a reactionary ideology not only as an authoritarian institution, but also on the strength of its own structure; it is the conveyor belt between the economic structure of conservative society and its ideological superstructure.[22]

The family not only produces a character structure that does not make a revolution; it produces men and women who wish to be dominated by authoritarian power.

> It creates the individual who is forever afraid of life and of authority and thus creates again and again the possibility that masses of people can be governed by a handful of powerful individuals.[23]

In this Freudian-Marxist analysis Reich has clearly taken us beyond fetishism, helplessness, and passivity to active self-renunciation.

> Hitler promised the abolition of the freedom of the individual and the establishment of the "freedom of the nation." Enthusiastically, the masses of people exchanged their potentialities for individual freedom for *illusionary* freedom. . . . They craved a *"freedom" which the Fuhrer should conquer for them and guarantee to them:* the freedom to howl, to escape from the truth into a fundamental falsehood, to be sadistic, to brag—though one was in actuality a cipher—about one's superior race, . . . to sacrifice oneself for imperialistic goals instead of the actual struggles of everyday life.[24]

So Reich, and later Fromm, introduced the theme of "escape from freedom" that was to play so large a role in explanations of the rise of fascism. The use to which Reich, Fromm, Marcuse, and the members of the Frankfurt school put Freud's theory takes us beyond Marx's view of ideology; but it leads to a critical paradox. We need to recall Baran's claim that "Marx and Engels . . . seriously underestimated the extent to which man's wants can be influenced and shaped by the social order within which he is enclosed." And yet, we have suggested that a corrective to this limitation of Marxist theory lies in Freud's theory—a system of thought built fundamentally upon the notions of inherited instincts, unconscious domination, and the perpetual repetition of archaic patterns of individual and social structure. How is such an apparently antidialectical and "asocial" system as that of Freud likely to illuminate the issue we have posed—the stultification of the dialectic in contemporary capitalist society?

Are Marx and Freud compatible? How? In what respects? If not, how do their theories conflict? Must we make a choice between them, or is there some procedure that will permit integration? And what precisely does "integration" mean? Can we draw equally from both systems, must we move beyond both to some larger position from which they are both intelligible, or can one be made the basis upon which the other is incorporated? And most important, what is the political dimension of this question? If we cannot answer this last question, the others are of little consequence.

PART I

Marx and Freud: Convergence and Antagonism

CHAPTER ONE

Convergence

Freud and Marx were heirs of the enlightenment. The whole of their approach bears this imprint. Both regard themselves as advancing the movement of scientific rationality into new areas of human inquiry. The first sentence of Freud's first major theoretical work (1895) carries the purpose of his life's work: "The intention of this project is to furnish us with a psychology which shall be a natural science."[1] As Ricoeur notes, Freud will never disavow this fundamental conviction.

> Like all his Vienna and Berlin teachers, Freud sees and will continue to see in science the sole discipline of knowledge, the single rule of all intellectual honesty, a world view that excluded all other views, especially that of the old religion.[2]

And what, precisely, is the claim of science? Freud explains:

> It asserts that there is no other source of knowledge of the universe, but the intellectual manipulation of carefully verified observations, in fact, what is called research, and that no knowledge can be obtained from revelation, intuition or inspiration.[3]

And is this not an arrogant usurpation of traditional modes of authenticating belief?

> The bare fact is that truth cannot be tolerant and cannot admit compromise or limitations, that scientific research looks on the whole field of human activity as its own, and must adopt an uncompromisingly critical attitude towards any other power that seeks to usurp any part of its province.[4]

The sense of science as a total vocation (in Weber's sense of the term) is equally strong in Marx. His remark, cited in Paul Lafargue's reminiscences, could equally well have come from Freud:

> Science should not be an egoistic pleasure. Those who are fortunate enough to be able to devote themselves to scientific work should be the first to apply their knowledge to the service of humanity.[5]

Certainly Engels's view was that Marx, with his great "discoveries," had transformed socialism from a set of utopian (infantile?) wishes into a *science*. Marx is more cautious about the use of the term because of the reactionary, ideological construction that had been placed upon it. But in objecting to those who wish to give socialism a "higher ideal orientation . . . that is, to replace the materialist basis which requires serious objective study if one is to use it, by a modern mythology"[6] he is in essential agreement with the spirit of Freud's intentions. In the *Paris Manuscripts* he asserts:

> History is itself a *real* part of *natural history*, of the development of nature into man. Natural science will one day incorporate the science of man, just as the science of man will incorporate natural science; there will be a *single* science.[7]

This view is repeated in the *German Ideology*. "We know only a single science, the science of history."

There is a similarly striking agreement between Marx and Freud in their rejection of religion. Both view religion as an expression of human inadequacy, a compensatory need which arises against the suffering of mortal human existence.

> Religion is the relation of man to his own nature . . . but to his nature not recognized as his own, but regarded as another nature. . . . Herein lies its untruth, its limitation, its contradiction to reason and morality; herein lies the noxious source of religious fanaticism . . . of all the atrocities . . . in the tragedy of religious history.[8]

Religion arises out of the difficulty of the human condition, and reflects the fact that human beings do not control their situation. Freud and Marx agree that while societies were formed, in part, to protect human life against the ravages of nature, they became an independent source of suffering for their creators.[9] So, Engels wrote,

> it was not long before, side by side with the forces of nature, social forces began to be active—forces which confront man as equally alien and at first equally inexplicable, dominating him with the same apparent natural neces-

sity as the forces of nature themselves. The fantastic figures, which at first only reflected the mysterious forces of nature, at this point acquire social attributes, become representatives of the forces of history.[10]

And Freud asks:

> But how does he [the individual] defend himself against the supremacy of nature, of fate, which threatens him, as it threatens all?
>
> Culture relieves him of this task: it performs it in the same way for everyone. . . .
>
> In the course of time the first observations of law and order in natural phenomena are made, and therewith the forces of nature lose their human traits. . . . The gods retain their threefold task: they must exorcise the terrors of nature, they must reconcile one to the cruelty of fate . . . and they must make amends for the sufferings and privations that the communal life of culture has imposed on man.[11]

Religion arises to console humanity for the social pain it has incurred in the process of attempting to alleviate itself of the terrors of nature. But the attempt is a pitiable delusion, a wish, a fantasy.

> The whole thing is so patently infantile, so foreign to reality, that to anyone with a friendly attitude toward humanity, it is painful to think that the great majority of mortals will never be able to rise above this view of life.[12]

> Where was the way out, salvation, for the enslaved, oppressed and impoverished, a way out common to all these groups of people whose interests were mutually alien or even opposed? And yet it had to be found if a great revolutionary movement was to embrace them all.
>
> This way out was found. *But not in the world* . . . a way out was found which would lead the laboring and burdened from this vale of woe to eternal paradise (emphasis added].[13]

What is the remedy? To remake the world so that the consolation of fantasy is no longer required. Freud says:

> Thus by withdrawing his expectations from the other world and concentrating all his liberated energies on this earthly life he will probably attain to a state of things in which life will be tolerable for all and *no one will be oppressed by culture any more* [emphasis added].[14]

And Marx says:

> Religious distress is at the same time the expression of real distress and the protest against real distress. Religion is the sigh of *the oppressed* creature. . . . It is the opium of the people.
>
> The abolition of religion as the illusory happiness of the people is required for their real happiness. The demand to give up the illusion about its condition is the demand to give up a condition which needs illusions. The criticism of religion is therefore in embryo the criticism of the vale of woe, the halo of which is religion.[15]

So passionate is Freud's commitment to the enlightenment conception of rationality as against religion that it not only draws from him the un-characteristic phrase, noted above—"no one will be oppressed by culture any more"—but leads him to remarks that are practically indistinguishable from those of John Stuart Mill:

> Since men are so slightly amenable to reasonable arguments, so completely are they ruled by their instinctual wishes, why should one want to take away from them a means of satisfying their instincts and replace it by reasonable arguments? Certainly men are like this, but have you asked yourself whether they need be so, whether their inmost nature necessitates it? Can an anthropologist give the cranial index of a people whose custom it is to deform their children's heads by bandaging them from their earliest years? Think of the distressing contrast between the radiant intelligence of a healthy child and the feeble mentality of the average adult. . . .
>
> We may insist as much as we like that the human intellect is weak in comparison with human instincts, and be right in doing so. But nevertheless there is something peculiar about this weakness. The voice of the intellect is a soft one, but it does not rest until it has gained a hearing. Ultimately, after endlessly repeated rebuffs, it succeeds.[16]

The insistence on rationality would be of no import, however, if it were not closely tied to its converse: the equally profound insistence upon the irrationality of the prevailing human condition. It is not rationality as such that is put in question, but the reliability of conscious human intention. Both Freud and Marx severely limit the credibility that can be assigned to the "rational" accounts that men and women provide of their own activity. They thoroughly undermine the naïve conception which humanity offers of the grounds of its own activity. They regard men and women as driven by forces they do not comprehend and cannot control.

The categorical distinction between appearance and reality is absolutely crucial to their views of human existence. What people take themselves to be doing, the reasons they assign to their own activity, is no more than the surface manifestation of underlying forces of which the purported "agents" are almost wholly unaware. Ordinary consciousness is revelatory, but not to the "actors" who are consciously the subjects of their own experience. Human existence can only be grasped from the vantage point of a theory at odds with the conceptions that people commonly entertain. This shared comprehension of the illusion of rational consciousness is one of the fundamental propositions that unite the work of Marx and Freud, and is perhaps the basic ground for the view that finds them ultimately compatible.

Engels argues:

> In one point, however, the history of the development of society proves to be essentially different from that of nature. In nature . . . there are only blind,

unconscious agencies acting upon one another, out of whose interplay the general law comes into operation. Nothing of all that happens . . . as a consciously desired aim. In the history of society, on the contrary, the actors are all endowed with consciousness, are men acting with deliberation or passion, working towards definite goals; nothing happens without a conscious purpose, without an intended aim. But this distinction, important as it is for historical investigation, particularly of single epochs and events, cannot alter the fact that the course of history is governed by inner general laws. For here, also, on the whole, in spite of consciously desired aims of all individuals, accident apparently reigns on the surface. That which is willed happens but rarely; in the majority of instances the numerous desired ends cross and conflict with one another, or these ends themselves are from the outset incapable of realization or the means of attaining them are insufficient. Thus the conflicts of innumerable individual wills and individual actions in the domain of history produce a state of affairs entirely analogous to that prevailing in *the realm of unconscious nature* [emphasis added].[17]

Engels is clear; the structure of human action is systematically discordant with its intended purpose. Human beings are the manifestations of social forces. The motives of individuals are more the expression than the cause of social reality. Our sense of ourselves as rational agents, as the initiators of activity in the world, is essentially a manifestation of false consciousness.

Freud says of the ego's certainty of itself:

Normally, there is nothing of which we are more certain than the feeling of our self, of our own ego. This ego appears to us as something autonomous and unitary, marked off distinctly from everything else. That such an appearance is deceptive, and that on the contrary the ego is continued inwards, without any sharp delimitation, into an unconscious mental entity which we designate as the id and for which it serves as a kind of façade—this was a discovery first made by psychoanalytic research.[18]

Literally speaking, Freud is undoubtedly correct. Psychoanalysis alone investigates the relationship between the ego and the id. But insofar as the basic thrust of the passage is to affirm that our sense of our rational autonomy is a mere façade which masks the presence of unknown forces operating upon us, Marxism must be credited with the same discovery. Reich captures the tone and significance of Freud's position; but with allowance for the difference of literal content, the same point is made in the Marxist perspective.

The subject of psychoanalysis was great and moving. To the thought of the average man, it came like a slap in the face. You imagine that you can determine your actions by your own free will? Indeed not! Your conscious actions are only a drop on the surface of an ocean of unconscious processes of which you can know nothing, and besides, you would be afraid of knowing them. . . . In brief, you are conditioned by processes which you do not control or even know, which you fear and misinterpret.[19]

As Bernfeld notes:

> Marx will declare that wartime patriotism is the ideological superstructure of
> the imperialist class interest, whereas Freud will detect an element of sadism
> in the enthusiasm of the individual wartime volunteer. In any event, neither
> of them will respectfully protect patriotism as a value independent from
> scientific analytic reduction.[20]

The convergence between Freud and Marx on the issue of false
consciousness goes even deeper. For appearance is not only different
from reality; it is most often the *opposite* of reality. Engels notes this when
commenting on the course of the French Revolution:

> But the new order of things, rational enough as compared with earlier condi-
> tions, turned out to be by no means absolutely rational. The state based upon
> reason completely collapsed. Rousseau's *contrat social* had found its realiza-
> tion in the Reign of Terror.... The promised eternal peace was turned into
> an endless war of conquest.... The antagonism between rich and poor,
> instead of dissolving into general prosperity, had become intensified.... The
> "freedom of property" from feudal fetters, now veritably accomplished,
> turned out to be, for the small capitalists and small proprietors, the freedom
> to sell their small property, crushed under the overmastering competition of
> the large capitalists and landlords, to these great lords, and thus, as far as the
> small capitalists and peasant proprietors were concerned, became "freedom
> from property.".... The "fraternity" of the revolutionary motto was realized
> in the chicanery and rivalries of the battle of competition.[21]

In short, "liberty, equality, and fraternity" reveal themselves as "compulsion, exploitation, and competition." The reasons for this transformation
are hardly adventitious. They derive from the structure of commodity relations as a system of fetishism as well as from the explicit manipula-
tions of the bourgeoisie, which in its efforts to overthrow the traditional
feudal aristocracy is required to appeal through "equality" to the constituency of peasants and the working class for the sake of alliance.[22] In
fact, the contradiction between reality and ideal is a distinguishing feature of capitalism. In ancient slave society or medieval feudalism the
professed system of hierarchical values corresponded to the hierarchical
stratification of power. In capitalist societies, the mode of production
and the dominant ideologies are necessarily contradictory.

Therefore, when Engels proceeds beyond his observation that in
society, despite the fact that "nothing happens without a conscious purpose," the result is a "state of affairs entirely analogous to that prevailing
in the realm of unconscious nature," he is driven to the following formulation:

> Men make their own history, whatever its outcome may be, in that each
> person follows his own consciously desired end.... But ... we have seen that
> the many individual wills active in history for the most part produce results
> quite other than those intended—often *quite the opposite*.[23]

The same "negation" is equally critical to the analysis offered in *Capital,* as in the marvelous, sardonic passage with which Marx closes Part II of the first volume:

> This sphere that we are deserting, within whose boundaries the sale and purchase of labor-power goes on, is in fact a very Eden of the innate rights of man. There alone rule Freedom, Equality, Property and Bentham. Freedom, because both buyer and seller of a commodity, say of labor-power, are constrained only by their own free will. They contract as free agents, and the agreement they come to, is but the form in which they give legal expression to their common will. Equality, because each enters into relation with the other, as with a simple owner of commodities, and they exchange equivalent for equivalent. Property, because each disposes only of what is his own. And Bentham, because each looks only to himself. The only force that brings them together and puts them in relation with each other, is the selfishness, the gain and private interests of each. Each looks to himself only, and no one troubles himself about the rest, and just because they do so, do they all, in accordance with the preestablished harmony of things, or under the auspices of an all-shrewd providence, work together to their mutual advantage, for the common weal and in the interest of all.[24]

The inverse relationship between reality and appearance is the foundation of Marx's irony. It is not only true that reality does not reveal itself; it hides itself. And what better disguise could it take on than the negation of its reality?

Abstractly, the spectacle can be viewed with contempt and derision, as Marx often does. But humor in all its forms is an abstract reflection. Concretely, the worker is paying with his life:

> In the expression "value of labor," the idea of value is not only completely obliterated, but actually *reversed.* It is an expression as imaginary as the value of the earth. These imaginary expressions arise, however, from the relations of production themselves. They are categories for the phenomenal forms of essential relations. That in their appearance things often represent themselves in *inverted form* is pretty well known in every science except political science.... The wage-form thus extinguishes every trace of the division of the working-day into necessary labor and surplus-labor, into paid and unpaid labor. All labor appears as paid labor....
>
> Hence, we may understand the decisive importance of the transformation of value and price of labor-power into the form of wages, or into the value and price of labor itself. This phenomenal form, which makes the actual relation invisible, and, indeed, shows *the direct opposite* of that relation, forms the basis of all the juridical notions of both laborer and capitalist, of all the mystifications of the capitalistic mode of production, of all its illusions as to liberty, of all the apologetic shifts of the vulgar economists [emphasis added].[25]

In other words, the wage-form extinguishes every trace of exploitation. The worker may still feel unfairly treated, but this is very different from understanding the nature of capitalist expropriation. Reality appears as its opposite, and this transformation founds "all the mystifications of the capitalist mode of production."

But of all the strands with which the fabric of illusion is woven, the most debilitating is that which transposes history into nature. The capitalist mode of production

> de-historicizes value and surplus-value, makes of them products of nature, and, in parallel fashion, regards the impersonal and objective form of capitalist social relations as an entirely natural state of affairs. It thus transforms the properties possessed by commodities, capital, etc., qua *social* objects, into qualities belonging naturally to them as things.[26]

By masking the opposition between the reality of exploitation and the appearance of "reason," capitalism tends to extinguish any opposition.

Rieff's observation on Freud's method underscores the same point: "In exposing the underside of the obvious, the Freudian strategy assumes that *what is hidden contradicts the obvious.*"[27] In *Wit and Its Relation to the Unconscious* Freud relates a story which seems characteristic of his method:

> Two Jews met in a train at a Galician railway station. "Where are you traveling?" asked one. "To Cracow," was the reply. "Now see here, what a liar you are!" said the first one, bristling. "When you say that you are traveling to Cracow, you really wish me to believe that you are traveling to Lemberg. Well, but I am sure that you are really traveling to Cracow, so why lie about it?"

And Freud comments that the story operates through a technique he calls "representation through the opposite, for, according to the uncontradicted assertion of the first, the second is lying when he speaks the truth, and speaks the truth by means of a lie."[28] Not only is one lying when one speaks the truth, but the surface of consciousness in which the lie is housed covers a contradictory reality which requires the disguise in question.

In *Civilization and Its Discontents* Freud considers the antagonistic relationship between civilization and sexuality. The clue to the disturbance lies in the ideal injunction, "Thou shalt love thy neighbor as thyself." Freud's analysis of the demand is revealing:

> Why should we do it? What good will it do us? But, above all, how shall we achieve it? How can it be possible? My love is something valuable to me which I ought not to throw away without reflection. . . .
>
> On closer inspection, I find still further difficulties. Not merely is this stranger in general unworthy of my love; I must honestly confess that he has more claim to my hostility and even my hatred. He seems not to have the least trace of love for me and shows me not the slightest consideration. . . . Indeed, if this grandiose commandment had run "Love thy neighbor as thy neighbor loves thee," I should not take exception to it.

The existence of this inclination to aggression, which we can detect in ourselves and justly assume to be present in others, is the factor which disturbs our relations with our neighbor and makes it necessary for culture to institute its high demands. . . . Civilization has to use its utmost efforts in order to set limits to man's aggressive instincts and to hold the manifestations of them in check by psychical *reaction-formations*. Hence, therefore, the use of methods intended to incite people into the restriction upon sexual life, and hence too the ideal's commandment to love one's neighbor as oneself—a commandment to which is really justified by the fact that nothing else runs so strongly *counter* to the original nature of man [emphasis added].[29]

We are introduced to a basic Freudian theme: the opposition of civilization and human nature. The antagonism can be interpreted logically as the negation (counter) of "original nature" by culture. The distinction between appearance and reality is for Freud, no less than for Marx, a necessary relation of opposites. Furthermore,

most pathological character traits correspond to the *reaction formation* type; that is, whereas normal character traits permit discharge, the majority of pathological traits primarily serve the purpose of keeping still existent opposite tendencies in the unconscious [emphasis added].[30]

The last two quoted passages link Freud's theory of individual pathology to his social theory of the antagonistic origins of false consciousness. No more than the ruling class can the ruling superego permit dangerous materials to announce themselves undisguised. In both cases, protest is a threat to "legitimate" power, and a mechanism intervenes to deny its actual significance. Were individual pain, militancy, or breakdown interpreted as deriving from the social system, the ruling class would stand accused. Instead, the ideology of individualism forces the grievance back upon itself; the victim is declared responsible for the crime. Were sexuality and aggression permitted entrance into consciousness, society would become subject to violent disruption. Instead, the superego forces the reprehensible material back into the self, thereby avoiding the pain of self-condemnation.

Thus the subject-matter of a repressed image or thought can make its way into consciousness on condition that it is *denied*. Negation is a way of taking account of what is repressed: indeed, it is actually a removal of the repression, though not, of course, an acceptance of what is repressed. . . . To deny something in one's judgment is at bottom the same thing as to say: "That is something that I would rather repress." A negative judgment is the intellectual substitute for repression. . . . By the help of the symbol of negation, the thinking-process frees itself from the limitations of repression.[31]

At root, affirmation and negation are expressions of the deepest dualism of human existence, the contradiction between life and death, Eros and Thanatos. "Affirmation, as being a substitute for union, belongs to Eros; while negation, the derivative of expulsion, belongs to the instinct of destruction."[32] It is not that the destructive energy contains negation in the very structure of the instinct; quite the contrary. For "we never discover a 'No' in the unconscious."[33] But the barriers of civility deny entrance to primitive desire, and its claim must be registered through the subterfuge of "expulsion."

Consequently, when Dora refused the advances of Herr K. Freud suspected that she actually desired him. Aversion is not the expression of desire, but of morality.

> The "No" uttered by a patient after a repressed thought has been presented to his conscious perception for the first time does no more than register the existence of a repression and its severity.... If this "No," instead of being regarded as the expression of an impartial judgment (of which, indeed, the patient is incapable), is ignored, and if work is continued, the first evidence soon begins to appear that in such a case "No" signifies the desired "Yes."[34]

If we ask for the grounds of false consciousness, we discover new convergences between Marx and Freud. In both cases mystification derives from powerlessness, and powerlessness is itself an expression of alienation. However the term "alienation" seems appropriate to Marx but somewhat artificial when applied to Freud. Although Freud does not use the word, he does employ an analytic concept that signifies the same process to which Marx calls our attention. The core of both positions is that our own life becomes separated from our control, and in its independent existence, passes through stages that are foreign to our intentions, beyond our understanding, and harmful to our interests.

Marx's position is well stated in the following passage:

> This crystallization of social activity, this consolidation of what we ourselves produce into an objective power above us, growing out of our control, thwarting our expectations, bringing to naught our calculations, is one of the chief factors in historical development up till now.... The social power, i.e., the multiplied productive force ... appears to these individuals, since their cooperation is not voluntary but natural, not as their own united power, but as an alien force existing outside them, of the origin and end of which they are ignorant, which they thus cannot control, which, on the contrary, passes through a peculiar series of phases and stages independent of the will and the action of man, nay even being the prime governor of these.[35]

Now consider the corresponding Freudian reflection:

> As a rule the instinctual impulse which is to be repressed remains isolated. Although the act of repression demonstrates the strength of the ego, in one particular it reveals the ego's powerlessness and reveals, too, how impervious to influence are the separate instinctual impulses of the id. For the mental process which has been turned into a symptom owing to repression maintains its existence *outside the organization of the ego* and *independently* of it. Indeed, it is not the process alone but all its derivatives which enjoy, as it were, the

privilege of *extraterritoriality;* and whenever they come into associative contact with a part of the ego-organization, it is not at all certain that they will not *draw that part over to themselves* and thus enlarge themselves at the expense of the ego [emphasis added].[36]

Freud's conception parallels Marx's notion that the labor-power of the working class is appropriated by the capitalist through his control over the means of production, and that this advantage permits the capitalist to exploit the laborer further through the apparatus of the latter's own exploited labor. To make the parallel exact we should have to find that the original act of repression was induced by a ruling function within the psyche, and that is what we do find when we explore the connection between repression, alienated psychic energy, and the dominating agency of the superego. We shall return to this issue later in our discussion. Something of the connection can be gleaned, however, from the following passage:

> The superego's relation to the subsequent modifications effected in the ego is roughly that of the primary sexual period in childhood to full-grown sexual activity after puberty. Although it is amenable to every later influence, it preserves throughout life the character given to it by its derivation from the father-complex, namely, *the capacity to stand apart from the ego and to rule it.* It is a memorial of the former *weakness and dependence* of the ego and the mature ego remains subject to its domination [emphasis added].[37]

This is an illuminating passage because it relates the alienation of the superego to the original helplessness and dependence of the child. What is revealed, in other words, is the dialectical interpenetration of dependence and the pathology of independence. A part of us becomes *other* to ourselves and independent of our control, because we are dependent upon *another* who is independent of our control, and who exercises critical power over the constitution of our selves.

Therefore, in both Marx and Freud, considerable attention is devoted to the cycle through which domination is perpetuated and augmented. Capitalist production develops on an increasing scale through the mechanism that converts capital into surplus-value and surplus-value into capital. Exploitation is materialized in self-perpetuity. It is not the only movement occurring in the system of capitalism. There is simultaneously a movement toward transcendence. This latter movement does not, however, deny the presence of the reproduction of alienation.

> If the exploitation of the laborers already employed does not increase, either extensively or intensively, then additional labor-power must be found. For this, the mechanism of capitalist production provides beforehand, by converting the working class into a class dependent on wages, a class whose ordinary wages suffice, not only for its maintenance, but for its increase. It is only necessary for capital to incorporate this additional labor-power, annu-

ally supplied by the working class in the shape of laborers of all ages, with the surplus means of production comprised in the annual produce, and the conversion of surplus-value into capital is complete. From a concrete point of view, accumulation resolves itself into the reproduction of capital *on a progressively increasing scale. The circle in which simple reproduction moves, alters its form, and, to use Sismondi's expression, changes into a spiral* [emphasis added].[38]

An analogous conception is put forward by Freud in commenting on the relationship between renunciation and conscience. In *Civilization and Its Discontents* he notes that

conscience (or more correctly, the anxiety which later becomes conscience) is indeed the cause of instinctual renunciation to begin with, but that later the relationship is reversed. Every renunciation of instinct now becomes a dynamic source of conscience and every fresh renunciation increases the latter's severity and intolerance. If we could only bring it into better harmony with what we already know about the history of the origin of conscience, we should be tempted to defend the paradoxical statement that *conscience is the result of instinctual renunciation, or that instinctual renunciation (imposed on us from without) creates conscience, which then demands further instinctual renunciation* [emphasis added].[39]

These views parallel each other; the alienated labor of the working class, appropriated by the capitalist, extends capital and the wage system, thereby furthering the extent and intensity of alienated labor; the superego demands renunciation of the id, whose repressed energy feeds the further tyranny of the superego. But the confluence of views goes considerably further than structural similarity. It is only a short step to combine these two positions in a way that deepens the separate contributions.

From Freud we can derive an understanding of how the process noted in Marx's account is reproduced internally in the psyche of the laborer, and from Marx's side we acquire illumination about the social circumstances around which the renunciation of instinctual desire is originally created. This sort of synthesis was one of the objects of the attempts at integrating Marx and Freud and is an example of the numerous complementary intersections between the two systems of thought. Whether it is ultimately satisfactory we will have to wait to decide. But it is easy enough to understand the basis for such attempts.

Even more specific psychoanalytic conceptions have a Marxist analogue. Fromm has called attention to the "close connection between the phenomenon of alienation and the phenomenon of transference which is one of the most fundamental concepts in Freud's system."[40] I should prefer to compare transference with fetishism, since both of these processes refer to the mistaken ascription of traits appropriate to one situation to another to which they do not in reality correspond. The mysterious character of commodities arises from the fact that relations among the producers are attributed to the products themselves: the actions of the producers appear to derive from the commodities they have themselves produced. In the case of transference, the patient attributes to the therapist characteristics that in fact derive from significant figures in the past. In this form, the comparison is more misleading than helpful. For in the Freudian model the movement of transference is from person to person while in Marx's account it is from social relations to material entities. And again, in the Freudian account the therapist exists independently, while for Marx the fetishized commodity only comes to be through the activity of its producers. And yet there is something behind Fromm's suggestion. It is, I believe, the relationship of powerlessness to memory and the dominance of the past.

The fetishized consciousness has lost the awareness of history. It regards the present as a natural fact, permanent and unalterable. Under capitalist alienation workers are separated from the results of their labor. Since they do not control the process of production they experience these products as having a life of their own. But it is a fixed and unchanging life, a contradiction in terms. The effect of ideology is to make this contradiction incomprehensible. It is suffered through, rather than understood. In Freudian language, it is repeated or acted out rather than recollected. For both Marx and Freud, an inability to comprehend the past condemns one to repeat it. And most significantly, to repeat it from the position of powerlessness through which it was originally constituted. Of course

> nature does not produce on the one side owners of money or commodities, and on the other men possessing nothing but their own labor-power. This relation has no natural basis; neither is its social basis one that is common to all historical periods. It is clearly *the result of a past historical development,* the product of many economic revolutions, of the extinction of a whole series of older forms of social production [emphasis added].[41]

In Marx's view there is a necessary connection between powerlessness and the illusion of permanence. Under conditions of alienated labor, subordination appears inevitable. To the extent that one is alienated one has lost the power to change, to experience one's self as a historical agent. Therefore, alienation produces the illusion of its own permanence.

In the first section of *The 18th Brumaire of Louis Bonaparte,* Marx offers some brilliant reflections on the reification of the past.

> Men make their own history, but they do not make it just as they please; they do not make it under circumstances chosen by themselves, but under circumstances directly encountered, given and *transmitted from the past. The tradition of all dead generations weighs like a nightmare on the brain of the living.* And just

when they seem engaged in revolutionizing themselves and things, in creating something that has never yet existed, precisely in such periods of revolutionary crisis *they anxiously conjure up the spirits of the past* to their service and borrow from the names, battle cries and costumes in order to present the new scene of world history in this time-honored disguise and this *borrowed language....* In like manner a beginner who has learnt a new language always *translates it back into his mother tongue* [emphasis added].[42]

So, the present is acted out under the alienated influence of the past: Luther appears in the mask of Paul, and the Revolution of 1789 "drapes itself" in the disguise of ancient Rome. We have in this account Marx's version of the repetition compulsion of history. The past must be understood so that it can be buried, and so that the present can speak in the poetry of its own unique and concrete need. However, while men and women do in fact change the world, it is only through "ideological forms" that they "become conscious of this conflict." So Marx suggests to us a striking image in which historical agents overthrow the past but conceive of the meaning of their activity in terms borrowed from the very conditions they are engaged in destroying.

For psychoanalysis, "one of the outstanding characteristics of transference reactions is their repetitiousness, their resistance to change, their tenacity."[43] This is the same account that Marx applied in his analysis of *The 18th Brumaire.* The repetitions that operate in transference point to the cardinal fact behind all neurotic behavior; patients fall ill because they have "chosen" not to remember their past:

> It is familiar ground that the work of analysis aims at inducing the patient to give up the repressions (using the word in the widest sense) belonging to his early life and to replace them by reactions of a sort that would correspond better to a psychically mature condition. It is with this purpose in view that he must be got to recollect certain experiences and the emotions called up by them which he has at the moment forgotten. We know that his present symptoms and inhibitions are the consequences of repressions of this kind: that is, that they are a substitute for these things that he has forgotten.[44]

Under conditions of alienation or repression, the life of the individual becomes external to itself; and yet one is always alienated from something that remains part of one's self. In the account of both Marx and Freud, the material that has been separated from conscious control continues, simultaneously, as something of myself, and something foreign to me. This process applies not only to labor, consciousness, and feeling, but to the modes of time. Past, present, and future cannot be expunged. But lacking power over the course of life, the subject no longer experiences time as cumulative phases of the passage of activity, but as separate, reified sectors of being. Memory which has been severed from conscious control continues to exist as a foreign presence. To return to

Freud's previous phrase, it enjoys the right of extraterritoriality. The past becomes an implacable and overwhelming fate.

> Our hysterical patients suffer from reminiscences. Their symptoms are the remnants and the memory symbols of certain (traumatic) experiences . . . *they cannot escape from the past, and neglect present reality in its favor.* This fixation of the mental life on the pathogenic traumata is an essential, and practically a most significant characteristic of the neurosis [emphasis added].[45]

The alienated and repressed are dominated by their past labor. They do not understand their history and so it continues to overwhelm them. Their past was born in helplessness and persists in this form until it is purposively reclaimed. Freud stresses both that symptoms are a substitute for what the patient has forgotten, and that the patient suffers from reminiscences. Neuroses are, in Greenson's nice phrase, a "repetition of the past, a reliving without memory."[46] But ambiguity appears in this line of inquiry if we ask what precisely is being relived without memory. For the answer may refer either to the past of the individual or to the past of humanity in its historical existence; either to ontogenesis or phylogenesis.

Marx believed in a progressive evolutionary scheme of historical development, in which periods followed each other in accordance with the laws of dialectical materialism.

> In broad outlines we can designate the Asiatic, the ancient, the feudal, and the modern bourgeois methods of production as so many epochs in the progress of the economic formation of society. The bourgeois relations of production are the last antagonistic form of the social process of production—antagonistic not in the sense of individual antagonism, but of one arising from conditions surrounding the life of individuals in society at the same time the productive forces developing in the womb of bourgeois society create the material conditions for the solution of the antagonism. This social formation constitutes, therefore, the closing chapter of the prehistoric stage of human society.[47]

So much is obvious, as is the fact that Marx seems just as clearly to lack any theory of the development of the individual. But the system of individual stages of growth is the heart of Freud's theory of libidinal development. The transition of sexual energy along the path of oral, anal, phallic, and genital phases charts the course of human growth and the potential arrest of that growth in regressive fixations. And yet there is a historical analysis present in Freud, which occasionally occurs as an analogy for the periods of human growth, as in the following passage from *Totem and Taboo,* where Freud notes the movement from individual to social reality, suggesting that

> the *animistic* phase would correspond to narcissism both chronologically and in its content; the *religious* phase would correspond to the stage of object-

choice of which the characteristic is a child's attachment to his parent; while the *scientific* phase would have an exact counterpart in the stage at which an individual has reached maturity, has renounced the pleasure principle, adjusted himself to reality and turned to the external world for the object of his desires.[48]

Of course, this is the familiar positivist scheme of Comte applied to the process of individual transformation. But Freud sometimes extends the analogy to a literal judgment of historical development.

> We know that the human child cannot well complete its development towards culture without passing through a more or less distinct phase of neurosis. . . . Most of these child neuroses are overcome spontaneously as one grows up, and this is especially true of the obsessional neurosis of childhood. . . . In just the same way one might assume that in its development through the ages mankind as a whole experiences conditions that are analogous to the neuroses, and this for the same reasons, because in the ages of its ignorance and intellectual weakness it achieved by purely affective means the instinctual renunciations, indispensable for man's communal existence. . . . Thus religion would be the universal obsessional neurosis of humanity. . . . According to this conception one might prophesy that the abandoning of religion must take place with the fateful inexorability of a process of growth, and that we are just now in the middle of this phase of development.[49]

While Marx does not refer to individual stages of development, he does note the connection between individual power or powerlessness and the awareness of the past. So much is clear in the passage cited from *The 18th Brumaire*. That work even adumbrates a distinction between the normal and pathological dependence on previous historical stages, the difference resting on whether a class uses ancient symbols to amplify its present historical mission or to conceal from itself the painful awareness of its impotence, "magnifying the given task in imagination," or "of fleeing from its solution in reality."[50]

While Marx lacks any theory of personal development he does point to an important relationship between individual development and the awareness or ignorance of *origins*. And it is the notion of origins that confers upon the role of history its critical significance:

> On the surface of bourgeois society the wage of the laborer appears as the price of labor, a certain quantity of money that is paid for a certain quantity of labor. . . .
>
> In the expression "value of labor," the idea of value is not only completely obliterated, but actually reversed. . . .
>
> We see, further . . . the wage-form thus extinguishes every trace of the division of the working-day into necessary labor and surplus-labor, into paid and unpaid labor. All labor appears as paid labor.[51]

The wage of the laborer can appear as "the price of labor" only because the wage-form tends to extinguish the awareness of the origins of exploitation. The working class suffers the result of its ignorance in the denigration and dehumanization of its daily life. But "ignorance" is the wrong term. The working class suffers not from a sheer privation of knowledge but from the presence of mystification, the persistence of fetishism.

We have briefly summarized the views of Marx and Freud on irrationality, mystification, inversion, alienation, and powerlessness. How is liberation to be achieved, under what circumstances, by which historical or personal agent? Since the deficiency that human beings face in their lives is rooted in the separation of themselves from their own control, that is, in the alienation and subordination to something that is still fundamentally their own, i.e., themselves, the cure must be the reintegration of the life that has been severed and lost to itself. The solution is the act of reclamation in which the self reappropriates its own fetishized existence and brings its own power back under the control of conscious, personal agency. The depersonalization of life, the result of human activity lost to itself, is transcended as the self repersonalizes its fetishized presence.

That is why the work of salvation must be carried on by the alienated being itself. It is not possible to be redeemed by external forces. External force flourishes precisely because we are powerless; it certainly can not be the source of self-constitution. Engels stated the matter with clarity and precision:

> Our notion, from the beginning, was that "the emancipation of the working class must be the act of the working class itself. . . ."
>
> Active social forces work exactly like natural forces: blindly, forcibly, destructively, so long as we do not understand, and reckon with, them. But once we understand them, when once we grasp their action, their direction, their effects, it depends only upon ourselves *to subject them more and more to our own will, and by means of them to reach our own ends. . . .* With this recognition, at last, of the real nature of the productive forces of today, the social anarchy of production gives place to a social regulation of production upon a definite plan, according to the needs of the community and of each individual. Then the capitalist mode of appropriation, *in which the product enslaves first the producer and then the appropriator,* is replaced by the mode of appropriation of the products that is based upon the nature of the modern means of production: upon the one hand, direct social appropriation as means to the maintenance and extension of production; on the other, direct individual appropriation as means of subsistence and enjoyment. . . .
>
> With the seizing of the means of production by society, production of commodities is replaced by systematic, definite organization. The struggle for individual existence disappears. Then for the first time *man, in a certain sense, is finally marked off from the rest of the animal kingdom and emerges from mere animal conditions of existence into really human ones. The whole sphere of the condi-*

tions of life which environ man, and which have hitherto ruled man, now comes under
the dominion and control of man, who for the first time becomes the real, conscious lord
of nature because he has now become the master of his own social organization. The
laws of his own social action, hitherto standing face to face with man as laws of nature
foreign to and dominating him, will now be used with full understanding, and so
mastered by him. Man's own social organization, hitherto confronting him as a neces-
sity imposed by nature and history, now becomes the result of his own free action. The
extraneous objective forces that have hitherto governed history pass under the control of
man himself. Only from that time will man himself, more and more consciously, make
his own history—only from that time will the social causes set in movement by him have,
in the main and in a constantly growing measure, the results intended by him. It is the
ascent of man from the kingdom of necessity to the kingdom of freedom [emphasis
added].[52]

This is one of the most majestic and passionate passages in the whole
Marxist literature on the transcendence of alienation. The connection
between knowledge, power, rational control, reappropriation, and self-
determination is beautifully stated. So long as we are dominated by
alienated structures, our own nature takes the form of external, impersonal historical necessity. Our action is governed by "causes" and we are
foreign to ourselves. But when we seize our power, we become luminous
to ourselves, beings of freedom and reason who regulate our lives
through our own self-determined ends.

For Freud, too, the difficulty to be overcome is the loss of the individual to its own being; the repression that maintains a barrier between
the rational ego and critical constituents of its own nature. At one point
Freud describes his patients as "alienated from both present and future.
They are marooned in their illness."[53] The heart of Freud's view is that
symptoms disappear when the unconscious antecedents of symptoms
have themselves been brought to the level of consciousness. "Our
therapy does its work by transforming something unconscious into
something conscious."[54]

But this knowledge that the patient requires for health cannot be
imposed by the analyst or even affected by the latter's articulation. For
"there is knowing and knowing. . . . Knowing on the part of the physician
is not the same thing as knowing on the part of the patient and does not
have the same effect."[55] The physician can initiate a process of cure, but
only the patient can complete the process through internal identification
with its end. "The necessary condition is that the knowledge must be
founded upon an inner change in the patient which can only come about
by a mental operation directed to that end."[56] Everything of the patient's
own life which is relevant to the illness and which has been forced out of
consciousness must now be reclaimed. This is the painful labor of personal transformation.

The task which the psychoanalytic method seeks to perform may be for-
mulated . . . thus: the task of the treatment is to remove the amnesias. When

all gaps in memory have been filled in, all the enigmatic products of mental life elucidated, the continuance and even a renewal of the morbid condition are made impossible. Or the formula may be expressed in this fashion: all repression must be undone . . . the task consists in making the unconscious accessible to consciousness, which is done by overcoming the resistances.[57]

Recalling the unconscious to consciousness is not merely a matter of acquiring information, however, as we have already seen. It is a matter of overcoming resistance:

The pathological factor is not his ignorance in itself, but the root of this ignorance in his inner resistances; it was they that first called this ignorance into being, and they still maintain it now. The task of the treatment lies in combating these resistances.[58]

Freud puts the matter very nicely in the following passage:

In actual fact, indeed, the neurotic patient presents us with a torn mind, divided by resistances. As we analyze it and remove the resistances, it grows together; the great unity which we call his ego fits into itself all the instinctual impulses which before had been split off and held apart from it.[59]

The repressed material is of the self; the ego, both conscious and unconscious, is of the self; and the act of repression is also of the self. Just as the self has split itself, so it must heal itself. The hand that inflicts the wound is the hand that heals it. This is the fundamental reason Freud relinquished hypnosis as a therapeutic technique for the development of analysis. "The first works cosmetically, the second surgically."[60] While the illness is external to the rational ego, to the self-conscious being of the self, it is nevertheless the patient's own being that forms the pathology. This is the root point for both Marx and Freud; alienated force is my own force severed from myself, it is myself existing beyond my control. Rieff says:

In the school in which Freud trained, the physician addressed himself only to the disease, as an alien which had somehow insinuated itself into the body of the patient. The pathos of the patient was only a distraction, and the physician, to guard against it, trained himself in a bedside manner, a standard mask of geniality and aloofness assumed for the benefit of patients and their friends and relatives alike. The patient, for his part, was merely obliged to be docile. Like a feudal lady, he was a spectator at the tournament for which he had engaged the physician as his champion. He was the accidental host of his disease, and the treatment—like the disease once contracted—was something to which he could only submit.[61]

For Freud, however, the disease was the patient himself, and it was the patient who must be treated if the illness were to be overcome. Patients must struggle against their repressions, against their terror at loss and anxiety in the face of rejection. The patient alone could affirm and disavow. This may seem an overly voluntaristic account of Freud's position, but we need only recall Freud's own comment on dreams to set the matter right:

> Obviously one must hold oneself responsible for the evil impulses of one's dreams. What else is one to do with them? Unless the content of the dream (rightly understood) is inspired by alien spirits, it is a part of my own being. If I seek to classify the impulses that are present in me according to social standards into good and bad, I must assume responsibility for both sorts; and if, in defense, I say that what is unknown, unconscious and repressed in me is not my "ego," then I shall not be basing my position upon psychoanalysis, I shall not have accepted its conclusions—and I shall perhaps be taught better by criticism of my fellow-men, by the disturbances in my actions and the confusion of my feelings. I shall perhaps learn that what I am disavowing not only "is" in me but sometimes "acts" from out of me as well.[62]

It is equally true that the patient cannot accomplish the cure without the aid of the therapist. Yet, while "the physician makes it possible for him to do this by suggestions which are in the nature of an *education*," it is still "the patient [who] has to accomplish it."[63] Habermas puts the matter very well:

> For the insight to which analysis is to lead is indeed only this: that the ego of the patient recognize itself in its other, represented by its illness, as in its own alienated self and identify with it.[64]

But it is equally true for Marx that transformation is not possible until the working class recognizes itself in the alienated objectification of its own labor, until it grasps its own dehumanized toil in the commodities and capital that confront it. The working class, too, has its resistances to overcome. For ideology is not merely imposed, it is also recreated within the being of the oppressed. It is constitutive of the working class that it views capitalism as a manifestation of "self-evident laws of nature." For our understanding of ourselves has been shaped against us, in opposition to our interests, and it is a long, slow, disciplined labor to win back our own comprehension as a liberating power. And didn't Marx also insist

> we tell the workers: "You have to endure and go through fifteen, twenty, fifty years of civil war in order to change the circumstances, *in order to make yourselves fit for power*" [emphasis added].[65]

A Note of Discord

It is not a difficult matter to continue noting the similarities between Marx and Freud. The list could easily be extended, but there is nothing useful to be gained by the exercise. The problem is to relate the various common themes to the equally important contradictions between them.

The following are representative reflections of Freud:

The liberty of the individual is no gift of civilization. It was greatest before there was any civilization, though then, it is true, it had for the most part no value, since the individual was in no position to defend it.[66]

In the process of individual development, as we have said, the main accent falls mostly on the egoistic urge (or the urge towards happiness); while the other urge, which may be described as a "cultural" one, is usually content with the role of imposing restrictions.[67]

The function of education, therefore, is to inhibit, forbid and suppress, and it has at all times carried out this function to admiration.[68]

Men are not gentle creatures who want to be loved, and who at the most can defend themselves if they are attacked; they are, on the contrary, creatures among whose instinctual endowments is to be reckoned a powerful share of aggressiveness. As a result, their neighbor is for them not only a potential helper or sexual object, but also someone who tempts them to satisfy their agressiveness on him, to exploit his capacity for work without compensation, to use him sexually without his consent, to seize his possessions, to humiliate him, to cause him pain, to torture and to kill him. *Homo homini lupus.*[69]

It is just as impossible to do without government of the masses by a minority as it is to dispense with coercion in the work of civilization, for the masses are lazy and unintelligent, they have no love for instinctual renunciation, they are not to be convinced of its inevitability by argument, and the individuals support each other in giving full play to their unruliness.[70]

It is quite impossible to understand how psychological factors can be over-looked when the reactions of living beings are involved; for not only were such factors already concerned in the establishment of these economic conditions, but even in obeying these conditions, men can do no more than set their original instinctual impulses in motion. . . . For sociology, which deals with the behavior of man in society, can be nothing other than applied psychology.[71]

The unconscious is the true psychical reality; in its innermost nature it is as much unknown to us as the reality of the external world. . . .[72] The sole quality that rules in the id is that of being unconscious. Id and unconscious are as intimately united as ego and preconscious; indeed, the former connection is even more exclusive. . . .[73] In popular language, we may say that the ego stands for reason and circumspection, while the id stands for the untamed passions. . . .[74] Thus in its relation to the id [the ego] is like a man on horseback, who has to hold in check the superior strength of the horse; with this difference, that the rider seeks to do so with his own strength while the ego uses borrowed forces. . . .[75] We can come nearer to the id with images, and call it a chaos, a cauldron of seething excitement. We suppose that it is somewhere in direct contact with somatic processes, and takes over from them instinctual needs. . . . These instincts fill it with energy, but it has no organization and no unified will. . . . The laws of logic—above all, the law of contradiction—do not hold for the processes in the id. . . . There is nothing in the id which can be compared to negation, and we are astonished to find in it an exception to the philosopher's assertion that space and time are necessary forms of our mental acts. In the id there is nothing corresponding to the idea of time, no recognition of the passage of time, and . . . no alteration of mental processes by the passage of time.[76]

This final goal of all organic striving can be stated too. It would be counter to the conservative nature of instinct if the goal of life were a state never hitherto reached. It must rather be an ancient starting point, which the living being left long ago, and to which it harks back again by all the circuitous paths of development. If we may assume as an experience admitting of no exception that everything living dies from causes within itself, and returns to the inorganic, we can only say "The goal of life is death," and casting back, "The inanimate was there before the animate."[77]

Now compare the previous citations with the following reflections of Marx:

Only in community do the means exist for every individual to cultivate his talents in all directions. Only in the community is personal freedom possible. In previous substitutes for the community, in the state, etc., personal freedom has existed only for the individuals who developed within the ruling class and only insofar as they belonged to this class. The illusory community, in which individuals have come together up till now, always took on an independent existence in relation to them and was at the same time not only a completely illusory community but a new fetter.[78]

It is but in the eighteenth century, in "bourgeois society," that the different forms of social union confront the individual as a mere means to his private ends, as an outward necessity. . . . Man is in the most literal sense of the word a *zoon politikon*, not only a social animal, but an animal which can develop into an individual only in society.[79] In place of the old bourgeois society, with its classes and class antagonisms, we shall have an association in which the free development of each is the condition for the free development of all.[80]

It has been objected that upon the abolition of private property all work will cease and universal laziness will overtake us.
    According to this, bourgeois society ought long ago have gone to the dogs through sheer idleness, for those of its members who work acquire nothing and those who acquire anything do not work.[81]

It can be seen that the history of *industry* and industry as it *objectively* exists is an *open* book of the *human faculties,* and a human *psychology* which can be sensuously apprehended. . . . No psychology for which this book. i.e., the most tangible and accessible part of history, remains closed, can become a *real* science with a genuine content.[82]

In bourgeois society living labor is but a means to increase accumulated labor. In communist society accumulated labor is but a means to widen, to enrich, to promote the existence of the laborer.

In bourgeois society, therefore, the past dominates the present; in communist society the present dominates the past. . . .[83] Once a need is satisfied, which requires the action of satisfying and the acquisition of the instrument for this purpose, new needs arise. The production of new needs is the first historical act.[84]

For labor, *life activity, productive life*, now appear to man only as *means* for the satisfaction of a need, the need to maintain his physical existence. Productive life is, however, species-life. It is life creating life. In the type of life activity resides the whole character of the species, its species-character; and free, conscious activity is the species character of human beings.[85]

It will be seen from this how, in place of the *wealth* and *poverty* of political economy, we have the wealthy man and the plenitude of *human* need. The wealthy man is at the same time one who *needs* a complex of human manifestations of life, and whose own self-realization exists as an inner necessity, a *need*.[86]

In fact, however, when the narrow bourgeois form has been peeled away, what is wealth if not the universality of needs, capacities, enjoyments, productive powers, etc., of individuals produced in universal exchange? What, if not the full development of human control over the forces of nature—those of his own as well as those of so-called "nature"? What, if not the absolute elaboration of his creative dispositions, without any preconditions other than antecedent historical evolution which makes the totality of this evolution— i.e., the evolution of all human powers as such unmeasured by any *previously established* yardstick—an end in itself? What is this, if not a situation where man does not reproduce himself in any determined form, but produces his totality? Where he does not seek to remain something formed by the past, but is the absolute movement of becoming.[87]

It is not merely that these statements can be arranged as pairs of contradictions. They originate from wholly different conceptions of human nature and society; their sense of lived dimension is as contrary as the theoretical perspectives from which they derive and in which they articulate their vision. Life and death, time and movement, hope and despair—the fundamental experiences of men and women are so differently lived through and defined. And yet, the similarities we noted have their own reality. To reconcile this apparent discrepancy we must turn to a more detailed account of the structure of Marxist and Freudian theory.

CHAPTER TWO

Antagonism

I will begin this chapter with a skeletal overview of the fundamental differences between Marx and Freud. I will then proceed to flesh in this bare outline, attending somewhat more to Freud than Marx. In the next chapter, I will continue the discussion with more attention paid to Marx. The remainder of this book will continue to concretize the basic differences, to raise the possibility of reconciliation and consider the question of practical implications.

The fundamental theoretical contradictions between Freud and Marx are the following:

1. Freud's method is dualistic; it is based on the view that there is a perennial conflict of opposing forces—both within the individual and between the individual and the social system.

Marx's method is dialectical; dualities are eschewed for a conception that views antagonistic factors as necessary aspects of a larger configuration which renders them partial and temporary.

2. Freud views the part as primary and the whole as a construction out of its elements; sociology is applied psychology.

For Marx, the social totality establishes the meaning of its aspects; psychology is a derivative of the pervasive social structure.

3. Freud's view is ahistorical; the id, which is our fundamental stratum, is timeless.

For Marx, transformation is the basic existential category; no specific feature of the human condition can make a claim to permanence. We are fated to historicity and cannot avoid the task.

4. Consequently, the prevalent motif in Freud's methodology is the recurrence of past events, the search for an identical foundation beneath apparent differences.

For Marx, novelty is genuine and teleology guides the comprehension of passage; that is, emergent characteristics have the capacity to determine the meaning of those events that preceded them.

5. More specifically, for Freud, the variety of social and historical occurrences masks the identity of underlying conflicts and compromise.

For Marx, it is the specific determinations of collective life that hold the key to adequate social explanation.

6. For Freud, human nature is homeostatic and tends toward equilibrium under conditions of freedom.

For Marx, human nature is intrinsically responsive to its self-realization and tends toward passivity only when defeated.

7. For Freud, human need is characterized by inadequacy, deprivation, and vulnerability.

For Marx, human need is ideally the source of opening to a growing participation in the world of humanized nature.

8. For Freud, human nature is essentially aggressive, competitive, envious, and self-serving.

For Marx, the destructiveness of human existence derives from an irrational social system and is open to transformation.

9. Civilization is basically repressive, in Freud's perspective; individual freedom and social structure are necessarily opposed.

For Marx, it is only through participation in the social order than human freedom arises as a potentiality.

10. Freud's conception of politics is essentially conservative—social conflict and suffering are inevitable and revolution an illusion of fundamental change.

For Marx it is revolution that most illuminates human existence and the disbelief in its possibility that most betrays the conditions of alienation.

11. It is Freud's contention that the ultimate hope against social oppression rests in the permanent rebelliousness of the instincts.

For Marx, the source of antagonism to social exploitation lies in the responsiveness of human beings to the emerging and antagonistic tendencies in the social system.

12. Freud's appraisal of political practice is meliorist; one can hope

for a somewhat better balance of antagonistic forces, but nothing radically different can be maturely entertained.

Marx maintains, on the contrary, that the belief in incremental changes is an expression of the ideology of accomodation to prevailing power.

13. For Freud, reason is merely a technical bureaucratic charge to carry out the requirements of the id, external reality, and the superego.

For Marx, reason makes substantial claims upon the world on behalf of human emancipation and possesses the capacity to grasp the emergence of its own reality by the developing standards of its own reflection.

14. For Freud, morality and reason, superego and ego, are distinct faculties.

For Marx, morality is the social self-reflection of humanity upon the conditions of its realization.

15. For Freud, the demystification of human nature follows the archeological paradigm of uncovering the past.

For Marx, the demystification of human existence follows the revolutionary paradigm of reconstituting the future.

Dualism and Dialectics

Freud's theory is *dualistic;* Marx's theory is *dialectical.* Freud delineates the world through a series of antinomies: individual vs. society, pleasure principle vs. reality principle, cathexis vs. countercathexis, free energy vs. bound energy, irrational id vs. rational ego, impulse vs. defense, ego instinct vs. sexual instinct, ego libido vs. object libido, eros vs. thanatos. The basic schema is that of antithetical forces, processes, or entities. But perhaps the most critical polarity Freud utilizes is that between reality and appearance:

> The unconscious is the true psychical reality; *in its inner nature it is as much unknown to us as the reality of the external world, and it is as incompletely presented by the data of consciousness as is the external world by the communications of our sense organs.*[1]

The external world and our own "true psychical reality" are both unknow*able* to us. A radical chasm separates appearance and reality. What is most profound about ourselves is least open to our own scrutiny. Freud vacillates between holding that this condition is due to temporary ignorance, and that it is a permanent condition. However, the second view predominates. For even if we could succeed in reducing our psychical reality to its underlying chemical basis (a view Freud sometimes entertains), that chemical structure, as part of the external world, would be "incomplately presented to us by our sense organs." Freud expresses his own conviction when he writes that "an instinct can never become an object of consciousness"[2] or that "reality will always remain unknowable."[3]

Marx also adheres to a distinction between underlying reality and manifest appearance. But Marx subscribes to Hegel's conviction that "the Essence must appear."[4] Marx's theory of false consciousness combines the themes of inversion and reflection. The "appearance" is simultaneously a distortion and a *revelation*.[5] To say that Marx's theory is dialectical is to assert that it eschews any notion of ultimate dualities. The distorted forms of our consciousness are the necessary manifestations of the alienated society in which we live.

> The Fetishism which attaches itself to the products of labour, so soon as they are produced as commodities, is therefore inseparable from the production of commodities.[6]

> The categories of bourgeois economy consist of . . . forms of thought *expressing with social validity* the conditions and relations of a definite, historically determined mode of production, viz. the production of commodities.[7]

It is not self-evident that capitalism should produce the appearance of fetishized commodities. Because appearance and reality are not identical, scientific inquiry is required to clarify their relationship. But neither are reality and appearance totally separable. For appearance is very different from "illusion," and reality itself cannot exist without its manifestations. The relationship between appearance and reality is dialectical precisely because the terms are neither identical nor intelligible in distinction from each other. As Lenin notes in a comment on Hegel: "The more petty philosophers dispute whether essence *or* that which is immediately given should be taken as basis. . . . Instead of *or*, Hegel puts *and*."[8]

Appearances are partial manifestations of reality. They are "illusory" to the extent that they are taken to be identical with the "reality" they express. The color of a flame is a real manifestation of its physical properties, but were we to identify the color we see with the flame, directly, without considering the nature of light, the atmosphere, the structure of our eye, our nervous system and our brain, we would be committing an error analogous to the fetishism. False consciousness arises when we regard an aspect of reality as identical with the whole. Two truths must be grasped together: the whole is more than its parts or their mere sum; but the whole has no being in separation from its parts.

While for Freud appearance and reality lie on two different planes of existence, for Marx they are continuous. The view that regards them as fundamentally distinct is, from a Marxist perspective, a manifestation of social estrangement. It is an illusion that arises when the subject experiences its activity as separated from its own control. The forms of bourgeois thought have "social validity," it is true; they possess the "reality" of the society they manifest. But that society is historically determined. Therefore, the underlying reality which hides itself behind appearance is subject to human change. And so, too, is the theoretical separation between appearance and reality a manifestation of this estranged epoch.

There is a further difference between Marx and Freud concerning dualism and false consciousness. I previously emphasized that both positions are deeply opposed to the views of common sense; neither accepts the claims of ordinary consciousness at face value. Nevertheless, their accounts of the genesis, function, and overcoming of false consciousness are fundamentally distinct.

For Freud, the truth that the patient would flee lies beneath the surface of the mind like the ruins of an ancient city.[9] This truth was once known, and is now forgotten; but it continues to endure. "Our patients suffer from reminiscences," Freud observed. We cannot escape the past simply because we turn our attention elsewhere. What is required in therapy is an act of excavation in which the broken remnants of our past are returned to the light of consciousness. We need to *recover* what we once covered over in terror. The truth of ourselves that we pursue lies crouched behind disguises of our own making. They are marked by a pathological identity, for they have remained fixed over time in the precise form in which they were first encountered. When we remember again, we come upon the small child in ourselves as the archeologist comes upon the preserved fixtures of some primitive time. We unearth the fossils and artifacts of our past as they have been preserved unchanged in the frozen glacier of our unconsciousness.

Freud holds an *archeological* theory of recovery. But for Marx the truth does not lie ossified in the past; it is still to be created in the future. Marx, of course, wrote that philosophers have only understood the world, while the point is to change it. But the world cannot be understood until it is changed. We live mystified because we lack power over our own lives. We are divided from ourselves and embodied in entities and institutions which, opaque to our power, are opaque to our comprehension. We can only truly understand what we freely make. But the world in which we persevere thwarts our ends, defeats our purpose, and forces our intentions malignly back upon ourselves. Since we are not free, we do not understand our lives. Our truth lies in the future:

> The life-process of society, which is based on the process of material production, does not strip off its mystical veil until it is treated as production by freely associated men, and is consciously regulated by them in accordance with a settled plan.[10]

Marx's theory of transcendence is not *archeological,* but *transformational* and *revolutionary.* For mystification resides in powerlessness and will not be expunged until we transform the world through revolutionary practice. This point sharply distinguishes Marxist theory from the various forms of therapy, mediation, religious encounter and "personal growth" so prevalent today. Not all of them follow Freud in looking backward to the truth. But all of them, in one way or another, look "inward," and all of them eschew confrontation with social reality. They are founded on the assumptions that social oppression is irrelevant to our understanding of ourselves and that society can be understood by understanding the individual lives of its members. Both of these contentions follow Freud more than Marx. But these contentions are not merely about the individual and society; they also contain a set of assumptions about basic human nature, history, and explanation. The easiest way to locate these presuppositions is once again to contrast the views of Marx and Freud.

Society and Individuals

> Society does not consist of individuals, but expresses the sum of interrelations, the relations within which these individuals stand.[11]

> For sociology, which deals with the behavior of man in society, can be nothing other than applied psychology. Strictly speaking, indeed, there are only two sciences—psychology, pure and applied, and natural science.[12]

For Freud, sociology is applied psychology. Freud begins with the individual, and views society as the sum of individual transactions. "Applied psychology" means applied *individual* psychology. Marx holds the contrary view that individuals are the result of historical and social development rather than the starting point of our explanation. Freud does not deny society, nor Marx the individual. But they ascribe different meanings to these terms, because they view them as differently constituted. Social reality is primary for Marx because society possesses a unity of its own which is not reducible to the combination of its parts. Even when Freud appears to approach this position his view is fundamentally different.

> If the individuals in the group are combined into a unity, there must surely be something to unite them.[13]

> Human life in common is only made possible when a majority comes together which is stronger than any separate individual and which remains united against all separate individuals.... The liberty of the individual is no gift of civilization. It was greatest before there was any civilization.... The development of civilization imposes restrictions upon it....[14]

Like Hobbes before him, Freud consistently utilizes the model of separate entities which must be combined or opposed by force. It was the model Freud inherited from the physics and chemistry of his early scientific training. In combination with the assumptions of bourgeois individualism which informed Freud's social perspective this mechanical view of structure became his primary vision of all reality.

The dualism that characterizes Freud's system is of course intimately related to its atomism. While Marx's account emphasizes the manner in which the aspects of a system mutually determine each other's nature, Freud's vision concentrates our attention on the separateness of units and the forces required to collect them in an aggregate. The individuals who constitute these collections have no intrinsic concern with each other's welfare. The principle that guides them is the reduction of the painful tension each feels within its own body. To move from this atomistic indifference to social antagonism it is only necessary to ascribe to these individual units an unwillingness to coalesce, or a primary interest in destructiveness. This is precisely Freud's move.

It is therefore no surprise to discover that Freud views the individual and society (the mass of other individuals) as being in permanent opposition. Civilization is founded on repression; its primary function is the renunciation of individual, instinctual demands and the transformation of originally hostile energy into socially acceptable forms. "The function of education, therefore, is to inhibit, forbid and suppress...."[15] The other individual can be an obstacle or an aid to my gratification. But the other never transcends the category of means to my end, for love and friendship are ultimately weakened forms of an originally selfish sexuality.

Certainly, Marx does not deny the existence of social antagonism. Class conflict is at the heart of his system. The critical issue concerns the permanence of this antagonism. Is it built into the human condition and therefore unalterable? Or is it subject to human transformation? We cannot even maintain that Marx and Freud agree in their description but disagree in their explanation. There is some provisional validity in this distinction, but the condition which both describe is so differently presented that the accounts appear to converge only if we attend to their abstract features. For the reason that men and women confront each other destructively is not a manifestation of their biologically rooted instincts for Marx, any more than for Freud it is an expression of class divisions. Rooting the destructiveness and conflict of human beings in their innate drives removes the phenomena from history and the possibility of transcendence. What Freud views as a primordial opposition is for Marx a particular, concrete moment in an evolving historical process. The notion that "the liberty of the individual is no gift of civilization" is as unacceptable to Marx as the following position would be to Freud:

In place of the old bourgeois society, with its classes and class antagonisms, we shall have an association in which the free development of each is the condition for the free development of all.[16]

From Freud's perspective, Marx's vision of a society devoid of destructiveness and marked instead by mutual respect and cooperation is an instance of infantile wish fulfillment. For Marx, Freud's view of civilization as the permanent antagonism of its members expresses the ideology of the ruling class, from whose privileged vantage point the existing system appears to be unalterable. The notion of the individual as *intrinsically* opposed to society is incomprehensible in a Marxist perspective, for "the essence of man is . . . the ensemble of social relations" (Sixth Thesis on Feuerbach).

Freudian and Marxist Method

The method and content of a theory are inseparable. What we see and how we see are two aspects of the same vision. Freud's view of knowledge was most influenced by what came to be known as the Helmholtz School of Physicalist Physiology.[17] The position of the school was conveyed to Freud by Brücke, to whom Freud referred as "the greatest authority who affected me more than any other in my whole life."[18] It rested on the thesis that "no other forces than the common physical-chemical ones are active within the organism."[19] These forces were held to be quantitative in nature, governed by attraction and repulsion, tending toward a state of inertia, and determined by several universal laws from whose combination the remaining features of the system could be deduced. In other words, this Helmholtzian system which so influenced Freud was a form of Newtonian physics applied to human beings. It would be absurd to say that this is the only perspective operating in Freud's system; it would also be absurd to insist that Freud ever freed himself of its influence.

Freud persisted in holding that human beings are regulated by the principle of the conservation of energy, and the chemical properties of their physical organism. But Freud imposed upon this mechanistic theory a totally different view of human beings as governed by intentions, meanings, and symbols. The two theories are juxtaposed but they never coalesce. In fact, they are fundamentally incompatible, another example of Freudian dualism (we return to this theme in the last section). The mechanistic theory prevails: ideas are not basic, but derive from instincts, which are fundamentally somatic in origin. So, in Freud's last work, in distinguishing the provinces of the mind, he declares that

to the oldest of these mental provinces or agencies we give the name of *id*. It contains everything that is inherited, that is present at birth, that is fixed in the constitution—above all, therefore, the instincts, which originate in the somatic organization and which find their first mental expression in the id in forms unknown to us.[20]

This "oldest portion" is also described as "the most important" because it "expresses the true purpose of the individual organism's life . . . the satisfaction of its innate needs."[21]

It is important to note the terms that are juxtaposed: "inherited," "fixed," "constitution," "somatic organization," and "oldest portion." These notions express Freud's methodology as much as any judgment based on observation of his patients. Freud's tendency to reify the human condition, that is, to consider the characteristics of present men and women as the immutable characteristics of all human beings, is rooted in the mechanistic positivism we have been delineating. Physics and chemistry are held to be basic. But the properties that form the proper subject matter of these physical sciences do not develop or grow; they have no history. Because in Freud's work mechanistic method remains basic, so the content of his system will also emphasize what is fixed and unalterable—what is inherited, oldest, and fixed in the somatic constitution. The tendency toward reification is therefore inseparable from the positivistic version of scientific method which is employed.

It is the logical outcome of Freud's whole procedure that he views what is most archaic and least distinctively human as rooted in an unalterable substratum. The ego represents reason, as we understand it, and is the portion of ourselves most in contact with the external world, but it "is essentially passive . . . and 'lived' by unknown and uncontrollable forces."[22] These forces emanate from the id, which is distinguished by the absence of development and history. It is described by Freud as "all that the ego is not":

> It has no organization and no unified will. . . . The laws of logic—above all the laws of contradiction—do not hold for processes in the id. There is nothing in the id which can be compared to negation. . . . In the id there is nothing corresponding to the ideas of time, no recognition of the passage of time, and . . . no alteration of mental processes by the passage of time.[23]

The method of Freudian explanation always looks back to the fixed properties of the past for the clue to the meaning of present events. That is why, as we noted above, Freud's manner of uncovering reality is *archeological*. The id is a psychical representative of purely material energy; as physics and chemistry are the basic sciences, the id, which is somatic at its base, is the fundamental human province. This perspective determines the entire meaning of explanation in the Freudian system. Bernfeld seems to me to be correct when he notes:

> Psychoanalysis differs from official psychology by its genetic standpoint. . . . It is the most consistent among the genetic psychological schools. . . . A phe-

nomenon is regarded as "understood" in psychoanalysis if its determinants have been *discovered in the pre-history of the phenomenon* [emphasis added].[24]

But the term "genetic" is questionable, for it usually connotes "development," and the basic insight of Bernfeld's observation is the recognition of how Freud undoes the ordinary notion of development by tracking the meaning of the present to its prehistory. The basic principle of explanation in Freud is the repetition of past events. The apparently autonomous and creative event is revealed to be the combination or recurrence of ancient experiences: "There is no love that does not reproduce infantile prototypes."[25] The infantile is always reproduced, by reiteration, denial, or disguise.

How striking is the contrast with Marx's contention: "Human anatomy contains a key to the anatomy of the ape."[26] This statement, as much as those of Freud, also derives from a total perspective which joins method and content. The basic propositions of the Marxist approach are: reality is rational, that is, intelligible; rationality is a process constituted by the creation and destruction of historical epochs; these epochs are "wholes" or "totalities." These totalities are structured so that (1) the aspects of these systems cannot be understood in isolation from each other, (2) because they are mutually determining (3) in historically specific forms; (4) through the predominance of the mode of production, (5) which determines and is determined by the other social institutions in their structured relationships, through (6) the emergence of crises that cannot be contained by the social forms that have produced them and that lead to their transcendence in a new series of social forces and structures with their own novel organization.

I believe that the Freudian contentions are driven more deeply into our theoretical unconsciousness than those of Marx. We have been induced by social practice and theoretical example to believe in explanation by repetition. To take Marxist method seriously, however, is to believe in the possibility of *emergent* properties and novel configurations:

> In fact, however, when the limited bourgeois form is stripped away, what is wealth other than the universality of individual needs, capacities, pleasures, productive forces, etc., created through universal exchange? The full development of human mastery over the forces of nature, those of so-called nature as well as of humanity's own nature? The absolute working out of his creative potentialities, with no presupposition other than the previous historic development, which makes this totality of development, i.e., the development of all human powers as such the end in itself, not measured on a *predetermined* yardstick? Where he does not reproduce himself in one specificity, but produces his totality? Strives not to remain something he has become but is in the absolute movement of becoming?[27]

Against the Freudian paradigm of "disguised repetition" stands Marx's vision of a striving to transcend what one has been made in "the absolute movement of becoming." And yet, how is it possible to understand a development which is not measured by a predetermined yardstick, but rather by criteria whose emergence cannot be divorced from the development they are required to measure? This question can only be answered through revolutionary practice. Any other answer looks to the past and is limited in its rationality by previous levels of development. In order to transcend our own reification it is critical that we restructure the principles of our own rationality.

We have noted how Freud's method leads him to the view that human reason is a limited capacity rooted in an ineradicable core of primitive illogic. At the center of our being there is no time, passage, alteration, or development. Marx recognizes the fact of unreason, but he refuses to transform the fact into a fate. He insists instead that reason and unreason emerge and develop historically. Even the meaning of these terms is transformed within the social systems in which they manifest themselves. What is rational for a primitive agricultural society is irrational under industrial capitalism. It is not merely that these systems have different means available to the satisfaction of their ends; they have different notions of "means" and "ends." For the very concept of reason as the adjustment of means to ends is a specific development of capitalist instrumentality.

Men and women, as Marx understands them, produce their own forms of reason and unreason as they produce the remainder of their social lives. The conditions under which this production takes place are not freely chosen; they are limited by previous developments. But we also transform what is imposed on us. As Engels notes,

> Man is the sole animal capable of working his way out of the merely animal state—his normal state is one appropriate to his consciousness, *one to be created by himself.*[28]

> Universally developed individuals, whose social relations, their own communal relations, are hence also subordinated to their own communal control, *are no product of nature, but of history.*[29]

As important as the notion of history is the Marxist emphasis on totality. For history is demarcated by the emergence of internally related systems, that is, by structures that are not reducible to any addition of their parts, that exhibit novelty as a whole, and that are constituted by elements whose meaning is determined by their place in this configuration.

> The result we arrive at is not that production, distribution, exchange, and consumption are identical, but that they are all members of one entity, different sides of one unit. ... A definite form of production thus determines the forms of consumption, distribution, exchange, and *also the mutual relations between these various elements.*[30]

These units, which are made up of "the reciprocal action of various sides on one another,"[31] are the fundamental historical forms. History is the emergence and development of totalities; the uniqueness of the totalities is what differentiates the moments of historical time.

The following passage, from a review of *Capital,* was quoted approvingly by Marx in the preface to the second edition:

> But it will be said, the general laws of economic life are one and the same, no matter whether they are applied to the present or the past. This Marx directly denies. According to him, such abstract laws do not exist. On the contrary, in his opinion every historical period has laws of its own. . . . As soon as society has outlived a given period of development, and is passing over from one given stage to another, it begins to be subject also to other laws. In a word, economic life offers us a phenomenon analogous to the history of evolution in other branches of biology. The old economists misunderstood the nature of economic laws when they likened them to the laws of physics and chemistry. A more thorough analysis of phenomena shows that social organisms differ among themselves as fundamentally as plants and animals. Nay, one and the same phenomenon falls under quite different laws in consequence of the different structure of those organisms as a whole.[32]

The uniqueness of historical periods and the specificity of historical laws are both compared with the development of biological forms. Freud can be likened here to "the old economists" who relied on the paradigm of physics and chemistry. The likeness is both literal and symbolic. For in considering the emergent forms of life, Freud underscores what is recurrent and Marx the creative aspect of the totality. It is of course true, for Marx, that "some determinations belong to all epochs," but this recognition will not carry us far, for

> even though the most developed languages have laws and characteristics in common with the least developed, nevertheless, just those things which determine their development, i.e., the elements which are not general and common, must be separated out from the determinations valid . . . as such, so that in their unity—which arises already from the identity of the subject, humanity, and the object nature—their essential difference is not forgotten.[33]

And Marx immediately follows this observation with the contention that "the whole profundity of those modern economists who demonstrate the eternity and harmoniousness of the existing social relations lies in this forgetting."

But here it is helpful to liken Freud to "the old economists" again. With one fundamental change: Freud demonstrates the eternity of the recurrent system by insisting precisely on its contradiction. And this is one of the novel themes of contemporary bourgeois ideology. For it would take a feat of ingenuity beyond sanity to argue the recurrence of harmony amidst the brutal strife of our age. Freud, therefore, reverses the traditional bourgeois contention and provides, instead, a rationalization for the eternity of conflict and opposition. But eternal conflict and eternal harmony come to the same thing. From the latter perspective nothing need be done; from the former, nothing can be done.

These views illustrate the intimate connection between theories of human nature and views of politics. Marx stresses the uniqueness, development, and creativity of human experience because in these historical characteristics he sees both the evidence and the hope of revolutionary transformation. Freud's political perspective grows out of a view of human nature which maintains that

> what was acquired by our ancestors is certainly an important part of what we inherit. When we speak of our "archaic heritage" we are generally thinking only of the id and we apparently assume that no ego is yet in existence at the beginning of the individual's life. But we must not overlook the fact that id and ego are originally one, and it does not imply a mystical overevaluation of heredity if we think it credible that, even before the ego exists, its subsequent lines of development, tendencies and reactions are already determined. The psychological peculiarities of families, races and nations, even in the attitude towards analysis, admit of no other explanation.[34]

The view expressed in this passage is continuous with the position that Freud enunciated in *Totem and Taboo,* according to which primal murder and guilt are the inheritance of every new generation. Each child repeats in fantasy the original act of the rebellious sons against their father. Philip Rieff notes that

> it was Freud's propensity to defer to acts of violence as the original repressed substrata of all social action. Compound the recapitulation theory with this belief, add his understanding of the basic wishes of children as egoistic and murderous, and you have Freud's reasoning that the later neurotic *wishes* coincide with the *deeds* of primitive men.[35]

But we needn't stop here. With the addition of two other Freudian contentions—that we all share the wishes of primitives and neurotics, and that the primordial horde which murdered the original father never overcame its original guilt and self-renunciation, we arrive at a critical political judgment: rebellion is futile. "Political-religious history is a record of man's irrational attempts to reinstate the primal father."[36] There may well have been an "advance" in the internalization of self-restraint. But the result is conclusive: each child of each generation must renounce its hatred of its father and reinstate the paternal authority in the world and in itself. As the past prevails, so the authority of the past prevails.

Freud maintained an exact parallel between the primitive and the child.[37] But the experience of childhood is the primary determinant of our lives. We are not so far from primitives ourselves; but what the first "horde" committed in fact we merely wish through dream and fantasy. For in our social life we share with the primitive an identical desire:

> Why the great man should rise to significance at all we have no doubt whatever. We know that the great majority of people have a strong need for authority which they can admire, to which they can submit, and which dominates and even ill-treats them. *We have learned from the psychology of the individual whence comes this need of the masses.* It is the longing for the father that lives in each of us from his childhood days [emphasis added].[38]

Children, like primitives, stand in terror of uncontrollable forces. The father they would destroy, or have destroyed, is the ultimate source of their protection. Therefore, we are all caught in an inexorable dilemma; we envy and hate the same being we rely upon for our security. Rebellion must be followed by counterrebellion, permission by renewed repression. The masses move between the desire to be dominated and envy of the power of those who dominate them.

Turning from the content of Freud's position to the method by which he maintains it, the first thing we note is the presupposition that the group can be understood on the basis of the psychology of the individual. For Freud persists in viewing society as the conjunction of distinctly formed individuals. "All emotions, Freud supposed, begin privately and are rationalized outward."[39] If we reconsider this contention through Marxist terms we understand that Freud has assumed the private realm of the bourgeoisie and transported the conflict between the elite individual and the masses back into some mythical, primordial past. Even the term "Massenpsychologie," which Freud adopted, like the use of the term "horde" in *Moses and Monotheism* and *Totem and Taboo*, is rich in reactionary connotations. The group is continually compared with savages and neurotics, and is described, like the id, as everything the ego is not. Not only is the group a mob, an irrational mass much like our irrational passions, but the mind itself is intelligible on the model of the mass threatening the individual and restrained by a ruling elite:

> Our mind, that precious instrument by whose means we maintain ourselves alive, is no peacefully self-contained unity. It is rather to be compared with a modern State in which a mob, eager for enjoyment and destruction, has to be held down forcibly by a prudent superior class.[40]

Freud's image of the mind was as much the result of his view of social conflict as his view of society resulted from projecting individual psychology onto the group. In fact, the positions are inseparable.

> In order to make a correct judgment upon the morals of groups, one must take into consideration the fact that when individuals come together in a group all their individual inhibitions fall away and all the cruel, brutal and destructive instincts, which lie dormant in individuals as relics of a primitive mob, are stirred up to find free gratification.[41]

The same complex of notions appears again: primitive, irrational, archaic, inherited—the ahistorical, recurrent core of our being. For we bring with us at birth "fragments of phylogenetic origin." We are intimately shaped by what we have inherited from primitive experience; our civilized egos not only disguise the power of our own individual irrationality, but of the archaic core of that libidinous heritage which forms the foundation of all our lives. This inherited state includes "not only dispositions, but also ideational contents, memory traces of the experiences of former generations."[42]

The introduction of the notion of inherited primitive memory permits Freud to connect the individual and the mass: *We have bridged the gap between individual and mass psychology and can treat peoples as we do the individual neurotic*" (emphasis added].[43] Individuals are rendered social through the inheritance of an act of patricide and remorse. This historical trauma is transmitted through the core of our being, and leads us either to the repetition of subordination or the singular power to dominate the group. Everything in Freud's method sinks to the primitive, the past, the dead. His biology rests on the tendency toward dissolution; his anthropology focuses on the persistence of impotence and futile rage. So Freud can only see the similarity of modern human beings with the mythical primitives of his theory. For the modern "also remains infantile and needs protection, even when . . . fully grown."[44]

But what are we to make of Freud's insistence on his Lamarckian ethnology in the face of later contrary evidence? He claims to be aware of the evidence that has been brought against the presuppositions of *Totem and Taboo;* he rejects it. His reason is arresting:

> Above all, however, I am not an ethnologist, but a psychologist. It was my good right to select from ethnological data what would serve me for my analytic work.[45]

Yes, but the working presuppositions of this analytic work were based to a very large extent on the carefully selected ethnographic data. Not all circles are vicious. But Freud's reliance upon anthropology for the elaboration of his individual psychology and his consequent construction of the anthropology upon the principles of the individual mind merely succeed in reifying the bourgeois present as a permanent feature of human existence. There is no real place for growth, development, or transcendence. *An Outline of Psychoanalysis,* one of Freud's last works, ends with a remarkable reflection:

> Those who have a liking for generalization and sharp distinctions may say that the external world, in which the individual finds himself exposed after being detached from his parents, represents the power of the present; that his id, with its inherited trends, represents the organic past; and that the superego, which comes to join them later, represents more than anything the

cultural past, an after-experiencing of which, as it were, the child has to pass through during the few years of his early life. It is scarcely likely that such generalizations can be wholly correct. Some of the cultural acquisitions have undoubtedly left a deposit behind in the *id;* much of what is contributed by the superego will awaken an echo in the id; many of the child's new experiences will be intensified because they are repetitions of some primeval phylogenetic experience.

> *Was du ererbt von deinen Vätern hast*
> *Erwirb es, um es zu besitzen.*

> (What thou hast inherited from thy fathers,
> Acquire to make it thine.—*Faust*)

Thus the superego takes up a kind of intermediate position between the id and the external world; it unites in itself the influences of the present and of the past. In the emergence of the superego we have before us, as it were, an example of the way in which *the present is turned into the past.*[46]

Marx speaks with a different voice:

> In bourgeois society living labor is but a means to increase accumulated labor. In communist society accumulated labor is but a means to widen, to enrich, to promote the existence of the laborer.
> In bourgeois society, therefore, *the past dominates the present; in communist society the present dominates the past. In bourgeois society capital is independent and has individuality, while the living person is dependent and has no individuality.*[47]

Freud's View of Human Nature

We have noted the main differences between Marx and Freud, but we have not yet directly treated their views of human nature. In what follows I am interested in isolating the features of their systems that are in fundamental contradiction. For Freud, human beings are characterized in the following way:[48]

- The human psyche is a system of energy, rooted in the physical/chemical processes of the body. This energy is a quantity whose "production, increase or diminution, distribution and displacement"[49] determines the condition of the individual.
- Human life is governed by instincts, the psychic representatives of the continually flowing excitation arising in the body. Instincts are "wholly determined by their origin in a somatic source,"[50] the aim of the instinct being the removal of this source of stimulation.[51]
- This energy is dualistic in form and can be characterized as sexual vs. self-preservative, self-directed vs. outer-directed, or erotic vs. aggressive. (These Freud's descriptions at different stages of his theoretical development.)[52]

- The id is the vital stratum of the mind, "a cauldron of seething excitement,"[53] the source of instincts and the repository of the experiences that have been repressed by the ego. The id is the exclusive source of our energy, and the carrier of inherited memories.
- The ego is that part of the id which has been modified by contact with the external world. "The ego represents what we call reason and sanity, in contrast to the id which contains the passions."[54] The ego "borrows its energy from the id" and "on the whole has to carry out the intentions of the id."[55] The ego has no purpose of its own.
- The id and the ego are governed by different principles: the id drives blindly toward the release of tension; the ego imposes restraint and delay upon the id. The basic laws of functioning of the id are called the primary processes and are regulated by the following principles:[56] (1) the *pleasure principle*—the id presses for the immediate discharge of tension and experiences pleasure as a result; (2) the *constancy principle*—the organism tends to maintain a state of equilibrium, that is, unchanging tension; (3) the *Nirvana principle*—the organism tends to reduce the amount of its internal tension to zero. The ordinary laws of logic do not apply. Instead the id is governed by (4) *displacement and condensation,* exemption from mutual contradiction, the replacement of reality by wish, and the tendency to repeat earlier experiences.
- The life and death instincts, sexuality and destructiveness, are first directed toward ourselves and only subsequently directed outward toward the world of things and people.

Narcissistic or ego-libido seems to be the great reservoir from which the object-cathexes are sent out and into which they are withdrawn once more; the narcissistic libidinal cathexis of the ego is the original state of things, realized in earliest childhood, and is merely covered by the later extrusions of libido, but in essentials persists behind them.[57]

The same description applies to the destructive energies; they are first directed toward ourselves and only later displaced toward the world.

- Love and affection are essentially aim-inhibited forms of sexuality; the other is a means to my satisfaction; love of another is a defense against excessive narcissism.[58]
- Human beings are intrinsically destructive; they take satisfaction in the subordination, humiliation, and destruction of other human beings whether these activities serve any "practical" function or not.[59]
- The function of the ego is to reconcile the erotic and destructive

demands of the id with the injunctions of the superego and the requirements of the external world.[60]

- Reason and moral judgment reside in two distinct agencies; moral reflection is less a function of reason than of the irrational superego. Freud enjoins us to "keep firmly to the . . . separation of the ego from an observing, critical, punishing agency."[61]

Now, or course, we cannot find any point by point Marxist rebuttal of these Freudian conceptions. But I think it is prima facie evident that Marx's historical-dialectical view of human social nature is incompatible with the previously outlined Freudian account, and the remainder of this work is an effort to substantiate that original impression. Nevertheless, the appearance of incompatibility between Marx and Freud has been challenged by an argument that very much requires our response. Simply put, the counterposition holds that Freud's account of the sexual instinct, in contrast to his view of the relative inflexibility of the ego instinct, emphasized the malleability of sexuality, and that this conception makes possible an agreement between the two theories on the critical issue of the transformation of human nature. Even as late as 1933, Freud wrote that:

> The sexual instincts are remarkable for their plasticity, for the facility with which they can change their aims, for their interchangeability—for the ease with which they can substitute one form of gratification for another, and for the way in which they can be held in suspense, as has been so well illustrated by the aim-inhibited instincts.[62]

To help resolve the issue, I should like to turn briefly to Freud's earlier essay "The Instincts and their Vicissitudes," which deals explicitly with the question before us. Freud begins by outlining four possible transformations of the sexual instinct: (1) reversal into its opposite; (2) turning around upon the subject; (3) repression; and (4) sublimation. These transformations are presented as particular instances of the fact that the sexual instincts have "in a high degree the capacity to act vicariously for one another and that they can readily change their object."[63] So it does seem, at first glance, that Freud's theory of instinct is much less fixed and mechanical than our account has acknowledged.

But it is crucial to recall Freud's view of instinct in this essay. The instinct is the "mental representative of the stimuli emenating from within the organism and penetrating to the mind, and . . . a measure of the demand made upon the energy of the latter in consequence of its connection with the body."[64] The instinct has four dimensions: (1) its impetus—the amount of force; (2) its aim—satisfaction, achieved through the abolition of the stimulation affecting the organism; (3) its object—that through which it achieves its aim; and (4) its source—the somatic process from which the stimuli arises, "that which gives the instinct its *distinct and essential character*"[65] (emphasis added). This last point is critical, for as Freud goes on to remark, "The differences in the mental effects produced by the different instincts may be traced to the differences in their sources."[66]

Freud is attempting to account for the fact that the instincts act for one another and change their object (note that he does not say that they can change their nature). The difficulty is that his metapsychology will not permit an explanation of this supposed occurrence. The problem derives from the manner in which Freud ties the aim of the instinct to its source: "Instincts are wholly determined by their origin in a somatic source, in mental life we know them only by their aims."[67] But the source of the instinct is specific; it is that which gives the instinct its *distinct* character. As Laplance and Potalis note:

> Even when he speaks of the instinct's "final aim" Freud is referring to a specific aim tied to a specific instinct . . . *Freud asserts the thesis of the specificity of aim of each component instinct* [emphasis added].[68]

If the aim of the instinct is specific—the removal of *this particular stimuli*—how can it be satisfied by anything other than its originally intended specific object. How can instincts "act vicariously for one another" when they are determined by the specific somatic source that defines them? The need for food, which is equally specific, cannot be satisfied by anything but food. I know that Freud claims that such a transformation takes place, but his metapsychology makes it impossible to understand the process. In fact it leads to the conclusion that no such process is possible. The same result occurs when we examine the two vicissitudes—reversal of aim and turning around on the subject. The first transformation is subdivided into two processes: "a change from active to passive and a reversal of content." An example of the first is the pair of opposites, sadism–masochism. But Freud notes, in a very significant phrase, that "the reversal here concerns only the aims of the instincts."[69] That is, nothing else changes—not the source, not the impetus, and, most critically, not the object. We reach the converse point by considering the turning around of the instinct upon the subject. In this case Freud notes that "the essence of the process is the change of the object, while the aim remains unchanged."[70]

In one case, then, we have a change in aim while the object remains constant and in the other we have a change in object while the aim remains constant. This is exactly what I intend by calling the supposed transformation mechanical rather than dialectical. Freud's analogy remains the transformation of liquid forced through a series of channels or pipes, a figure he actually used in "Three Essays on Sexuality."[71] None of this gives us any possible understanding of how masochism can satisfy a need for sadism defined as the removal of a stimulus in the somatic source. A force, like a stream of liquid, can flow in one direction or be deflected, but this does not really help us to understand human transformations. If an individual need was defined from the beginning as intentional and social—the need for reciprocity, for example—we could understand how both sadism and masochism could be viewed as disturbances of this particular desire. But on the account of instincts based on somatic sources, no such understanding is intelligible.

The only notion introduced by Freud that would seem to suggest genuine transformation is "sublimation," and that term is presented in the most sketchy and underdeveloped fashion. The use of the concept must answer the question of how energy that is sexual can be changed into artistic or intellectual energy. I don't believe Freud provided any answer. His specific studies, such as his analysis of Leonardo, tend to reduce aesthetic activity to its sexual origins rather than provide an account of the development of a new and autonomous function out of the old.

At one point in Fenichel's discussion of the issue he distinguishes (a) a child who learns to write well; (b) a child inhibited in writing; (c) a child who writes meticulously; and (d) a child who smears. All of them have "displaced anal-erotic instinctual quantities to the function of writing."[72] Only in the case of the first child has sublimation taken place. But what does the key term "displacement" mean?

> When a person suppresses an irritation and subsequently in another situation reacts violently to an insignificant provocation, it must be assumed that the first quantity of irritation, which was suppressed, was still at work. The energy of the forces behind the mental phenomena is displaceable.[73]

So we discover that displacement is involved in sublimation and that in displacement the first quantity of energy is still at work. In other words, anal-erotic energy is still at work in the case of the first child, who wishes to write. But if this is so, what is the nature of the supposed transformation and what can it possibly mean to say that joy in writing is the expression of anal-erotic impulses? The mechanical strain in Freud's position remains fixed.

CHAPTER THREE

Marx's View of Human Nature

Now that we have presented the basic structure of Freud's view of human nature, how shall we proceed with Marx? Since Freud held that men and women are intrinsically destructive, egoistic, and illogical, do we need merely to negate these characteristics to arrive at Marx's position? There is a strong tendency among those who have pierced the reified Freudian view of basic human evil to affirm in response that human beings are essentially good. According to this view we are fundamentally moral at the core of our being and would naturally move toward our own self-realization were we not frustrated by external impediments. This is neither a new contention nor a new debate. The philosophes of the Enlightenment asserted the same position against Luther and Calvin, as did Rousseau against the Hobbesian conviction of natural human ruthlessness.

There is one significant difference, however. In the past the proponents of natural goodness argued on the basis of an assumption of progressive social transformation. Today, the argument is raised more from a situation of social stagnation amidst bourgeois cynicism. It is an act of willed buoyancy; in the present age sanity rests upon hope. The contention of natural human goodness it is the result of a simplistic wish for ontological certitude where only political labor can provide grounds for confidence. Since the claim to natural goodness is more a compensation for the absence of a vital social movement than its articulation, its consequences tend to be politically regressive. There are two points worthy of note.

First, it is no less a reification of human nature to claim its "natural" goodness than its "natural" evil. The mode of predication remains fetishized. I do not intend this assertion as the denial of human nature. But that nature cannot be characterized in a Marxist mode as intrinsically predisposed toward any specifiable end. The heart of Marx's contribution to our understanding of human nature lies in his conviction that *we are neither wholly formed nor wholly unformed at birth.* We form ourselves in the process of social–historical production. We are simultaneously the impediments that prevent our self-realization, and beings capable of transcending these limitations. To be human is to be required, by the very absence of a fixed, instinctual disposition, to create one's own nature. But we are not predetermined by that requirement to realize ourselves or even to strive in any predefined direction.

Marx noted that the first stage of transition from one social epoch to another is marked by the introduction of new content within old forms.[1] This is precisely what occurs when the Freudian view of natural human viciousness is supposedly stood on its head. A new content is poured into the older vessel and adopts its shape. We are seen as entities of a *radically different sort;* but we remain *entities* nonetheless. It is in fact very difficult to believe seriously in human nature as self-productive. Our lives are so thoroughly alienated that we respond more quickly to the image of human nature as given and fixed than to our own slumbering sense of potentially transcendent creativity. In a society that affords little scope for self-initiation, it is not surprising that we conceive of ourselves as little different from the remainder of nature. We come to view our own characteristics, to return to Marx's phrase, "as self-evident laws of nature." A socialist movement, in which a Marxist theory and vision of human nature plays a vital part, has the obligation to oppose such reification. It is of the deepest practical significance to maintain the seriousness of Marx's view of human nature as self-transformative. To lose this vision, to become embarrassed by its rapture, is to contract in resignation before the density of the social world. It is to have lost any prospect of revolution.

This leads us to a second difficulty. The conviction that we are basically good tends to promote a strange complacency in regard to our own deformation. Those who view human nature as continually pressing toward moral growth are lulled into a false assurance of incorruptibility. The Freudian dualism of appearance and reality is reinstated, and we are consoled with the faith that under the current social pathology there is substantial reason for optimism. This view may take an explicitly negative form. Drawing on Freud's view of libido, Lionel Trilling can assert that "culture is not all-powerful. . . . There is a residue of human quality beyond the reach of cultural control, and . . . this residue of human quality, elemental as it may be, serves to bring culture itself under criticism and keeps it from being absolute."[2] Or the position can be given positive expression:

> Man demonstrates *in his own nature* a pressure toward fuller and fuller Being, more and more perfect actualization of his humanness in exactly the same naturalistic, scientific sense that an acorn may be said to be "pressing toward" being an oak tree, or that a tiger can be observed to "push toward" being tigerish, or a horse toward being equine. . . . The environment does not give him the potentialities of capacities; he *has* them in inchoate or embryonic form, just as he has embryonic arms and legs.[1]

> *Existence and the unfolding of the specific powers of an organism are one and the same.* All organisms have an inherent tendency to actualize their specific potentialities.[4]

These comments of Maslow and Fromm express the same reification they are designed to combat; they manifest that repetition of old modalities that Marx noted. A reductive conception of humanity and scientific method animates this perspective. For Marx there are no *specific* potentialities inherent in human beings; the analogy of the acorn and the oak could hardly have been better chosen to indicate precisely what is mistaken with the ontology of self-realization. For the human being at birth does not possess the internal itinerary that leads by preordained steps to the transformations that structure inorganic or merely animal nature.

What does mark us as unique is the capacity to transform our nature as given. The theory of self-realization is caught in a fatal difficulty. Either it holds that the end of human life is prestructured in the code of our genetic and psychic constitution at birth, or it denies any such view of "specific potentialities. But on the first alternative it must either ignore everything we have learned from historical and social study about the variability of the human condition, or it must pronounce one of these forms natural and the others unnatural deviations. The second alternative is no better. For if human nature at birth is intrinsically malleable and given its determinate form through concrete social activity, we are forced to acknowledge that the very existence and comprehension of "self," "actualization," and "fuller Being" are culturally divergent. We can then insist on the formula of universal self-realization, but we will have to recognize the emptiness of the abstraction to which we are committed.

It is of some comfort to see ourselves as constantly "pressing" toward our moral fulfillment. But such a vision leads us away from social practice to a new narcissism. If we are essentially good at our core, if under the surface of our fragmented and distorted lives the goal of our striving already exists, we are not so much in need of remaking the world as of delving inward to find our "true selves." This has been a major social tendency of the last decade, though it has taken very different forms. For some, the doctrine of primordial goodness has led away to new forms of solipsism, new efforts at immediate transcendence. The "growth movement" has made a fetish of the "true self" and abhorred political practice. Yet there is no "real person" behind our roles, character, and patterns of social action. We are our being in the world, though we are not fated to *this* world. The real self is the counterpart of that real world; neither can exist without the other. This is not to deny self-reflectiveness, but to locate the self within the world of other selves, and within the domain of labor, art, and public practice. But this world does not yet fully exist, and, consequently, neither do we.

For others whose lives have been concerned with political practice the present period has witnessed the exhausting fall from ahistorical optimism to despair. For the counterculture of the sixties, America, greening, was to come to fruition in uncorrupted innocence. The appeal was not to character as it had been shaped in the social world, but to the core of goodness which unites us all beyond class and power. For much of the left, there was a chiliastic vision trembling in anticipation of revolution. Behind every economic decline, every strike, every act of social disobedience or rebellion a burgeoning revolution was perceived. It was as if one were seated in a theatre constantly awaiting the revelation of the revolutionary players whom we would join in their triumph. And yet, the curtain fluttered so many times without being borne aloft. Finally, as it must, hope so poorly nurtured turned to despair, and the apathy of the present moment descended with the dimming of the lights. When the "core of goodness" refuses to reveal itself, there is nothing left but the surface of corruption, and that "surface" comes quickly to define the totality.

The Marxist Dialectic and Human Nature

Marx's view of human nature begins with human beings in their social relations:

> Individuals producing in society, and therefore a socially determined production by individuals, naturally constitutes the starting point.[5]

> But man is not an abstract being, squatting outside the world. Man is the world of men, the State and society.[6]

It is above all necessary to avoid postulating "society" once again as an abstraction confronting the individual. The individual *is* the *social being*. . . . Individual human life and species-life are not different things, even though the mode of existence of individual life is necessarily either a more *specific* or a more *general* mode of species-life, or that of species-life a *specific* or more *general* mode of individual life.[7]

The smallest intelligible unit of social explanation is human beings in specific social relations transforming the natural environment through historically determinate technology. These terms are "all members of one entity, different sides of one unit."[8] The reciprocal action of the various aspects of the totality is what I shall mean by the term "dialectic." The various sides of the totality are both different from each other and inseparable from each other. Each term derives its meaning from its place in the totality; each term fills out the meaning of the others.

Now, these phrases of Marx—"The individual *is* the social *being*." "Man is the world of men"—indicate that the individual and society are inseparable. But they are not identical; that is, the individual does not disappear within the social whole. For society is no more intelligible without the individual than is the individual without society. This is a simple but basic point. Some readers of Marx take such affirmations as "production is consumption and consumption simultaneously production" to mean an equivalence of terms. But the "is" in the proposition does not mean abstract self-identity; it means dialectical unity. Marx makes the point very clearly when he writes that "thought and being are indeed *distinct* but they also form a unity."[9] He himself underscores the term "distinct." "Being" is independent of thought. There was a time when the world existed without consciousness. Why then does Marx maintain that these two notions make up a unity? First, because it is the nature of this "being" to give rise to "thought" and it is the nature of thought to transform the being out of which it has been produced. Second, because "being" is an abstraction, and the character of being before thought is distinct from the being which thought transforms. Finally, each historical epoch conceives of this "being" distinctly.

The heart of the dialectic is the manner in which the aspects of the totality reciprocally transform each other and the totality. This is what distinguishes a dialectical process from mere mechanical interaction. The more mechanistic a system, the more its aggregate properties can be deduced from the nature and laws of its component parts. If we drive one billiard ball into a group they will scatter in such a way that their new locations are theoretically deducible from the application of a general law to their initial positions. The kind of change they undergo is additive and external. They may be marked or dented by the collision, but they do not change their nature as a result of it. Their collective weight, mass and motion are intelligible on the basis of a combination of their separate properties. Each remains basically in the aggregate what it was outside of it.

Freud's system remains mechanical because he does not see the individual essentially transformed through social life. That is why concrete historical change plays no part in his analysis. Human beings are fundamentally the same in primitive agricultural societies and in contemporary corporate capitalism. Of course instinct is channeled toward socially acceptable ends. But Freud cannot give up the mechanical analogy which insists that the entities still retain their original identity under their complicated interactions.

> People give the name "love" to the relation between a man and a woman whose genital needs have led them to found a family; but they also give the name "love" to the positive feelings between parents and children, and between the brothers and sisters of a family, although we are obliged to describe this as "aim-inhibited love" or "affection." Love with an inhibited aim was in fact originally *fully sensual love, and it is still so in man's unconscious* [emphasis added].[10]

At one point in an argument designed to prove that Freud's thought is dialectical, Reich gives the case away: "As development progresses the old element is not entirely lost through transformation. While a part of the trait *develops into its opposite,* another continues to exist *unchanged* (emphasis added).[11] In a dialectical process no original part remains unchanged. An acorn develops into a tree, but no dissection of the tree will discover an acorn still contained beneath the tree's exterior. And what of the part of the trait that develops into its opposite?

> Transformation into the opposite is a property which, Freud says, all the instincts in general possess. In such reversal *the original instinct is not destroyed but is fully maintained in its opposite* [emphasis added].[12]

One part of the instinct remains the same, another changes into its opposite. But the part that is transformed *is fully maintained in its opposite.* This description does not characterize a dialectical development. The paradigm of Freud's notion of change is derived from physics or hydraulics. The analogy is to a particle reversing its charge, or a fluid diverted into a new channel.

> We therefore have to conclude that the sexual impulse-excitations are exceptionally "plastic," if I may use the word. One of them can step in place of another; if satisfaction of one is denied in reality, satisfaction of another can offer full recompense. They are related to one another *like a network of communicating canals filled with fluid* [emphasis added].[13]

The fluid does not develop; it merely changes position. The way in which Freud defines id and instinct precludes the possibility of their development. They can be detoured in novel ways, but they remain the same.

> It should be apparent from what has been said so far that Freud conceived the psychic apparatus primarily as a closed system. . . . Of course, streams of influence reach it from the external world. But once these have activated it, the apparatus proceeds to operate within its own intrapsychic territory according to its own autonomous laws. *Its connection with the world is not one of essential involvement, but only of casual interplay* [emphasis added].[14]

This is a perfect description of a mechanical system. For Marx, on the contrary, human beings are *essentially involved* with the structure of their social world.

This reference to an "essential characteristic" of human nature may expose us to the charge that we are violating the principle of concreteness which we ourselves insisted upon in criticizing the "universalism" of self-realization. If, in Marx's view, human beings must be understood in their sociohistorical context, and if the mode of social life has varied as dramatically as Marx himself insisted, what can be meant by the reference to essential human nature, even if that nature is defined as "dialectical," "social," or the "free conscious activity of the species"?

Two points: first, the difficulty with self-realization is not that it is an abstraction, but that it is the wrong abstraction. Second, the present objection seems to assume that we are forced to choose between a wholly abstract and a wholly concrete designation of human nature. But no such choice is required. In Marx's method, terms can only be understood in reference to each other, and particularly in relation to what appears as their opposite. The concept "concrete" can consequently only be understood in reference to the concept "abstract." The simplest way to grasp this point is to note that "concrete" is in itself an abstract concept. Nothing is concrete in itself, but only in reference to a particular perspective. Therefore it is crucial to understand the basic perspective from which the designation "concrete" proceeds. This perspective will, of course, contain abstract terms. So, the concrete can only be understood in reference to abstract categories.

If you should now object that the preceding paragraph is itself too abstract, if you should insist that merely saying that the concrete must be referred to the abstract does not indicate which abstraction to begin with—you would be correct. We cannot begin with something purely concrete; nor can we begin with the truism that we need to use abstractions. The question is: which abstraction is the appropriate starting point?

Since it would take a separate essay to discuss this issue, let us simply refer to Marx's own work. He began his analysis in *Capital* not with "the secret of private accumulation," which might be thought the more specific and historical origin of capitalism, but with the commodity. His choice can claim two particular advantages; first, that the notion "commodity" is the most specific abstraction we require to understand the foundations of capitalism. Anything more abstract would not single out capitalism; anything less abstract would fail to grasp what all capitalist systems have in common.

Second, if we analyze the concept "commodity" we will be led to the other concepts through which to analyze the capitalist system—use value, exchange value, exchange, money, capital, surplus value, wages, and accumulation. Although it would be a mistake to think that the order of these concepts paralleled a similar historical order, it is nevertheless true that the derivation of these concepts from each other makes possible the understanding of historical change.

> Whenever we speak of production, then, what is meant is always production at a definite stage of social development—production by social individuals. It might seem, therefore, that in order to talk about production at all we must either pursue the process of historic development through its different phases, or declare beforehand that we are dealing with a specific historic epoch such as, e.g., modern bourgeois production, which is indeed our particular theme. However, all epochs of production have certain common traits, common characteristics. *Production in general* is an abstraction, but a rational abstraction in so far as it really brings out and fixes the common element and thus saves us repetition. Still, this *general* category, this common element sifted out by comparison, is itself segmented many times over and splits into different determinations. Some determinations belong to all epochs, others only to a few.[15]

The Need for a Concept of Human Nature

The notion that human nature is essentially mediated by social relations, tools, and the natural environment is also abstract. The question is whether it is a *rational abstraction*. I have chosen to emphasize this point because, as I have noted, it is sometimes held that Marx wholly denied any abstract human nature. Instead, he is supposed to have held that human beings are totally malleable and derive whatever nature they possess from their concrete social–historical environment. Furthermore, it is argued, speaking of abstract human nature is ideological, because it converts a particular characteristic of men and women into an essential characteristic of all human beings.

But the rebuttal to this last point is as clear as the need for employing abstractions: if we omit a general conception of human nature we stand in jeopardy of reification for a reason opposite to the one just proposed. If we lack an abstract criterion of the distinguishing features of human nature we deny ourselves a standard by which to judge whether the phenomenon before us is human or not. Everything becomes indiscriminately "equal"; no manifestation is more human than the next.

> Bentham is a purely English phenomenon. Not even excepting our philosopher Christian Wolf, in no time and in no country has the most homespun commonplace every strutted about in so self-satisfied a way. . . . The principle of utility was no discovery of Bentham. He simply reproduced in a dull way what Helvetius and other Frenchmen had said with esprit in the 18th century. To know what is useful for a dog, one must study dog-nature. This nature is not to be deduced from the principle of utility. Applying this to man, he that would criticize all human acts, movements, relations, etc., by the principle of utility, *must first deal with human nature in general, and then with human nature in each historical epoch* [emphasis added].[16]

To understand human beings in any epoch we must have an abstract concept of "human nature." This contention rests on two arguments. The first can be gleaned by simply paying close attention to Marx's actual language. Note precisely what Marx asserts: "He that would *criticize* all human acts . . ." We cannot ground our estimate of human beings in their social relations unless we possess a normative principle of human nature. Unless we have some notion of what it is to be a fully developed human being, we have no ground whatever for condemning any social system or set of institutional arrangements: we cannot employ such notions as "alienation" or "exploitation"; we cannot recommend socialism as a "richer" or "higher" form of human existence. In short, unless we possess a normative criterion—a principle for distinguishing and grading the manifestations of human beings in the world—we are without a standard that would justify our political commitment to socialism. This is the way I understand Marx's contention, and I believe he was correct. A neutral, scientific, positivistic Marxism is a contradiction in terms. The fundamental Marxist categories are simultaneously descriptive and prescriptive; fact and value make up a dialectical unity. They are neither identical nor intelligible in separation from each other.

But there is a second argument on behalf of the need for articulating an abstract concept of human nature. Paradoxically, it derives from its apparent opposite, the total plasticity of concrete human nature. Consider two statements of this second position:

> All history is nothing but a continuous transformation of human nature.[17]

> Man is the sole animal capable of working his way out of the merely animal state—his normal state is one appropriate to his consciousness, *one to be created by himself*.[18]

Once again the specific language is crucial. Marx refers to the *transformation* of human nature. But "transformation" is different from mere "change." Only that which persists can be transformed, for unless the differences are rooted in something more fundamental than sheer variety there is nothing to be transformed at all. *Transformation,* in other words, requires *persistence* as well as *modification.*

The second quote makes the case even clearer. Engels contends that man is the sole animal capable of creating the condition appropriate to himself. Now the term "appropriate" is once again normative. But the point takes us further, for it rests on the necessary assumption that something distinguishes human beings from other animals. What precisely is it about ourselves as human beings that permits us to transcend our "merely animal state" and produce ourselves in accordance with conditions appropriate to our own consciousness? Other animals cannot accomplish this transformation. There is some capacity, some power, some creativity that distinguishes human nature as such. It is this quality of self-generation that continually transforms human nature in history. What is common to all human beings is their capacity to reconstitute their own being. So, the arguments for human malleability and for an abstract human nature do not contradict each other. They are two aspects of a dialectical unity; *our distinguishing characteristic as human beings is our capacity to give ourselves specific determinations in social time.* Neither a merely abstract nor a wholly concrete being is humanly intelligible. Marx rejects the position of nominalists for whom only the "immediate" is real. He also denies the contentions of abstract humanists and "metaphysical philosophers" for whom the common property is of sole concern.

In saying that the abstract and concrete are aspects of one structure, we have advanced our argument. But we have advanced to a new abstraction which, though more determinate than before, needs still to be specified further.

> Labour is, in the first place, a process in which both man and Nature participate, and in which man of his own accord starts, regulates, and controls the material reactions between himself and Nature. He opposes himself to Nature as one of her own forces, setting in motion arms and legs, head and hands, the natural forces of his body, in order to appropriate Nature's productions in a form adopted to his own wants. By this acting on the external world and changing it, he at the same time changes his own nature. He develops his slumbering powers and compels them to act in obedience to his sway. We are not now dealing with those primitive instinctive forms of labour that remind us of the mere animal. . . . We presuppose labour in a form that stamps it as exclusively human.[19]

This statement makes an admirable beginning for our analysis. Marx notes two points: first, that human beings are natural, embodied, material beings; and second, that we are capable of will, imagination, and creativity. The root of Marx's anthropology is in the double contention that we are of nature and more than mere nature. (Whenever Marxist praxis is in decay one of these sides prevails to the exclusion of the other.) Human history is "differentiated from natural history as the evolutionary process of self-conscious organisms."[20] The animal uses nature, but man masters it. "Unlike the hunter, the wolf does not spare the doe which would provide it with young deer in the next year."[21] We possess this superiority over other animals only because we can comprehend the laws of nature and apply them in practice. Therefore, while

> a spider conducts operations that resemble those of a weaver, and a bee puts to shame many an architect in the construction of her cells . . . what distinguishes the worst architect from the best of bees is this, that the architect raises his structure in the imagination before he erects it in reality. At the end of every labour-process, we get a result that already existed in the imagination of the labourer at its commencement. He not only effects a change of form in the material on which he works, but he also realizes a purpose of his own that gives the law to his modus operandi, and to which he must subordinate his will.[22]

We carry out a purpose of our own and through its completion make ourselves determinate. We are forced to shape a recalcitrant nature which is both like us, since we are "one of her own forces," but not yet formed in a manner "adopted to our own wants." In fact, *we* do not yet exist in a form adopted to our own wants. But since we are natural, we can only reconstitute ourselves by remaking the world of which we are an aspect. Because we have the power of imagination we can transcend the immediately given; but because we are natural, we cannot transcend it any way we please. Since our purpose is realized in the world it posesses a structure to which we must "subordinate our will." Both realism and idealism are contributions to the truth.

The motion of Freud's view of human nature is centripetal: everything is drawn toward the body and its instinctual satiation. But the Marxist vector is centrifugal: we cannot, in his view, locate ourselves within the confines of physical boundaries. Our "nature is outside ourselves." We are copresent with our worlds because our nature consists of a field of forces through which we relate ourselves to the natural and social dimensions of *our own being*. The origin of this field can be located "within us," but the terminus of our movement is the natural–social world. The food we consume in hunger is not merely an external means to our internal drives. It is first ours in imagination and then, if we are successful, it is ours—of us—in fact. So, to say that we are purposeful and natural is to say that we are directed toward the world as a continuation of our selves. "To say that man *lives* from nature means that nature is his *body* with which he must remain in a continuous interchange in order not to die."[23] Our ability to transform our slumbering powers into actual forces constitutes our creativity. Marx emphasized intentionality and purpose as much as any phenomenologist or "object-relational" therapist. But he understood that we and our "object" are social from our inception, and that the class structure of this social system has the power to thwart our intentionality as well as to realize it. Our selves are not "given" in a fixed form at birth, but are rather the result of our continuous transformation of the natural–social world.

Marx distinguished between natural characteristics—those attributes, powers, and tendencies we share with the remainder of the natural and animal world—and our species being, those features that differentiate us from other natural beings.[24]

> Man is directly a natural being. As a natural being, and as a living natural being he is, on the one hand, endowed with natural powers and faculties, which exist in him as tendencies and abilities, as drives. On the other hand, as a natural, embodied, sentient, objective being he is a suffering being, conditioned and limited being, like animals and plants. The objects of his drives exist outside himself as objects independent of him, yet they are objects of his needs, essential objects which are indispensable to the exercise and confirmation of his faculties. . . . A being which does not have *its nature outside itself* is not a natural being and does not share in the being of nature. A being which has no object outside itself is not an objective being.[25]

The plant cannot exist without the sun. But neither can the sun be what it is unless, in the context of nature, it promotes the growth of the plant. The plant is one of the determinations of the sun, just as this dyad is itself a determination of the soil, the atmosphere, and the remainder of nature. In this, human beings are no different from the remainder of nature. As human beings, however, we *experience* an essential connection with the objects of our needs, and thereby experience our separation from our own completion. What we lack is not merely the object, as independent, but our own self in its relation to the object we seek. We are conscious of having our nature outside of ourselves in a double sense: the objects we need are beyond our present possession, and our own capacities are similarly beyond our determination because they are intrinsically linked to the independence of the objective realm.

In contradiction to the bourgeois view, which tends to regard self-consciousness as a personal capacity for direct self-awareness, Marx views self-reflection as grounded in human community. It is in a community that we become selves through the social process of being so defined by others. In recognizing that we belong to the same species as those who define us as human, we experience the mediation between others and ourselves. In self-consciousness we adopt the attitude of others toward ourselves. We learn to do what others do—to refer to ourselves as beings in the world. But our knowledge is mediated through the standard of humanity that prevails in our social life. And this criterion defines us as human only through the continual activity of becoming human in social praxis.

But man is not merely a natural being; he is a *human* natural being. He is a being for himself, and, therefore, a *species-being;* and as such he has to authenticate himself in being as well as in thought. Consequently, *human objects* are not natural objects as they present themselves directly, nor is *human sense,* as it is immediately and objectively given, *human* sensibility and human objectivity. Neither objective nature nor subjective nature is directly presented in a form adequate to the *human* being.[26]

This passage links factors separated in the bourgeois perspective: our dependence on nature; our transcendence of nature; our self-consciousness as mediated through our awareness of our species as governed by criteria that define "humanity" as an achievement rather than a natural fact. In Freud's view we satisfy our natural instincts through natural objects. For Marx, we constitute objects as "human objects" by subjecting them to principles of human significance in the process of their appropriation. That is why, for Marx, production in the world and the self-production of human nature are intrinsically linked. We are compelled by our lack of predetermined instinctual nature to create ourselves in the course of imbuing the "natural" world with our own social being. We never confront nature, either in the external world or within our own organism, unmediated by our self-constituted social existence.

The human self is constituted in the world. This contention distinguishes the Marxist position from every religious or therapeutic movement that claims to transform the self without transforming the natural–social world. It is sometimes held that the cultivation of self-awareness is a distinct contribution of bourgeois culture which socialism, with its emphasis on collective life, would destroy. This view confuses two distinct notions: our awareness of ourselves, and introspection as the sole device for knowing ourselves. In other words, self-consciousness is identified with its privatistic bourgeois form. To be self-conscious is literally to be conscious of our self, and nothing more. The critical question concerns the nature of our self.

Capitalist culture isolates us from the world and other human beings. We are forced into an interior enclave. A virtue is then made of necessity and we are counseled to prize our seclusiveness as a unique cultural achievement. Since we believe with some justice that we stand in danger of losing ourselves in the world, we are inclined to believe that we can only "find ourselves" by turning our backs to the social realm and moving more deeply into our "real" self. Current attempts to purify the self before returning to the world miss the critical truth in Merleau-Ponty's observation:

We must reject that prejudice which makes "inner realities" out of love, hate, or anger, leaving them accessible to one single witness: the person who feels them. Anger, shame, hate, and love are not psychic facts hidden at the bottom of another's consciousness; they are types of behavior or styles of conduct which are visible from the outside. . . . *Emotion is not a psychic internal fact but rather a variation in our relations with others and the world.*[27]

No matter how profoundly we penetrate into the subject, we always find the world.[28]

This position is overstated, but it is the necessary counter to subjectivism.

One of the persistent themes of contemporary life asserts that our actions in the world, the roles we "play," are mere masquerades of our deeper reality. Buried beneath our social selves is our real "homuncular" self. We are admonished to strip away these artificial encumbrances so that we might reach the pristine essence behind social illusion. Fritz Perls states one of the basic assumptions of the contemporary therapy movement when he announces: "I am talking about the organism *per se*. I am not talking about ourselves as social beings. I don't talk about *pseudo*existence, but of the basic natural existence, the foundation of our being."[29] Perls is not condemning this particular society for its pseudoexistence. He is reproducing a particularly privatistic version of Freud's archeological perspective. The solution proposed, not surprisingly—since the social world is rejected—is a return to our biological being, our natural foundation.

Unfortunately, there is no *natural* biology to embrace, for there are no bodily functions that are not permeated with social meaning. Freud himself established this point for eating, sexuality, and defecation. Reich added the dimensions of posture, musculature, and breathing. Every historical epoch creates its own version of natural, primitive existence. The difficulty in our lives does not stem from the generic fact of "social roles." Roles are our *characteristic presence* in the world, an indication of our capacity to pursue organized processes in our social relations. A being that could not engage in social roles would be relegated to chaotic impulsiveness, routine, or reflex behavior. The destruction of the self does not derive from the sheer fact of "role," but from the *particular role* we are required to "play" in this society. The word "play" gives the case away. Since we experience our roles as alienating us from ourselves, we attempt to deny their significance by relegating them to triviality. Since our culture determines that work is "important" and play "insignificant," we construct the illusion that what we are in fact compelled to do in order to survive and flourish is of no real consequence. We would like to escape these odious social routines. The way out into the world is blocked; it is, in fact, the realm we wish to avoid. There seems no place to turn but into ourselves, to seek out some peaceful, loving core of the world, where social burdens are left behind.

Once, men and women sought to escape the pain of the world in religious fantasy. But secular society has destroyed this avenue of compensatory grace. Freud was right when he noted that "the neurosis takes, in our time, the place of the cloister."[30] The dichotomy between this world and "the other" has been reproduced in our lives as the schism between the real private self and the public other. We reserve what is most precious in ourselves for our personal existence, because the public realm is so foreign to our human desires. But we constantly discover that what we had marked off as our refuge from the world, our private being, is simply the form of social existence through which capitalist social relations establish their ubiquity.

Wealth and Scarcity

We have argued that the self and the social world are dialectically joined. Marx also maintained that self-consciousness is only possible in community, and that a distinguishing feature of this capacity is our recognition that our lives are inadequate in their given form. The same social life that articulates the standards we employ to judge ourselves as human, provides us with the capacity to measure our distance from our appropriate relationship to the world.

> The animal is one with its life activity. It does not distinguish the activity from itself. It is *its activity*. But man makes his life activity itself an object of his will and consciousness. He has a conscious life activity. It is not a determination with which he is completely identified. Conscious life activity distinguishes man from the life activity of animals . . . he is only a self-conscious being, i.e., his own life is an object for him, because he is a species-being.[31]

Just as we are of nature and other than nature, so we are our lives and other than our lives. This is the source of our freedom. We are not fixed in any specific determination. To the extent that we enjoy control over our social world, we have the capacity to regulate the emergence of our specific character. Community, freedom, self-consciousness, and transcendence are dialectically related. But, of course, this is the ideal condition. For us to be able to treat ourselves as "universal and consequently free beings"[32] we must have collective power over our own social life.

> In the type of *life activity* resides the whole character of a species, its species character; and free, conscious activity is the species character of human beings [emphasis added].[33]

Our character resides in our life activity, our social practice. It is through our social labor that we determine and transcend ourselves and construct the form of our consciousness. The more alienated the form of our labor, the more fetishized our consciousness, the less able are we to conceive of ourselves as other than we presently are. Though Marx is occasionally driven into pessimism by the tendency of capitalism to fetishize consciousness, his basic position is that we never wholly lose our capacity for "free, conscious activity," for "we presuppose labor in a form that stamps it as exclusively human."

> The practical construction of an *objective world*, the *manipulation* of inorganic nature, is the confirmation of man as a conscious species-being.... The object of labour is, therefore, the *objectification of man's species-life;* for he no longer reproduces himself merely intellectually, as in consciousness, but actively and in a real sense, and he sees his own reflection in a world he has constructed.[34]

We are not identical with our given determinations and we are dialectically related to the world. It must follow that the world in which we embody our labor is equally indeterminate. Since we have our nature "outside" ourselves and the objects of this labor "are not natural objects as they present themselves directly," it must be a basic human task to construct this objective world as an appropriate place for our objectification. Kant maintained that the human subject imposes various judgments upon experience and thereby constitutes its cognitive order. Marx maintained that *practical labor* imposes its categories upon the natural world and thereby constitutes its meaning for us as human beings. We are not *presented* with natural objects because we *construct* what we respond to. We "appropriate" the natural world, which means that we do not receive it passively but shape it through our activity.[35]

Nature is simultaneously the limit to our construction and the means through which our objectification takes place. Nature is both obdurate and compliant. To the extent that we are free we realize ourselves in the world and "man himself becomes the object."[36] The natural world always bears the imprint of human activity, but there is all the difference between activity that is stunted and minimally human, and that which is collectively controlled and directed toward the realization of our creativity, our species-being. The natural world must be so *constructed* that it can serve *human* need, for it is not "directly presented in a form adequate to the *human* being." The role that nature plays in human life is determined by the form of society that imposes its role.

These considerations set the context for a quite remarkable passage which becomes even more significant in contrast with the views of Freud:

> It will be seen from this how, in place of the *wealth* and poverty of political economy, we have the *wealthy* man and the plenitude of human *need*. The

wealthy man is at the same time one who *needs* a complex of human manifestations of life, and whose self-realization exists as an inner necessity and need. Not only the wealth but also the *poverty* of man acquires, in a socialist perspective, a *human* and thus social meaning. Poverty is the passive bond which leads man to experience a need for the greatest wealth, the *other* person. The sway of the objective entity within me, the sensuous eruption of my life-activity, is the passion which here becomes the *activity* of my being.[37]

Freud holds the same basic view of "wealth" and "poverty" as the political economy Marx here criticizes. He applied the term "economic" to his own view of the distribution of psychic energy: "We have seen that culture obeys the laws of psychological economic necessity."[38] Freud related the use of his concepts to physics, not economics, for he determined to use the notion of psychical energy "in the same sense as the physicist employs the hypothesis of a flow of electric fluid."[39] But there is a striking parallel between the basic structures of classical physics and classical economics, and although Freud's theory borrows directly from the former, his clinical application more closely resembles the latter.

The theme of scarcity and distribution which deeply concerned European capitalism in the nineteenth century is directly evident in Freud's perspective. He constructed a theory of fixed libidinal energy that is identical in form to the wage fund theory of the classical economists. According to this view there is a limited quantity of wages to be divided among competing working-class interests; a gain for one group automatically means a loss for another. The total sum cannot be expanded, so distribution must be the fundamental concern. The notions of "surplus" and "exploitation" are minimized or eliminated and the prospect of a collective improvement for the working class is held to be logically impossible.

Freud makes a similarly conservative use of the theory:

> Since man has not an unlimited amount of mental energy at his disposal, he must accomplish his tasks by distributing his libido to the best advantage.[40]

> We perceive ... a certain reciprocity between ego-libido and object-libido. The more that is absorbed by the one, the more *impoverished* does the other become. The highest form of ... object-libido is ... being in love, when the subject seems to yield up his whole personality in favor of the object cathexis. ...
>   At the same time the ego has put forth its libidinal object-cathexes. It becomes *impoverished* in consequence of these cathexes [emphasis added].[41]

Marx defines as *wealth* precisely what Freud defines as *impoverishment.* But Freud is describing capitalist society and Marx is referring to human nature under socialism. Both are correct up to this pont. Under capitalism, a "plenitude of human need" signifies a "plenitude" of incompleteness, deprivation, vulnerability, and impoverishment.

We have seen the importance which must be attributed, in a socialist perspective, to *the wealth of human needs,* and consequently also to a new mode of production and to a new object of production. . . . *Within the system of private property it has the opposite meaning.* Every man speculates upon creating a new need in order to force him to a new sacrifice, to place him in a new *dependence* [emphasis added].[42]

Since capitalism requires each individual to create a new dependence in others, it promotes a character structure that is simultaneously aggressive and fearful of the other's incursions. Freud's theory reifies both sides of the situation. On the one hand, the instinct theory views hostility as a permanent biological disposition, independent of social origins. On the other, we are admonished not to become overly involved in loving others. For the more "object-cathexis" we put forward the less we retain for ourselves; the more dependent and impoverished we become. To be "wealthy" in Freudian terms is to stand self-contained within the citadel-self. The economics of emotion and desire parallel the arguments advanced for the sanctity of private property.

And yet this fortress offers little refuge. Self-scrutiny is continuously required to warn of the possibility of rebellion from wihin. And so, both love and hatred become personal afflictions which the individual can only tolerate by refracting outward toward the world. In order that we "may not fall ill . . ." we are impelled to love "when the cathexis of the ego with libido exceeds a certain degree."[43] Similarly, we would be overwhelmed by our own self-destructiveness if we did not expel it from our own organism. So much despair is generated in this view of the self that Freud is moved to deny not only instinctual dependence on the object, but instinct itself. Thanatos is more than a longing for dominance and pain; it is a longing for dissolution. Walled off against the world, the fortress bears slow witness to death within its confinements.

Under capitalism, need is continually transformed into "neediness." Since desire is more and more satisfied through commodities, we find ourselves required to barter or purchase the entities or techniques that are necessary for our gratification. On the one hand we become instruments of our own self-manipulation. On the other, we become dependent upon "skilled experts" for the provision of culture, "common sense," entertainment, pleasure in sport or sexual intimacy. But these needs are continually more standardized through commodities which must be literally bought from others. And since the purpose of this commodity production is to exploit us for commercial gain we quite reasonably become suspicious of the commodities we depend on and, eventually, of commoditized needs themselves. We prefer, often, not to "need" at all, since we perceive helplessness in the condition of need.

So, when Freud writes of a desire to abolish stimulation and turn to equilibrium, he is noting a pervasive characteristic of our society. But it is

a characteristic that is often obscured by the countertendency to renewed and increasingly more powerful stimulation. The less able we are
to satisfy ourselves through commodities the more strongly we desire
"genuine" or "authentic" fulfillment. The whole panoply of therapeutic
and religious growth movements is an attempt to satiate this growing
hunger for "use value" as against exchange. But the greater the "demand" for pristine, "uncommoditized" experience, the greater the opportunity for those suppliers who rush into the vacuum with more
sophisticated products.

Romantic love is a paradigm of this transformation. Since the public
realm of work is recognized as inhuman, hope of meaningful recognition and nurturance is relegated to the private sphere of the intimacy of
pairs of lovers. They are there to make good in the intensity and passion
of their feelings what cannot be expected in the outside world. But there
is simply too much to make up. After the initial euphoria mingled with
terror in which romantic love originates, every sign of the world is
greeted with some disillusionment. But, of course, the lovers are also
shaped in this world, and so they are forced to bring to their enclave the
materials they are seeking to flee.

Furthermore, when love becomes commoditized, it takes on the
characteristic of any product. Its value becomes inversely proportionate
to its supply: dating is basically an initiation into the rites of husbanding
one's affection while attracting the largest supply from others.

> Romantic love is one scarcity mechanism that deserves special comment.
> Indeed, its only function and meaning is to transmute that which is plentiful
> into that which is in short supply. This is done in two ways: first, by inculcat-
> ing the belief that only one object can satisfy a person's erotic and affectional
> desires; and second, by fostering a preference for unconsummated, unre-
> quited, interrupted, or otherwise tragic relationships.[44]

This perceptive comment by Philip Slater seems to me to exaggerate the
extent to which love is in fact "plentiful" in capitalist society. He therefore overstates how much "fostering" needs to be done. A competitive,
atomistic society will itself *impose* unconsummated relationships. What
needs to be "fostered" is the *belief* that this situation is both inevitable and
the highest stage of human existence.

There is an interesting passage in Marx which prefigures a tendency
that has perhaps only reached its apogee in our own time:

> We arrive at the result that man (the worker) feels himself to be freely active
> only in his animal function—eating, drinking and procreating, or at most
> also in his dwelling and personal adornment—while in his human functions
> he is reduced to an animal. The animal becomes human and the human
> becomes animal.

Eating, drinking and procreating are of course also genuine human functions. But abstractly considered, apart from the environment of human activities, and turned into final and sole ends, they are animal functions.[45]

I take this passage to mean that when ends that have been relegated to privacy become compensatory satisfactions for the alienation of appropriately human functions, i.e., satisfactions in which our "species nature" has been reduced to the function of mere survival, they become abstract, inhuman activities. In contemporary language, they become compulsory and obsessional. Rather than offering us refuge from exploitation they become a new tyranny. The nameless protagonist in *Last Tango in Paris*, in flight from the external social world which has abused and terrorized him at every turn, makes a desperate attempt to replace social pathology with primitive, "animal" functions. But forced back to anality, there is no further recess of the sheerly biological realm of the body in which to hide. Yet the public world is no more hospitable. In its frantic rituals of compensation and amnesia—in the last tango—he grows weaker and moves toward death. Finally he lies curled as a fetus, turned in upon himself, unable to find life in the world or beyond it.

When we cannot participate as human beings in the public polity, when we cannot shape the social realm through our mutual labor, our society offers as one compensatory fantasy the idolatrous recession into the primitive. Marx underscores the manner in which frustrated productive labor is transformed into private ends, a reversal of Freud's claim that ungratified sexuality turns to the public world for satisfaction.

For Freud, work plays a critical role in the "economics of the libido":

> No other technique for the conduct of life attaches the individual so firmly to reality as laying emphasis on work; for his work at least gives him a secure place in a portion of reality, in the human community. The possibility it offers of displacing a large amount of libidinal components, whether narcissistic, aggressive or even erotic, on to professional work and on to the human relations connected with it lends it a value by no means second to what it enjoys as something indispensable to the preservation and justification of existence in society. Professional activity is a source of special satisfaction if it is a freely chosen one—if, that is to say, by means of sublimation, it makes possible the use of existing inclinations, of persisting or constitutionally reinforced instinctual impulses. And yet, as a path to happiness, work is not highly prized by men.[46]

For all his incredible tenacity in undermining the ordinary claims of common experience, Freud showed a singular lack of curiosity in regard to the significance of the last assertion of this passage. It is certainly true that Freud generally regarded work as a grim necessity for the preservation of human life. And in this he was certainly historically correct. But this passage speaks to something beyond the utilitarian importance of work. Here Freud considers its "libidinal" value as a sublimation for "narcissistic, aggressive or even erotic" needs.

> "Sublimation" is a concept that contains a judgment of value. Actually it signifies the application to another field in which socially more valuable achievements are possible.[47]

Does Freud mean to identify work with "professional work," thereby eliminating the category of wage-labor, the predominant form of work in capitalist society? Or does Freud intend to distinguish "professional work" from "freely chosen professional work," the former operating according to the defense mechanism of displacement, while the latter, alone, is capable of the loftier transformation provided by sublimation? Does the phrase "special satisfaction" mean that all work offers considerable satisfaction, even if it falls short of that optimum available only to those who are specially privileged? It is difficult to answer these questions, but a clue is provided in a letter Freud wrote a half century earlier:

> The mob gives vent to their impulses, and we deprive ourselves. We do so in order to maintain our integrity. We economize with our health, our capacity for enjoyment, our forces: we save up for something, not knowing ourselves for what. And this habit of constant suppression of natural instincts gives us the character of refinement. We also feel more deeply and therefore dare not demand much of ourselves. . . . Why don't we make a friend of everyone? Because the loss of him or any misfortune happening to him would bitterly affect us. Thus our striving is more concerned with avoiding pain than with creating enjoyment. . . . Our whole conduct of life presupposes that we shall be sheltered from the direst poverty, that it is always open to us to free ourselves increasingly from the evils of our social structure. The poor, the common people, could not exist without their thick skin and their easygoing ways. Why should they feel their desires intensely when all that the afflictions of nature and society have in store is directed against those they love: why should they scorn a momentary pleasure when no other awaits them? The poor are too powerless, too exposed to do as we do. When I see the people doing themselves well, putting all seriousness aside, it makes me think it is their compensation for being so unprotected against all the imposts, epidemics, diseases, and the evil conditions of our social organization. . . . There is a psychology of the common man which is somewhat different from ours. Such people also have more feeling of community than we do; it is only they who are alive to the way in which one life is the continuation of the next, whereas for each of us the world vanishes with his death.[48]

I find this one of the most remarkable passages in Freud's work. Its analysis is worth a short volume. Freud never came closer to realizing the social constitution of the contemporary psyche, nor the class structure of the dynamics of repression and release. For all its obfuscation, Freud's commentary cannot disguise social dissolution beneath the personal despair and theoretical pessimism of bourgeois culture. This reflection expresses a view of mind analogous to the structure of social classes:

> Our mind, that precious instrument by whose means we maintain ourselves alive, is no peacefully self-contained unity. It is rather to be compared with a modern State in which a mob, eager for enjoyment and destruction, has to be held down forcibly by a prudent superior class.[49]

Freud's early letter reveals the nature of this "prudent superior class." As the mob concentrates within itself the functions of id and libido, the privileged class represents the executive functions of the ego and the moral authority of ego-ideals and superego. It deprives itself, economizes its capacity for life, and saves for unknown ends. In this process it develops a superior refinement, though it cannot risk its deep feeling in the world. We have already noted this theory of capitalist accumulation applied to the psyche. But here Freud adds the other side of the orthodox bourgeois theory: the view of the profligate masses. At one point he is severe; at another, sympathetic. But the "mob," for whatever reason, is moved from impulse and the desire for immediate release. It moves either because it is incapable of anything more or because it is perceptive enough to recognize, in this momentary pleasure, the limited compensations for its suffering.

These are illuminating considerations, once they are demystified. The additional "deprivation" of the professional stratum permits it to rationalize its political authority, just as the superior wealth of the capitalist class was once regarded by bourgeois economists as a reward for superior savings. There is a dialectic in all our lives which buys self-justification at the expense of deprivation. And while Freud notes that the privileged classes can gain protection from the worst poverty and social evil, we can draw the relevant implications from the fact that these advantages require the unprotected labor of the masses. The idlike mob must be "held down forcibly by a prudent superior class." It must be controlled against its will; or, more accurately, it must be controlled by having its own will turned against it. The "superior class" uses the energy of the masses against it, just as the superego turns the hostility of destructive impulses into fetters upon their expression. We can see that Freud's theory of the individual psyche accurately represents the extent to which the layers of our selves are formed out of the system of antagonistic social forces.

Our desires are, as Freud describes them, short-lived, ruthless, peremptory, and seething with irrational demands. But this is not, as Freud believed, because of their constitutional nature. In our society drives are mediated through social relationships so as to produce real dependence behind a façade of freedom. There is little chance that the child's first inclinations will be slowly and lovingly nurtured and articulated as it enters more fully into the social world. The disfigurations of childhood are repeated in the remaining institutions of capitalist society—in school, media, and work, thereby providing the social determination of what Freud took to be the repetition compulsion of our biological being.

In Freud's account it is not desire that develops, but the mechanisms of repression and control. Again, there is a perverted insight in this account. Our social needs remain unsatisfied while our manipulated wants are stimulated to frenetic excess. Our "private" desires can be compared with a mob, because they are formed in an irrational society which devalues true social life and instigates instead insatiable longing, self-hatred, and despair.

When we transform Freud's figure, the analogy between the modern state and the individual psyche is clear: those who can control their own internal passions are given the privilege of controlling others. Desire versus control is the dominant motif for both the individual psyche and the social system. Yet Freud cannot decide whether the privileged class governs by sublimation or deprivation. And he cannot shake off the awareness of isolation that forms the bourgeois mentality, its pervasive discontinuity and fear of total annihilation in death. The masses flee their vulnerability in the security of crude gratification. The privileged deny themselves gratification and, in their refinement, make themselves vulnerable to pain and death.

In a socialist society my need can be my opportunity for fulfillment rather than my vulnerability. Such needs are humanly formed and can therefore be humanly realized. If the world of social nature is myself, "outside myself," the deeper and richer my engagement in this world, the greater my human enlargement. For Freud, the other is not only not myself, but my antagonist. We cannot help but see ourselves in the world we have constructed. Everything depends on the form of this construction. The significance of nature for us resides in the character of the society that has imbued it with meaning. Under capitalism, nature becomes a battleground for competing interests. But if, in the object, humanity becomes acquainted with itself, and if the object is *itself objectified,* then it follows that in my relationship with nature I will be ingesting the labor, stunted or fulfilled, of other human beings. This is what Marx intends when he holds that "the sense and minds of other men have become my *own* appropriation."[50]

> The whole of history is a preparation for "man" to become an object of sense perception, and for the development of human needs (the needs of man as such).[51]

The Development of Human Needs

The phrase "development of human needs" echoes a position we have already noted: "By thus acting on the external world and changing it, [man] at the same time changes his own nature." Human beings are self-mediating and historical; because we have no determinate nature at birth we are required to produce ourselves concretely over time.

> Men have a history because they must *produce* their life.... Once a need is satisfied, which requires the action of satisfying and the acquisition of the instrument for this purpose, new needs arise. *The production of new needs is the first historical act....*
>
> The diverse shaping of material life is always dependent on needs already developed, and the production as well as satisfaction of these needs is itself a historical process not found with a sheep or a dog [emphasis added].[52]

Marx is not asserting that needs change only as the *direct* result of economic satisfaction, nor that the "instrument" of change is a material tool. He is speaking of our human self-production, an activity which is much larger in scope and more variegated than material production narrowly defined.

> Most often, needs arise directly from production or from *a state of affairs based on production.* World trade turns almost entirely round the needs, not of individual consumption, but of production. Thus ... does not the need for lawyers suppose a given civil law which is but the *expression* of a certain development of property, that is to say, of production [emphasis added]?[53]

Law is also an instrument of our self-production, a way in which we mediate ourselves. Civil law is not merely an external institution. The concepts of rightful ownership, duty, contract, liability, etc., are aspects of our sense of ourselves as human beings. When Mill writes "Over himself, over his own body and mind, the individual is sovereign,"[54] he is expressing the sense of bourgeois proprietorship that permeates our self-consciousness. The idea that we possess our own mind, that we have sovereign property rights to its use, as we do to a material entity that belongs to us, is a historically peculiar notion. We create the institutions of law and we are, in turn, created through such institutions. We make ourselves into particular, determinate beings through the distinct form of our activity in the world.

For Marx, the basic human characteristic is our ability to transform our original nature by creating the objective world in which we acquire our specific nature. This position seems to me to be important and correct though it is obviously much too general as it stands. What is contained in this notion of "species-being" that makes intelligible the fact of human self-transformation? This problem requires a Marxist "psychology," in order: (1) to enunciate the system of universal needs—biological, social, intellectual, aesthetic, and moral—which we share in the process of our common labor in the world; and (2) to investigate the capacities in thought, language, self-reflection, and creativity through which we create and realize these needs. This whole enterprise must be kept historically specific and responsive to changing forms of the division of labor, and ideology. The insistence on the dialectic between abstract tendencies and their concrete manifestations is one of the primary contributions of a Marxist view of human nature to an adequate psychology and a viable political methodology.

The hope that must inform political activity rests on the conviction of the possible historical transformation of human need. The view that our society expresses the deepest stratum of human nature ends all movement toward a new life. On the first page of *One-Dimensional Man* the following assertion appears: "To the degree to which freedom from want, *the concrete substance of all freedom,* is becoming a real possibility, the liberties which pertain to a state of lower productivity are losing their former content" [emphasis added].[55] If we conjoin with this view the additional proposition that modern technology is constantly better able to satisfy our wants—a position Marcuse accepts—we will have established the main lines of an argument that proves no socialist agency remains in contemporary capitalist society.

But everything depends on what view of human nature and its needs is postulated. If there is some fixed biological core of "want" whose satisfaction is the "concrete substance of freedom," then increasing productivity will eventually satisfy our desire for freedom. But if "wants," "freedom," and "productivity" are aspects of a historical dialectic, their nature and meaning will change with history. Marcuse's analysis obliterates Marx's contention that "once a need is satisfied . . . new needs arise." Marx insisted that since "our wants and pleasures have their origin in society . . . we therefore measure them in relation to society."[56]

There is movement in history precisely because societies produce needs they cannot satisfy. Even the idea of physical subsistence has no fixed meaning. Some peoples have lived for centuries in the constant presence of toil and misery, while others have found in affluence and luxury the grounds of discontent and rebellion. Marcuse's analysis reifies our despair. Marx points in a different direction:

> Just as the savage must wrestle with Nature to satisfy his wants, to maintain and reproduce life, so must civilized man, and he must do so in all social formations and under all possible modes of production. With his development this realm of physical necessity expands as a result of his wants: but, at the same time, the forces of production which satisfy these wants also increase. Freedom in this field can only consist in socialized man, the associated

producers, rationally regulating their interchange with Nature, bringing it under their common control, instead of being ruled by it as by the blind forces of Nature; and achieving this with the least expenditure of energy and under conditions most favorable to, and worthy of, their human nature. But it nevertheless remains a realm of necessity. Beyond it begins that development of human energy which is an end in itself, the true realm of freedom, which, however, can blossom forth only with this realm of necessity as its basis.[57]

On the basis of a new mode of production a new form of freedom becomes possible. The material means exist for human beings to devote themselves to the realization of their nature. Our common human capacity to transform ourselves now becomes available as a power that can be cultivated for its own sake. Whether this possibility can be realized depends on whether we can elicit from each other "a need for self-realization as an inner necessity." If we persist in reified views of ourselves we shall never be in a position to test this possibility. The explanation of the facts of alienation and powerlessness that dominates works like *One-Dimensional Man* only reinforces the hegemony of the facts. Ironically, it produces an easy rest. Nothing can be done, nothing need be attempted. We can rest "content."

The heart of Marx's position is captured in the term "apropriation," a notion both objective and subjective in its reference. While the Freudian bourgeois manipulates the external world to overcome tension and reinstate an earlier equilibrium, the species-being of whom Marx writes proceeds differently:

> Man appropriates his manifold being in an all-inclusive way and thus as a whole man. All his *human* relations to the world—seeing, hearing, smelling, tasting, touching, thinking, observing, feeling, desiring, acting, loving—in short, all the organs of his individuality . . . are in their objective action (their *action in relation to the object*) the appropriation of this object, the appropriation of human reality.[58]

"The appropriation of this object, the appropriation of human reality"; the terms are reciprocal. As the object is given its meaning through social action, so is human nature. There are, of course, structures and parameters that define the limits of human transformation. Just as the external world is both obdurate and malleable, so is human nature. But the very idea of "limit" is a human construction. Its meaning varies from one period to another. The most obvious limit is "death," but people die differently in different societies, just as they are born differently. The meaning of these universal biological acts is not a constant meaning. Marx wrote to Annenkov: "Machinery is no more an economic category than the ox which draws the plow."[59] Neither is biology a human category. For just as "the way in which machinery is utilized is distinct from the machinery itself," so the manner in which we utilize our "given" dispositions is totally different from the physical facts themselves.

The Production and Consumption of Needs

In the introduction to the *Grundrisse* Marx discusses the relation between production and consumption in a manner that throws further light on our inquiry. He begins by noting that these two functions reciprocally determine each other. Consumption produces production because "the product first becomes a real product in consumption" and because consumption creates the "necessity for new production by providing the ideal, inward, impelling cause which constitutes the prerequisite of production.... It is clear that while production furnishes the material object of consumption, consumption provides the ideal object of production, as its image, its want, its impulse and purpose."[60] On the other hand, production furnishes consumption with its material, and also gives consumption "its definite outline, its character, its finish":

> For the object is not simply an object in general, but a definite object, which is consumed in a certain definite manner prescribed in its turn by production. *Hunger is hunger; but the hunger that is gratified by cooked meat eaten with fork and knife is a different hunger from that which bolts down raw meat with the aid of hand, nail and tooth* [emphasis added].[61]

The manner in which an object is consumed produces a need for that object, for

> Production not only supplies the want with material, but supplies the material with a want. When consumption emerges from its first stage of natural crudeness and directness ... it is itself furthered by its object *as a moving spring*. The want of it which consumption experiences is created by its appreciation of the product [emphasis added].[62]

These reflections are the foundation of any Marxist social psychology. Their significance can best be gauged in comparison with psychoanalytic assumptions. As we have noted, it is sometimes maintained that Marxist critics have misunderstood Freud's insistence on the malleability of human instinct. The theme of "instincts and their vicissitudes" speaks it is said, to the plasticity of our basic inclinations:

> It has been brought to our notice that we have been in the habit of regarding the connection between the sexual instinct and the sexual object as more intimate than it in fact is. Experience of the cases that are considered abnormal has shown us that in them the sexual instinct and the sexual object are merely soldered together—a fact which we have been in danger of overlooking in consequence of the uniformity of the normal picture, where the object

appears to form part and parcel of the instinct. We are thus warned to loosen the bond that exists in our thoughts between instinct and object. It seems probable that the sexual instinct is in the first instance independent of its object; nor is its origin likely to be due to its object's attractions.[63]

This passage reveals a position radically different from Marx's. For the instinct and object are given no intrinsic connection with each other; they are "merely soldered together." Since the instinct is not formed through the "object's attraction," its aim must be constitutionally predetermined or left to chance. Either alternative differs basically from Marx's dialectic of object and need. Freud merely succeeds in isolating the individual from the social context of desire and gratification. The object is merely the means for gratification rather than a constitutive aspect of its nature.

Many who have incorporated Freud in a larger "social" perspective believe they have taken account of what is true in Marx. Their common position can be stated as follows: Though we affirm the existence of inborn human needs and drives, we are not insensitive to society's effects. For we acknowledge that different societies provide different channels for the expression of these given tendencies. In one place anger may be released in sport, in another warfare may serve the same function, and in a third, the fallen chief may become the object of hostility. While a boy in our society is hostile toward his father, the Trobriand boy may direct this feeling toward his uncle. We do not deny that the objects of human drives are various and that the structure of permission produces real differences in social life.

This *is not* Marx's position, and it is *mistaken at its root*. The political economy of Marx's day also attempted a strict division between production and distribution. The first domain was supposedly marked by immutable laws; the second was open to transformation. Marx rejected the dichotomy for the same general reason that the reigning psychological view needs to be rejected. Human drives cannot be separated from the channels of their release. "Consumption provides the ideal object of production, as its image, its want, its impulse and purpose." The drive is formed through its object, which is itself shaped through its place in the network of social relations. That is why the hunger that is gratified with cooked meat is different in kind from the hunger that "bolts down raw meat." *It is not the same hunger, with different objects; it is "a different hunger."*

Freud holds that instincts aim at abolishing "the condition of stimulation in the source of the instinct," while the source is defined as "that somatic process in an organ or part of the body from which there results a stimulus represented in life by an instinct."[64] In other words, Freud holds the view that physical instincts are gratified by making good a state of privation in the body. This is a fundamental mistake. What is overlooked is the manner in which the bodily impulse is *defined through social processes*. In satisfying "a physical need" are we simultaneously satisfying the social conventions that structure the significance of the need.

In capitalist society our view of the body, and its "needs and requirements," is instrumental. The traditional "industrial" notion of sleeping and eating regards these functions as preparations for the next day's labor. We treat ourselves somewhat like a machine that must be refueled and made ready. With the recent rise of a cult of "deserved gratification" these values are themselves in transition. Though there is less drama surrounding eating than sexuality, the same conflict arises between regarding the act as useful for the promotion of other ends, and engaging in it as a highly charged end in itself. It is not a discipline, as it was for the Japanese, nor is it usually a casual, sensuous relaxation. It is suffused with considerable compensatory value as a substitute for love, recognition, sacrifice (in cooking), stimulation, or reward. Since it is mediated by advertising, it also bears the imprint of status, style, and conspicuous display.

The same point obviously holds for needs that do not derive from the body.

> Money is therefore not only *an* object, but is *the* object of greed. . . . Greed as such, as a particular form of the drive, i.e., as distinct from the craving for a particular kind of wealth, e.g., for clothes, weapons, jewels, women, wine, etc., is possible only when general wealth, wealth as such, has become individualized in a particular thing, i.e., as soon as money is posited in its third quality. Money is therefore not only the object but also the fountainhead of greed. The mania for possessions is possible without money; but greed itself is the product of a definite social development, not *natural,* as opposed to *historical.*[65]

Money and greed stand in a dialectical relationship. They imply each other, just as money itself derives from a total system of production. Once again, it is not the same drive with a different object, but a different drive. There is no universal drive for possession because there is no universal form of possessiveness, i.e., of property relations, through which such a drive could be articulated.

The difference between a Marxist view of the matter and the orthodox social psychology position is the difference between dialectics and interaction. In a dialectical relationship the terms are reciprocally transformed. Human needs are shaped through the process in which they are *simultaneously generated and released.* Bourgeois theory speaks of the *discharge* of drive without specifying the process through which the drive is *charged,* that is, formed, shaped, and constructed. Hunger is hunger, as sexuality is sexuality. But the sexuality that is satisfied through the relatively uninhibited and public institutions of Trobriand society is different from the sexuality that is constructed through the monogamous, patriarchal, private, repressive family structure of Freud's clients.

Marxism denies that the ultimate source of conflict in human life is an inherent antagonism between primary biological drives and repressive social institutions. The pervasive antagonisms of our lives have their origin in the contraditions inherent in our society. When we experience ourselves drawn simultaneously toward immediate gratification on the one hand, and a need for permanent relations on the other, we are reflecting social movements beneath the immediate surface of our own lives. A scrutiny of our biology will not advance our understanding of this dilemma one whit. But a historical explanation of the social roots of isolation, the changing nature of the family, and the pressures of the contemporary market will offer some illumination.[66]

The Striving Toward Self-Realization: Summary and Review

In denying the existence of primordial human drives, are we not cutting the ground from under our own argument? Doesn't Marxist anthropology rest squarely on the view that human beings possess an inherent tendency toward their self-realization? And doesn't Marxism equate the possibility of self-realization with the introduction of a communist society in which "the free development of each is the condition of the free development of all"? Furthermore, haven't we eliminated the common bond that unites all men and women and makes it possible to understand each other across wide chasms of historical time? It is all well and good to note distinctions, but are we not remarkably similar still, as great works of literature attest when they move us *despite enormous differences* in their historical origins? We have already discussed this question somewhat polemically. We can now reconsider the issue from a more developed Marxist vantage point here. But first let us briefly respond to the assertion of a common human nature.

We have no reason to deny this contention. First, we have already acknowledged the existence of general powers and needs which are constitutive of all human beings. And second, the very fact that human nature is formed in society means that to the extent that various social systems resemble each other, so will the lives of those who are members of these similar systems. Consider these two passages:

> *Gold? yellow glittering, precious gold? No. Gods,*
> *I am no idle votarist: roots, you clear heavens!*
> *Thus much of this will make black, white; foul, fair;*
> *Wrong, right; base, noble; old, young; coward, valiant.*

.... Why this
Will lug your priests and servants from your sides;
Pluck stout men's pillows from below their heads:
This yellow slave
Will knit and break religions; bless th'accurst;
Make the hoar leprosy ador'd; place thieves,
And give them title, knee, and approbation,
With senators on the bench. . . .

Money wins friendship, honour, place and power,
And sets man next to the proud tyrant's throne.
All trodden paths and paths untrod before
Are scaled by nimble riches, where the poor
Can never hope to win the heart's desire.
A man ill-formed by nature and ill-spoken
Money shall make him fair to eye and ear.
Money earns man his health and happiness,
And only money cloaks iniquity.

The first passage is from Shakespeare's *Timon of Athens;* the second is a fragment of Sophocles. The immediate appearance of this juxtaposition argues against our contention, for though they are some two thousand years apart, they are certainly remarkable for their similarity. But the form of social life can account for the resemblance. The period of Sophocles' work, in the fourth century B.C., was in important respects like that during which Shakespeare wrote. In both cases the basic form of wealth changed from political control over land by aristocratic, hereditary strata, to individual posession of exchangeable property in the commercial market.

The Elizabethan sense of guilt and responsibility was quite different from that of the Greeks, and ours is different still. I do not believe that a modern audience can ultimately understand how Oedipus can be held responsible for crimes he was fated to commit. The Greeks could inherit responsibility in a manner that is unintelligible to us; their sense of continuity with the past, of identification with family, of the immortality and intrusive presences of ancestors marks off their lived, objective world. But this network of social relations is not an abstractly chosen system of ideals; it is ingredient in the state of production, in class divisions, and in the character of land, commerce, and politics.

Human subjectivity is an irreducible fact, but this subjectivity is formed through the objective system of production and reproduction that *in*forms it. So Marx wrote:

It can be seen that the history of *industry* and industry as it objectively exists is an *open* book of the *human faculties*, and human *psychology* which can be

sensuously apprehended. This history has not so far been conceived in relation to human *nature,* but only from a superficial utilitarian point of view. . . .
No psychology for which this book, i.e., the most tangible and accessible part
of history, remains closed, can become a *real* science with a genuine content.[67]

We have thus far had superficial utilitarian accounts of industry *and*
superficial accounts of psychology. This distortion in theory expresses
the fetishized split between public work and private consciousness which
informs bourgeois society. Marx does not deny the relevance of human
nature; in fact, he criticizes previous accounts of industry precisely because they have not been seen as an expression of human nature. Since
we so heavily identify psychology with introspection, Marx's contention
may seem perverse to us. The reference to industry as "human psychology sensuously apprehended" gives us pause. But this is merely the
consistent articulation of a dialectical perspective which insists that our
consciousness and our objective labor are mutually self-determining.

The question of whether objectivity or subjectivity is primary is unintelligible because it rests on a mistaken assumption. It either betrays a
belief that human beings can be understood on the model of "tabula
rasa," in which case the objective world is seen as imprinting itself on the
mind; or it accepts the model of human activity driven by instincts, in
which case our mind is viewed as imposing itself on nature. In fact, we
objectify ourselves and assimilate our own objectifications; we are simultaneously objective and subjective, though the meaning of these terms
changes in different historical circumstances.

It is now possible to return to our previous question: is there inherent
in primordial human nature a striving toward self-realization? I think
there can be no doubt that Marx judged the development of human
societies by this criterion.

> The transformation of . . . personal powers (relationships) into material
> powers, cannot be dispelled by dismissing the general idea of it from one's
> mind, but can only be abolished by the individuals again subjecting these
> material powers to themselves and abolishing the division of labor. This is
> not possible without the community. Only in community [with others has
> each] individual the means of *cultivating his gifts in all directions: only in commu-
> nity, therefore, is personal freedom possible.*[68]

> While in the earlier periods *self-activity* and the production of material life
> were separated, in that they devolved on different persons, and while, on
> account of the narrowness of the individuals themselves, the production of
> material life was considered as a subordinate mode of self-activity, they now
> diverge to such an extent that altogether material life appears as the end, and
> what produces this material life, labour (which is now the only possible but, as
> we see, *negative form of self-activity*), as the means. . . . The appropriation of
> these forces is itself nothing more than *the development of the individual*

capacities corresponding to the material conditions of production. . . . Only the proletarians of the present day . . . are in a position to achieve a complete and no longer restricted self-activity, which consists in the appropriation of a totality of productive forces and in the . . . postulated *development of a totality of capacities.*[69]

The cultivation of human capacities is not merely an ideal moral imperative but a historical fact. Sometimes this realization occurs in so distorted, narrow, and alienated a context that it appears as merely a "negative form of self-activity." But no matter how inadequate the realization, if we are considering human beings we are in the presence of beings capable of some form of self-activity. In the short run, any given period may reveal very little growth. But in the longest overview of history, human beings can be seen to develop their "slumbering powers" and to "bring out new qualities in themselves, develop themselves in production, transform themselves, develop new powers and ideas, new modes of intercourse, new needs and new language."[70]

Nevertheless, it is one thing to judge human development by the criterion of self-realization and quite another to claim that human beings are driven by some internal imperative to fulfill their moral capacities. Marxism is not an abstract ontology; it does not attribute basic, determinate tendencies to being, or to human being. Marx does ascribe characteristics to human nature, as we have seen. There are both capacities and tendencies which mark off the sphere of human existence. But the genius of Marx's approach is an insight into the dialectical reciprocity of anthropology—basic human nature—and social structure. The ontologizing of Marx misses the point, which is the way in which basic categories are determined through social relations.

Freud held that individuals react to social domination with neurosis, psychosis, or, uncharacteristically, with political self-determination: "No doubt he will always defend his claim to individual liberty against the will of the group."[71] And it was such a conception in Freud that proved attractive to Horkheimer, for whom "libido . . . implied a stratum of human existence stubbornly out of reach of total social control."[72] The ontological theory of self-realization, the view that human beings necessarily strive toward their personal freedom, is a contention that often arises in a period of totalitarian domination and social despair. It expresses an unwillingness to relinquish hope. Marx maintained that the impetus for revolutionary transcendence arose from the contradictions within society. When those contradictions seem totally overwhelmed by political tyranny, the only point of faith that appears to remain is the innermost stubbornness of the human will. But the "human will" is an abstraction that has no historical presence.

It is true that as human we have the capacity to transcend our given nature. But the meaning of this freedom—its goal, its instrument, and its significance—is specified in the historical moment in which we live. Solutions are historically concrete because they are responses to situations that are historically concrete: "Individuals have always built on themselves, but naturally on themselves *within their given historical conditions and relationships, not on the 'pure' individual in the sense of the ideologists.*"[73] For genuine self-realization to become a real historical possibility, that is, for human beings to experience their condition as a motive of their action, the abstract capacity for self-transcendence must intersect a specific mode of production in which this condition arises as an immanent tendency. Human nature and the mode of social production must reproduce each other. Our anthropological capacity to realize ourselves as full, "universal" beings must inform a system of labor in which universal mastery is a historical possibility. Capitalism is the distorted presence of this full possibility.

> Universally developed individuals, whose social relations, as their own communal relations, are hence also subordinated to their own communal control, are *no product of nature, but of history.* The degree of universality of the development of wealth where this individuality becomes possible supposes production on the basis of exchange values as a prior condition, whose universality produces not only the alienation of the individual from himself and from others, but also the *universality* and *comprehensiveness* of his *relations* and *capacities.*[74]

That is why Marx insisted that "only the proletarians of the present day . . . are in a position to achieve a complete and no longer restricted self-activity, which consists in the appropriation of a totality of productive forces and the thus postulated development of a totality of capacities."[75]

In transforming ourselves we make use of the tools and materials that have been bequeathed us from the past. The ideal draws on this past as it points to the future. Each period has its own conception of appropriation and self-realization. Capitalism produces alienation, but this alienation is simultaneously the truncated presence of "comprehensive capacity." It is not possible to determine in advance how human beings will realize themselves. For the ideal of "self-realization" is itself transformed in the process of its attainment. In a fully dialectical system no aspect of the whole remains unchanged, particularly the notion of change itself.

> In fact, however, when the limited bourgeois form is stripped away, what is wealth other than the universality of human needs, capacities, pleasures, productive forces, etc., created through universal exchange? The full development of human mastery over the forces of nature, those of so called nature as well as of humanity's own nature? The absolute working out of his creative potentialities, with no presupposition other than the previous historical development, i.e., *the development of all human powers as such the end in itself, not as measured on a predetermined yardstick?* Where he does not reproduce

himself in one specificity, but produces his totality? Strives not to remain something he has become, but is *the absolute movement of becoming?* [76]

It is impossible to comprehend Marx's anthropology without fully crediting his radical insistence on emergence. Marx denies that the goal of self-realization is predetermined. *It therefore cannot be constitutionally present in the "being" of human nature.* Marx rejects views such as Freud's which reduce the future to the past, and he similarly eschews such "voluntarism" as would make human will independent of historical constraints.

But, if the ontological view of self-realization is mistaken, what is Marx's alternative? The heart of Marx's position is his view of human nature as *self-mediating* as "a *"a moving spring."* Human beings possess the capacity to expand appropriation, social organization, and the system of cultural ideals that direct this process. Self-realization is a historical achievement. It is accomplished through the production of "objects" which both *embody* human needs as they are presently constituted and *incite* incipient needs for which appropriate "objects" are not yet available. The process of self-fulfillment follows the rhythm of objectification and assimilation; we mediate our own development through the creation of a world that manifests us as we are and urges us toward aspects of ourselves that are merely adumbrated. There are views, like that of Freud, that reduce society to the addtion of individual psychologies. On the other hand, there is a "sociologistic" position which reduces the individual to the product of social action. Both views deny that the individual is intrinsically social, or that society is the ensemble of socially related individuals. The doctrine "that men are products of circumstances and upbringing, and that, therefore, changed men are products of other circumstances and changed upbringing, forgets that it is men that change circumstances, and that the educator himself needs educating."[77] Need and object are dialectically related; they reciprocally determine each other. The "objects" which satisfy our needs are ourselves as objectified. In manifesting our given nature they are continuous with what we are, but in eliciting from us new propensities and abilities they are continuous with what we might become.

> The eye has become a *human* eye when its *object* has become a human, social object, created by man and destined for him. The senses . . . relate themselves to the thing for the sake of the thing, but the thing itself is an *objective human* relation to itself and to man, and vice versa. . . .
>
> It is evident that the human eye appreciates things in a different way from the crude, non-human eye, the human ear differently from the crude ear. . . .
>
> Let us next consider the subjective aspect. Man's musical sense is only *awakened* by music. The most beautiful music has no meaning for the non-

musical ear, is not an object for it, because my object can only be the confirmation of one of my own faculties.[78]

This Marxist dialectic is wholly contrary to the Freudian paradigm. I am not overlooking the fact that terms like "object relation," "incorporation," "introjection," and "projection" signify a process by which we assimilate others into ourselves and reciprocally propel certain aspects of ourselves and of incorporated others outward again. I am aware that Freud wrote that "the character of the ego is a precipitate of abandoned object-cathexes and that it contains a record of past object-choices.[79] But Freud does not use the phrase "object-cathexes" to signify an autonomous relationship with another person. The other is a means to our relationship with ourselves. That is why the idea of oral incorporation becomes the model for "identification," a procedure that explains nothing, as is sometimes acknowledged: "We know nothing about the specific nature of this identification."[80] Ingestion is a biological analogy which is irrelevant in regard to social relations. Identification is less a process of taking others into ourselves than of taking ourselves into others. But for this process there is no good Freudian analogy. There is nothing in his system that resembles Marx's view of historical self-creation of the human species:

> For it is not only the five senses, but also the so-called spiritual senses, the practical sense (desiring, loving, etc.), in brief, human sensibility and the human character of the senses, which can only come into being through the existence of its object, through humanized nature. The cultivation of the five senses is the work of all previous history.[81]

There is nothing in Freud that corresponds to Marx's notion that our musical sense is only *awakened* by music. The Freudian conception of awakening is an archeological conception of recall. The element of creativity is absent, and so, therefore, is history.

PART II

The Transcendence
of Psychoanalysis

CHAPTER FOUR

The Demystification of Freudian Theory

Saving the Good Freud

Freud's theory is in no way *revolutionary*. Though it certainly contains what can be called rebellious or oppositional tendencies, in the total context of Freud's system these radical elements are suspended, canceled or totally engulfed by contrary considerations. Freud's metapsychology is a conjunction of psychophysical dualism, Neo-Kantian vitalism, neurological determinism, entropic and cyclical biophysics, positivistic quantification, and hydraulic energy circuits. His politics combines Enlightenment rationality and a critique of excessive sexual restraint on the one hand with a conviction of the necessity of repression, a reactionary fear of the majority, an insistence on the need for elite authority, and a profound cynicism regarding the possibility of fundamental human transformation on the other. His view of human nature is marked by compassion for suffering and despair at the prospect of its elimination, by a mechanistic perspective on which he erected a view of human intentionality that extended the realm of symbolic meaning and purpose far beyond their previous limits. His work displays a wide sensitivity to culture and an extreme narrowness in interpretation, egoistic reductionism and a pervasive scarcity mentality culminating in

99

philosophical antirationalism that resonates through Schoppenhaur and the least progressive contributions of Nietzsche. His overall view of civilization weaves together a critique of hypocrisy, bourgeois exhaustion at self-denying sublimation, the nobility of the self-sacrifice of superiors, a profound ahistoricism, and a reification of the prevailing capitalist claim of a necessary contradiction between the individual and society. As J. M. Brohm noted:

> Freud's work develops in fact out of the end of the era of bourgeois revolutions, at the moment when the bourgeoisie has long since lost every revolutionary calling. His work consequently combines in a dialectical manner the rationalist materialism of the era of bourgeois revolutions (the progressive and critical materialism of a bourgeois revolutionary idology which calls its objects by their names) with the ideology of the imperialist period, the period of ideological and theoretical disintegration.[1]

The term "dialectical" is inappropriate and the passage is too simple, but it nevertheless captures a contradiction that permeated all of Freud's contributions.

What is most important about the Freudian contradiction is that within its combination of progressive and conservative elements are embodied concepts that are indispensable to a Marxist understanding of social domination and transcendence. As we shall see, Freud provided critical components of a theory of alienation and false consciousness. But his own understanding of these factors was often reified, and consequently a perspective that intends both to learn from Freud and transcend his deficiencies must demystify Freud's contribution in the process of incorporating its insights. *The fundamental question I am concerned with at this stage of analysis is the manner in which this demystification is to be accomplished.*

I argued earlier that the works of Freud and Marx bore striking resemblances as well as irreducible contradictions. It would greatly simplify the task of understanding the relationship of their theories if we could split the works of Freud and Marx into component "parts" and proceed to line up the similarities and differences. Then we could characterize the notions of science, atheism, self-determination, and rationality as the points of identity and the concepts of social class, revolution, instinct, repetition, and human self-transformation as the points of difference. Insofar as Marxism absorbs what is progressive in the world view of the bourgeoisie we would have explained the convergence between Marx and Freud, and insofar as Marxism rejects the necessary alienation and mystification of bourgeois domination we would have grounded their incompatibility.

There is some validity in this approach; the difficulty is that the aspects of a theoretical system are not "parts" which retain their separable meanings when removed from their place in a larger configuration.

They are not like bricks in a wall or patches in a quilt. The notions of "rationality," "science," and "self-determination" have different meanings in the totality of the systems of Marx and Freud and a less mechanistic procedure must be utilized to adequately grasp their relationship. I intend to retain the notions of convergence and disparity, of course, but I reject the possibility of laying one set of concepts over the other and tracing their contours. Instead, I adopt the view that theories embody (however indirectly) the tendencies of the social classes and specialized cadres that propound and defend them, and these tendencies may move in similar directions when viewed from a limited vantage point, but along very different paths when sighted from a more inclusive location.

Just as the original humanism of the capitalist Enlightenment flourished through its onslaught upon the backwardness of a clerical aristocracy languishing in the lengthening shadows of its feudal structure, so Freud's attack upon the reactionary medical mysticism and sexual duplicity of his age also grew upon that which it destroyed and replaced. But as the bourgeoisie came eventually to the point at which it would have either to reject its class privilege for the sake of its ideals, or refashion its ideals to justify its privilege, so Freud too came upon the limits of a therapeutic humanism grounded in the underlying assumptions of late capitalism. Like Weber, Freud found the culture of capitalism deficient. And like Weber, unable or unwilling to commit himself to the only critique that could move beyond this aversion—that is, to socialism—Freud was condemned to a narrowing circle of theoretical abstraction and practical despair. Like all condemnations that do not comprehend the roots of the evil they deplore, Freud absorbed in his critique vital elements of the system he rejected. His uncritical acceptance of the postulates of capitalism are never so obvious as when he is involved in a "universal" analysis of culture or a specific characterization of primitive society. And without a way open before him, Freud could only follow the path of similar antibourgeois critiques into a reactionary ahistorical mysticism. Helmholtz's materialism gave way to Nietzsche's eternal occurrence, and the explorations of an earlier scientific coalition were slowly extinguished by fantasies of primal murder and cosmological manichaeism. The furthest reach of Freud's amelioristic ambition, which is simultaneously the limit of his vision, is well stated by Philip Rieff as

> a better balancing of profit and loss among the emotions. His is the iron law of analysis: culture develops at the expense of the instincts; and neither revolution nor religion can save man the eternal wear of conflict.[2]

Those who have wished to maintain allegiance to Freud have either taken over the system as a whole or attempted to isolate its virtues from its defects. The most prevalent form of this immaculate dissection is that which divides Freud's metapsychology from his clinical perspective. But it is not possible to say immediately which of these dimensions is preserved or eliminated, for it depends entirely upon who is performing the operation. In the current revisions of psychoanalytic theory by its practitioners, it is the metapsychology that is the anachronism and clinical practice the saving remnant. In the writings of various Neo-Marxists, particularly Marcuse and Jacoby, however, the evaluation is reversed. For the latter, therapy is of necessity adjustment to a corrupt society while the transcendent concepts of Freud's metatheory provide a perspective from which contemporary capitalist culture can be comprehended and condemned.

It is not surprising that analysts should wish to amputate Freud's metapsychology. There are several factors relevant to this decision. First, metaphysics is clearly out of favor. This is an age of idealistic positivism, and analysts are more likely to ground their theories in Wittgenstein, phenomenology, and information theory than Helmholtz and Haeckel. It generally takes analysts a decade or two to integrate the prevailing philosophical tradition, which, like an exploding star, has ceased to exist by the time its outline is discernible.

Second, it is quite clear that earlier hopes for psychoanalytic practice have proved grandiose. Rates of cure through psychoanalysis, on available empirical evidence, are no higher than elsewhere, and remain considerably more expensive. It is not merely that analysts are threatened economically on occasion by increased competition from the variety of quick-cure franchise operations that have arisen like mushrooms in the shade of disintegrating social shadows. The intellectual prestige of psychoanalysis has been challenged with a growing realization that its theory of human existence has lost its once dominant power, while its clinical practice serves less adequately for a diminishing portion of the population.

Finally, Freud's metapsychology resonates with a universe of scarcity, deprivation, and painful repetition that is incompatible with contemporary American attitudes toward immediate gratification and perennial progress. Freud's roots in traditional European culture—not merely its works of art, but its values of hierarchy, conflictual resignation, and privileged sublimation—do not flourish readily in the surburban version of the analytic alliance.

Theory against Therapy

It is more difficult to account for the Marxist dichotomization of Freud carried out by writers like Marcuse and Jacoby. A theory deriving so explicitly from the tradition of "internal relations" would seem an unlikely source for the view that Freud's work can be split into halves, one to be saved and the other discarded. Marx's acerbic condemnation of Proudhon's misunderstanding of the dialectic should serve as a warning at this point:

> For him, M. Proudhon, every economic category has two sides—one good, the other bad. He looks upon these categories as the petty bourgeois looks upon the great men of history: Napoleon was a great man; he did a lot of good; he also did a lot of harm.
>
> The problem to be solved: to keep the good side while eliminating the bad. . . .
>
> What would M. Proudhon do to save slavery? He would formulate the *problem* thus: preserve the good side of this economic category, eliminate the bad.[3]

Nevertheless, Russell Jacoby's judgment, following Marcuse, is clear: "Psychoanalysis as individual therapy necessarily participates *within* the realm of social unfreedom, while psychoanalysis as theory is free to transcend and criticize this realm."[4] How a theory could be so asceptically conceived should give us pause to wonder.

I have already explored (Chapter 1) some of the factors that drew critical theory to Freud: I shall simply recall here that Marxism had ignored perversions of the subjective realm while psychoanalysis spoke to these disfigurations. The absence of a radical Marxist alternative that might account for the pathologies of Stalin and Hitler led critical theory back into a nostalgic recreation of the virtues of bourgeois culture and its theory.

> The greatness of Freud consists in that, like all great bourgeois thinkers, he left standing undissolved such contradictions and disdained the assertion of pretended harmony where the thing itself is contradictory. He revealed the antagonistic character of the social reality.[5]

Freud saw a dark reality that Marxism had all too often ignored. But Freud did not *reveal* the structure of this reality. His vision reified what it observed, a fact which Jacoby, following critical theory, seems unable to concede.

The work of this chapter is devoted to showing that Freud cannot be preserved by dichotomizing his system. In criticizing both the Freudian and Marxist versions of this effort, I intend to lay the groundwork for a theory that will permit the incorporation of Freud into a Marxist perspective, both in its theoretical and its therapeutic dimensions.

The alleged duality of Freud's theory and practice to which Jacoby alludes is aligned with another postulated duality, which Jacoby terms the "two logics." It is Jacoby's contention that Marxists have recently attempted to compensate for a previous disregard of subjective phenomena by harmonizing Marx and Freud.

> This manner of posing the problem suggests that the task is to make agreeable the incompatibility by a round-table discussion that tables the contradictions. A harmonious synthesis of Marxism and psychoanalysis *presupposes* that society is without the antagonisms that are its essence [emphasis added].[6]

Instead of "synchronizing" contradictions, or bifurcating them, "critical theory seeks to articulate them; the task is not to homogenize the insolubles, but, as it were, to culture the differences."[7] If Jacoby, following critical theory, wishes to culture the differences between Marx and Freud, it is crucial that these differences be articulated. The contents of the theories are never specified, however. Instead, the theoretical antagonism between the views is misleadingly reduced to a reflection of social antagonisms. In this move two separate categories are conflated, and Jacoby is spared the problem of analyzing the theoretical differences in question.

A harmonious synthesis between Marx and Freud *presupposes nothing,* least of all a harmonious society, for the simple reason that such a harmonious synthesis of *theories* is absolutely impossible. An alleged antagonism between Freudian and Marxist *theory* is a wholly different issue than the antagonism between individuals in capitalist *society.* Critical theory continually falls into this confusion; however, no *social change* can alter the antagonism between the theories of Marx and Freud because the theories disagree as to whether such a change is possible, and would offer conflicting interpretations if the resolution actually appeared to occur.

> To culture the differences entails pursuing two different logics simultaneously, the logic of society and the logic of the psyche. . . . The various efforts to interpret Marx and Freud have been plagued by reductionism; the inability to retain the tension between the individual and society, psychology and political economy.[8]

Once again rhetoric overwhelms analysis. First, what is meant by "two logics"? This is hardly a trivial question, for everything depends on precisely how separable the individual and society in fact are. If the term "two" simply indicates that the concepts "individual" and "society" are different from each other, no harm is done: but nothing is gained. If the term means something significant, however, and is taken to indicate that each logic is intelligible in separation from the other, the account is profoundly mistaken. If the term is taken to be different from both of these possibilities, it is certainly never made clear what it does intend.

Difficulties are further compounded by the fact that Jacoby has himself previously claimed that Freud "unearthed the objective roots of the private subject—its social content."[9] But if Freud did in fact undo the "primal bourgeois distinction between private and public, *the individual and society*,"[10] what becomes the fate of the alleged "two logics" and the tension between psychology and political economy? Again, if "psychologism (the reduction of social concepts to individual and psychological concepts) remains false in all its forms"[11] society must have properties that cannot be deduced from the characteristics of its individual members. But this is precisely what Freud denied. Freud never could have shown the social roots of the individual because it violated his basic conception of the relationship between society and its individual members: "For *sociology*, which deals with the behavior of man in society, can be nothing other than *applied psychology*. Strictly speaking, indeed, there are only two sciences—psychology, pure and applied, and natural science."[12] For Freud, the individual is basic and society a derivation. It is not possible to cite Freud in behalf of the two logics for he espouses only one—psychology.

Therefore, despite Jacoby's endorsement of Adorno's assertion that "psychoanalysis and historical materialism must co-exist,"[19] the position must be rejected. For on the interpretation psychoanalysis itself offers of the relationship between the individual and society the fundamental distinction between them is reduced to the very different duality between pure and applied psychology: that is, between *pure individual* psychology and *applied individual* psychology. Psychoanalysis and Marxism cannot coexist unless psychoanalysis is radically reinterpreted, a task Jacoby does not attempt.

In its concern to authenticate the individual against the ravages of totalitarian society, critical theory mistakenly concluded that a "logic of the individual psyche" is required. Now, it is one thing to wish to protect the individual against mass domination. It is a wholly different matter to equate this desire with a *theory* based on the "logic of the individual psyche." For if the phrase is taken nontrivially to indicate that there are actual properties of individuals that can be understood independently of the social structure the view is significantly misleading. The notions of "individual" and "society" are dialectically related; that is, while not identical neither are they separable. We cannot begin to understand either without immediately referring to the other. The smallest intelligible unit of explanation is the social individual. It is true that the individual brings to social existence a system of abstract structures and general tendencies. But these are in turn specified through concrete social arrangements that are themselves constituted out of the network of determinate human beings who compose them. Although human nature possesses abstract limitations and potentialities, even these cannot be specified outside of their social manifestation. Therefore, a defense of "the individual psyche" against its social reduction is a defense of every form of social system that has ever existed. For each of them is grounded in its individual members and would be unintelligible without them.

On *the plane of theoretical understanding,* then, the individual and society cannot be in opposition. Of course, a given society can be so structured that some set of individuals opposes another, or even so that all individuals but one oppose a single member. These are not, however, antagonisms between society and the asocial individual but between some *social individuals* and *others.* We could find Jacoby's account intelligible only if the notion of a determinate *asocial* individual were plausible. Such a perspective is fundamental to Freud and is rejected by Marx, for whom the tension between the individual and society is grounded in the contradictions within a given sociohistorical structure. To conceptualize the relationship between Freud and Marx through the motif of the two logics is to deny the Marxist perspective in the very process of adjudicating the dispute in question. In fact, what is most curious about Jacoby's account is that he himself approvingly cites the following passage from Marx:

> [The] private interest is already *a socially determined interest,* which can be achieved only within the conditions laid down by society and with the means provided by society. . . . It is the interest of private persons; but its *content,* as well as the *form* and *means* of its realization, is given by social conditions independent of all [emphasis added].[14]

And yet, the clear meaning of this passage—that the realm of the private is socially constituted in its form and content—is not merely ignored by Jacoby but negated.

Logically speaking, since neither the individual nor society can exist without each other, we must conclude that they are specified out of a *single logic.* Nor is it intelligible to assign priority to either. Adorno leads us astray when he asserts that

> we have never doubted the primacy of objective factors over psychological. . . . We say socio-psychology as a subjective mediation of an objective social system; without its mechanism the subject would not be able to be held on the leash.[15]

The reference to the leash is illuminating because it serves to remind us of the fusion of political and theoretical categories. In reality, however, objective factors cannot have priority over psychological factors for the simple reason that objective factors are themselves simultaneously psychological. What are the objective factors in any case if not the network of "sociopsychological" individuals who constitute the socioeconomic structure? Jacoby's approving citation of Reich and Fromm only compounds the error:

Between the two terminal points—the economic structure of society at one end, the ideological superstructure at the other . . . psychoanalysis sees a number of intermediate stages.

[psychoanalysis] can show in what manner particular economic conditions influence the psychic apparatus of men and produce particular ideological results; it can provide information on the "how" of the dependence of ideological facts on particular configurations.[16]

But psychology cannot be assigned this task of elucidating "intermediate stages" or the causal influences of economic structures on the psychic apparatus for the basic reason that *economic structures are themselves sociopsychological categories.* Neither Reich nor Fromm ever overcame the basic duality of individual and society which is the persistent mystifying heritage of psychoanalysis. They could do no more than ameliorate as best they could the dichotomy between individual and social, psychological and economic, which they were never able to transcend.

It is now necessary to return to the first of Jacoby's dichotomies—that between Freud's theory and practice. The argument here is that psychoanalytic *theory* transcends the capitalist order that subverts its *therapy.* To credit this position we need to believe that the same capitalist society whose ubiquitous corruption of every other aspect of social existence is minutely traced by critical theory and reiterated by Jacoby reigns itself in at the border of psychoanalytic theory. The position is not plausible a priori; nor does Jacoby offer any argument on its behalf. Instead, the basic theory-practice duality is elaborated through a presentation that adds further confusion to the original error.

Freud's subversiveness is derived from his concepts and not from his stated political opinions. This disjunction is absolutely crucial to recognize: the disjunction between the political, social, and truth content of concepts *and* the political–social outlook of those using the concepts. They are not identical: they often stand in contradiction [emphasis added].[17]

This passage, whose importance Jacoby himself underscores, is remarkably unclear. Concepts are distinguished from political outlook: neither is defined, however, and the obvious rejoinder that political outlooks are themselves comprised of concepts is not addressed. The concepts in question are perhaps those of "repression, sexuality, unconscious, Oedipal complex, and infantile sexuality," which Jacoby takes to be "the fundamental core of Freudian theory."[18] Not only does Jacoby fail to show how the concepts are subversive, but his "disjunction," which at one pole identifies the political, social, and truth content of these concepts, is further obfuscating. The traditional "genetic fallacy," which distinguished between the origin and validity of a theory, was at least clear. But Jacoby's analysis appears to identify these two features and set them together in opposition to the outlook of its user.

Have we any way of discovering Freud's outlook independently of examining the social and political content of his theory? What is the purported ground of his radicalism?

> Freud undid the primal bourgeois distinction between the private and public, the individual and society; he unearthed the objective roots of the private subject—its social content.[19]

From this Jacoby concludes that if Freud was "conservative in his immediate disregard of society, his concepts are radical in their pursuit of society where it allegedly does not exist."[20] If this account were true of Freud (which it is not), it would suffer the reductio ad absurdum of immediately reconstituting every conservative from Plato through Durkheim and beyond, as radical. Conservatism agrees with Marxism that the individual cannot be understood except as intrinsically social. Therefore, even if we can bracket the fact that Freud's "immediate disregard of society"—which Jacoby acknowledges as conservative—is clearly part of the "political, social, and truth content" of his concepts, we cannot fail to realize that had Freud in fact discovered the social in the individual, this would not support Jacoby's claim of radicalism. Freud's actual "accomplishment" consisted in replacing a wholly superficial, optimistic bourgeois illusion regarding individual autonomy with a more sophisticated, pessimistic version of the same theory. Jacoby succumbs to Freud's mystification on this point; it is important to get the issue clear.

Levels of Mystification

Capitalism requires individuals who are legally free and able to enter into and out of contractual relationships. Such individuals cannot be slaves or serfs. Nor can they possess the means of their own reproduction, or they would lack any incentive to exchange their labor power for wages. The capitalist takes all this for granted, but he translates the fact of contractual exchange based on *necessity* into the ideology of *free* movement and *individual* liberty. While the capitalist is clearly part of a complex social system that is essential for his own survival, the anarchic and unplanned character of production tends to promote the fantasy that individuals are independent of each other. The particular set of social relations that defines the structure of capitalism does not appear on the surface of economic life, *but behind the backs of its agents.* The fact that the capitalist is not legally or morally obligated to consider others is confused with the contention that he is not dependent upon them. His relationship to society remains disjunctive and anonymous and this aids the capitalist in promoting the general illusion of personal autonomy. Society appears not as a necessary structure dependent on a vast complex of involuntary social transactions but as the sum of the private acts of self-interested individuals.

For the capitalist, then, passionately committed to the denial of social dependency, the individual is not the product of social existence but a universal fact of nature, possessing an identical character throughout history. Freud's position is similar and equally naïve. The social contract therefore rests on the properties of "natural man," and social explanation consists in showing how these isolated figures are drawn or driven into social relations with each other. (At this point Freud's account begins to display its greater acuity in its recognition of the family as a noncontractual unit, but his vision of the larger social system retains the bourgeois perspective.) Social existence is then deduced from the natural properties of its members in contractual conjunction. For Rousseau the natural individual is motivated by moral self-realization and sympathy; for Hobbes, by destructiveness and exclusive self-interest. Freud concurs with Hobbes.

Since the economic structure of capitalism is not consciously determined by a common plan but by individual units of competitive power (however these units change historically), the activities of others appear not as a potentiality for mutual enrichment but as a sheer hostile facticity to be manipulated for survival and profit. The "self-realization" of others constitutes a threat to my existence, although the ideology of the system claims the very opposite. So capitalist theory is perpetually rent by the contradictions between freedom and necessity, self and other, individual reason and social calamity; in short, by the fact that self-interest is socially destructive.

It must be acknowledged by all, however, including the bourgeoisie, that individuals impinge upon each other, that they are affected by their social existence. *The notion of natural man does not exclude the fact that individuals have a social existence and develop new characteristics in society.* On the contrary, both Hobbes and Rousseau insist that individuals take on the mantle of civilization, and acquire a set of social customs that overlay their original constitution. But the surface is not what is seems and never eradicates the primal reality it disguises. Whether human beings are naturally good and corrupted by society into the adoption of evil (Rousseau) or naturally evil and forced to assume some semblance of good (Hobbes) the duality between eternal nature and its social appearance is retained. Rousseau was typically concerned to distinguish what is "fundamental" in human nature from the "changes and additions" that circumstances have introduced to "modify his primitive condition."

Now it is clear that Freud follows in this bourgeois tradition. But he adds to the general bourgeois assumptions that he inherits an ingenious, complex, and subtle account of precisely how this primal instinctual nature undergoes the specific "vicissitudes" which transform the original infant into the member of a civilized culture. By developing a "scientific" explanation of the influence of individuals upon each other— particularly through the stages of psychosexual development in children—Freud establishes that the bourgeois pretense of individual autonomy is fallacious. His theory affirms that individuals are clearly affected by their social existence. But this social existence is merely the result of multiplying and conjoining their original nature, which does not fundamentally change in the process of social construction. Individual character is the intersection of primary instinct and social repression. Its vicissitudes, however esoteric, are the conjunction of two forces which *do not themselves undergo any historical transformation but remain fundamentally everywhere the same.*

This is the crucial fact of Freud's theory, the root both of his unmasking of superficial bourgeois illusions and his reiteration of reified capitalist categories. The "independent," free, rational individual disappears, only to be replaced by the necessary warfare of each with all, the inherent destructiveness of social existence, and the unalterable opposition between the irrational individual and the repressive social order. This aspect of Freud's theory does not distinguish him from Hobbes. But then Freud adds a dimension to this account no previous bourgeois or conservative thinker before him could do more than adumbrate; Freud indicates how this individual–social antagonism is reproduced *within the individual* and manifested throughout social life. In short, Freud grasped a reality that operated "behind the backs" of unsuspecting individuals. But he interpreted this overpowering force, which is ultimately social in nature, as emanating from the fixed nature of private individuals. Through this schema Freud rejected the bourgeois perspective through its own categories.

Freud's "immediate disregard of society" follows precisely from the fact that the concrete structure of the social world is irrelevant to his account. He is concerned solely with what is "universal"; the "immediate" is precisely what needs to be penetrated and discarded. Jacoby is himself forced to acknowledge that "the loyalties of Freud himself lay with modified repression"[21] and that in the end he "justifies civilization."[22] Jacoby can still accept Freudian theory as revolutionary, however, because he takes Freud to have "said enough about [civilization's] antagonistic and repressive *essence* to put it in question" (emphasis added).[23] But this defense brings us to the heart of the difficulty. For if civilization is *essentially antagonistic and repressive,* no particular social or political transformation can do more than modify the most extreme instances of its pathology. The essence of repression remains the same; permanent and inexorable, the perennial dark side of the liberal vision.

But so intent is Jacoby on the resurrection of revolutionary Freud that he in fact cites and then fundamentally misinterprets a vital key to the understanding of Freud's project:

> Observing the prevalence of "inner resolution and craving for authority" Freud stated that one of its principal causes was "the impoverishment of the ego due to the tremendous effort in repression *demanded of every individual by culture*" [emphasis added].[24]

Jacoby draws from this passage the conclusion that "personal insecurity is a direct response to collective repression. It is not a universal component of man's essence."[25] I believe, however, that Freud intends precisely the opposite of Jacoby's interpretation: that is, that repression is demanded of *every individual* by culture. For Freud, culture demands repression and is inconceivable without it. It is no doubt true that repression causes various human pathologies, insecurity among them. The dilemma for Freud is that without cultural repression human life would not only be insecure but totally impossible.

The result of Jacoby's extreme dualism of transcendent theory and manipulated practice not only leads to a misunderstanding of Freud's theory but, predictably, to the paradox of total accommodation to present therapeutic forms. The "cure" of the individual and the "cure" of civilization are absolutely severed. Nothing that occurs within the realm of therapy can serve as more than adjustment, for psychoanalysis as a form of therapy "necessarily participates *within* the realm of social unfreedom." But then again, what human activity does not participate within the social realm? The question is not whether we participate, but how? There are forms of action that solidify the social system and those that introduce the seeds of transcendence. We are haunted here by the phantom of one dimensionality; a critique so transcendent, of a society so corrupt, that no dialectical passage can be conceived from the one to the other.

> Individual therapy must necessarily forget the whole so as to aid its individual victim; how exactly it does this *is in part* irrelevant to theory. As Brown, whose discussion parallels Marcuse's, wrote, psychoanalytic therapy as a "technique . . . can be judged only pragmatically. Anything goes if it works." This is not to be criticized—or if criticized, only when that which "works" is called liberation or growth. Theoretically, what Adorno wrote remains true: "In adjusting to the mad whole the cured patient becomes really sick."[26]

I do not take issue with Jacoby on the question of whether contemporary therapy can be termed "liberation." In the overwhelming majority of instances therapy is accommodation. Three aspects of the argument are dangerously misleading, however. First, we are offered no meaningful definition of "pragmatic" success, so that all forms of therapy become acceptable regardless of the degree of adjustment or even reaction they promote in their clients. The total dichotomization of theory and therapy eliminates any comparative estimate of different forms of therapy so long as they provide individual relief, however that notion is defined. We have here another illustration of the fact that every form of transcendent idealism ends with accommodation to the world as it is.

Second, the reliance of therapy upon theoretical assumptions is totally ignored.

> From his early writings to his last no attempt is made to reconcile individual therapy with the "metatheory" of psychoanalysis; they exist in contradiction. Insofar as civilization was repression, individual therapy was education in repression, albeit conscious repression.[27]

Individual therapy is education in repression not because "civilization was repression" but because psychoanalytic theory *viewed* civilization as repression. Freud's therapeutic practice followed with great cogency from this metatheoretical perspective. He counseled conscious repression because it was the best that could be achieved within civilization, *as he understood it. "Psychoanalysis is a theory of an unfree society that necessitates psychoanalysis as a therapy."*[28] This is a lovely aphorism but it needs to be recast: "Psychoanalysis is a theory of an unfree society that reproduces that unfreedom and necessitates psychoanalysis as an *unfree* therapy." Psychoanalysis, in other words, reifies capitalist alienation, and logically deduces the necessity of self-alienation from its erroneous premise.

Finally, the severing of theory and practice obviates the necessity of examining Freud's clinical practice to discover its actual dependence on metatheoretical assumptions. Marxist theory has tended to ignore the specifics of Freudian therapy and the resulting global judgments have often lacked credibility. It is the purpose of this work to fill in something of that lacuna. But it is first necessary to dispose of the counterclaim of contemporary analytic theory—that the practice of therapy is independent of metapsychology and valid on its own terms.

Current Attempts to Save Practice from Theory

I want to be very clear about the intention of the next section of this analysis. In taking up the issue of the relationship between clinical practice and metapsychological theory it is not my purpose to pursue an exhaustive review of the current literature. My concern is: (1) to show that clinical practice and metapsychology cannot be separated; and (2) to consider the hypothesis that the particular relationship between Freud's metapsychology and his clinical practice was mediated by his sociopolitical assumptions regarding human nature. (This point will be discussed in a later chapter.) These contentions are the necessary aspects of an argument designed to show that Freud's insights cannot be preserved by rejecting one *sector* of his work—the metapsychology or clinical practice—for the sake of preserving the other. Instead, I will argue that the most useful paradigm for restructuring Freudian theory within a larger social framework is Marx's conception of *the fetishism of consciousness,* which depends on a dialectic of totality as exemplified in Marx's critique of Hegel and the political economists.

A significant number of contemporary psychoanalysts would subscribe to the following statement:

> Freud's work shows two separate theories of psychic structure-formation, one of which belongs to the clinical side of psychoanalysis and the other to the metapsychology: the first is a theory of meanings; the second, a theory of forces.[29]

The dichotomy between forces and meanings as explanations of human activity has a long history. At the turn of the century the argument, focused through the writing of Dilthey, Windleband, and Weber, concerned the role of hermeneutics and verstehen (empathy) as distinguishing marks of appropriate inquiry into human existence. In the recent debates within the Anglo-Saxon tradition, arguments regarding the relationship between the language of science and of common sense have reopened the discussion concerning appropriate categories of human explanation. Within psychoanalytic circles an argument put forward by H. J. Home in 1966 seems to have considerably influenced later discussions of the subject. Home insisted that there were two distinct ways of studying human beings: the first based on traditional forms of science deriving from physics and employing deductive models of explanation which emphasize lawful regularity, and the second concerned with the human enterprise as unique, creative, and idiosyncratic.

> In discovering that the symptom had meaning and basing his treatment on this hypothesis, Freud took the psycho-analytic study of neurosis *out of the world of science* into the world of the humanities, because a meaning is not the product of causes but the creation of a subject. This is a major difference; for the logic and method of the humanities is radically different from that of science, though no less respectable and rational, and of course much longer established.[30]

And what is the distinct logic and method of the humanities as contrasted with science? It is the difference between humanistic *interpretation* and scientific *explanation*. Science, according to Home, asks questions about how various mechanisms *cause* the occurrence of particular phenomena; humanistic inquiry asks why human activity occurred and answers in terms of motives understood as *reasons*.

These distinctions have been taken up by a growing body of psychoanalytic theorists, whom I will refer to for heuristic purposes as clinical psychoanalysts to distinguish them from figures like Rapaport who maintain allegiance to the basic structure of Freud's metapsychology. For the clinical school the key notions in psychoanalytic theory are "meaning," "intention," "purpose," and "phenomenological description" as they are exemplified in actual clinical practice. Psychoanalysis is understood by the clinical theorists to embody two distinct theories—one clinical and the other metapsychological—or, in Rapaport's account, "clinical principles" and "general psychological theory." There is common agreement among the clinical psychoanalysts that Freud's metapsychology is not the critical part of psychoanalysis.

> Now it should give us pause to be told that metapsychology . . . is the most basic theory of psychoanalysis, for it is surely *not* the part of psychoanalysis that stimulated, excited, and revolutionized twentieth-century culture. It was the so-called "clinical" part of the enterprise which sparked the revolution. Psychoanalysis as a scientific system appealed to many people, including those outside psychology, because of its elegance and beauty in accounting for behavior. Relatively few simple principles enabled us to see meanings in the most varied and apparently incomprehensible or senseless behaviors, such as dreams, jokes, mistakes, and symptoms. Yet, as analysts came to formulate their ideas systematically, they abandoned this level and assumed the aims and mannerisms of natural scientists talking about energies, forces, cathexes, systems, layers, mechanisms, and physical analogies, rather than meanings. Thus, today, psychoanalysis presents itself in two guises: the psychology in terms of which Freud interpreted dreams and symptoms and slips of the tongue—the distinctive meanings that behaviors acquire when interpreted in terms of sexual and aggressive wishes, conscious and unconscious events, displacement of aims, transference, unconscious fantasy, and related principles; and on the other hand a theory—the theory of metapsychology—which explains the clinical theory.[31]

There are some for whom a theory of metapsychology (as developed by Freud) is either meaningless or mistaken and others, like Kline, who regard it as "simply *irrelevant* to the clinical psychoanalytic enterprise."[32] The difference here is a matter of degree. But the same thing cannot be said in regard to the very important question of whether clinical theory is autonomous or depends upon a new metapsychology to replace the classic theory of mechanical forces and systems of psychical energy. According to the advocates of what I shall call pure clinical theory (as opposed to the neometapsychologists) the concepts crucial to successful clinical practice can be gathered from careful reflection upon the process of therapy and require no new metapsychological deductions, postulations, or philosophical inferences to ground their proceedings. Holt's comment is typical:

I am unable to follow or agree with Arlow's contention that the model of the ego and the id is part of the clinical theory (as opposed to metapsychology) or that it is more intimately connected to clinical observation than the topographic model. The concept of ego is no more observable than that of the *system Pcs.* and the inferential chain between clinical observation and either set of concepts is of equal length. *Concepts like projection, and isolation, unconscious guilt, and regressive impulses are close to direct observation and undoubtedly integral parts of the clinical theory* [emphasis added].[33]

Now although Holt does not say that concepts like "projection" are directly observable, he clearly means to distinguish such concepts from those like "ego" which depend upon an "inferential chain" for their validation. Whatever the notion of "close to observation" means, and however it could apply to a concept like "unconscious guilt," for example, a basic distinction between the realm of observation and metaphysical postulation is implicit in Holt's account. This factor is made perfectly clear in Holt's positive comment on the work of Roy Schafer, who is described as

seeking a relatively modest objective—to formulate *not a new metapsychology* or basic model but *a language that will be free of metapsychology's* besetting errors and fallacies, consistent and appropriate for clinical use [emphasis added].[34]

I believe this is a very dubious account of what Schafer is in fact doing, but the key aspect of the comment seems to me the interpretation of Schafer's work as constituting a language that is free of metapsychology. The basic structure of the argument of the "pure" clinical theorists is precisely this alleged division between experience and clinical practice on the one hand and metapsychology on the other.

But before proceeding with our inquiry into the possibility of eliminating metapsychology from clinical theory, it is important to pause for a moment over the obvious need to define the term "metapsychology" itself. This is not an easy matter, for Freud's statements are ambivalent, reflecting on different occasions first his view that psychoanalytic theory will one day be replaced by physiological explanation, and at other times vehemently denying this same proposition.[35] Rather than pursue the technicalities of Freud's position through all its ramifications I will, instead, utilize the following account as basic to Freud's perspective:

Besides the dynamic and topographical points of view, we have adopted the *economic* one. This endeavors to follow out the vicissitudes of amounts of excitation and to arrive at least at some *relative* estimate of their magnitude.

It will not be unreasonable to give a special name to this whole way of regarding our subject matter, for it is the consummation of psycho-analytic research. I propose that when we have succeeded in describing a psychical process in its dynamic, topographical and economic aspects, we should speak of it as *metapsychological* presentation.[36]

I believe that by the term "metapsychology" Freud meant the conjunction of the dynamic, topographic, and economic perspectives, allowing for the fact that the topographic perspective was later replaced by a structural account of psychic life.[37] On Freud's view, then, in denying the metapsychological point of view, one would appear to be denying that psychological phenomena are only finally intelligible as the expression of underlying forces, particularly those in opposition; that behavior is regulated by the flow of energy whose quantity is constant and whose tendency is toward discharge until a state of constancy or stability is attained; that mental life is made up of different strata, regions, or structures having very different characteristics and laws of operation that involve distinctions between primary and secondary processes, the division of the psyche into id, ego and superego, and a large number of propositions of a similar level of generality. This appears to be what *Freud* meant.

The main issue, however, is not the exact definitions of metapsychology and clinical experience but the relationship between them. Consequently, the following statement of Freud's takes on enormous significance:

> We seek not merely to describe and to classify phenomena, but to understand them *as signs of an interplay of forces* in the mind, as a manifestation of purposeful intentions working concurrently or in mutual opposition. We are concerned with a dynamic view of mental phenomena. On our view *the phenomena that are perceived must yield in importance to trends which are only hypothetical* [emphasis added].[38]

Freud explicitly contends that metapsychology is a realm of hypothetical construction rather than description. But instead of denigrating metapsychology through this account Freud makes it clear that description acquires its meaning from the fact that it is a sign of underlying forces, and that perception must yield to hypothetical trends when necessary. Whatever a sheer descriptive account might be, it would certainly not satisfy Freud's conception of the nature or achievement of psychoanalysis, whose "consummation," to use Freud's term, lies precisely in the principles of metapsychology.

For the current pure clinicians Freud's underlying principles can be retained to the extent that they are clinically required. Arlow, whom Holt previously criticized on this point, exemplifies the perspective when he notes:

> First of all, I wish to emphasize the fact that the conceptual innovations proposed in the *Ego and the Id* were above all clinically determined. What was

new and different was introduced for the purpose of bringing theory in line with clinical observations.[39]

What was metapsychological inference (at best) for Holt, namely, Freud's later structural model, is clinically determined by observation for Arlow. But Arlow has a similar distinction in mind, as the following passage makes clear:

> Economic concepts, for example, based on the principles of thermodynamics borrowed from physics, constitute a priori assumptions when applied to psychoanalysis. The genetic viewpoint, on the other hand, derives from empirical findings.[40]

So, while the ego and the id are speculative for Holt they are observational for Arlow, for whom, in turn, economic concepts are a priori and opposed to genetic principles, which "derive" from empirical findings. These references might be taken to show nothing more than the obvious fact that those espousing the doctrine of pure clinical psychoanalysis disagree among themselves. But I believe the dispute indicates that there is considerable confusion regarding terms like "derived from experience," "close to observation," and "clinically determined." The problem is not gratuitous, but springs from the mistaken assumption that it is logically possible to delineate a realm of "direct clinical experience." Yet experience of any kind is necessarily ordered in some transcendent conceptual framework—a fact that renders all attempts to separate a realm of "pure observation" from "mere conjecture" structurally impossible. No observation can be theory-free.

I believe that the point is inadvertently illustrated by Wallerstein in commenting favorably on a reflection of Gill's which

> draws the distinction between defense mechanisms (clearly in the nonexperiential realm) and defenses (equally clearly—to me—in the experiential realm). For a defense mechanism is nothing but a construct that denotes a way of functioning of the mind. It is a construct invoked to explain how behaviors, affects, and ideas serve to inhibit, avert, delay, or otherwise modulate unwanted impulse discharge. Defenses, on the other hand, are the actual *behaviors, affects,* and *ideas* that serve defensive purposes.[41]

The difficulty with this separation of experiential and nonexperiential realms lies in the fact that behaviors, affects, and ideas, which are described as experiential, can only be regarded as defenses to the extent that they serve defensive purposes. But whether any aspect of experience serves defensive purposes is not itself directly experiential. Wallerstein acknowledges as much when he notes that the functioning of "*behaviors, affects,* and *ideas* ... is explained *in terms of* the operation of defense mechanisms."[42] In other words, the characterization that applies within experience derives its meaning from the postulated defense mechanisms that lie beyond experience. Without the postulations of such extraexperiential mechanisms the behaviors and experiences in question could not be understood as defenses at all.

The question of what lies within the realm of experience and what lies beyond it is too complex a philosophical issue to explore very deeply in this essay; but unfortunately, the political implications of the distinction are too crucial to go completely without comment. For to the extent that experience is understood as simply *given* rather than *constructed* (or *taken*, to use Dewey's word), to that extent the social and political presuppositions that order experience and clinical practice go unacknowledged. Analysts who adopt the pure clinical theory are likely to be particularly unaware of the societal foundation of their own perspective. For the more one interprets experience as speaking to us directly and unadorned, the less one has reason to engage in the necessary self-reflection that seeks after the contribution of our own values and expectations in the constitution of what we recognize as direct experience.

And yet, a vital and inexpungable element of what constitutes experience is due to our own "theoretical" contribution—metaphysical, scientific, social, and political. This fact is true of all experience, even the most simple and commonplace; it is especially true of a practice like psychotherapy, which is specifically designed to alter human activity in accordance with very particular value directives, whether these be explicitly recognized or not. Behind the appearance of immediacy lies the mediation of institutions of control and domination.

The starting point of any valid analysis is the truth contained in the following statement of C. I. Lewis:

> The two elements to be distinguished in knowledge are the concept, which is the product of the activity of thought, and the sensuously given, which is independent of such activity.[43]

What precisely each of these factors contributes to the whole enterprise of knowledge is the difficulty a proper analysis would need to explicate; furthermore, I do not accept the implication that concepts—as the products of thought—are also wholly the invention of thought. To understand the defects of the pure clinical approach, however, it is enough to grasp the validity of the contrast Lewis sets out between "the immediate data, such as those of sense, which are presented or given to the mind, and a form, construction, or interpretation, which represents the activity of thought"[44]

The most direct and basic realm of experience, the world of material objects, is already constituted by the most audacious flights of theoretical construction. The very notion of a "material object" is a metaphysical elaboration that transcends immediate evidence. We always mean more by a material object than by anything we can establish through an appeal to our senses. We begin the constitution of the world with metaphysical conjectures concerning causality, continuity, and the public availability of identical objects to diverse subjects. As the notion of "material world" is slowly constructed, these conceptions are progressively brought into play. When we are capable of identifying a material "thing" we have constructed a metaphysics that asserts at least the following: that objects continue to exist when they are not perceived; that they can continuously exercise causal agency when not observed; that diverse subjects, differentially located in space and time, can grasp the identical characteristics of a common entity; and that some material "substrate" is the underlying source of unity of the diverse experiences reached through our incommensurate senses. We add to this original ontology a set of implicit judgments derived from past science, current theory, and ancient stock of "common sense," and from a slowly accumulating awareness of the social meaning attributed to things, which in time permeates their nature and delineates their "thinghood."

We organize the world on the basis of principles derived from the innate tendencies of our own minds, from reflection on the common characteristics of experienced reality, and from the requirements and perspectives of our concrete place in a specific social order. If nothing were given to mind, knowledge would become a purely arbitrary decision, which would negate the very distinction between truth and error and make knowledge itself impossible. If nothing were contributed by mind, error and illusion would become impossible, the distinction between truth and error would dissolve, and knowledge would again become impossible.

Reality is a social construction, but this does not lead to the conclusion that either the given, the taken, or the relationship between them is arbitrary. Nor does it lead us to deny that there is a fundamental difference between appearance and reality, with "dreams" and "illusions" harbored in the first region, and public (real) entities in the second. The concepts we apply to experience are not adventitious; our conceptualization is limited by the characteristics of the given itself. In constructing our theoretical framework we discriminate from among the real properties of the world. This means that on the one hand we are not forced into any particular selection out of the range of possible categories, while on the other, that we are restricted by our original determinations.

For example, we are free to classify "velvet" and "feathers" together as "soft," and "steel" and "rock" as "hard." Or we can classify "velvet" and "steel" as "produced by human beings" while we regard "rock" and "feathers" as "natural." But if we make the first choice we are not then free to regard "glass" as "soft" without making other transformations in the structure of our classifications. The seductiveness with which our own construction presents itself within the constitution of the world itself necessitates continual socioepistemic self-reflection into the character and meaning of our elaborations. The most difficult fetishism of consciousness to unmask is that which insinuates itself within the world as its fundamental reality.

The most basic operations of common sense are metaphysical. As we move beyond this fundamental realm to the more complex and elaborate domain of therapeutic interaction we add to the store of our material postulates new conjectures about action, language, meaning, personal agency, and social communication. There is no discipline for which this fact should be more obvious than psychoanalysis, for the very foundation of its unique practice is the notion of the unconscious, a concept that by definition is precluded from empirical verification. I am not judging the soundness of *inferences* to the existence of an unconscious but simply noting that the meaning of the term requires a status that transcends any observation that can be claimed as a ground for its deduction.

All psychoanalytic clinical practice begins with the notion of the unconscious—that is, with a metapsychological construction. Without such a concept the actual practice would obviously proceed in a very different manner. But the unconscious is not the only transcendent notion involved in therapy. The *interpretation* of dreams is another obvious example. Exactly which additional notions are required is a matter that varies from one theorist to another. For Freud, however, every clinical conception he utilized was dependent upon metapsychological foundations. In some cases this fact is obvious: the idea of actual neurosis depends on the conception of a toxic energy substance trapped within the organism; the imposition of abstinence in therapy rests on theory of a fixed amount of available libido, as does the pessimistic diagnosis regarding the cure of schizophrenia. But the same consideration holds for "substitute gratification," "transference," "melancholia"—due to an inhibition of libido, "defenses"—since they require cathexis and countercathexis, "autism," "work," "conflict," and "displacement," which implies that there is a "something" to be displaced, that it can move from one function to another, and that an original impulse can be "satisfied" in attenuated form.[45] This point becomes unavoidable when we remember that Freud understood phenomena as "signs of an interplay of forces," so that he viewed the entire realm of experience in therapy as constituted by notions of a metapsychological sort.

Since phenomena are a "signs" of underlying processes, description and explanation cannot be separated. For the meaning of the phenomenon is determined by what it signifies, and this determination necessarily involves reference to transecendent conceptions. Any description that is pursued to its appropriate foundation will thereby reveal itself simultaneously as an explanation. Conversely, a description that barricades itself within the phenomenal realm will merely disguise the ground of its own conceptualization. On this important point Freud seems to me to have been correct. It is a separable issue as to whether Freud's *particular* metapsychological perspective was valid or useful; but his account of the relationship between the two realms seems persuasive. An alternative view of the functioning of mind is certainly possible, but I fail to understand how such a view can be consistently maintained from within a psychoanalytic perspective, since its whole purpose is to reveal the ultimate unconscious determinants of presented experience.

Rapaport and Gill introduce some considerations that help to illuminate this issue.[46] In setting out a formal presentation of the basic propositions of metapsychology they distinguish among: (1) empirical propositions; (2) specific psychoanalytic propositions; (3) general psychoanalytic propositions; and (4) propositions stating metapsychological assumptions. An example of the first is: "Around the fourth year of life boys regard their fathers as rivals." An example of the second: The solution of the Oedipal situation is a decisive determinant of character formation and pathology." Of the third: "Structure formation by means of identification and anticathexis explains theoretically the consequence of the 'decline' of the Oedipus complex," while the propositions of the fourth realm "which explain the Oedipal situation and the decline of the Oedipus complex involve dynamic, economic, structural, genetic and adaptive assumptions."[47]

I believe that it is clear, on reflection, how the second proposition depends upon the third, which in turn derives its meaning from metapsychoanalytic assumptions. That is, notions like "identification" and "anticathexis" are necessary to explicate the meaning of phrases like "solution of the Oedipal situation" and "character formation." Where the account is misleading, however, is in the suggestion that the first proposition does not itself rest on more general considerations but can be investigated directly by nonpsychoanalytic methods. The difficulty with this proposal is that the notion of "rivalry" derives its specific meaning from the remaining propositions in the psychoanalytic system. For the verification of the claim that rivalry does in fact exist involves reference to data that psychoanalytic theory interprets according to the more general propositions of its own perspective. In other words, the data would not indicate the existence of rivalry unless it were regarded from a psychoanalytic perspective. For evidence of rivalry can come from the interpretation of dreams, from the symbolic nature of play, and even from the fact that the boy shows an "abnormal" lack of rivalry toward his father, a phenomenon that might be explained by reaction formation— but only on the basis of psychoanalytic assumptions.

I alluded earlier to a group of neometapsychoanalytic theorists and I wish to comment briefly on their work before setting aside the present topic. This work is not the place to carry out an examination of some of the newer attempts to provide a metapsychology to replace the original Freudian system of mechanical–hydraulic energy. Needless to say I am sympathetic to the general intention of this enterprise, although I do not find any of the present attempts successful, and some seem to me headed in the wrong direction. Some writers like Peterfreund[48] and Rubinstein[49] are moving toward neurophysiological information-processing models, while Schafer[50] has developed an action theory, and Klein,[51] an informational-meaning theory. I see two major difficulties in these new attempts: (1) they are *insufficiently* metapsychological; and (2) they are fundamentally deficient in their grasp of the social origins of human relationships.

The first objection will hopefully seem less outrageous after our critique of the pure clinical school. For if it is impossible to eliminate metapsychological considerations from a proper psychology and an adequate clinical practice, the only question that remains is the specific metapsychology. Freud's basic errors in this realm derived from his failure to pursue his own metapsychological presuppositions to their logical conclusion. It is not the concept of energy, for example, that is at fault in Freud's metapsychology, but the particular notion of energy derived from the physical sciences with their assumptions of quantity, constancy, and entropy. A notion of energy is indispensable to the comprehension of human existence; it is more likely to be illuminated through Bergson's reflections on *qualitative* magnitudes, however, than by the exemplars of nineteenth-century physics.

But the theorists of the neometapsychological school, while cognizant of Freud's limitations, have not begun to approach a new foundation for their own discipline. Klein, who is certainly one of the more sophisticated of the newer advocates, notes sharply: "The information model of conscious experience implied here will not be spelled out in this book but it is taken for granted."[52] This is an honest disclaimer and I have no objection to it; nobody can be expected to explicate every concept contained in his theoretical work. It is something else in the theory that needs to be noted—not an explicit statement that certain positions will be taken for granted, but what I believe is a failure to grasp the sort of question that needs to be pursued to make the new position fully intelligible.

Reversal and Ideology in George Klein

Klein is one of the ablest theorists of intentionality, and the following passage is crucial to his perspective:

The central objective of psychoanalytic clinical explanation is the *reading of intentionality;* behavior, experience, testimony are studied for meaning in this sense, as jointly exemplifying directive "tensions," avowed, disavowed, repressed, defended. This orientation to explanation generates concepts that reflect a picture of individual development as a problem-solving, meaning-seeking, meaning-organizing venture, involving and resulting from the constant reslution of incompatible aims and tendencies.[53]

This perspective, which "aims at specifying the subject's own vantage point,"[54] is sharply distinguished from traditional psychoanalytic meta-psychology, which approaches the person as an observed physical process. The second approach is external, impersonal, physical, and mechanistic; it leaves behind the realm of meaning, purpose, and the subject's experienced intention. The two approaches locate themselves in totally different perspectives, employ different concepts, give wholly different interpretations to the same term, and are satisfied by radically different criteria of explanation. It is perfectly clear which of these orientations is central to Klein:

My point is that it is the clinical orientation to explanation, and the concepts anchored to it, that are the most distinctively psychoanalytic—more relevant to psychotherapy and more applicable to other humanistic endeavors in which reading the directionality of man's behavior is central.[55]

Klein is equally clear that "clinical concepts are as abstract, and as theoretical, as metapsychology"[56] and that a crucial distinction is necessary "between experiential and functional concepts, i.e., between intraphenomenological concepts."[57] If the basic data of the therapeutic encounter are the therapist's inferences to the client's experience, this material is interpreted through concepts that transcend the client's lived experience.

Concepts like projection, introjection, and repression, which point to something in the mind of the patient which the patient does not experience but is part of his reality, are functional or extraphenomenological concepts. These are the class of concepts which are meant to account for, or in some way to illuminate or elucidate, those experiences of the patient which are not accessible directly. The analyst plunges into phenomenology, but goes beyond it to generalizations that connect accessible and inaccessible levels of experience.[58]

The extraphenomenological concepts are meant to illuminate the experiences the analyst attributes to the client. It is precisely at this point that difficulties arise. For the basic functional concepts that articulate the significance of the client's experience are clearly beyond the client's experience. The client's own vantage point, whose elucidation was previously described as the distinguishing mark of psychoanalytic explanation—"All the explorations and probes as well as concepts of the clinical theory are dedicated to this effort"—cannot be maintained. However much Klein may wish to preserve the notions of meaning and purpose as the basic functional explanatory concepts, these terms cannot retain the significance they possess in the realm of consciousness. The new metapsychology is required to explicate the meaning of "unconscious meaning" and supply an intelligible account of the relationship between this extraphenomenological realm and the vantage point of the client's lived experience. The theory seems to me to fail in this respect.

The difficulty derives from a central contention of Klein's account, the notion of "two theories." With the idea that psychoanalysis contains two perspectives, one clinical and the other metapsychological, I have no quarrel. The critical issue is the relationship between them. Klein, and those who have adopted his dualism, have severed the two aspects of psychoanalysis so completely that not only the content but the methodology of the two approaches have been reconstituted as each other's opposite. The quickest way to confront this point is in the set of dichotomies Klein embraces: the division between why and how, and the separation of meaning from cause. The adoption of these polarities makes it impossible to understand the connection between the functional, extraphenomenological concepts, which are required to illuminate the *significance* of lived experience, and the meaning for the client of that experience as undergone. One can simply disavow "how" questions, that is, decide to reject the very relevance of mediating mechanisms that link unobserved factors to experience, but the penalty for this declaration is the fact that the connection is rendered unintelligible. If we do not understand the relationship between unconscious and conscious purpose, we are hardly in a position to understand what purpose means and how it is embodied in the lives of human beings. If we cannot reproduce the mediations that tie our conscious experience to the more disguised foundations of our being, we have no right to attribute our experience to such underlying factors.

The most unfortunate aspect of Klein's approach to this point is that it is unnecessary. There are mediations besides those operating in the realm of physics. Just as the notion of energy has a perfectly intelligible meaning within human experience, so do the variety of notions which could serve to bridge the gap between functional concepts and phenomenological presentation, even if these concepts need to be reconstituted to become intelligible as mediations.

Klein contends that the extraphenomenological conceptions utilized in clinical psychoanalysis—notions like development, defense, resolution, repression, and transference—have not much to do with mechanisms. But it is perfectly reasonable to ask how transference operates and to insist that one does not understand the term without the explanation.

The difficulty is augmented by the second dichotomy: cause vs. meaning:

> Psychoanalysis is, therefore, in the class of theories that concern themselves with the "why" of behavior, that try to state reasons rather than causes, that try to say that a behavior has a certain meaning, derived from the *history* of this meaning in the person's life, that try to speak of the psychical *functions* through which the meaning is expressed. Thus to say that a wish is repressed explains a behavior without specifying *how* repression is accomplished.[59]

But, the split between meaning and cause only compounds the difficulty and threatens to turn a legitimate concern with meanings and intentions into sheer mystification or a plea for ignorance. Meanings and causes are not contradictory notions. Causality sometimes operates through physical forces and other times through human comprehension and purpose. If there were not causal agency operating through meaning all learning would become impossible and human consciousness itself, unintelligible. The common experience of being required by the evidence to assert a given conclusion is sufficient warrant for believing that our grasp of meaning on one occasion has causal influence over our meaningful judgments on others.

Furthermore, if meanings were not causally linked, their real concatenations and distortions in the actual lives of human beings would be unintelligible. To say that behavior has "a meaning *derived* from the history of this meaning in the person's life" either begs the question through tautology or simply reintroduces the notion of cause under the rubric of "derivation."

> An array of events becomes coherent (1) when a leading element, an organizing principle of the array, can be specified, and (2) when *the clues or carriers* of this leading element   *its mediation*   can also be specified.[60]

This comment of Klein's seems to me an acknowledgment of the role of causal mediation in the construction of intelligible account of human activity.

I believe that Klein obscures this point because he focuses on particular intentions and meanings rather than the notion of "intention" or "meaning" itself. A new metapsychology which intends to ground clinical practice cannot avoid this task. Klein touches this issue in his interesting and important discussion of repression. The heart of his approach to repression is the replacement of the energy model of cathexis and anticathexis with the notion of "a gap in comprehension."[61] This notion involves a "meaning schema" which continues to influence conscious thought and behavior, though its effects are uncomprehended. The schema remains dissociated from the person's self-conception. "A dynamically unconscious idea is denied the attributes of self-relatedness, is excluded from the self as *agent,* self as *object,* and self as *locus."*[62] The crux of the process is not the banishment of an idea from consciousness, but a failure to comprehend the meaning of the idea, which continues to operate in the quest for gratification, but without responsiveness to the consequences of the person's acts.

There is a great deal in this account that marks a real improvement over traditional psychoanalytic emphasis on forbidden and banished forces. The view has strong affinities with a Marxist notion of alienation as the loss of control over the direction of the agent's continued activity. But the fundamental issue of the metapsychology of meaning remains unresolved. Klein cites approvingly Merleau-Ponty's contention that while meaning is always lived out consciously, "not all such 'lived' meanings are *understood,* i.e., cognitively represented." To say that a meaning is being lived out only "unconsciously" can only mean that "comprehension of the leading element of a schema is lacking."[63] Thus, although meaning is always lived out in experience, these "experiences may not include comprehension of their meaning."[64]

We are therefore left with a dichotomy between consciously lived out meanings and consciously lived out meanings that are not understood. The problem is confounded by the fact that "consciousness is taken to mean an experienced integration of meaning."[65] What, however, can we make of the notion of an "uncomprehended meaning," or an "experienced integration of meaning" that is not understood? Are we being offered a form of Platonic theory in which meanings can persist independently of the agent who would entertain them? Perhaps the notion is plausible. It is at least clear that the idea of such a detached meaning raises questions that need to be pursued, and it is equally clear that Klein does not pursue them. That is why I conclude that the foundation of the new metapsychology has not been completed.

I alluded a few pages earlier to a second major difficulty in the newer attempts at metapsychology: their almost total avoidance of the social dimension of human activity. In regard to the neurophysical theories this lacunae is no surprise; the body is hardly a place to perceive the origins, as distinct from the effects, of social existence. It is somewhat more surprising that writers like Schafer and Klein remain within so limited a perspective. More than any other consideration this repetition of traditional psychoanalytic parochialism indicates how tenaciously Freud's reductionism has persisted in what appear to be novel forms. The substitution of object relations and interpersonal meanings for Freudian tension reduction merely instinctualizes some variant of the nuclear family, a position already present in Freud's account. The source of meaning is as narrowly prescribed as the source of cathectic behavior in the orthodox position. Two brief illustrations will have to suffice.

In distinguishing his own position from that of existentialism Klein notes that the

> analyst will not rest with the assumption that intentionality is exhausted in what the patient is able to avow consciously; he does not believe that he is abandoning the objective of reading the patient's own vantage point when he looks for directives which even the patient himself cannot admit.... However, any account of such disavowed aims must encompass what the subject can experience or insists upon as *the* "real" reasons.[66]

Nowhere is it suggested that social mystification may make it impossible for the client or the analyst to grasp the connection between accessible and inaccessible dimensions of experience. It is assumed that psychoanalytic practice is sufficient to raise the veil that separates the agent's meaning from the larger existence of the social world. In other words, the reasons for our acts are viewed as not only residing in our individual psyches but as originating in individual consciousness as well.

An even more mystifying illustration of the same social naïveté occurs in the course of Klein's discussion of active reversal of passive experience—the capacity of the individual to initiate experiences that have previously been imposed. The significance of repetition is not that it is an expression of a primary drive to constancy, nirvana, and death; rather, it represents the tendency to "recreate in an active mode an event that has been passively experienced as in some respect unacceptable, unrelated' or alien to the self."[67] By actively creating what was previously a matter of alien imposition, the self becomes integrated, syntonic, and capable of mastery of its world.

> The functional importance of such repetition of experience is that it produces a form of *control* or *integration:* the self is able to *make* the experience happen. The basic aim is to "*own*" the experience, its *alien* status and disconnectedness from the self are reduced by a *self-governed* re-experiencing of it.[68]

> Thus a basic assumption of the principle is that to "*make sense out of*" things and to bring them into connection with a continuing self-identity is a fundamental tendency of development. *We "own" our experiences as we own an object.* Conversely, an object may be perceived as strange or uncanny, with an accompanying feeling of "not making sense," of discontinuity. Just as the hammer in one's hand to make a table is a tool experienced as an extension of the self, so can the table be experienced as "*my table*" as against a "table made for me." When events have been thoroughly self-accommodated they are no longer focally experienced. It is when discordance appears—experiences that cannot be "placed," that "don't fit," in short, that have no ready reference point to the self—that we have a condition for focal awareness, with consequent efforts toward making the discrepancy self-syntonic [emphasis added].[69]

These are marvelously illuminating passages—when read in their social context. That we do indeed "own our experiences as we own an object" is the heart of the matter. For the form of ownership to which we are subject is precisely the form of commodity fetishism—the tendency for our social relations to take the character of entities imposed on us, beyond our choice and understanding. So, on Klein's account, we should expect our selves to be equally reified. But this fetishism, which converts our agency into passivity, is not a private aberration derived from the misfortunes of childhood. It is a necessary form of the pathology of capitalism, a form of mystification "which has its origin . . . in the peculiar social character of the labour that produces [it]."[70]

To own our experience as we own such commodities is to stand in a fetishized relationship to our own selves; to perceive ourselves under the form of the commodity—private, alien, imposed, and beyond human determination. But what of the reversal of voice, the change from passivity to agency? Pathetically, such reversal is the exact form of self-subordination of capitalist democracy, the procedure by which we come to adopt, as "our own," the forms of domination previously imposed upon us. Because Klein deals only with the superficial form of reversal, the deeper structure and fundamental content of the system is ignored.

Yet bourgeois democracy operates precisely through the mechanism that requires individuals to impose upon themselves "voluntarily" what has been previously inflicted by the power of others. It is the illusion of self-determination that is the heart of liberal ideology. Our selves, unhappily, are as much or as little our own as the commodities that surround and infiltrate our being. On this point Klein is certainly correct. The social relations through which our selves are produced are the same social relations through which we ostensibly "grow" and are "humanized." These are social relations that function as the simultaneous ground of domination and the illusion of self-mastery. We learn to "make happen" on our "own" what is required for the reproduction of the system in which our forced compliance is a continuing necessity.

It is striking that Klein refers to the extension of selfhood in the hammer as a tool and the table as an artifact of our construction. For if applied to the massive forms of corporate property which in fact dominate our lives, the illustrations would immediately announce their absurdity.

> With increasing bureaucratization, it becomes plain to all who would see that man is to a very important degree controlled by his social relations to the instruments of production. This can no longer seem only a tenet of Marxism, but a stubborn fact to be acknowledged by all, quite apart from their ideological persuasion. Bureaucratization makes readily visible what was previously dim and obscure. More and more people discover that to *work*, they must be

employed. For to *work*, one must have *tools* and *equipment*. And the tools and equipment are increasingly available only in *bureaucracies*, private or public [emphasis added].[71]

It is only through the guise of individual subjectivity, the illusion that what appears to us in our consciousness is the determining force of social life rather than its outcome, that the reference to tool and table makes any claim to sense. Unfortunately, the hammer and the table are forms of property as consumption, the results of a system of production whose power over us is so massively alien as to defy the parameters of Klein's considerations. It is not merely that the wood and the hammer must themselves be purchased at prices that are imposed, or that the table we construct is made for a home whose social properties and costs fluctuate beyond our will. These are minor points. The basic fact is that what we make privately, what we consume through our own efforts, takes its meaning from the converse realm of alienated power, of corporate property and bureaucratic domination against whose impervious presence the very meaning of private self-determination receives its fragile illusion.

What is particularly striking in Klein's account is its illuminating, if inadvertent, revelation of the ideological functions of individual therapy. Therapy is the paradigm of self-delusion in an age of democratic capitalism. For in therapy the ultimate forms of power which shape selfhood are bracketed. The changes admittedly wrought in the lives of individuals through therapeutic encounters are presented through the powerful, if unspoken, assumption that such transformations are the basic forms of human development. In the quiet seclusion of a private office, through the means of contractual exchange, a journey is undertaken into the self through the retracing of its history, the excavation of its childhood, the reliving of its ancient chaos. The realms of being are suspended; the stubborn obduracy of social life detached; the modes of culture, history, public life, and political obligation severed from the interior passage of the self through its own incommensurate labyrinth. In the immense dyad of the therapist and client the minuscule infinity of the world is effaced. The cries of the wretched are more difficult to hear; the new alchemy of private transubstantiation need not be distracted by their intervention. The alien power of the world has been contained, though "tragically" affirmed, through the power of rational technique to remake the human psyche. Individuals, in their *separateness*, can declare themselves, again, the ultimate source of their own being, the ultimate power of their own affliction and transformation. What can be individually purchased, lived and possessed is marked again as the measure of reality. Like the tool and the artifact, therapy is itself another form of private consumption:

> The categories of bourgeois economy ... consist of forms of thought expressing with social validity the conditions and relations of a definite, historically determined mode of production, viz., the production of commodities.[72]

We need only replace the reference to bourgeois economy with bourgeois therapy to maintain the relevance of Marx's account. For therapy remains the paradigmatic illustration of the reversal of voices, expressing with "social validity," that is, as an accurate reflection of the relations of pathological social power, the relegation of individual self-control to a realm of subordinate self-deception.

It is now possible to look back upon the two criticisms I have made of the neometapsychology and note their connection. The fact that the new position does not trace its metapsychological assumptions to their roots simplifies the avoidance of social categories. It becomes stylish to talk of meanings, purposes, and intentions without noting the particular manner in which human agency is structured in its social dimension, its class context, its economic exploitation. The cast of humanism is worn easily through the lightness of its mantle. It is particularly ironic for psychoanalytic thought, which congratulates itself so effusively for its tragic view of life, its willingness—as opposed to the brief, and superficial counterfeit therapies—to look hard into the eyes of truth, to remain so smugly unaware of the grounds of social evil that surround its modest enclave. We need by all means to look at human agency and meaning. But we need to see them as they are disfigured in the world which simultaneously forms them and receives them again in contours beyond their "original" intention.

In conclusion, we have determined that Freud's work cannot be dichotomized. Neither the metapsychology nor the clinical practice can be independently preserved. The demystification of Freud's theory must proceed differently, and it is to this task that we now proceed.

CHAPTER FIVE

Clinical Practice:
The Case of Dora

In this chapter I will proceed with the demystification of Freud's clinical practice and with some aspects of the theory in which it was grounded. A critical reading of one of Freud's better known cases will serve to focus the discussion in a particularly relevant way. For here we are brought face to face not only with an individual life but with the family nexus in which this life was supposedly shaped. And since many of Freud's basic theses find their locus in the family—the stages of psychosexual development, the formation of individual identity, the resolution of the Oedipus complex, and the etiology of character formation, for example—it will be particularly helpful to pursue the nature of individual life in the setting of its origin. Furthermore, in his account of the family Freud undoubtedly discovered important aspects of the structure of contemporary bourgeois life. Unfortunately, as we shall see, he was unable to comprehend the fundamental meaning of his own insight. He often observed features of individual existence under capitalism which he noted but could not integrate into the structure of his theory. Or, put another way, Freud could not grasp the significance of his own discovery because his basic social assumptions led him to reify his insights and to attribute either to biology, physics, or universal anthropology what was, in fact, the precipitate of bourgeois social relations.

I choose to examine Freud's "Fragment of an Analysis of a Case of Hysteria," known popularly as the case of Dora, because it so perfectly illuminates Freud's basic assumptions and because Freud himself regarded it as the vindication of his theory of the pathogenesis of hysterical symptoms. Before Freud cites the details of Dora's therapeutic history, he reflects on the very issue raised by the revelation of individual intimacy. He fears that where he was previously accused of giving too little information about his therapeutic work, so that his hypotheses could not be verified by other specialists, he will now be indicted for revealing what ought properly to remain hidden. The problem is quite real for Freud and "hard for me to solve." For

> if it is true that causes of hysterical disorders are to be found in the intimacies of the patient's psychosexual life, that hysterical symptoms are the expression of their most secret and repressed wishes, then the complete exposition of a case of hysteria is bound to involve the revelations of those intimacies and the betrayal of those secrets. . . . But in my opinion the physician has taken upon himself duties not only towards the individual patient but towards science as well; and his duties towards science mean ultimately nothing else than his duties towards the many other patients who are suffering or will some day suffer from the same disorder.[1]

These remarks, which may seem to us merely ceremonial and somewhat more anguished than our age requires, are in fact an admirable entry into the context of the presentation. For they range from the domain of science, with its universal commitment to the truth and to truth's client, humanity, to the realm of intimacy, secrecy, sexuality, and repression; in short, the Victorian sphere of individual boundaries. It is striking that the impersonal canons of science are brought to bear on the pathology of everyday life, to minister to the most trivial and commonplace complaints of individual "life ineptitude."[2] The importance attributed to the minutiae of commonplace occurrences by the bourgeoisie is fully matched by the concentration of concern in psychoanalytic theory. Matters that would previously have been dismissed as the banal constituents of existence are now the object of studious inquiry and intended transformation. Inefficency in work, headaches, failure in studies, a troublesome mistress, fatigue, a persistent cough—all of these everyday occurences are symptomatic. It is like passing from the panoramas of Leonardo and Michelangelo to those meticulous interiors of the Dutch and Flemish schools of the seventeenth century in which bourgeois life is rendered precious by its dedication to its own self-conscious material detail. And yet, though the intention of psychoanalysis is to free the individual from such symptomatic involvement, the course of treatment begins in the private meeting of two isolated figures, immersed in the petty detail of daily existence.

The particular object of Freud's participation is to uncover the patient's past, "to bring to the light of day after their long burial the priceless though mutilated relics of antiquity."[3] Freud likens himself to a "conscientious archeologist" engaged in the reconstruction of the missing remnant. He had previously presented his account of the process of restoration in "The Interpretation of Dreams" and had thought of entitling the Dora case "Dreams and Hysteria." The link is simply that hysterical symptoms, like dreams, have their meaning, which can be interpreted and understood, and that these symptoms too originate in a process of repression in which the patient's own mental life, owing to its content, has been cut off from consciousness and rendered pathogenic. The "patient," in this case Dora, cannot reproduce her own history. First, she intentionally holds back, through timidity and shame, relevant material she is quite well aware of. Second, part of what she knows actually disappears during the telling. Finally there are "true amnesias," gaps in memory, and paramnesia, contructions employed to fill in those gaps. "That this state of affairs should exist in regard to the memories relating to the history of the illness is *a necessary correlate of the symptoms and one which is theoretically requisite.*"[4]

Since the hysterical symptom represents a compromise between desire and repression, it signifies that the self has alienated a part of its own nature by rendering it unintelligible. Unable to understand her own desire, the patient is not *directly* threatened by its consequences. The self has rendered itself opaque, foreign, or "ego-alien." The cause of the pathology and the broken manner of its presentation are necessarily related. The repression that produced the symptom continues in the distortion of its communication. The capacity to tell one's story whole is an achievement that is accomplished by the cure that renders one's memory available. For this to occur the original repression, with its accompanying censorship, must be overcome. Then the patient can speak and be heard, not only to others but to herself. For as the individual has become self-alienated, so has her speech. Every dream and symptom expresses a conflict in which "the communicating agency has, it is true, been able to say what it wanted but not in the way it wanted—only in a softened down, distorted and unrecognized form."[5] The individual is not only excluded from public communication but from intelligible discourse with herself. The symbolism of such dreams and symptoms is so privatized that they cease, in Freud's words, to be "social utterances, not a means of giving information."[6]

Being unable to speak luminously to others is equivalent to being unable to understand one's self. So, the significance of Freud's commitment to scientific universality becomes clearer; for it is precisely the intersubjectivity of science, the communality of its understanding, the elucidation of a public mode of discourse that transcends the idiosyncrasies of individual vicissitudes that render the *science* of psychoanalysis fruitful. The universality of scientific understanding can be applied therapeutically to deprivatize individual discourse and render it meaningful.

The Social Function of Self-Deception

While Freud brilliantly illuminates the relationship between repression and communicative distortion he does not locate its social dimension. He views society as simply the abstract external cause of internalized repression. But just as the origin of the patient's symptom in repression and the inability of the patient to tell a coherent story are connected, so is the incomprehensibility of the self's monologue and its social inability to convey information to others. The mediations lie in the structure of capitalism. The privatization of social life and the privatization of speech are not unrelated. The ground of the difficulty is the irrational, unplanned, and ideological nature of capitalist society.

The requirements of speech in this society involve the communication of information and the disguise of intention. For despite the semblance of cooperation the reality of the child's education consists in learning to dissemble and to protect itself against the deceits of others. A competitive society, through the agency of an atomized, nuclear family system, constitutes its individual members as privatized models of self-interested demand. The sentiment of shame, which bound the members of traditional societies to public custom, is replaced by the "feeling" of guilt, which sets up the separate individual as the "master" of his own self-denial. Each is given autonomy, even over the process of self-negation.

Because selfhood is constituted out of public discourse, the state of the individual's self-comprehension will embody the state of prevailing social communication. Under capitalism, this state is contradictory. Enough truth must be told to support the illusion of self-determination. Since every significant bourgeois social need will require its contrary pretense—rivalry–friendliness, sexual domination–familial piety, compulsive accumulation–self-divesting altruism—the child must be introduced simultaneously into strategies of reality and illusion. What the child needs to know and be, but cannot be acknowledged to know or be, makes up the realm of repression. It is not that society must contain and extinguish the barbarism of the individual but that *capitalism must create the barbarism of the individual while simultaneously producing the facade of its denial.*

But much of this process would not distinguish capitalism from other repressive societies. What is unique to the capitalist order is the culture of liberalism and the illusion of self-determination. The individual must come to believe that the structures of capitalist domination have been freely chosen. The ideological hegemony of bourgeois life rests entirely on the pretense of democratic participation. But as the self has been produced as much in the shadow of the ideal as its reflection, it consists always of needs and impulses that threaten the illusion of individual compliance. Therefore one must learn not only to embrace the ideology but to extinguish all signs of the countervailing reality. One must repress the structures of real exploitation, and then, as Laing has noted, one must repress the awareness that one is repressing this deceit. What is publicly acknowledged in social life is self-consciously initiated in the individual. What is publicly demanded but necessarily denied in social life must also be initiated by the individual, but in the mode of self-deception. The difference between these two modes must itself be extinguished. If the child were aware of the festering rebelliousness which it bore toward authority, its compliance with public power would be based on calculating self interest and the desire to avoid punishment, rather than on voluntary identification with social ideals. But such a system of motivation would be incompatible with liberal ideology and capitalist power; it is replaced by the system of familial distortions that are endemic in our social life.

Intersubjectivity is maintained by forcing the individual to bear the pathology of the social order. The price of "agreeing" not to act against public power is that one cannot understand one's own cries of protests. The individual is made to bear the burden of capitalist pathology. In the ancient fable the messenger of ill tidings suffered the loss of his tongue. In the present reality, the witness to ill tidings suffers the mutilation of speech and hearing—of self-comprehension. The public order is maintained in tact because the privatization of capitalist exploitation requires the individual to bear the cost of social exploitation. Or, more concretely, we are permitted so much intelligible discourse as is necessary for the reproduction of social domination. As Habermas notes:

> What happens is that the neurotic, even under conditions of repression, takes care to maintain the intersubjectivity of mutual understanding in everyday life and accords with sanctioned expectations. But for this undisturbed communication under conditions of denial, he pays the price of communication disturbances within himself.[7]

What this means is that a society permeated by objective false consciousness forces the disturbance of understanding within the individual who is made incapable of grasping his or her own intention. The real distortions of individual reflection are the cost of the apparent intelligibility of social discourse.

When the sacrifice to the public realm becomes too costly or threatening, therapy is introduced to render these broken texts intelligible and their bearers, social once more. Scientific rationality, itself immanently related to the rise of the capitalist system that has produced the mutilation of meaning, is now enlisted as a human technology to render discourse whole again. The critical issue therefore becomes the character of this new technique and the nature of its demystifications.

It is promising when Freud notes, early in his presentation, that

> we are obliged to pay as much attention in our case histories to the purely human and social circumstances of our patients as to the somatic data and the symptoms of the disorder. Above all, our interest will be directed towards their family circumstances—and not only, as will be seen later, for the purpose of inquiring into their heredity.[8]

The immediate social circumstances of Dora's situation focused on her relationship with four primary figures: her father and mother and their close friends Herr and Frau K. Dora's father

> was the *dominating figure in this circle owing to his intelligence and his character as much as to the circumstances of his life* . . . a man of rather unusual activity and talents, a large manufacturer in very comfortable circumstances. His daughter was most tenderly attached to him, *and for that reason her critical powers which were developed early, took all the more offense at many of his actions and peculiarities* [emphasis added].[9]

He was, however, a man of poor health whom Freud had previously treated for syphilis and diffuse vascular infection, and who in the course of Dora's development had suffered from tuberculosis, a detached retina, "a confusional attack, followed by symptoms of paralysis and slight mental disturbance."[10]

> It was no doubt owing to this fortunate intervention of mine that four years later he brought his daughter, who had meanwhile grown unmistakably neurotic, and introduced her to me, that after another two years he handed her over to me for psychoanalytic treatment.[11]

Dora's mother was, on the accounts given Freud by Dora and her father, a drab, uncultivated woman totally immersed in domestic affairs who might best be described as suffering from

> "housewife's psychosis." She had no understanding of her children's more active interests, and was occupied all day long in cleaning the house with its furniture and utensils and in keeping them clean—to such an extent as to make it impossible to use or enjoy them. This condition, traces of which are to be found often enough in normal housewives, inevitably reminds one of forms of obsessional washing and other kinds of obsessional cleanliness.[12]

It is consequently clear to Freud that Dora derived her "intellectual precocity" and her gifts from her father's family, as well as the predisposition to her illness. For in regard to the latter point it is relevant to note that Freud has also met a sister of Dora's father who "gave clear evidence of a severe form of psychoneurosis without any characteristically hysterical symptoms"[13] and that an older brother of the father was a "hypochondriacal bachelor."

It was due to the father's illness that the family had moved from Vienna to a provincial town where they had made the acquaintance of Herr and Frau K, who became close friends and even shared quarters during periods of holiday. Frau K was considerably more vivacious than Dora's mother and quickly established herself as an older sister–mother surrogate and intimate, sexual confidante; Dora cared for Frau K's children and clearly worshiped her early in their relationship, before the occasion of the incidents that led Dora into therapy with Freud. According to the father, Frau K was quite unhappy with her husband, "of whom, by the way, I have no very high opinion," a somewhat charming though passive man who occasionally engaged in sexual affairs with the serving girls in his household. Frau K first made herself the primary friend and nurse to Dora's father, who soon became her lover as well as her patient, thereby abandoning his daughter to the developing interests of Herr K.

Dora, at the age of twelve, had begun to suffer from migraine headaches and nervous coughing. The first difficulty disappeared in time but the second became more intense. When she first came to Freud at the age of sixteen, the fits of coughing had developed in occasional loss of voice. At the age of eighteen, when Dora began her treatment with Freud, she was a "mature young woman of independent judgment—

> a girl of intelligent and engaging looks. But she was a source of heavy trials for her parents. Low spirits and an alteration in her character had now become the main features of her illness. She was clearly satisfied neither with herself nor with her family; her attitude toward her father was unfriendly, and she was on very bad terms with her mother, who was bent upon drawing her into taking a share in the work of the house. She tried to avoid social intercourse and employed herself . . . with attending lectures for women and with carrying on more or less serious studies.[14]

Now, it would be easy enough to fault Freud for what he omits from his presentation—the specific structure of economic relationships and their connection with the characteristics of the members of this therapeutic group, the social role and status of men and women, the prevailing conditions of illness and their distinctive class symptoms, etc. I do not, however, wish to begin these comments in so external a mode of criticism: it is too foreign to Freud's own method and it would miss a very important feature of his presentation—the very abundant social material which Freud *does in fact include* in his account. What is particularly striking to me is that Freud continually refers to significant social aspects of Dora's situation which he then divorces from his analysis of the etiology of her "illness."

It is as though two perspectives are operating simultaneously; one which registers interesting social phenomena and another which reduces the level of social observation through an individually psychologistic model of explanation. Both what Freud includes and what he omits from his account follow from the necessity of the reduction of social structure to the transformations of personal life. For, such social arrangements as appear on the surface of daily life—the "housewife's psychosis" of Dora's mother for example—are noted by Freud, but in such a manner that sociopolitical roles are reduced to psychiatric categories, while such categories of socioeconomic existence as are not immediately obvious— the relationship between class structure, sexual role domination, and familial antagonisms, for instance—are wholly neglected.

The structure of Freud's procedure can be analogized to a figure of three concentric circles: the largest sphere, (a) the basic pattern of socioeconomic arrangements is totally screened out of the presentation; the intervening sphere, (b) of presented social phenomena is included through a mode of explanation that reduces it to (c) the instinctual vicissitudes of the individual. If I were to rewrite these last few sentences in a Freudian mode I would have to say that Freud defended himself against his awareness of capitalist exploitation by dissociating his awareness of individual and social factors. This would be a wholly misleading account, however, for Freud in fact had no such social knowledge for reasons that are basically political rather than individual in nature.

Two particular incidents motivated Dora's father to initiate her treatment with Freud. First, the discovery "upon the girl's writing desk, or inside it," of a letter in which she threatened suicide, and then, after a heated discussion between father and daughter, an attack in which Dora lost consciousness. The connection between the "circumstances of the patient's life and her illness"[15] were readily supplied by her father. In the course of the relationship between the two families, while Frau K had tenderly nursed her patient, Herr K had been most solicitous of Dora, spending a great deal of time with her and providing her with numerous small presents. During the course of these relationships, when she was sixteen, Dora had announced to her mother, so that it might be communicated to her father, that Herr K had in fact propositioned her. He was called to account by her father and uncle and vehemently denied Dora's interpretation. He then proceeded to undermine Dora's credibility and soundness of mind by relating that he heard from Frau K that Dora was preoccupied with sex, that she used to read Mantegazza's *Physiology of Love*, and that she was most likely "overexcited" by such reading and had invented the entire incident. It was, in the father's judgment, this incident that was responsible for Dora's irritation and depression, and for her insistence that he break off all contact with Herr K and, even more strikingly, with his wife.

The Mechanics of Passion

Freud is very clear in noting that he approaches Dora's story on the basis of the theory of hysteria that he previously elaborated with Breuer and according to which hysteria is the result of three factors: "a psychic trauma, a conflict of affects, and—an additional factor which I brought forward in later publications—a disturbance in the sphere of sexuality."[16] The incident with Herr K seems to provide the psychic trauma. But this does not take us very far. The trauma itself would not have occurred were it not for other events that had transpired earlier in Dora's childhood.

In the course of tracking these prior conditions Dora had told Freud of an incident with Herr K that had occurred when she was fourteen. On that occasion Herr K had arranged to meet Dora alone in his offices and when she appeared had kissed her passionately on the mouth.

> This was surely just the situation to call up a distinct feeling of sexual excitement in a girl of fourteen who had never before been approached. But Dora had at that moment a violent feeling of disgust, tore herself free from the man, and hurried past him to the staircase and from there to the street door. She nevertheless continued to meet Herr K. Neither of them ever mentioned the little scene; and according to her account Dora kept it a secret till her confession during the treatment.
>
> In this scene—second in order of mention, but first in order of time—the behavior of this child of fourteen was already entirely hysterical. I should without question consider a person hysterical in whom an occasion for sexual excitement elicited feelings that were preponderantly or exclusively unpleasurable; and I should do so whether or not the person were capable of producing somatic symptoms. The elucidation of the mechanism of the *reversal of affect* is one of the most important and at the same time of the most difficult problems in the psychology of neurosis.[17]

But not only does Dora suffer a reversal of affect; she also undergoes a *displacement* of sensation. For instead of experiencing "the genital sensation which would certainly have been felt by a healthy girl in such circumstances" Dora was overcome by disgust.

On the basis of these speculations "in accordance with certain rules of symptom formation I have come to know,"[18] and given Dora's recurring experience of a "sensory hallucination" in which she could still feel Herr K's embrace upon the upper part of her body, and of a desire to avoid men in animated conversation with women, Freud develops the following reconstruction of the scene: During the embrace Dora felt Herr K's erection pressing against her. The experience was revolting and was repressed, replaced by the "innocent" sensation in her thorax, which was unusually intense due to its repressed source. In short, we have three transformations of an originally repressed erotic experience: the disgust which was a symptom of repression in the "erotogenic oral zone" which had been overindulged in Dora's childhood: the displacement of her own clitoral excitement to the sensation in her thorax; and the phobia in regard to men, which is a defense mechanism designed to ward off the repressed experience.

Once we have assimilated the unique combination of Freud's ingenuity and fancy, we are next struck by the introduction of the mechanical paradigm—the separability of idea and affect, the transformation of this sexual energy from one state to another, reversed, displaced, and converted into bodily form. Freud follows the line of analysis he set down as early as 1904 where he first suggested three possible avenues for repressed sexual energy: discharge into the body—conversion; continuation in the psychic sphere with resulting obsessions; or, if the affect attaches to other ideas, phobic reaction.[19]

The point becomes even clearer if we pursue the derivation of disgust in more detail. In Freud's reconstruction such feelings are originally a reaction to the smell and sight of excrement, which becomes connected with the genital which are reminders of these functions, particularly the penis, which is an organ of micturation—in fact, originally known only as such—as well as sexual function. Now if we put aside our skepticism as to precisely how, in Freud's account, the originally pleasant excremental function is actually transformed into disgust without social factors playing the critical role, or how we can reconcile Freud's insistence on the micturational function of the penis with its important sexual function in penis envy, etc., we are struck by the fact that the basis of the whole procedure appears to be the utilization of a simple associationist principle that carries us along a route of reversed, displaced, and converted *associations* from what Freud posits as the original experience to its present manifestations. But Freud notes that a "knowledge of the paths does not render less necessary a knowledge of the forces which actually travel along them."[20] Concentrating on either paths or forces is likely to blind us to an important consideration, however,—that the only reason Freud invokes this notion in the first instance is his contention that "I should without question consider a person hysterical in whom an occasion for sexual excitement elicited feelings that were preponderantly unpleasurable."

There are two points to be made about this suggestion: First, it is preposterous, totally ignoring any of the social circumstances to which Freud previously alluded as crucial to an understanding of Dora's situation. And second, it is an instance of a dimension of Freud's analysis that fits neither the model of mechanical forces nor of intentional meanings. It is simply an example of Freud's social convictions about human nature and a revealing gauge of their ideological status. The reductionism that leads Freud to interpret Dora's disgust with Herr K as a refusal to acknowledge her sexual attraction is based on a prior view that reduces complex social experiences like the avoidance by an adolescent girl of the socially inappropriate sexual advances of a friend of her father to simple alterations of individual experience. In other words, between the mechanical force and the meaningful symptom stands a body of readily accepted social assumption, which not only mediates between these forces and meanings but establishes the necessity of their mediation and the condition that constitute the issue to be resolved.

Barter and Betrayal

Freud notes that it was difficult to direct Dora's attention to her relationship with Herr K. The "uppermost layer of her associations"[21] was always connected with her father and with his continuing relationship with Herr and Frau K, for which she could not forgive him. For "she viewed those relations in a very different light from that in which her father wished them to appear. In her mind there was no doubt that what bound her father to this young and beautiful woman was a common love affair."[22] The affair became so obvious, in fact, that Herr K complained to Dora's mother about what was becoming a matter of general observation. Dora noted that her father had begun to shower Frau K with gifts, and then, in an effort to disguise his activity, had become especially generous with her mother and herself. Dora accused her father of insincerity, falseness of character, egoism, and a tendency to view matters in such light as pleased him.

> I could not in general dispute Dora's characterization of her father; and there was one particular respect in which it was easy to see that her reproaches were justified. When she was feeling embittered she used to be overcome by the idea that *she had been handed over to Herr K as the price of his tolerating the relations between her father and his wife;* and her rage at her father's making such a *use of her* was visible behind her affection for him. At other times she was quite well aware that she had been guilty of exaggeration in talking like this. The two men had of course never made a formal agreement in which she was treated as an *object for barter;* her father in particular would have been horrified at any such suggestion. But he was one of those men who know how to evade a dilemma by falsifying their judgment upon one of the conflicting alternatives . . . each of the two men avoided drawing any conclusions from the other's behavior which would have been awkward for his own plans. [emphasis added][23]

This passage is of inestimable value in understanding Freud's therapeutic methodology. And we discover, as we will continue to discover, the same inclusion and bracketing of significant social relations to which I previously alluded. To begin with, the phrase "handed over" may reverberate in the reader's mind; it is the same phrase that Freud employed when he described how Dora's father "handed her over to me for psychotherapeutic treatment." The phrase is not an accident. Instead, it points to the fact that an identical structure lies behind the initiation of Dora's therapy by her father and his tacit bribe of Herr K through the "gift" of his daughter. Dora's father wanted simply to be let alone and he contrived to accomplish this task by bartering his daughter to Herr K on the one hand, and by seeking Freud's assistance in making Dora herself more compliant, on the other. But Freud does not, for all his ingenuity in hounding words to their hidden origins, note the repetition of the phrase "handed over." To have done so would have raised an important question about his own relationship to Dora's situation. Yet, the string of terms is impressive: "handed over," "making such a use of her," "the price of his tolerating the relations," and, finally, "an object for barter." The exchange of women for the sake of continued masculine domination, either as price affixed to a commodity or in the form of barter as an equivalent of "items of exchange," is almost too obvious to ignore.

Freud seems to struggle against the consequence of his own participation when he misdirects the entire inquiry by noting that the two men had never "made a formal agreement." But then Dora's father had not made a formal agreement with Freud when he handed Dora over to him, nor had they discussed the terms of the therapy or the criteria of its successful resolution. Nevertheless, Freud's conceptions and those of Dora's father are wholly consonant. On the one hand Freud notes that Dora's reproaches were justified, and on the other he observes that she was guilty of exaggeration. Can it fail to have entered Freud's mind that he, like Dora's father, could evade his own dilemma by avoiding drawing any conclusions from the other's behavior? Freud knew too much to avoid the issue completely.

Toward the conclusion of the presentation Freud says of Dora's father:

> He had given his support to the treatment so long as he could hope that I should "talk" Dora out of her belief that there was something more than a friendship between him and Frau K. His interest faded when he observed that it was not my intention to bring about that result.[24]

What was Freud's ultimate intention in this issue? That is not so easy to determine, as we shall see.

At the heart of Dora's situation was the overwhelming fact of betrayal. The corrupt bartering of Dora to Herr K by her father was only the last of a series of incidents that previously involved his neglect and rejection of this once favored companion and confidante, and that ultimately stretched back to his contraction of syphilis. But this betrayal, rather than an isolated incident, was part of a pattern of exploitation and hypocrisy engaged in by every powerful adult in Dora's life, all of whom used her in one way or another to achieve purposes for which she was merely a means of convenience. From her mother she received nothing but the dreary repetition of despair and household compulsion. The fact that she herself had been deceived and replaced by Frau K did not evoke compassion from Dora. The roles available to Dora, mirroring her mother or Frau K, were as victim or victimizer. One could vivaciously "steal away" the father and husband of other women, as Frau K, or suffer the encroachments of a woman more skilled at seduction than one's self, as her mother. But in neither case could one live openly in the world nurtured by the secure love of others, as one had been instructed by these "loving" parties themselves.

It was Dora's governess who had first attempted to reveal the truth of Frau K's relation with her father. This woman, who was "well-read and of advanced views,"[25] insisted to Dora's mother that it was undignified for her to tolerate the relationship that was occurring in her presence and she offered the same account to Dora herself. For a while all was well between them, despite the fact that Dora continued to deny the accusation and to remain devoted to Frau K. But eventually she became hostile to the governess when she realized that her motive, too, had been the love of Dora's father:

> She did not become angry until she observed that she herself was a subject of complete indifference to the governess, whose pretended affection for her was really meant for her father.[26]

It was for possession of her father that she was betrayed; for this father who replaced her with another in his affections, who disbelieved her account of the advances of Herr K, who lied to her and persisted in his lie, whose syphilis was a threat to her health, who nevertheless remained her access to the social world, "the dominating figure in this circle, owing to his *intelligence and character.*"

Nor did she fare much better at the hands of Frau K. At one point the two of them had been extremely intimate. When Dora visited the K's she used to share a bedroom with Frau K while Herr K slept elsewhere. Dora had become Frau K's "confidante and advisor in all the difficulties of her married life."[27] They talked about everything and Dora praised Frau K in terms that seemed to Freud more appropriate for a lover than an older friend. And yet, how had Frau K dealt with Dora? Remember that after Dora had accused Herr K of indecent advances toward her he had responded by meeting with her father and vehemently denying her accusations. Although he first spoke of his high regard for Dora, his tone soon changed to disparagement and in this context he accused her of a perverted interest in sexual matters as illustrated by her reading of Mantegazza.

> Frau K., therefore had betrayed her and had calumniated her; for it had only been with her that she had read Mantegazza and discussed forbidden topics. It was a repetition of what had happened with the governess: Frau K had sacrificed her without a moment's hesitation so that her relations with her father might not be disturbed.[28]

It is not accidental that Frau K repeats the betrayal by the governess. Women in Dora's life deny each other in time of need and do not hesitate to sacrifice each other to their interests with men. Their rivalry is masked by the pretension of affection, which serves to hide both the domination of men and the true nature of the purported concern for each other. Nothing could have been better calculated to teach Dora her sexual subservience than to have witnessed its acting out by Frau K, who not only colluded with the deceitful neglect of her father, but who revealed at the same time the ideological significance of the sweet, comraderly ties of these women to each other. That Frau K revealed her intimacies with Dora to her husband must have meant that she knew of Herr K's liaison with the young girl and was prepared for the sake of her own affair to support his groundless accusations against her regardless of the cost to Dora's life.

The final repetition of sacrifice and self-aggrandizement occurs again in the case of Herr K. Whatever Dora's ambivalent feelings toward his charming flattery and painful deceit, her meaning to Herr K was imposed upon her unmistakably by an incident Freud related toward the end of the analysis. There was a governess of the K's who two days before the incident of Herr K's proposal to Dora at the lake had taken her aside to relate how Herr K had made advances toward her at a time when his wife was away. He pursued her passionately and remarked specifically "that he got nothing from his wife."

> "Why, those are the very words he used afterwards, when he made his proposal to you and you gave him the slap in the face."—"Yes. She had given way to him, but after a little while he had ceased to care for her, and since then she hated him."

> "Now I know your motive for the slap in the face with which you answered Herr K's proposal. It was not that you were offended at his suggestions; you were actuated by jealousy and revenge. At the time when the governess was telling you her story you were still able to make use of your gift for putting on one side everything that is not agreeable to your feelings. But at the moment when Herr K used the words 'I get nothing out of my wife'—which were the

same words he had used to the governess—fresh emotions were aroused in you and tipped the balance. 'Does he dare,' you said to yourself, 'to treat me like a governess, like a servant?' "[29]

Just as Freud does not respond to the repetition of the words "handed over" so too, Herr K's statement that he "gets nothing out of his wife," used each time in a context of seduction, is met with silence. To obtain Dora and the governess Herr K must denigrate Frau K for *her lack of contribution to him*. They, apparently, will yield him up better results. Herr K does not deny the criterion of female usefulness to men, but suggests, instead, that Dora will fare better by this standard than Frau K herself. Women are measured by their ability to satisfy men. Still Freud can conclude that "she was not offended by his suggestions." Once again the pattern of sexual domination is obscured, and Herr K's manipulation of Dora is replaced with an account of her role in bringing about the feelings for which she is now made responsible.

It is impossible for Freud to ignore the structure of power without simultaneously shifting the balance of responsibility from the social corruption of sexual roles under capitalism to Dora's participation in her own subservience. In this ideological perspective even the truth of the charge of Dora's compliance is totally mystified. For Freud is wholly incapable of understanding Dora's dissimulation as the last line of defense in a world significantly devoid of the possibility of her acting directly in accordance with the truth. It is this ideological blindness that skews Freud's considerable insight and renders his genius in grasping the nature of self-deception another device to be employed against the victims of exploitation. Freud offers no criticism of what Dora includes in her account: "I could not in general dispute Dora's characterization of her father."[30] Instead, he adopts a different approach:

> When the patient brings forward a sound incontestable train of argument during psycho-analytic treatment, the physician is liable to feel a moment's embarrassment, and the patient may take advantage of it by asking: "This is all perfectly correct and true, isn't it? What do you want to change in it now that I've told it you?" But it soon becomes evident that the patient uses thoughts of this kind, which the analysis cannot attack, for the purpose of cloaking others which are anxious to escape from criticism and from consciousness. A string of reproaches against other people leads one to suspect the existence of a string of self-reproaches with the same content.[31]

Truth and Power

Now, the notion that the truth can be used as a defense against self-accusation, though surprising, perhaps, is undoubtedly correct. The important question concerns the truths that are acknowledged, the truths that are hidden, and their connection. Freud may well be right in his contention that Dora means to erect defenses against self-reproach. What is striking is that Freud abstracts the entire issue from the structure of social hypocrisy that forms the parameters of her situation. As I have previously suggested, Freud sharply separates the realm of individual action from the social circumstances in which it occurs. So, self-defense is isolated from the obvious system of social illusion which runs as a persistent thread through all the lives and transactions of this case. Self-defense is isolated from the structure of attacks against which it is a defense. Like Dora's father and Herr K, Freud too "avoids drawing any conclusions" *of a social kind*. The issue of discovery and deceit is made wholly personal; Dora is right in accusing her father and Herr K, but she is deceived in avoiding her own accusation against herself. The idea that there are structures of deceit that define the roles of the agents is no part of Freud's consideration. He is unaware of ideology.

Before pursuing the details of Freud's unmasking of Dora's pretense, therefore, it is important to summarize her situation. Brought up in a social class that nominally values both fidelity and honesty—ideals it identifies with the sanctity of the family and male and female honor—Dora discovers the consistent violation of these principles. When she confronts those whom she has been taught to respect, she is met with lies, cruel self-interest, and groundless attack. Society protects itself against Dora's insight into her father's corruption, Frau K's betrayal, Herr K's shallow self-indulgence, her mother's retreat from life, and her governess's manipulation. Assuming for the moment that Freud is correct in his claim that there is a still deeper stratum of truth composed of Dora's sexual love for her father, for Herr K and Frau K, and for her masturbatory self-indulgence, what consequences could we expect to occur in the wake of such disclosures, were they made by Dora either to herself or to others? Dora now defends herself with such difficult and unacknowledged truth as is required for her intellectual integrity and moral sanity, and even this "limited" truth forces her into a position of solitary opposition, rejection and "neurosis." It is all well and good for Freud to probe still further and encourage the revelation of still more dangerous insights. But it is theoretically and politically abberant for Freud to abstract this pursuit from the context that renders it necessary and that determines both the nature of that material which is to be unmasked and the motives of its original oppression.

Psychoanalysis derives a great deal of its sense of profound disclosure from such revelations as the self-reproach that lies behind the reproach of others. There can be no doubt that such disguise is endemic in our society, and it is therefore a commonplace therapeutic strategy to discover the roots of self-avoidance which are masked through externalization—through projecting onto others what we wish to deny in ourselves. However, these terms, "externalization" and "projection," are themselves disguised social theories. They replicate the distinction between the individual and society that is the dominant motif of bourgeois ideology. Behind this psychoanalytically inspired vocabulary is the assumption that the social derives ultimately from the external displacements of initially internal factors, a perfect inversion of the actual situation. So, while it is certainly the case that individuals focus upon each other to avoid themselves, this move only represents one turn of the dialectic, and concentrating upon it exclusively, as Freud does, loses the meaning of the turn itself. Externalization is a distorted attempt to reconstitute the social world that has produced the original internalization from which the individual wishes to escape. It marks a move in the right direction, but one that is forced off its path by the structure of forces that has given rise to its need.

Dora cannot recognize herself because social repression has necessarily constituted her as self-repressing. Her avoidance of the truth of herself is merely the individualized counterpart of the system of social ideology her avoidance serves. Therefore, encouraging her self-disclosure requires the simultaneous encouragement of social disclosure, that is, it requires the elimination of structural repression: a radical social transformation. Freud resists any such move. Instead, he minimizes Dora's attack on the forces of her own repression by calling her back to the private domain of her own collusion. But as this private locus is itself the result of social forces, the whole enterprise has the effect of obscuring the social function of private deception. Freud's work with Dora represents a stage of disclosure that cannot complete its journey because it is blind to the meaning of the repression it would disclose. Dora's adumbrated social critique represents a distorted attempt to work her way back into the social sphere from which her self-deceit, as Freud would have it, derives. Dora has both too much need for survival and too much integrity to acknowledge the sphere of her internal illusions, whatever it may be, in the presence of a system that denies the need of her repression. Externalization is the distorted attempt to relocate the social origin of the distorting source of one's internalization.

There is an obvious truth to the view strongly asserted by Critical Theory that psychoanalysis unmasks the illusion of individuality. Freud discovers another realm behind Dora's rational, autonomous critique of others. Her apparently persuasive indictment, clearly articulated and based on overwhelming evidence, is nevertheless a disguise for her own sexual displacement, her own unacceptable entanglements in the erotic lives of powerful and prohibited figures. The difficulty is that Freud accomplishes his archeological discovery with tools still firmly fashioned in a bourgeois mold. It is the idea of individual instinct that grounds Freud's disclosure of the superficiality of individual bourgeois "rights."

Freud replaces the artificial system of bourgeois contractual expectations with a "deeper" account of private and primitive instinctual determinations. However, he is unable to grasp the structure of capitalist exploitations that underlies both the surface and the depth of his own revelation.

Freud begins his inquiry into Dora's self-deception by suggesting that her anger at the governess had roots in a similar self-deception. "What the governess had from time to time been to Dora, Dora had been to Herr K's children."[32] Her preoccupation with these children was a "cloak" for her love toward Herr K, whom she admitted she may have been in love with before the incident of the kiss. Dora's reproach against her father, that he used the pretext of his illness for his own purposes, "concealed a whole section of her own secret history."[33] Dora had learned, from observing those about her, the uses to which illness could be put. Herr K, for example, spent a good deal of time traveling. Upon his return he invariably found his wife in ill health, although Dora well knew that she had been fine only the day before. It was not difficult for her to realize that Frau K's illness served as the excuse she wanted to avoid sexual relations with her husband.

> Dora had had a very large number of attacks of coughing accompanied by loss of voice. Could it be that the presence or absence of the man she loved had had an influence upon the appearance and disappearance of the symptoms of her illness? . . . I asked her what the average length of these attacks had been. "From three to six weeks, perhaps." How long had Herr K's absences lasted? "Three to six weeks, too" she was obliged to admit. Her illness was therefore a demonstration of her love for K, just as his wife's was a demonstration of her dislike.[34]

> Dora's aphonia, then, allowed of the following *symbolic* interpretation. When the person she loved was away she gave up speaking; speech had lost its value since she could not speak to him. On the other hand, writing gained in importance as being the only means of communication with the absent person [emphasis added].[35]

At this point it is clear that Freud's presentation enters a new stage. He moves from his previous emphasis on the transformations of repressed sexual excitation (generating disgust, obsession, and phobia) to a concern with the symbolic significance of the symptom. In short, Freud shifts the mode of analysis from forces to meanings. Of course, there is nothing surprising in this change; it conforms exactly with the contemporary interpretation of Freud's theory. But there is a feature of Freud's theory of meanings, illuminated at this juncture of the analysis, which often goes unnoticed: Freud's theory of meaning is actually a theory of disguise. That is, Freud does not develop a theory of meaning as such. All of his reflections deal with the distortion of meaning, the repression of meaning, the compromise of meaning. *The Interpretation of Dreams,* the most elaborate and detailed instance of Freud's theory of the transformations of meaning, is actually a theory of censorship and self-deception.

Since the theory of meanings is in fact a theory of censored disguises, it is a theory of political power and ideological distortion. But it does not recognize itself as such. Instead of pursuing the origins of self-deception to their social roots, it rests with a very vague and often contradictory theory of the status of meaning which serves to obscure its political dimension and the role of the analyst in the process of its ellucidation. In short, Freud's theory is isomorphic with the practice of bourgeois life. For just as Dora's father and Herr K avoided "drawing any conclusions" of a practical sort about the web of corruption they had constructed, so Freud avoids drawing any theoretical conclusions about the social context of their situation or the political dimension of his relationship to them. There is hardly a better illustration of Marx's observation, made originally in regard to the representatives of the bourgeois, but applicable here to Freud's relation with Dora's protagonists:

> What makes them representatives of the petty bourgeoisie is the fact that in their minds they do not get beyond the limits which the latter do not get beyond in life, that they are consequently driven, theoretically, to the same problems and solutions to which material interest and social position drive the latter practically. That is, in general, the relationship between the *political* and *literary representatives* of a class and the class they represent.[36]

How does Freud assess the relative influence of forces to meanings?

> As far as I can see, every hysterical symptom involves the participation of both sides. It cannot occur without the presence of a certain degree of *somatic compliance* offered by some normal or pathological process in or connected with one of the bodily organs. And it cannot occur more than once—and the capacity for repeating itself is one of the characteristics of a hysterical symptom—unless it has a psychical significance, a meaning. The hysterical symptom does not carry this meaning with it, but the meaning is lent to it, welded on to it, as it were; and in every instance the meaning can be a different one, according to the nature of the suppressed thought which are struggling for expression.[37]

Both the somatic and psychical dimensions are involved, but it is the unconscious thoughts that have the somatic factors "at their disposal."[38] This reflection seems to give priority to the psychical and this speculation is borne out by Freud's reflection that for

> therapeutic purposes the most important determinants are those given by the contingent psychical material; the clearing-up of the symptoms is achieved by looking for their psychical significance.[39]

The somatic factors (which as a rule Freud also regards as constitutional), necessary as they are, do not constitute the core of the symptom's origin or of psychoanalytic treatment. It was Dora's intention, in this case, her desire to separate her father from Frau K, that generated her illness. She had not been able to achieve this end by "prayer or argument."

> I felt quite convinced that she would recover at once if only her father were to tell her that he had sacrificed Frau K for the sake of her health. But, I added, I hoped that he would not let himself be persuaded to do this, for then she would have learned what a powerful weapon she had in her hands, and she would certainly not fail on every future occasion to make use once more of her liability to ill-health.[40]

This striking comment of Freud's provides a valuable insight into the political implications of his intervention. First, if Freud is correct in his speculation, Dora's malady could have been cured simply by changing her external situation. The long, painful course of the analysis would have become unnecessary. This is a devastating comment in itself. Then again, the idea that Frau K would have been "sacrificed" assumes the prior legitimacy of her relationship with her malingering lover. But most significant is Freud's concern that her illness provides her with a weapon of inestimable power in her relationship with her father, a judgment that totally obscures the prevailing structure of power and the paucity of Dora's means of attack upon it.

Freud's contracted client is Dora, not capitalist society, the politics of sexuality, or even the immediate circle of Dora's protagonists. He ascribes agency solely to her, both in theory and practice. He takes the prevailing system of power as given and adheres to it. Dora's intention is viewed as rebellion against authorized authority. It is Dora who must be prevented from threatening the current structure of power by the device of her illness. It is clear that Freud assumes that the prevailing power structure is irrelevant, or that it is justified, or that Dora can transform it by rational, "non-neurotic" means. All three possibilities are mistaken and ideological. Freud is thoroughly involved in the maintenance of prevailing power, and shifting the burden of proof to Dora's deception merely exemplifies this fact.

Freud next proceeded to discuss in more detail the part played in hysteria by the motive for illness. In the text he maintains: "A *motive* for being ill is sharply to be distinguished as a concept from a *liability* to being ill—from the materials out of which the symptom is formed."[41] But in the footnote added in 1923 he corrects himself with the introduction of a distinction between the *primary* (the paranosic gain) and the *secondary* (epinosic gain) from illness:

In the first place, falling ill involves *a saving of psychical effort;* it emerges as being *economically the most convenient solution* when there is a mental conflict . . . [emphasis added]. This element of the paranosic gain may be described as the *internal* or psychological one, and it is, so to say, a constant one. But beyond this, external factors (such as in the instance given above of the situation of a woman subjugated by her husband) may contribute motives for falling ill; and these will constitute the *external* elements in the paranosic gain.[42]

In the midst of the theory of meaning we are abruptly thrust back into the earlier view of psychic economics and the saving of energy. Although the somatic factor was previously put at the disposal of the psychic, the priority is now reversed. As meaning in motive points toward society, Freud returns to psychic forces. It is the paranosic gain that is primary, for it is economic and constant. Let us overlook Freud's ambivalence for the moment and concentrate on his analysis of secondary gain. His illustration of this concept is extremely interesting: let us suppose, he suggests, a worker who has been crippled and now earns his living through begging. Suppose through a miracle he could be made whole again. It would be a mistake to imagine that the worker would respond with joyful anticipation. For now, "the very thing which in the first instance threw him out of employment has become his source of income; he lives by his disablement. If that is taken from him he may become totally helpless. He has in the meantime forgotten his trade and lost his habits of industry."[43]

Once again it is clear that Freud's practice is consonant with the assumptions of prevailing power—with the conviction that one would rather be idle than work, that living by disablement is preferable to living by creative labor; observations which may have the sense of shrewd observation, but which rest on an unreflective reification of the nature of alienated labor in capitalist society.

The Social Function of Illness

But nothing better illustrates the political dimension of Freud's therapy than the following passage in which he arrives at the borderline of recognizing the social origin of symptom and illness:

The motives for being ill often begin to be active even in childhood. A child in its greed for love does not enjoy having to share the affection of its parents with its brothers and sisters; and it notices that the whole of their affection is lavished upon it once more whenever it arouses their anxiety by falling ill. . . . When such a child has grown up to be a woman she may find all the demands she used to make in her childhood countered owing to her marriage with an inconsiderate husband, who may subjugate her will, mercilessly exploit her capacity for work, and lavish neither his affection nor his money upon her. In that case, ill-health will be her one weapon for maintaining her position. It will procure the care she longs for; it will force her husband to make pecuniary sacrifices for her and to show her consideration, as he would never have done while she was well; and it will compel him to treat her with solicitude if she recovers, for otherwise a relapse will threaten. Her state of ill-health will have every appearance of being objective and involuntary ... and for that reason she will not need to feel any conscious self-reproaches at making such successful use of a means which she had found effective in her years of childhood.[44]

This remarkable passage has a truly contemporary ring to it and represents Freud's acumen at its zenith. But placed in the context of Freud's larger theory, it will also illuminate the way in which Freud's assumptions act to deny him the implications of his own discoveries.

First, this account, which appears to be drawn from observations of the situation of women in the Victorian family, seems entirely sufficient to explain the origin of Dora's symptom. We need not explore the exact relationship of somatic to intentional factors, for Freud himself acknowledges that somatic compliance may be contributed by perfectly "normal" bodily functions. The body is relevant, but not through any particular set of functions; for it is not the body's *malfunction* that is germane to the symptom. Dora's purpose, her desire to fall ill, would, if Freud is describing it accurately, be quite sufficient to explain her difficulty. Of course, Freud is unwilling to endorse the primacy of meanings and fails to free himself from a systematic vacillation between mechanical and intentional considerations.

Second, and this may be the reason for his vacillation, the content of Freud's hypothesis takes us immediately into the power structure of bourgeois society, and into Freud's ideological representation of that structure. No elaborate analysis is required to note the connection drawn here between powerlessness—particularly of women and children—and the manipulation of "authorized" defectiveness. The whole structure of bourgeois culture is implicated in this scenario in which the subservient elements of society—explicitly, children and women; implicitly, the economically and morally indigent—are granted a certain compensation for their *natural* inferiority, so long as they are willing to plead their case on grounds of personal deficiency. It remains to be seen, of course, what transpires when these defectives refuse to adopt the official doctrine of their corruption and forcibly challenge the society that dominates them. This bourgeoisified version of Christian charity functions to maintain the social structure of domination through the obfuscating pretense of kindness in its social transactions.

The meanings and functions of Victorian illness were, of course,

socially defined. The basis of the definition was the hierarchical structure of paternalistic capitalism, which combined humanistic concern
with ideological mystification. The ideological practice was explicitly articulated by a specific profession, medicine, which determined the meaning of "health" and "illness" and delineated its "causes" and "cures."
Medicine always mediates between the body and social power to gener-
ate an ethos of biological politics, which distinguishes the "well" from the
"ill" and genuine "healers" from their spurious counterparts. The specific content of these terms depended on many factors, of which the
most relevant for our purposes were class and sex. Women have peren-
nially been viewed as incomplete, weak, defective, inadequate versions of
men, in short, as characterologically-physiologically "diseased."[45] Preg-
nancy, menopause, menstruation, and childbirth have long been regarded with some mixture of repugnance and terror. Women, therefore, have generally been identified with impurity.

But the form of contemporary "corruption" depends very much on
class position within the changing structure of capitalism. Transformations in the mode of production and a growing need for women in the
labor force will necessitate a transformation of the justification of wom-
en's subservience. During World War II, for example, the image of
fragile women gave place to the familiar poster figure of the strong,
competent, and happy industrial worker, an image that was immediately
replaced in the postwar years with the popularization of the crucial role
of motherhood and the horrors of childhood separation. The need for
capitalist society to divorce and unite power and ideology has led to the
strategy of identifying bourgeois women with culture and spiritual refinement; they are believed to function as the purgation of necessary
male brutality in the world of dehumanizing competition. So, in the
insulated shelter of the bourgeois family, women, and spirituality were
pedestaled out of common reach.

For women of the lower class, where spirituality is "irrelevant," the
woman is identified, as is her male counterpart, with the recalcitrant
matter toward which the church, school, psychiatric system, or legal
apparatus are directed to ply their power of social change, or, when
necessary, incarceration.

> The social roles of women in these two classes [upper middle and industrial
> laboring classes] were almost diametrically opposed. For the affluent women,
> society prescribed lives of leisured indolence; for the working-class women,
> backbreaking toil. No *single* ideology of sexism could embrace both realities
> or justify both social roles. Hence, biomedical thought had to provide two
> distinct views of women; one appropriate to the upper middle class (and the
> middle class that aspired to an upper-middle class life style), and one appro-
> priate to poor and working-class women.
> It was as if there were two different human species of females. Affluent

women were seen as inherently sick, too weak and delicate for anything but the mildest pastimes, while working-class women were believed to be inherently healthy and robust. The reality was very different. Working-class women, who put in long hours of work and received inadequate rest and nutrition, suffered far more than wealthy women from contagious diseases and complications of childbirth.

But doctors reversed the causality and found the soft, "civilized" life of the upper classes more health-threatening and medically interesting than hard work and privation.[46]

Of course, Freud's theory fits this general pattern, viewing civilization as a source of psychic illness to which the lower classes are more often immune.

In Freud's account, the social lives of Dora's father and mother and of Herr and Frau K are simply taken for granted. The wives of these successful businessmen provided the visual display and the "sensitive" emotional nurturance of their husbands' industrial achievements; in their expected fragility, delicacy, and excruciating sensitivity lay the roots of their cultural and biological conspicuous "consumption." The sickness of affluent women became a way of life, a subculture of invalidism which pervaded art, dress, appearance, and physical and mental health. It was considered "natural and almost laudable to break down under all conceivable varieties of strain."[47] But whether women literally broke down or not, their nature was socially identified with fragility and dependence, a very good reason for their continued reliance on the power and wisdom of men. Where Freud takes us beyond this bourgeois fantasy is in his recognition of the category of "inconsiderate husband"; that is, with the recognition that the ideology of the system is often in contradiction with social reality. For the male is expected to offer genuine protection in return for the woman's subservience, much as the system of fealty that obtained in the feudal order. But as Ibsen noted in *A Doll's House,* the pretense of care was too often unmasked by disregard of the interests of the woman when they conflicted with the man's economic needs—a perfect illustration of the actual relationship between reality and "spirituality," power and "ideals."

In this particular context of patriarchal domination women at times used the definition of their helplessness as a weapon against their own oppression. By exaggerating the socially constructed fragility that had been imposed upon them, women could turn their subservience against their oppressors. This was most often the case in the realm of sexuality and childbirth, and represents the truth behind the legion of jokes connecting sexual reluctance with physical ailment, most notoriously, headache; a popular recognition of the psychosocial origins of hysteria. Hysteria became a recognized pattern of social life that some physicians came to interpret as a form of manipulation, "this most confusing, mysterious and *rebellious* of diseases" (emphasis added).[48] Some doctors noted that women did not have fits when alone or faint when there was nothing present to cushion their fall. On the whole the medical profession vacillated between regarding hysteria as due to the genuine physical inadequacy of women or as a form of subterfuge utilized by this manipulative sex to gain special favors.

Freud transcended the debate about intentions by interpreting the phenomena as unconscious and involuntary, so that the issue of malingering, in its ordinary sense, was made irrelevant. Paradoxically, Freud's humanism in this instance rests on the fact of social domination; as girls became women they increased their power by making their helplessness involuntary—by losing control over their manipulation of others. And we must remember Freud's stern insistence that it would be a serious mistake to support Dora in her "blackmail" of her father. Freud remained oblivious to the social structure and meaning of affluent invalidism and continued to urge the confession and atonement for rebelliousness as the final cure.

The Creation of the Child

Freud carries out the task of encouraging Dora's confession not only through the specific therapeutic interpretations, which we have already noted, but in the general metapsychological account he offers of the origins of agency. Typically, it is the child who is held responsible: "a child in its greed for love does not enjoy having to share the affections of its parents with brothers and sisters" and discovers that it can receive the whole of their affection by falling ill. Becasue Freud believes in a mechanistic relationship between need and its object, he is incapable of attributing any real agency to the "objects"—individuals—who make up the family system. That is why his early promise to "pay as much attention . . . to the purely human and social circumstances of our patients as to the somatic data" so quickly collapses. The Other, for Freud, is the object of an instinct already formed, not the agency through which a very general tendency is given its particular shape and significance. Dora's mother and father are not seen as contributing to her character and consciousness, but rather as forming the natural terminus of her already predetermined nature. As Schatzman has noted:

> Psychoanalysts say their patients (and all people) relate to *objects*, internal and external. By objects they nearly always mean persons or parts of persons— not things—who are the objects of their patients' (and other people's) acts or feelings. When psychoanalysts call a person an object, it is a person of a kind who is not and could not be alive. For instance, the object, in psychoanalytic theory, never acts or experiences; it cannot affect or be affected by anyone; it

cannot see, feel, know, plan, wish, hope, or act. Psychoanalysts use the term to represent a person, but the person it represents is not real.[49]

This passage is overstated but contains a truth that is significantly obscured by psychoanalysis. Freud consistently ignores the contribution of the child's parents to its development. This child is represented as "choosing" to act toward them on the basis of its original disposition. The child is *naturally greedy* for love and *naturally attracted* toward the parent of the opposite sex—Dora toward her father, and Dora's brother toward his mother. I have insisted throughout this work that the child is "chosen" by the parents, who determine, as society's representatives, the meaning of its dispositions, needs, and capacities and, therefore, its nature as a social being. But what I wish to emphasize now is the fact that Freud *notes* this fact himself, though he is incapable of grasping the meaning of his own observation.

Consider this account of Dora's attraction toward her father:

> The nature of her disposition had always drawn her towards her father, and his numerous illnesses were bound to have increased her affection for him. In many of these illnesses he would allow no one but her to discharge the lighter duties of nursing. He had been so proud of the early growth of her intelligence that he had made her his confidante while she was still a child.[50]

We begin with Freud's dominant view that "her disposition had always drawn her toward her father." Agency resides in Dora. But why do his illnesses increase her affection for him? Incisively Freud notes that *Dora's father had selected her* to care for him. *He made her* his confidante and his favorite, in the context of his illness. The functions of illness and intimacy were socially learned and associated. The already compressed sphere of the nuclear, bourgeois family was further condensed through her father's isolation of their dyad from the rest of the family and the world. His illness, that is, his helplessness, dependence, need for physical intimacy and care, were focused on Dora alone as their ministering agent. Her social dependence on him as her father is strangely counterveiled by his dependence upon her as caretaker. In other words, Dora is selected by her father as the agent of a highly intimate, caring, eroticized relationship. On this occasion, at least, it was not Dora who greedily sought out her father but her father who greedily lavished his attention and physical dependence exclusively upon her. For note that "*he would allow no one but her* to discharge the lighter duties of nursing." The exclusivity and possessiveness of the bourgeois family is taught to the child by its parents, in this case, characteristically, the parent of the opposite sex.

Greed for love is not part of the child's original nature. It is a political construction constituted out of social assault, individual isolation, guilt over the need for nurturance, and a very real poverty of supportive figures, who are not only limited to the immediate family, but further reduced by heterosexual role typing. So the self becomes its own dearest possession; the anxiety in which it is baptized as "separate" forms the ground of its relations with others. The secret of the resolution of the Oedipus complex is that individualism is born in terror. The male child agrees both to separation and "autonomy" under the threat of castration—mutilation. The "independent" male figure is launched on his journey toward selfhood as a compensation for the denial of intimacy, and as a bargain struck with power. Independence is *separation from* those whose nurturance one desires and *compliance with* those who hold terrifying power and who agree to transmit it on the child's promise to delay its own right to exclusive possession. So is the real helplessness behind bourgeois illusions of independence constructed.

The passage quoted above, though it violates the basic emphasis of Freud's theory of instinctual determination, is by no means unique.

> Children's relations to their parents, as we learn alike from direct observations of children and from later analytic examination of adults, are by no means free from elements of accompanying sexual excitation. *The child takes both of its parents*, and more particularly one of them, *as the object of its erotic wishes*. In so doing, it usually follows some indication from its parents, *whose affection bears the clearest characteristics of a sexual activity*, even though of one that is inhibited in its aims. As a rule *a father prefers his daughter and a mother her son;* the child reacts to this by wishing, if he is a son, to take his father's place, and, if she is a daughter, her mother's [emphasis added].[51]

This is an extraordinary passage. Freud begins, typically, by ascribing agency to the child, which supposedly takes its parents as its erotic objects. But he atypically inverts the explanation by noting the manner in which the parent actively constructs itself as the appropriate object of the child's sexual interest. In fact, the term "object" soon gives way to a very different notion, that of "role model," which, while not Freud's term, nevertheless captures his meaning; for it is the parent's indications that constitute the child's sexuality. The mother, in other words, has taught the son to prefer women and to wish to be like his father in this regard. Dora's father has explicitly initiated her into a realm of eroticized role divisions. Not only is the notion of an initial Oedipal instinct unnecessary, but it is contradicted by the account Freud here provides. To make this account even more relevant to Dora we would only need to consider what, in fact, her father, by word and action, taught her about women, about her mother, and consequently, about herself.

Freud intermittently provides the clues to his own transcendence. On those rare occasions where he observes the social construction of the child he points us away from a theory of instincts, with their predetermined objects, toward a theory of social-class determination of childhood. The passages are rarely clear; they follow the general structure of the quote above, which begins in one voice and ends in another.[52] But if one were to proceed slowly through Freud's writings (more slowly than I can proceed here), selecting those passages that are sensitive to the social formation, a very interesting picture of the bourgeois family would begin to emerge.

Consider Freud's reflections on the origins of illness in women, which I cited above, in conjunction with the following passage from the essay " 'Civilized' Sexual Morality and Modern Nervousness":

> As a mother, the neurotic woman who is unsatisfied by her husband is over-tender and over-anxious in regard to the child, to whom she transfers her need for love, thus *awakening* in it its sexual procosity. The bad relations between the parents then *stimulate* the emotional life of the child, and cause it to experience intensities of love, hate and jealousy while yet in its infancy. The strict training which tolerates no sort of expression of this precocious sexual state lends support to the forces of suppression, and the conflict of this age contains all the elements needed to cause lifelong neurosis [emphasis added].[53]

Once again the woman's lack of satisfaction in her marriage is "transferred." But whereas in the previous account it was "displaced" to her own physical incapacity in the form of conversion symptoms, it is here imposed on the child. The result is the awakening of the child's sexual precosity. Once again, it is the parent that induces the child's particular sexuality. The isolated, nuclear family, monopolizing all forms of erotic intimacy in the briefest possible compass, forces the parent's attempts at substitute gratification for their failed relationship with each other onto the child, who, Freud notes, is made to "experience intensities of love, hate and jealousy while yet in its infancy." But it is not the intensity alone that is crucial; the particular form of the emotional situation is one of failure, rejection, unmet need, jealousy, and oversolicitousness. So Freud provides us with a concrete glimpse of the manner in which the bourgeois family cripples its children and reproduces the cycle of family inadequacy–childhood displacement–neurosis and defective family.

The child becomes the receptacle of parental illusion, of hopes and promises that served as the ideological inducement for the marital relationship but that have long since betrayed their mockery. The child's experience derives from the social contradictions through which its parents suffer. Marriage, founded on a dream of tender solicitude, reveals its actual base: on the one hand, men who have been raised to deny tenderness so that they might be more proficient as competitors in a world in which gentleness and intimate concern are at best relics and at worst impediments to success: on the other, women who have been charged to raise these children but who are too deformed by their own induced fragility and insulated need for affection to contribute much to their children's well-being. It is no wonder Freud notes that the situation "contains all the elements needed to cause a lifelong neurosis." For on his account both women and men are incapable of meeting the requirements of marriage as it is defined by bourgeois culture.

The woman is so sexually repressed and socially intimidated that upon entering marriage, when sexual satisfaction is finally to be made available to her, she is psychically

> still attached to her parents, whose authority has brought about the suppression of the sexual feeling; and psychically she shows herself frigid, which prevents her husband finding any great enjoyment in relations with her.[54]

Husbands, however, are no better prepared for the marital relationship. In his important essay "The Most Prevalent Form of Degradation in Erotic Life," Freud notes that men in modern society are systematically incapable of fusing the feelings of tenderness and sexuality:

> The erotic life of such people remains dissociated, divided between two channels, the same two that are personified in art as heavenly and earthly (or animal) love. Where such men love they have no desire and where they desire they cannot love.[55]

Freud recognizes an objection that will be raised against his theory, namely, that it would seem to require that the state of psychic impotence be at least general, if not universal:

> Since all the factors that appear to be involved, the strong fixation in childhood, the incest-barrier, and the frustration in the years of development after puberty, are demonstrably present in all civilized persons, one would be justified in expecting that psychical impotence was universally prevalent in civilized countries and not a disease of particular individuals.[56]

Freud accepts the challenge and replies that in fact psychic impotence is indeed general in civilized society:

> In only very few people *of culture* are the two strains of tenderness and sensuality duly fused into one; the man almost always feels his sexual activity hampered by his respect for the woman and only develops full sexual potency when he finds himself in the presence of a lower type of sexual object [emphasis added].[57]

So men and women are almost perfectly constructed as unsuitable for each other as measured by the individual expectations for happiness that have originally led them to marriage. Freud attributes the difficulty to civilization as such, rather than to the specific capitalist form of civilization he in fact encountered in the lives of his clients. Since, by implication, people who lack the *culture* of Freud's circle may be spared the difficulty in question, he might have been moved to seek out the social context of such factors as "the strong fixation in childhood" that contribute to the malady. But even though he has provided some clue in his reference to the nuclear pattern of displaced parental need, that reflection is dissociated from the present consideration to prevent any critical social theory from arising. When Freud recognizes differences in cultures and classes his criterion is wholly quantitative—the degree of repression of sexuality imposed. He systematically ignores the social structure in which the supposed suppression occurs. It is for this reason that he never grasps the social meaning of sexual suppression, for he continues to view it as a denial of a predetermined libidinal energy rather than as the social determination of a capacity whose specific impetus is generated out of the very procedures that grant it release and denial and that determine its appropriate personal channels.

The Making and Masking of Sexuality

For as is now abundantly clear on Freud's own account, the parents not only repress the child's sexuality, they also induce, awaken, and stimulate it. It is the relation between inducement and denial that constitutes one important structure of sexuality in a given society and in the psyche of its members. Marxism provides a direction for understanding this issue that is wholly beyond Freud's comprehension. For Marx suggests that the form of family and the character structure of its members will embody the social relations required to reproduce the general economic structure of a given society. Capitalism atomizes social relations through the family, locates base and superstructure in the roles men and women are assigned, constitutes woman's spirituality as the mask of male exploitation, and constructs an Oedipal drama in which the boy's identification with his father is mediated precisely through the category of deferred gratification. And this pattern is then transmitted to the child in the form of an exclusive relationship in which the child is made the intense surrogate of its parent's frustration. The family, in short, as much incites the child to a dependent fantasy of erotic parental identification as it frustrates the satisfaction of this aim-inhibited need.

In fact, the two phases are one: It is only by directing sexual attention wholly to the opposite parent that the child can be bound to the conception of exclusive sexual intimacy; and it is only by simultaneously denying the satisfaction of this constructed need that desire, discontent, dependence, deferral, and intimacy can be joined. It is a relationship constituted to produce anxious sexual energy in the child needful of intimacy and simultaneously apprehensive, directed toward another human being who like one's self is driven precisely where need and denial have been made to coalesce.

Freud's occasional comments in this direction are too scattered to inform each other, and when he does note a connection he too often inverts the relationship:

> The more closely the members of a family are attached to one another, the more often do they tend to cut themselves off from others, and the more difficult it is for them to enter the wider circle of life.[58]

This observation is true for one side of the dialectic of social life: the nuclear family does make it more difficult to form bonds with similarly nuclear individuals. But Freud characteristically takes this move as the origin of the process and therefore constructs the social whole out of the family relationship which is in fact its product. Freud continually displays a tendency to reduce the social structure to the family, the family to the individual, and the individual ultimately to natural, mechanical forces. This procedure is perhaps most portentous in reflections on sexuality in a therapeutic context, for there Freud interprets as the natural tendencies of men and women what are in fact socially determined functions. In other words, the three stages of reduction are collapsed and the social roles of women are reified in the family on the basis of a theory which attributes the social characteristics in question to certain spontaneous recognitions of the value of anatomical differences.

So, when Freud continues his reflections on the internal (paranosic) versus the external (epinosic) gains of illness he observes:

> Motives that support the patient in being ill are probably to be found in all fully developed cases. But there are cases in which the motives are purely internal—such as the desire for self-punishment, that is, penitence and remorse. It will be found much easier to solve the therapeutical problem in such cases than in those in which the illness is related to the attainment of some external aim. In Dora's case that aim was clearly to touch her father's heart and to detach him from Frau K.[59]

Two points stand out: The external and internal aims are sharply distinguished so that the desire for self-punishment is isolated from the social–external character of the gain; and, Freud acknowledges that the internal motives are easier to resolve than those with an external aim. This last reflection could lead to a very different assessment than Freud's subjectivized view of society as the displacement and repetition of originally individual factors, but he moves back along his traditional route.

What most embittered Dora was her father's insistence that her account of the scene by the lake was a matter of her imagination. Freud refuses to take Dora's protestations at face value, "for a reproach which misses the mark gives no lasting offense."[60] Again, what is noteworthy in this comment is not merely the total disregard of the significance of Dora's father's lack of trust in her, but Freud's limited unmasking of motives which drives the ostensive deceit back no further than individual avoidance. Freud is convinced that the meaning of Dora's coughing lies, like all symptoms, in the realization of a sexual fantasy.[61] The opportunity for such an interpretation presented itself on an occasion Freud describes as follows:

> She had once again been insisting that Frau K only loved her father because he was "ein vermogender Mann" ("a man of means"). Certain details of the way in which she expressed herself (which I pass over here, like most other purely technical parts of the analysis) led me to see that behind this phrase its opposite lay concealed, namely, that her father was "ein unvermogender Mann" ("a man without means"). This could only be meant in a sexual sense—that her father, as a man, was without means, was impotent. Dora confirmed this interpretation from her conscious knowledge; whereupon I pointed out the contradiction she was involved in if on the one hand she continued to insist that her father's relation with Frau K was a common love-affair, and on the other hand maintained that her father was impotent, or in other words incapable of carrying on an affair of such a kind.[62]

I would very much like to know how Freud divined that "behind this phrase its opposite lay concealed," and precisely how Dora confirmed the interpretation. We are dependent upon Freud for the account, a dubious procedure. For we are beginning to enter the treacherous ground of reversed meanings, in which statements are taken for their opposites. It is crucial therefore to note when such reversals are made use of and when, on the other hand, statements are indeed taken at face value. This is particularly so because Freud's account here differs from the previous explanation by displacement. There is really no contradiction according to Freud, because Dora knows of the possibility of oral intercourse.

> I could then go on to say that in that case she must be thinking of precisely those parts of the body which in her case were in a state of irritation—the throat and the oral cavity.[63]

How the throat and the oral cavity are involved is anything but clear, for the simple reason that the entire explanation was introduced to explain how her impotent father could carry on a sexual relationship with Frau K. It is his orality that is relevant, not the oral cavity, which would only be significant if Frau K were orally active and Dora's father passive. But this issue is not discussed. Freud simply assumes that the relevant sexual posture is the sucking of the male organ, a convenient move which both permits the confirmation of his account of Dora's coughing and obviates the need of imagining Dora's father as involved in the sexual "perversion." It is an interesting example, too, of how quickly Freud can jettison his usual equation of masculinity with activity and femininity with passivity when the social situation requires.

Neutral Science Defines Sexual Normalcy

Freud introduces the notion of perversion in the context of a defense of medical neutrality both in regard to his own discussion of sexuality with Dora and also in regard to Dora's sexual fantasies. He defends his right to such a discussion, so long as it is done "in a particular way," and similarly rejects any "passionate condemnation" of Dora. His view "upon the aberrations of the sexual instincts" is quite mixed, and this is important:

> We must learn to speak without indignation of what we call the sexual perversions—*instances in which the sexual function has transgressed its limits in respect either to the part of the body concerned or to the sexual object chosen* [emphasis added]. The uncertainty in regard to the boundaries of what is to be called normal sexual life, when we take the different races and different epochs into account, should in itself be enough to cool the zealot's ardor.... The perversions are neither bestial nor degenerate in the emotional sense of the word. They are a development of germs all of which are contained in the undifferentiated sexual predisposition of the child, and which, by being suppressed or by being diverted to higher, asexual aims—by being *sublimated*— are destined to provide the energy for a great number of our cultural achievements.[64]

This passage reveals the profound importance of Freud's view of "normal" sexuality for the development of his therapeutic practice. On the one hand, traditional views are rejected: "The perversions are neither bestial nor degenerate." Orthodox moral–religious comdemnation is inappropriate. Nevertheless, Freud retains the notion of a sexual "transgression of limits in regard to parts and objects," and continues to hold to a notion of "aberrant instincts" which must be sublimated to reach a "higher, asexual" aim. The form of Freud's discourse is as important as its content.

The mode of speech is cool and detached, an expression of the new authority of "scientific impartiality" which has replaced the previous form of theological discourse. What the change provides is not the elimination of value judgment but its disguise. A "transgression" is still involved; but it is no longer directed against divine law. It is the appropriate "limit" of the sexual instinct itself that has been transgressed, although how this proper limit is defined scientifically is not revealed in the passage. In fact, Freud merely incorporates into his account of perversions the enlightened view of sexuality that obtained in his day—that sexuality is appropriate when it culminates in intercourse with a person of the opposite sex for the sake of procreation.[65] On the basis of this definition of normalcy he both evaluates Dora's activity and, more significantly, recreates the etiology of her disturbance.

For Freud's theory of the origin of Dora's hysteria is dependent upon an implicit bourgeois theodicy. The bourgeois opposition of individual and society is translated into the negation–reversal of the individual by society. As instinct and culture are incompatible, the present structure of repression reveals the primordial inclinations that would transgress it. The theory of evolution is played—in reverse. Since he claims to discover behind every *negation*, the inexpungable *assertion* of unconscious demands, Freud retrodicts Dora's original nature on the basis of current prohibitions. Of course there is truth in this account, for the child is in fact created in accordance with the social meaning imposed upon it. But Freud characteristically inverts the relationship between nature and society, between force and meaning, and claims for the material process what in fact resides only in the social definition of nature. As Marx notes: "Just as each century has its own nature, so it produces its own primitives."[66] Freud regards Dora's sexuality as primitive—perverse—because he regards it as directed more toward childhood fixations and self-gratification than the orderly recreation of the bourgeois family. The clue to this damaged etiology is Dora's failure to accept authority as constituted, for if she were "mature," her acceptance of her role would manifest itself in her acceptance of the extension of the role of the penis in the person of the male figure who is its possessor.

It is impossible to overemphasize the importance of this last point. For Dora's behavior to be regarded as "aberrant" and requiring treatment it must have incorporated an unconscious sexual fantasy; for the fantasy to be unconscious it must have been repressed; to have been repressed it must have been socially inappropriate; and to have become inappropriate it must have retained childish sexual dispositions *which are so defined* because they interfere with the orderly procreation of the human species and rob society of the energy it requires for "a great number of our cultural achievements."[67] The psychoneuroses are "the negative of the perversions." To become a pervert is to remain a child, and the neurotic is therefore regarded as a rebellious, arrested being who has been unable or unwilling to incorporate necessary social limitations. Beneath the veneer of scientific objectivity is a theory of social authority, appropriate sexual roles, scarce cultural energy, and elite assumptions of sublimation. In neurotics, the original perverse tendencies that others transcend are, by virtue of their sexual constitution and various accidents, retained. "A stream of water which meets with an obstacle in the river-bed is dammed up and flows back into old channels which had formerly seemed fated to run dry."[68] The old hydraulic theory is reintroduced to serve as the basis of Freud's scrutiny of Dora's past. The object is to discover the original fixation of her oral activity which now serves to fuel the fantasy of "perverse" sexuality which is the source of her hysterical coughing.

Before proceeding any further with the account, however, it is crucial to realize both the tenuousness of the argument and the ideological function it serves. Even if we agree that Dora's coughing is to be given a psychosocial meaning, a considerable number of alternatives are available. We might begin by examining Dora's betrayal, her protest, and the systematic denial of her account by those around her; in short, we could simply begin with the social violation of her being and her speech. But this is not the point. What is of moment is *Freud's presentation,* and what marks it off so sharply is its seamless intermixture of social theorizing, political judgment, and a claim to strict scientific transparency. By persistently denying any direct political involvement in the theory, Freud would have us believe that he is simply delivering "the truth" through the instrument of science. So he fits the pattern of positivism to the ends of reification. The social character of bourgeois domination is presented as a natural occurrence through the device of fitting a theory of "authorized" meanings to a foundation of material hydraulics. The whole social structure is thereby included in the causal explanation of Dora's "aberration" and simultaneously bracketed out of view by the sheer "medical" devotion of its advocate.

Since an originally "perverted" nature is the foundation of a later hysterical fantasy, that is, of an unsuccessful sexual repression, Freud looks back to an early childhood stage to discover Dora's specific predisposition. He locates this factor in her excessive thumb sucking and notes:

> No one will feel inclined to dispute, I think, that the mucous membrane of the lips and mouth is to be regarded as a primary *erotogenic zone,* since it preserves this earlier significance in the act of kissing, which is looked upon as normal. An intense activity of this erotogenic zone at an early age thus determines the subsequent presence of a somatic compliance on the part of the tract of mucous membrane which begins at the lips. Thus, at a time when the true sexual object, that is, the male organ, has already become known, circumstances may arise which once more increase the excitation of the oral zone, whose erotogenic character has, as we have seen, been retained.[69]

Here we have a concentrated fusion of bourgeois metapsychology and social–clinical speculation. The irritation in Dora's throat is traced back to her thumb sucking and its eventual substitution in the "true sexual object," the penis. The original issue, the sexual activity of Dora's supposedly impotent father, has been totally lost sight of and replaced with a consideration of Dora's orality. If we combine the authority of Dora's father—"the dominating figure in this circle"—with the superiority of the penis, the illness which is seen to reside in Dora's perversion, and her hysterical symptom, we can persuade ourselves that Dora's coughing manifests her own repressed sexual longing. If we then couch this male-oriented speculation in the scientific language of erotogenic zones—wholly ignoring the fact that the term "erotogenic zone" is not observable but a consequence of the nonempirical theory of libidinal stages—we can conclude with Freud this "excessively repulsive and perverted phantasy of sucking at a penis"[70] had its origin in Dora's childhood experience. Actually, the account here offered seems to me to have its origin as much in Freud's later consideration that

> in females we find that . . . it is their lack of a penis that forces them into their Oedipus complex. It does little harm to a woman if she remains in her feminine Oedipus attitude. . . . She will in that case choose her husband for his paternal characteristics and be ready to recognize his authority. Her longing to possess a penis, which is in fact unappeasable, may find satisfaction if she can succeed in completing her love for the organ by extending it to the bearer of the organ, just as happened earlier when she progressed from her mother's breast to her mother as a whole person.[71]

Since, in Freud's view, the deepest current of Dora's sexual life was her homosexual attachment to Frau K, she obviously remained arrested in her development. Her pathology was rooted in her refusal to accept the penis-father-husband-authority which would have constituted her normalcy. Freud is very clear; Dora's "arrested" development stems from her unwillingness or inability to accept paternal authority. She refuses, and the normal movement toward subservience is deflected.

Dora's life seems to me a very complex fusion of accepted and rejected authority. This ambivalence can be explained in large measure by the hypocritical nature of the authority she was expected to countenance. For while she is drawn to the power and privilege of the masculine role (the penis in Freud's reified account), she cannot help but despise the bearers of this role—her father and Herr K—who critically fail to meet the standards of the role itself. The honor due her father for the social function he ideally performs is totally undermined by his actual behavior. Since he systematically destroys the ground of his own authority, it is little wonder that Dora cannot establish any consistent relationship with his claim to dominance. Freud bypasses the entire issue by ontologizing the social relationship, which is then presented as a set of instinctual–biological factors. But Freud's honesty and incisiveness intrude on his own account, though, once again, he is thoroughly incapable of grasping the import of his own revelation:

> Her declaration that she had been able to keep abreast with her brother up to the time of her first illness, but that after that she had fallen behind him in her studies, was in a certain sense also a "screen-memory." It was as though she had been a boy up till that moment, and had then become girlish for the first time. She had in truth been a wild creature; but after the "asthma" she became quiet and well-behaved. That illness formed the boundary between the two phases of her sexual life, of which the first was masculine in character, and the second feminine.[72]

To get the real issue of this passage we need first to put aside Freud's transformation of the facts. There is no evidence that Dora was a wild creature and then became docile. Her father required her nursing care from the time she was six years old and her own illness did not occur until she was twelve. Her illness marked her initiation into the politics of feminine subservience. Her father's various maladies, given his initial power, could be utilized to enhance his opportunities. But Dora's illness was basically defensive in nature, an attempt to win back through helplessness what she could not directly gain through her own activity. Twelve is a crucial age because it marks her direct entrance into womanhood. The basic issue does not seem to be whether Dora was originally a "boy" and later became "girlish." She was certainly feminine in her function as a nurse to her father. At twelve she is required to define herself in regard to adult possibilities. She must become a woman with such limitations as define the political, social, sexual, and emotional possibilities of womanhood. There is a great deal in Dora's position and her awareness of her position to explain this break in her spirit, or, as Freud would have it, her entrance into a characteristic "quiet, good behavior." So she very typically falls behind the brother, whose equal she had clearly been to this point, and continues the struggle against her exploitation as a young woman.

Limitations of space will not permit me to continue this sort of running exegesis on Freud analysis. A great deal more remains to be said, but the procedure to be followed seems to me clear enough. We need simply to pursue Freud's interpretations back to their social origins. I have no dispute with the abstract statement of Freud's major contentions, particularly his discovery of the unconscious and his charting of the defense mechanisms. That Dora is repressing some significant aspect of her life is undoubtedly true, as it is also the case that the material she is denying to consciousness has something to do with her sexuality, her role as a woman, her hatred for her father, and her ambivalence toward both men and women. But nothing Freud describes in this analysis seems to me to require his specific explanation in terms of either original sexual forces or meanings; instinctual attractions; the splitting and conversion of affect; or the remaining strategems of conversion, displacement, and mechanical association. It is not merely that Freud continually reifies the social conditions of his time, and presents as an inherent constituent of Dora's nature what is in fact a very specific, historically variable set of social circumstances. His methodology also suffers in the process as he very loosely employs the notion of reversal so that on some occasions Dora's overt behavior is taken as a sign of its opposite in her unconscious, while in apparently similar circumstances her manifest activity is simply accepted as revealing her true purpose.[73]

The Social Construction of Meaning

To have unearthed the realm of the symbolic unconscious was Freud's monumental achievement. For Freud not only located this previously adumbrated territory; he essayed the first and most significant explication of its processes. Freud's voyage is that of an explorer who discovers a previously uncharted continent but mistakes the actual place and meaning of this new region. Freud disclosed something of the forced self-alienation of men and women under capitalism and believed, instead, that he had ventured into the universal nature of instinctual drives and meanings. Everything Freud accomplished in the therapeutic realm participates in this contradictory alignment. I wish to present two quick illustrations of this procedure before bringing this chapter to a close.

The first and minor example occurs in the course of Freud's interpretation of Dora's symbolic expression of her desire to masturbate. Freud's views on the subject of the effect of Dora's mastrubation upon her hysteria seem to me totally unfounded. But his reflections on the symbolic manifestation of the desire itself are extremely interesting. On one particular occasion

> she wore at her waist—a thing she never did on any other occasion before or after—a small reticule of a shape which had just come into fashion; and, as she lay on the sofa and talked, she kept playing with it—opening it, putting a finger into it, shutting it again, and so on. I looked on for some time, and then explained to her the nature of a *symptomatic act*.[74]

Now we are all perfectly familiar with this sort of interpretation which makes of the reticule *nothing but* a representation of the female genitals. It is easy enough to be impressed by Freud's distinct originality or to find the entire account ludicrous. In my own reading of Freud I often find myself swinging fitfully from one response to the other. It is more important for the moment to note precisely how Freud proceeds.

The key to the representation is the purported similarity of the reticule and the vagina. However, the reticule is external, metallic, hard, cold, mechanical, and rectangular. The female genitals are quite the opposite. Yet it is crucial for Freud's theory of symbolism that the one represent the other. But the obvious retort will certainly be that the reticule and the vagina share one crucial similarity which is sufficient for their symbolic relationship—the fact of emptiness. And certainly it is this that confers persuasiveness upon all Freud's interpretations of voids, holes, vacancies, etc., as representative of the vagina. However, the reticule is not merely an empty box. In fact, it is not empty at all. It is permeated by the social significance of female ornamentation and display, and of privacy, secrecy, and internality. But this last characteristic is not a biological expression of the anatomy of the womb. It is, rather, an expression of the social function of the family as divorced from the masculine function of economic–political control in the world of practice. The reticule contains the reality and fantasy of Dora's social location in the division of capitalist labor.

When Freud's hydraulic theory is rejected for his intentional–symbolic presentation it is precisely this sort of symbolic–phenomonological reading the the reticule that is adduced on Freud's behalf. And yet the entire account is antiphenomenological, and as mechanical an explanation of the realm of symbols as the economics of energy in the realm of psychic mechanics. For the truth is that experientially the vagina is not an absence at all. It is a very clear presence, a very distinct qualia to sight, touch, and our other senses. It is perfectly true that it can be entered into, but then so can the male mouth and anus, neither of which is regarded as inherently feminine for that reason. In the experience of intercourse or masturbation it is not the absence that is significant but the concrete presence of (a) particular sensations that mark off these acts as pleasurable and (b) the social code that marks off pleasure itself as proper or inappropriate. What is missing in Freud's account is an unstated mediation, an implicit assumption that the male is whole because of the presence of the penis while the female is incomplete because of the absence of this organ. It is the penis that embodies power, mobility, action, and initiative and it is the absence of these characteristics in the female that constitute her as dependent and needing to be filled.

Absence is not a natural fact but a social determination. The female lacks a penis; the male lacks a vagina. Freud regards womanhood as a lack of male power and virtue, and it is this preconception that lends the necessary but unwarrented credibility to Freud's explanation. In the course of his persistent reification Freud reduces the social subordination of women to a category of nature and presents a politically structured relationship of domination and subservience as a natural, anatomical fact. Freud hypostasizes a socially constructed relationship as a natural occurrence, thereby totally obscuring the realm of human activity that lies behind this alleged "fact." The helplessness individuals feel in the presence of their own sexual natures is expressed in the form of natural determination. The realm of meaning, as a dimension of human existence, is not only contracted but thoroughly decimated. Freud's account mystifies the human significance of purpose and intention, for it presents them as reflexes of a more basic necessity over which human beings have no ultimate control. In this manner Freud manifests the alienation of bourgeois society in an alienated form; he attributes to natural imposition what is a socially, humanly elaborated structure of political relationships.

The second point I wish to note is that Freud continues in the domain of theory what is taken for granted in the domain of bourgeois practice. Bourgeois parents do not recognize that they constitute the meaning of their children's genitals through the process of incitement and denial. Freud confirms this invisible construction by asserting the social result as a natural fact. A striking illustration occurs in another of Freud's cases, Little Hans.[75] In a situation heavy with the threat of castration and the loss of love, Freud offers the following reflection:

> This morning Hans was given his usual daily bath by his mother and afterwards dried and powdered. As mother was powdering round his penis and *taking care not to touch it*, Hans said: "Why don't you put your finger there?" Mother: "Because tha'd be piggish" [emphasis added].[76]

In this exchange the penis is constituted as a very specific social fact; as an object of parental interest and concern, as distinct in its significance from the remainder of the body, as an object of shame, as a source of unacceptable pleasure, and, finally, as an absence or negation that attaches to the organ and its function as its repressed and therefore hidden nature. The relationship between loss, desire, negation, and insatiability is suggestively adumbrated, and no deciphering of Lacanian hieroglyphics is required to understand the negated social construction of the body.

Freud's therapeutic intervention legitimizes the structure of bourgeois domination by "certifying" its basic presuppositions. For as Freud brings to consciousness what had previously been repressed, he acts to reconstitute the rebellious inclination by introducing it into the fabric of normal, acceptable social relationships. In this way its destructive power is dissipated and it is rendered harmless. As Freud notes, in the course of justifying his frank discussion of sexual matters with Dora:

> With the exercise of a little caution all that is done is to translate into conscious ideas what was already known in the unconscious; and, after all, the whole effectiveness of the treatment is based upon our knowledge that the affect attached to an unconscious idea operates more strongly and, *since it cannot be inhibited*, more injuriously than the affect attached to a conscious one [emphasis added].[77]

Freud's intervention makes it possible to incorporate into the social system what had previously been a recalcitrant opposition. Society has the power to repress various "instinctual" tendencies, but it has not the power to repress the effects of this repression. That is why psychoanalysis is so crucial a form of social control, and why it is so appropriate to the bourgeois order. It is not that it involves domination, nor ideology, nor the acceptance by the oppressed of the system that oppresses them; all these facts are as ancient as class society. What is novel in the system of bourgeois-psychoanalytic ideology is the belief of the exploited (a) not merely that they are not exploited at all but (b) that they have in fact freely chosen the situation in which they find themselves. The serf of the Middle Ages believed in the appropriateness of his subordination; it was God's will that society be hierarchically organized. But the typical bourgeois and, with the growth of capitalism, the typical worker believe that if their circumstances are not equal in power and privilege to those more fortunate, it is their own activity that has rendered them so subordinate.

What is unique in bourgeois ideology is the credo of personal responsibility—the belief that individuals freely select their own social status. I am not claiming that this ideology is uncontested; merely that it is a persistent and powerful force against which an enormous amount of counterenergy must be mobilized. As Freud notes:

> For analysis does not undo the *effects* of repression. The instincts which were formerly suppressed remain suppressed; but the same effect is produced in a different way. Analysis replaces the process of repression, which is an automatic and excessive one, by a temperate and purposeful control on the part of the highest mental faculties. In a word, *analysis replaces repression by condemnation.*[78]

The client, through the higher mental faculties of rational self-determination, chooses the suppression of instinct which had previously been externally imposed.

The therapist mediates this "self-determination" by directing the process of rational condemnation. The case of Dora did not reach a successful conclusion, and Freud's reflection on the outcome is instructive. In regard to the last visit Dora made to him he notes:

> I knew Dora would not come back again. Her breaking off so unexpectedly, just when my hopes of a successful termination of the treatment were at their highest, and her thus bringing these hopes to nothing—this was an unmistakable act of vengeance on her part. Her purpose of self injury also profited by this action. No one who, like me, conjures up the most evil of those half-tamed demons that inhabit the human breast, and seeks to wrestle with them, can expect to come through the struggle unscathed. Might I perhaps have kept the girl under my treatment if I myself had acted a part, if I had exaggerated the importance to me of her staying on, and had shown a warm personal interest in her—a course which, even after allowing for my position as her physician, would have been tantamount to providing her with a substitute for the affection she longed for? I do not know. Since in every case a part of the factors that are encountered under the form of resistance remains unknown, I have always avoided acting a part, and have contented myself with practising the humbler arts of psychology. In spite of every theoretical interest and of every endeavor to be of assistance as a physician, I kept the fact in mind that there must be some limits set to the extent to which psychological influence may be used, and I respect as one of these limits the patient's own will and understanding.[79]

The abrupt termination of the analysis is here attributed to Dora's vengeance against Freud. His lack of "warm personal affection," on the other hand, is attributed to his unwillingness to "act a part" and to his respect for the will and understanding of the client. But just why Freud's reserve—his insistence on Dora's restricted importance to him—is any less a "psychological influence" than an expression of warm personal affection is impossible to determine. The claim to respect for Dora's will and intelligence must be seen in the light of Freud's observations in the postscript to the case. There he candidly acknowledges that "I did not succeed in mastering the transference in good time."[80]

Freud noted from the beginning that he was replacing Dora's father in her imagination, for

> she was even constantly comparing me with him consciously, and kept anxiously trying to make sure whether I was being quite straightforward with her, for her father "always preferred secrecy and roundabout ways."[81]

Later, Freud comments, when Dora's transference to him proceeded from Herr K, he might have directed her attention to the fact that she was preparing to leave him as she had her previous suitor. But the comparison of Freud with Dora's father and Herr K in the transference raises the crucial question of the *real* grounds of comparison between them. According to Freud,

> the transference took me unawares, and, because of the unknown quantity in me which reminded Dora of Herr K, she took her revenge on me as she wanted to take her revenge on him, and deserted me as she believed herself to have been deceived and deserted by him. Thus she *acted* an essential part of her recollections and phantasies instead of reproducing it in the treatment. What this unknown quantity was I naturally cannot tell. I suspect it had to do with money or with jealousy.[82]

The key phrase in this passage is "as she *believed* herself to have been deceived and deserted by him." For she was, *in fact,* deceived and deserted by Herr K. Was Freud's behavior so absolutely dissimilar? He, like Herr K and her father, while not overtly deceiving her, refused to acknowledge her "truth," the persistent character of exploitation and betrayal in her life. And, like Herr K, Freud also refused to pursue her in treatment, to "show warm personal affection" toward her at the moment of her resistance.

But do we not need to keep in mind Freud's respect for Dora's will and intelligence?

> Moreover, the relation of transference brings with it two further advantages. If the patient puts the analyst in the place of his father (or mother), he is also giving him the power which his super-ego exercises over his ego, since his parents were, as we know, the origin of his super-ego. The new super-ego now has an opportunity for a sort of *after-education* of the neurotic; it can

correct mistakes for which his parents were responsible in educating him. But at this point a warning must be given against misusing this new influence. However much the analyst may be tempted to become a teacher, a model and ideal for other people and to create men in his own image, he should not forget that that is not his task in the analytic relationship, and indeed that he will be disloyal to his task if he allows himself to be led on by his inclinations. If he does, he will only be repeating a mistake of the parents who crushed their child's independence by their influence, and he will only be replacing the patient's earlier dependence by a new one. In all his attempts at improving and educating the patient the analyst should respect his individuality. The amount of influence which he may legitimately allow himself will be determined by the degree of developmental inhibition present in the patient. Some neurotics have remained so infantile that in analysis too they can only be treated as children.[83]

The amount of influence that may be exercised is determined by the degree of "developmental inhibition" present in the client. There can be no doubt that Dora was so inhibited; she had no awareness, for example, "that her homosexual love for Frau K was the strongest unconscious current in her mental life."[84] How, than, can we justify Freud's failure to intervene more directly in Dora's therapy on the basis of his supposed respect for her "own will and understanding." The difficulty is that according to Freud's own account, Dora did not yet possess her own will and understanding, and Freud's severe scientific "neutrality" can add nothing to its development.

Freud's ambivalence is rooted in the paradox of liberal education. The child–patient is acknowledged to have been determined by the parents' dominating influence and the therapist is admonished to respect the patient's "individuality." But if the analyst refuses to adopt the role of "teacher, model or ideal," how will he transform the crippling influence which the parents first exercised? If he were to be neutral—a stance we have seen to be both practically and theoretically impossible—he would merely perpetuate the child's helpless dependence. The standard response is that the analyst merely helps the patient to uncover repressed inclinations and leaves it to the patient to determine their value and freely adopt or reject them. But we have seen that the unearthing of hidden motives occurs in the context of an interpretation that cannot be impartial in terms of its ascription of responsibility to the individual or the social system, and that also cannot avoid the legitimization of one form of social relationship over another. The therapist's task is to counter the dependence of the client–child, which, as it was formed in a particular social arrangement, must be counterposed by a new social system dedicated to the independence of its members. This would require that the therapist be antiauthoritarian, antipaternalistic, and, consequently, anticapitalist, though it does not dictate the strategy by which this alternative vision is to be included in the therapeutic process.

CHAPTER SIX

The Sociology of Metapsychology

The key to demystifying Freudian theory is the translation of its "natural" categories into their social meaning. I have offered some suggestions as to how this task is to be accomplished in regard to Freud's clinical practice. However this practice itself rests on metapsychological assumptions which have not as yet been dereified; it is the purpose of this chapter to pursue that project.

We have already noted the contemporary dispute that rages around the significance of Freud's metapsychology. There are those who still employ such basic Freudian conceptions as homeostatic energy and others who have wholly abandoned such an approach for an exclusive emphasis on meaning, intention, and purpose. It is crucial for us to keep in mind that we are dealing here with Freud and not with his multitudinous followers. It will be a sufficiently useful contribution, in my view, to clarify what *Freud* meant and to follow out its consequences. From this vantage point I have no doubt that Freud's theory is fundamentally dualistic, and that it moves on different occasions from an energy model to a meaning model and back again. But it is equally clear that only the energy model had a developed metapsychological structure. The meaning theory, though it was employed often by Freud, not only in clinical practice but also in his more abstract conceptual formulations, was never given the same theoretical attention that underlay the theory of quanta-tive, homeostatic energy. There is no Freudian work that grounds the theory of meaning in the manner in which the "Scientific Project" grounds a theory of energic transactions. The only possible exception that might be proposed—"The Interpretation of Dreams"—falls back on an explicitly mechanical metapsychology for its theoretical foundation.

This condition is not accidental but stems from the postulates of Freud's theory of instincts.

> By an "instinct" is provisionally to be understood the psychical *representative* of an endosomatic, continuously flowing source of stimulation. . . . The con-cept of instinct is thus one of those lying on the frontier between the mental and the physical. The simplest and likeliest assumption as to the nature of instincts would seem to be that in itself an instinct is without quality, and, so far as mental life is concerned, is only to be regarded as a measure of the demand made upon the mind for work. What distinguishes the instincts from one another and endows them with specific qualities is *their relation to their somatice sources* and to their aims. The source of an instinct is a process of excitation occurring in an organ and the immediate aim of the instinct lies in the removal of this organic stimulus [emphasis added].[1]

The instinct is a psychical representative of a physiological process. Consequently, the aim is also a representative of organic causes. The aim, that is, the purpose of the instinct, has no independent, autonomous status. It is *epiphenomenal*. But certainly it is in the aim of the instinct that its meaning and intention would originate. Perhaps we are misreading Freud; haven't we just quoted him to the effect that instincts are distin-guished from each other by their "somatic sources *and . . . their aims*"? But the source and the aim are not of equivalent status as Freud clearly notes when he states that "instincts are wholly determined by their origin in a somatic source," although "in mental life we know them only by their aims."

So, while for our heuristic purposes it may be sufficient to concen-trate upon the aim and even to infer the organic source from mental representations, in fact, "What distinguishes from one another the men-tal effects produced by the various instincts may be traced to the dif-ference in their sources."[2] It seems clear that aims, intentions, purposes, and meanings are the epiphenomena derived from more basic physiological sources. The theory of meanings, then, can have no inde-pendent status in Freud's theory.

The absence of a theory of meaning reveals itself in a variety of difficulties. I shall select two for purposes of illustration. First, there is a serious ambiguity regarding the status of meaning, for it can have two very different interpretations. On the first, the subject means something by his or her intentional reference to the world through the use of a symbolic structure. On the second and very different view, the subject's activity, i.e., symptom, means something *to an external observer* who can relate the outcome of the act to its genesis.

An illustration of the first view occurs in the course of a typical discussion of the assertion that slips of the tongue and similar errors "make sense."

> Now what does it mean when we say "it makes sense"? Well, it means that the result of the slip may perhaps have a right to be regarded *in itself* as a valid mental process *following out its own purpose,* and as an expression having content and meaning [emphasis added].[3]

This is a very familiar sort of passage and could easily be duplicated from literally hundreds of other similar citations. However, it is not the same sort of account as the following, which Freud offers:

> The investigations which lay at the root of Breuer and Freud's studies led above all to two results, and these have not been shaken by subsequent experience; first, that hysterical symptoms have sense and meaning, being substitutes for normal mental acts, and secondly, that the uncovering of this unknown meaning is accompanied by the removal of the symptoms.... From the very beginning the factor of *affect* was brought into the fore-ground; hysterical symptoms, the authors maintained, came into existence when a mental process with a heavy charge of affect was in any way pre-vented from equalizing that charge by passing along the normal paths lead-ing to consciousness and movement (i.e., from being "*abreacted*"), as a result of which the affect, which was in a sense "*strangulated*," was diverted on to the wrong paths and found its discharge into the somatic innervation (a process named "*conversion*").[4]

Now, in this passage the presentation of the meaning of a symptom is nothing but the old hydraulic view of channeled and detoured energy-affects. The "sense and meaning" conveyed here is similar to that in which "smoke means fire." The fact that the symptom is a substitute for an "affective charge" is not the intention of the subject, either con-sciously or unconsciously, but merely something that occurs in the ner-vous system when the affective charge is too heavy to be borne by normal processes. The diversion of energy means something to the acute eye of Freud, but this is totally different from saying that it is meaningful to the subject undergoing the conversion.

A second difficulty concerns the issue of psychic representation. This problem stems directly from the epiphenomenal view of instinctual aims to which I referred above. Freud's epistemology is a form of Lockean representative dualism. The position is never clearly articulated but it is evident that Freud regards the contents of consciousness as "represent-ing" a material world with properties radically different from those that are directly revealed in conscious experience. Two questions arise: First, what is the object of cathexes in Freud's theory? Is it the external world or the mental representative? Brenner's comment inadvertently cuts to the heart of the matter:

> Freud continued the analogy between his psychological hypotheses and those of physics by speaking of the quantum of psychic energy with which a particular *object* or *person* was invested. For this concept Freud used the German word Besetzung, which has been translated into English by the word "cathexis." The accurate definition "cathexis" is the amount of psychic energy which is directed toward or attached to *the mental representative* of a person or thing. That is to say, the drive and its energy are considered to be *purely intrapsychic phenomena*. The energy *cannot flow out through space and cathect or attach itself to the external object directly*. What are cathected of course are the various memories, thoughts, and fantasies of the object which comprise what we call its mental or psychic representatives [emphasis added].[5]

Brenner begins by referring us to the "person" or "object" to which the cathexis is directed and ends by noting that it is in fact only the intrapsychic "representative" that can receive the charge of energy. Since Freud is explicit in maintaining that "By the medium of consciousness each one of us becomes aware *only* of his own states of mind" (emphasis added)[6] his immediately following reference to Kant's agnosticism is directly to the point at issue. But precisely how, on this view, do we in fact ever make contact with the external world? This objection to the theory is perennial, but that does not make it any the less troublesome. The shadow of solopsism which falls over the intrapsychic theory darkens the entire view of meanings, since a fundamental aspect of any such theory is the relationship between meanings and that to which they refer or "mean," and as to this difficulty, Freud is silent.

These latter difficulties derive from the relationship between quantity and quality in Freud's metapsychology. In the "Project for a Scientific Psychology" he observes:

> Hitherto, nothing whatever has been said of the fact that every psychological theory, apart from what it achieves from the point of view of natural science, must fulfill yet another major requirement. It should explain to us what we are aware of, in the most puzzling fashion, through our "consciousness"; and, since this consciousness knows nothing of what we have so far been assuming—quantities and neurones—it should explain this lack of knowledge to us as well.[7]

The issue resides in the fact that consciousness is qualitative whereas the neurophysiological processes that form the foundation of Freud's system are of a radically different character:

> Where do qualities originate? Not in the external world. For, out there, according to the view of our *natural science, to which psychology too must be subjected here,* there are only masses in motion and nothing else [emphasis added].[8]

The real question seems to me to be not where qualities originate—a question too ill-conceived to admit of an answer—but, rather, how do conscious qualities "represent" masses in motion. Before the difficulty is dismissed as due merely to the early state of Freud's conception at the time of the "Project," it is worth remembering that in the later *Three Essays on Sexuality,* a work Freud revised throughout his lifetime, instinct is described as being "without quality,"[9] a characteristic that does not, in Freud's view, prevent its qualitative presentation in consciousness.

Not only does Freud fail to join the theory of meaning to the metapsychology of hydraulic forces, but at times he himself recognizes the incompatibility between them:

> As will be remembered, we have conceived the principle which governs all mental processes as a special case of Fechner's *tendency to stability,* and consequently have ascribed to the mental apparatus the aim of extinguishing, or at least of maintaining at as low a level as possible, the quantities of excitation flowing into it. . . . From this it would follow that every "pain" coincides with a heightening, every pleasure with a lowering, of the stimulus-tension existing in the mind. . . . Unfortunately, this view cannot be correct. It seems that we experience the ebb and flow of quantities of stimuli directly in perceptions of tension which form a series, and it cannot be doubted that there is such a thing as both pleasurable tension and "painful" lowering of tension.[10]

Nor is it merely a confusion of categories to maintain that we experience quantities of stimuli directly; more significantly, our conscious experience contradicts the underlying mechanistic theory. This difficulty does not lead Freud to abandon the theory, however, although it is difficult to know how it can be maintained in the face of such "evidence" to the contrary.

The Reification of the Unconscious

Early in *The Ego and the Id* Freud offers the following judgment:

> It is easy to see that the ego is that part of the id which has been modified by the direct influence of the external world. . . . The ego represents what may be called reason and common sense, in contrast to the id, which contains the passions.[11]

To demystify the Freudian metapsychology it is necessary to reverse this pronouncement so that it reads instead: The id is that portion of ourselves which we alienate from our own conscious awareness under the pressure of intolerable social forces: it is the region of our being in which we flee from these aspects of ourselves which threaten us with dissolution.

When some aspect of ourselves is so defined that its presence in consciousness is intolerable to us, we withdraw it from our scrutiny, and in this act of forced divestiture construct those unconscious powers which, while of us, are never really ours. Our ego and superego are elaborated out of the same process, so that the divisions of the self are the product of social and historical agencies, not only in their specific content but in the nature of their structures as well. This is the fundamental starting point for a Marxist critique of Freudian metapsychology and for the elaboration of a Marxist psychology in its own right.

Once again we are face to face with the fundamental tendency to reification in Freud's theory. His description of the idlike portion of ourselves as marked by peremptory demand, insatiability, repetition, and "illogical" functioning contains an important element of the truth. But Freud's account of origins is once again inverted. He takes the effect for the cause; an error that not only makes crucial aspects of his theory unintelligible but which also portends a conservative or, at times, reactionary political perspective. On rare occasions Freud approached a very different view and provided an account that bears significant similarities to Marx's notion of alienation.

> For the mental process which has been turned into a symptom owing to repression now maintains its existence outside the organization of the ego and independently of it. Indeed, it is not that process alone but all its derivatives which enjoy the privilege of extra-territoriality; and whenever they come into associative contact with a part of the ego-organization, it is not at all certain that they will not draw that part over to themselves and thus enlarge themselves at the expense of the ego.[12]

But this is not Freud's persistent view of the subject. Instead, he holds that there is a system or region substantively and originally distinct from the character of rational consciousness in which the result of alienation is not only secreted, but from which it ultimately derives. To indicate what must be done to overturn the Freudian paradigm and set it properly on its social foundation, it is useful to follow Freud through the insoluble difficulties of his own exposition.

I will focus on two moments of the development of Freud's analysis: his topographic division of the psyche into systems of conscious, unconscious, and preconscious characteristics, and the later structural partition into the ego, id, and superego. The problem with both accounts is that the origin of the parts cannot be explained, nor their relationship to each other made intelligible.

The unconscious is of course identified with

> the older primary processes, the residues of a phase of development in which they were the only kind of mental processes. . . . These processes strive towards gaining pleasure; from any operation which might arouse unpleasantness ("pain") mental activity draws back (repression).[13]

Originally, then, when the state of our equilibrium was disturbed by the "peremptory demands of inner needs, . . . whatever was thought of (desired) was simply imagined in an hallucinatory form."

> This attempt at satisfaction by means of hallucination was abandoned only in consequence of the absence of the experienced gratification. . . . A new principle of mental functioning was thus introduced; what was conceived was no longer that which was pleasant, but that which was real, even if it should be unpleasant. This institution of the *reality principle* proved a momentous step.[14]

The problem is that the step is so momentous as to prove unintelligible. Since it is the "older, primary processes" that follow the pleasure principle and draw back from "any operation which might arouse unpleasantness"—including logical thought—it is incumbent upon Freud's theory to make the transition to a radically different form of mental functioning comprehensible. It is not enough to assert that the derivation takes place. Nor is it a question of whether it might prove useful to the pleasure principle to recognize reality and master it. Rather, the question is how a principle of irrational functioning organized solely around pleasure can ever come to conceive of reality and subordinate its own distinct character to a wholly different, radically opposed principle of organization.

Of course any genetic theory is committed to the notion that mature competence is not given at birth and comes only gradually to fruition. But Freud is claiming something else. Recall that he maintains that the primary processes were once "the only kind of mental processes." It is this judgment that is the key to Freud's difficulty; for whether the claim is made for individual development or for the history of humankind, it is inconceivable. No human individual could have been governed exclusively by the "primary processes" defined as the absence of the reality principle, because (1) the simplest acts of survival such as locating the breast or recalling the vague features of previous experience would be impossible on this account, and (2) because no development out of such a stage is conceivable.

Freud's account is teleological in the pejorative sense of the term. Because it is apparently useful to the organism to develop a capacity to judge reality, so, the capacity develops. This hardly constitutes a genetic explanation. And it does not help matters when Freud informs us that "actually, the substitution of the reality-principle for the pleasure-principle denotes no dethronement of the pleasure-principle, but only a safeguarding of it."[15] For the pleasure-principle was previously described as avoiding "*any* operation which might arouse pain." The pleasure-principle which is *served* by the reality-principle cannot be the same principle that Freud originally postulated.

Underlying these difficulties is the ultimate fact that for Freud the primary processes, and later the id itself, do not develop. They retain their original features throughout life. Another principle may come to reside on the foundation of the primary process, and the system of defenses which restrains the underlying pleasure principle may be said to develop, but this original system remains in perpetuity what it was at birth. This contention implies that the distinctive features of the primary process, condensation and displacement. are innately constituted and derive nothing from the developing experience of the child, a proposition that becomes all the more portentious when we realize that for Freud "every mental act begins as an unconscious one, and it may either remain so or go on developing into consciousness."[16] The analogy Freud himself suggests is perfectly suitable; every photograph begins as a negative and some "which have held good in examination" are admitted to consciousness. But the psychic "negative" is defined by the absence of features which characterize the "photograph," rendering an understanding of the "development" of one from the other incomprehensible.

The difficulty reappears in Freud's comparison of the nature of the unconscious, on the one hand, and the preconscious–conscious, on the other. In regard to the former:

> We know for certain that they have abundant points of contact with conscious mental processes; on being submitted to a certain method of operation they may be transformed into or replaced by conscious process, and all the categories which we employ to describe conscious mental acts, such as ideas, purposes, resolutions and so forth, can be applied to them. Indeed, of many of these latent states we have to assert that the only point in which they differ from states which are conscious is just in the lack of consciousness of them.[17]

And yet, in the very same essay, "The Unconscious," Freud attributes to system Ucs "characteristics which are *not again met with* in the system immediately above it."

> The kernel of the system Ucs consists of instinct-presentations whose aim is to *discharge their cathexis;* that is to say, they are wish-impulses. These instinctual impulses are co-ordinate with one another, exist independently side by side, and are *exempt from mutual contradiction.* When two wishes whose aims must appear to us incompatible become simultaneously active, the two impulses, do not detract one from the other or cancel each other, but combine to form an intermediate aim, a compromise.
>
> There is in this system *no negation,* no dubiety, *no varying degree of certainty:* all this is only imported by the work of the censorship which exists between the Ucs and Pcs. . . . By the process of displacement one idea may surrender to another the whole volume of its cathexis; by that of condensation it may appropriate the whole cathexis of several other ideas. I have proposed to regard these two processes as distinguishing marks of the so-

called "primary process" in the mind. In the systems Pcs the "secondary process" holds sway.

The processes of the system Ucs are *timeless;* i.e., they are *not ordered temporally, are not altered* by the passage of time, in fact *bear no relation to time* at all. [emphasis added].[18]

I have italicized those phrases that are incompatible with the earlier claim that the two systems are fundamentally similar. But this only marks the beginning of Freud's confusion. The real difficulty lies in the fact that the Ucs cannot be made intelligible on the basis of Freud's description. Consider the characteristic of "purpose" that was earlier attributed to the Ucs. In view of the contention that contradiction, negation, time, and sequential ordering are all absent from the Ucs, how can the concept be understood? Intrinsic to our very idea of purpose is the notion of an end or outcome of our action which is this particular termination rather than that, and which procedes along a path of temporal accumulation from one necessary stage to another. None of these characteristics can hold for "purpose" as Freud has characterized the system Ucs. In short, purpose requires stages which require time; but Freud has eliminated these properties from the system unconscious. The term is, therefore, simply dissolved.

Perhaps that is why Freud replaces "purpose" with the term "wish-impulse" instead. But the same difficulty recurs. Either the term has some meaning that we can grasp on the basis of our conscious experience or it is a mere vacuity. And our dissatisfaction with the presentation grows more pronounced when we realize that Freud's whole account is more relevant to psychic forces than to meanings, intentions, and purposes, in any case. For when Freud notes that two "incompatible" impulse combine "to form a compromise" we realize that the relevant paradigm is the mutual deflection of forces as in the parallelograms of vectors which are appropriate in physics. No "compromise" in the strict sense is intelligible without judgment, and judgment depends on the possibility of negation and contradiction. This suspicion is borne out by the language Freud employs to describe displacement and condensation, the two processes that are held to uniquely characterize the system Ucs. For his description merely alludes to the circulation of cathexis, to volumes of excitation which move from one instinct representation to another, a totally different matter from that of analogy or metaphor understood as conceptual processes.

I believe that Freud is somewhat aware of the difficulty to which his description of the Ucs leads, for in the section of the work immediately following his account of the special features of the Ucs he strongly insists that it would be a mistake to regard this system as "something finished with, a vestigial organ, a residuum from the process of evolution," And, he continues, it would be a mistake to believe that communication between the two systems is impossible. "On the contrary, the Ucs is living and capable of development and maintains a number of other relations to the Pcs, among them that of cooperation."[19] But these are mere assertion; they have no intelligible foundation and are undermined by Freud's previous characterization. The reason for Freud's insistence on contact between the systems is clear enough; not only would ordinary mental life be unimaginable on the grounds he has provided, but therapy in particular, which depends for its effect upon the influence that can be exerted by the consciousness of the analyst upon the Ucs of the patient, would be particularly unfathomable. Freud may insist that while negation is unavailable in the Ucs it is *imported* by the work of censorship. But it remains impossible to understand how so alien an emigrant can take up quarters in so inhospitable a climate.

Freud's additional efforts to clarify the distinction between the two systems seem to me to add nothing but new perplexities, and yet they are interesting for reasons that are worth commentary:

> What we could permissibly call the conscious ideas of the object can now be split up into *the idea of the word* (verbal idea) and *the idea of the thing* (concrete idea): the latter consists in the cathexis, if not the direct memory-images of the thing, at least of remoter memory-traces derived from these. It strikes us all at once that now we know what is the difference between a conscious and an unconscious idea. The two are not as we supposed, different records of the same content . . . but the conscious idea comprises the concrete idea plus the verbal idea corresponding to it, whilst the unconscious idea is that of the thing alone. The system Ucs contains the thing-cathexes of the object, the first and true object-cathexis, the system Pcs originates in hyper-cathexis of this concrete idea by a linking up of it with the verbal idea of the words corresponding to it.[20]

"The unconscious idea is that of the thing alone . . . the first and true object cathexis." Freud here makes explicit an assumption that runs through much of his topography—that there is some nonverbal form of cognition that reaches the object itself without conceptual intermediary. But this contention is unintelligible. For, since an idea represents the common character of a class, the notion of a "concrete idea" or an idea of a "thing alone" would seem a contradiction in terms. Even if we could understand how a thing is presented, we are given no idea of how it could be grasped.

For Freud there are apparently no words, and, by implication, no concepts in the unconscious. It is difficult enough to understand how there can be a direct, unmediated grasp of an object by the Ucs, but the difficulty grows worse when we realize that the Ucs is without negation, which would apparently be a prerequisite for any act of mind that had the power to discriminate one object for cathexis rather than another. Freud has to grant the Ucs (and later, the id) cognitive powers his own explication renders impossible. If the Ucs cannot conceptualize, it cannot discriminate and cannot selectively direct its cathexis. In short, it cannot discriminate the objects of its discharge.

It is precisely because thought is required to demarcate distinct features of the world from each other that we must reverse Freud's account and argue, instead, that no substantive Ucs is possible until such time as the child acquires sufficient conceptual capacity as to be able to discriminate from amidst the plethora of experiences those which are the object of terror and the eventual content of the act of repression. In this sense Lacan is correct in noting the relationship between language and unconscious. But we must equally insist that language use is developed in the world of social discourse rather than preexisting as an innate structural imposition.

The preceding string of confusions and contradictions in Freud's analysis points to several important considerations. First, as I have previously argued, Freud's underlying metapsychology strongly conflicts with the current view which would sutstitute meanings and purposes for mechanical energy transformations. Freud's view of the system Ucs is strikingly anticonceptual and anti-intentional. It is very difficult to understand how even the primary processes of displacement and condensation can themselves be made intelligible on this account. Freud's theory precludes a transformational account of the unconscious manifested in analogy and metaphor because these processes are postconceptual rather than preconceptual.

Freud continually contradicts himself on this issue. In the course of an analysis of "The Antithetical Sense of Primal Words," he notes:

> The word "No" does not seem to exist for a dream. Dreams show a special tendency to reduce two opposites to a unity or to represent them as one thing. Dreams even take the liberty, moreover, of representing any element whatever by the opposite wish.[21]

How dreams can operate upon opposites without the concept of negation is simply bypassed, leaving us to speculate that the entire account is fundamentally awry. The following comment by Frank Cioffi nicely summarizes this part of the difficulty:

> An extended exposition of this property of the unconscious (that it contains no contradictions) occurs on the following occasion: Freud is anticipating an objection that his account of a patient's symptoms as due to an unconscious wish to be penetrated by his father's penis and bear him a child plus an unconscious conviction that castration was a precondition of this wish being fulfilled conflicted with another interpretation which presupposed that the

patient was unconsciously convinced that the anus was the orifice of intercourse and birth; "That it should have been possible . . . for a fear of castration to exist side by side with an identification with women by means of the
bowel admittedly involved a contradiction. But it was only a logical
contradiction—which is not saying much. On the contrary, the whole process
is characteristic of the way in which the unconscious works." But the first of
the two accounts which Freud attempts to reconcile by this device itself presupposes that the unconscious is aware of contradiction, for it is this which
brings the desire to play a passive sexual role vis-à-vis the father in conflict
with the desire to retain the penis. And one cannot help noticing that the
unconscious, which "has no logic" and knows nothing of contradictions, is
nevertheless constantly involved in the drawing of inferences. For example,
in the case history of Hans, Freud describes the following as a "typical unconscious train of thought"; "Could it be that living beings really did exist which
did not possess widdlers? If so, it would no longer be so incredible that they
could take his one widdler away and, as it were, make him into a woman."
But if there is no "No" in the unconscious . . . then there can be no "If," "So,"
or "Thus" either.[22]

Second, and a point we need to return to later in our exposition, the
difficulties in Freud's analysis strongly suggest that his fundamental mistake lies in turning the unconscious into an ontological region with
characteristics that are neither derived from social experience nor even
influenced by its modalities. We need to consider the possibility of once
again reversing the account offered by Freud, and of conceiving of the
unconscious as derivative from the procedures of socially imposed repression.

The Creation of the Repressed Unconscious

With one aspect of Freud's theory—his claim of a repressed unconscious governed by irrational, peremptory, insatiable demands which act
beyond our understanding and behind our conscious choice—there can
be no quarrel. This was, in fact, Freud's monumental discovery. It is in
the explanation of the origin and nature of this force that the difficulty
resides. It is in reifying the Ucs as a topography, or structure, a fixed,
innate, distinctly constituted region with its own unique and compelling
organization and content, that Freud mystifies the issue. And the result
of this move on his part is not only to attribute portentious powers to the
Ucs, but to confuse our understanding of consciousness (Cs) in the process. We shall return to this matter in time but at the moment we can
suggest the problem by noting that in the papers on metapsychology
Freud has already developed two views in regard to the Cs (later ego)
which he never reconciled: (1) that the Cs is the highest in a series of

systems in which the Ucs is the primitive foundation; and (2) that "the conception of the Cs as a receptor sense organ clearly precludes its having contents."[23]

The major internal difficulty in Freud's account is that by the criteria he himself has established for distinguishing the two major systems—Ucs/(id) and Cs-Pcs/(ego)—important mental phenomena cannot be accorded any unique location. Whether we define the original topography in terms of the relationship of contents to consciousness, to the nature of energy, or to the mode of functioning, these phenomena lack univocal existence. By one criterion they belong to the Ucs, by another to the Pcs-Cs. And to compound the difficulty, the criteria conflict.

For example, Freud himself indicated that there were mental phenomena whose mode of organization was characterized by primary-process formation but which were nevertheless conscious. Such material is present in dreams, hallucinations and "the ideational components of symptoms."[24] On the other hand, there are contents—fantasies—which are organized according to secondary processes and are nonetheless dynamically unconscious. The following reflection of Freud's adumbrates the difficulty:

> Among the derivatives of the Ucs instinctual impulses, of the sort we have described, there are some which unite in themselves characters of an opposite kind. On the one hand, they are highly organized, free from self-contradiction, have made use of every acquisition of the system Cs and would hardly be distinguished in our judgment from the formations of that system. On the other hand they are unconscious and are incapable of becoming conscious. Thus *qualitatively* they belong to the system Pcs, but *factually* to the Ucs.[25]

This passage echoes Freud's earlier attempt to bridge the two systems, and seems to me to fail because the task is impossible as Freud has constructed the dichotomy between the systems. But Freud does not withdraw the characterization. He continues to struggle laboriously with the original topographic and later structural compartmentalizations, and with the major difficulty posed by his ontological division—that in some manner the repressing force and repressed content must both emanate from the same source and yet be fundamentally opposed as two distinct and incompatible principles. Since Freud was incapable of understanding that both the repressed desire and the repressing counterforce were socially determined, having thereby a common though contradictory social origin, he could not resolve the difficulty his theory posed at this juncture. We shall return to this issue. For the moment I wish simply to note in passing what is at stake in the argument.

Freud noted a crucial difference between two aspects of our mental life and proceeded to ontologize the distinction. He made functions into regions, and regions into substantive, permanent, innate facts of human nature. His dualism of Cs–Ucs and Ego–id did not merely oppose one type of activity to another, but one ineradicable reality to another. The irrational, peremptory, and insatiable we shall have always among us. We shall always be governed by forces we cannot control. Psychoanalysis itself may prove a respite, but its possibilities are limited. Wisdom lies rather in recognizing the boundaries of existence, grounded as they are in the unalterable constitution of our psychic life.

This is not a neutral or harmless doctrine. It is a political meta-psychology masquerading as psychological theory. It converts the history of oppression into a timeless region. No emancipatory vision can flouish in this doleful topography. Instead, we participate in our own alienation through our conviction that we are without the power to transcend our present selves. In simplest terms, Freud failed even to question the possibility that we are *made* irrational and "unconsious." He typically assumed that what we manifest as illogical functioning must be derived from an intrinsically illogical realm. This error is the source both of his theoretical confusion and his political regressiveness.

As important as it is to avoid Freud's reification of our pathology, however, it is equally important to recognize its presence. We do harbor in ourselves a pathology that overwhelms our illusions of autonomy. The fact that we understand this presence differently from Freud does not permit us to avoid the task of struggling with the ubiquity of its existence. A Marxist theory that does not credit the tyranny of the irrational is irrelevant. And here, once we have cut away from the dominant context of Freud's conception of the phenomena, we need to set our own vision against his so that we can satisfy ourselves that we have not avoided the hard recognition of what he so forcefully, if misleadingly, called to our attention.

The moments in which Freud himself provides clues to a very different interpretation of his own presentation seem to me particularly valuable. Therefore when Freud notes:

> Under the rule of the unconscious system this material found an elaboration—the condensation and displacement—which is unknown or *only exceptionally admissible* in normal mental life [emphasis added].[26]

The door is consequently open to us to force the issue of this exception, and to question how we can be dealing with distinct regions in view of the reality of phenomena that so clearly escape their ostensible confinement. In fact, we are required to consider that the distinction Freud is struggling with is totally a matter of degree of repression, or from a Marxist perspective, of the mode of alienation, and that no substantive, primordial, dualistic organization is involved. Or put conversely, what is displayed in the unconscious is also displayed in consciousness, so that whatever the difference between them comes to, it cannot be explained by their residence in mutually exclusive ontological realms. And if we should conclude that the unconscious comes to acquire its character and predominant power through social procedures, it is open to us to restructure society in such a way that its destructiveness is minimized or wholly eliminated. The Ucs as Freud construes it, however, is an irradicable fate, which we have some small power to manipulate but no capacity to transcend.

Freud made an absolutely vital discovery in noting a connection between conscious and unconscious processes, the mode of mental organization and the nature of the defense mechanisms. Nor is this simply an interesting fact about individual human beings. It is simultaneously a crucial dimension of social life, because the ensemble of public–private relations that constitute the structure of the social world is also constituted out of diverse levels of mental organization. There has been almost no recognition of this fact in Marxist theory—one of its most critical defects. Institutions are maintained, however, not only through (a) the formal and explicit rules that define their practice; (b) the implicit and informal procedures that both bind and interpret the meaning of these codified principles; (c) the structural mandates one aspect of the system imposes upon other sectors of the totality; but also (d) through the powerfully adhesive forces of the repressed, unconscious meanings and processes that bind each social agent to the preceding dimensions of the public realm.

Though there is a significant Marxist notion of the unconscious, which we will turn to in the next chapter, there is in the Freudian contribution an insight that cannot be ignored. The processes of alienation, which Marx had attributed to the relationship of human beings to their products, tools, activities, and their fellow human beings he also attributed to their reflexive self-production; that is, to their relationship to themselves.[27] But, though he occasionally spoke of the struggle of human beings against "their own internal priest, against their own priestly nature,"[28] and explicitly held that "man himself is no longer in a condition of external tension with the external substance of private property; he has himself become the tension-ridden being of private property,"[29] it would take an act of idolatrous self-mystification to believe that Marx had any particular notion (or even interest) in how these internal processes of alienation operated. Freud's significance for us lies precisely in the fact that with some elaboration we can employ his observations in the service of a more fruitful understanding.

But we must first be perfectly clear about what is mistaken in Freud's explanation. The basic misconception is the replacement of differentiated functions with an innate ontology. A dialectically differentiated system is converted into a metaphysical polarity. There are two ways in which this difficulty manifests itself; First, either Freud cannot account for the point of contact between the polar categories he has established, or he is forced to designate mental phenomena by contradictory characteristics. We have already observed instances of this horn of the dilemma. Or second, to avoid this difficulty he is compelled to attribute rationality, judgment, conceptual organization, and structure to the Ucs or the id, thus violating his original description. Let us consider this second mode of difficulty.

In a discussion of topographic regression, the tendency of material at the level of Pcs to be reorganized according to the principle of the Ucs, Freud emphasizes the transformation of thoughts into images. It would be easy at this point to define the regression as proceeding from secondary to primary process and from word-idea to thing. But Freud seems to believe that these latter processes can occur only after the movement from thought to image has taken place:

> When regression has been completed, a number of cathexes are left over in the system *Ucs.*—cathexes of memories of *things.* The primary psychical process is brought to bear on these memories, till by condensation of them and displacement between their respective cathexes, it has shaped the manifest dream-content.[30]

But a comment by Gill inadvertantly underscores the difficulty:

> It must be borne in mind that dream formation involves not merely the transformation of thoughts into images but also the acceptance of these images as real—that is, a dream is a hallucination.[31]

For if the image is accepted as real, then some form of judgment must be involved in attributing reality to the image. Whatever the nature of this act it transcends the mere presentation of images as such and remains unintellible on Freud's irrationalistic account of the Ucs. Images in the unconscious have already been elaborated by thought. If this were not the case they could not bear the characteristic of "threat" or "trauma" and could not function in the development of mechanisms of defense. For images are not dangerous in themselves but only through a recognition of their significance in the social matrix.

Now it might be thought that Freud corrected these difficulties when he rejected the topographic for the structural mode. Freud seemed to understand that this original criteria were inadequate to differentiate the two provinces of the original topography:

> The reason for all these difficulties is to be found in the circumstance that the attribute of being conscious, which is the only characteristic of psychical processes that is directly presented to us, is in no way suited to serve as a criterion for the differentiation of systems. . . . The truth is that it is not only the psychically repressed that remains alien to consciousness, but also some

of the impulses which dominate our ego—something, therefore, that forms the strongest functional antithesis to the repressed.[32]

By moving to the structural model of ego, id and superego, Freud seemed able to locate the repressing force and the repressed content in the same region—the dynamic unconscious—and thereby avoid the previous dilemma. However, the gain is more apparent than real as Freud is forced to acknowledge:

> Large portions of the ego, and in particular of the superego, which cannot be denied the characteristic of being preconscious, none the less remain for the most part unconscious in the phenomonological sense of the word.[33]

As Gill notes:

> Freud was forced to call the ego at one and the same time preconscious and unconscious because all of the ego was preconscious by the definition in terms of binding and mode of organization, but part of it was unconscious by the definition in terms of the relationship of mental contents to consciousness.[34]

> The structural theory . . . has built in contradictions. First, since primary-process functioning is found in the unconscious defenses attributed to the ego, then either some of the defenses cannot really belong to the ego, or the ego does not operate entirely according to the secondary processes. Second, the conception of the id as totally without structure is inconsistent with Freud's statements that the id includes ideas, memories, symbols, and mechanisms.[35]

It is Gill's second observation that is crucial to our argument, however, because it is an objection that can only be met by reversing the fundamental thrust of Freud's metapsychology and restructuring the id as the product, rather than the inception, of the structural unconscious. The id can then be grasped as that aspect of the self alienated under contradictory social influence.

To complete the argument it is necessary to rely on an inversion of Freud's theory of repression. Once the defenses are viewed as the agency through which the self divests itself of intolerable threats to its continued identity, rather than the compromise of two warring, incompatible structures, it becomes possible to afford them the same high regard they were assigned by Freud in his theory without reifying them.

> The theory of repression is the corner-stone on which the whole structure of psycho-analysis rests. It is the most essential part of it.
> If anyone sought to place the theory of repression and resistance among the *premises* instead of the *findings* of psycho-analysis, I should oppose him most emphatically . . . the theory of repression is a product of psycho-analytic work, a theoretical inference legitimately drawn from innumerable observations.[36]

On occasion, Freud seemed to suggest an account of repression that is closer to the interpretation I am here offering:

> We have come upon something (resistance) in the ego itself which is also unconscious, which behaves exactly like the repressed—that is, which produces powerful effects without itself being conscious . . . we land in endless obscurities and difficulties if we keep to our habitual forms of expression and try, for instance, to derive neurosis from a conflict between the conscious and the unconscious. We shall have to substitute for this antithesis another, taken from our insight into the structural conditions of the mind—the antithesis between *the coherent ego and the repressed which is split off from it* [emphasis added].[37]

This is a view which would seem to identify the Ucs with repressed desire, and there are a number of passages in Freud that could be adduced in behalf of this position.[38]

But Freud often writes from a contradictory perspective:

> The content of the *Ucs.* may be compared with an aboriginal population in the mind. If inherited mental formations exist in the human being—something analogous to instinct in animals—these constitute the nucleus of the *Ucs.*[39]

> The sole quality that rules in the id is that of being unconscious. Id and unconscious are as intimately united as ego and preconscious; indeed, the former connection is even more exclusive. If we look back at the developmental history of the individual and of his psychic apparatus, we shall be able to make an important distinction in the id. Originally, of course, everything was id, the ego was developed out of the id by the continual influence of the external world. In the course of this slow development certain material was transformed into the preconconscious condition and was thus taken into the ego. *Other material remained unaltered in the id, as its hardly accessible nucleus* [emphasis added].[40]

And it is precisely this perspective which must be rejected, for it leads to the contradictions in the structural theory and to the unintelligible claim of a wholly unstructured energy from which the organization of the self arises.

Once again we are forced to the conclusion that primary and secondary processes, id and ego, reason and instinct, agency of defense and repressed content—that these distinctions cannot be relegated to distinct spheres of existence. They are, rather, continuous with each other and formed simultaneously out of the social articulation of malleable inclinations. We come here to the heart of the matter. Defenses are not barriers against preexisting instincts which deflect an original aim through a series of detouring vicissitudes. The elaboration of defenses shapes the inclinations "against which" the defenses are ostensibly required. Force and counterforce, the paradigm of Freud's metapsychology on either an economic or symbolic interpretation, are dialectically defined through the imposition of contradictory social criteria.

An aspect of mental life becomes a defense to the extent that the inclination it is employed to structure is defined as socially prohibitory. And an originally amorphous inclination becomes a determinate unconscous motive, drive, or "instinct" to the extent that it is defined as "censorable," and so forced away from the self-consciousness of the self and into the literally alien province of the id-unconscious.

Motive and countermotive have no existence independent of each other. Both are socially constructed out of a process which construes each only in contrast with the other. The contradictions or coherence of the self follow the inducements set out in the sphere of social life. Since capitalism requires the production of contradictory institutional forces, it requires the construction of contradictions "internal" to the self. But nothing in this process is innate or ineradicable.

Freud could not locate the contradictions of the self in distinct ontological regions because they do not originate there. The dichotomies that divest us of ourselves and fissure our being are the legacy of an irrational society. It is there that the explanation resides. It is there that the transformation must be effected.

At one point in his very helpful discussion of Freud, Habermas makes the following observation:

> The institutions of social intercourse sanction only certain motives of action. Other need dispositions, likewise attached to interpretations in ordinary language, are denied the route to manifest action, whether by the direct power of an interaction partner or the sanction of recognized social norms. These conflicts, at first external, are perpetuated intrapsychically; insofar as they are not manifested consciously, this perpetuation takes place as a permanent conflict between a defensive agency representing social repression and unrealizable motives of action.[41]

Two correctives to this interpretation are necessary: (1) Conflicts are not first "external" and then "internalized"; they are simultaneously social and personal, external and intrapsychic, and (2) the conflict is not between "a defensive agency representing social repression" and an "unrealizable motive of action," but between a social defense agency and a socially constituted-as-unrealizable motive of action. There are no conflicts perpetuated in the self that are not mediated through the conflicting structures of a particular social system.

It is in the course of accommodating to social institutions that the individual is forced into the self-divestiture that constitutes personal alienation—what Freud referred to as repression and the splitting of the self. Therefore, the production of the self, of social institutions, and of the peremptory power of the irrational unconscious are dialectically related. As has often been noted, Freud's specific choice of the terms *"das Ich" "das Es"* and their translation into ego and id is of real importance.

Das Ich means *I* and *das Es* means *the it:* That is, they refer to the antithesis between reflexive, personal subjectivity and reified, impersonal objectivity. Freud's famous statement of the goal of psychoanalysis, "Wo Es war, soll Ich werden," should read in English, "Where it was, I shall become," or perhaps, "Where it-ness was, I-ness shall come into being."[42]

The term "I-ness" seems to me self-defeating, but the reference to *das Es* as "itness" is illuminating because it so clearly calls Freud's account back into proximity with the Marxist theories of alienation, fetishism, and reification.

The id is formed, or better, malformed, out of the necessity of social self-diremption. The specific "itlike" quality of the unconscious is due to the specific manner of its alienation. Freud's analysis of the self in *The Ego and the Id* is undermined by his failure to realize that the id is the result, not the precondition, of repression. He is thereby forced into dualisms from which there is no escape:

> You must not expect me to tell you much that is new about the id, except its name. It is the obscure inaccessible part of our personality . . . and can only be described as being *all that the ego is not.* We can come nearer to the id with images, and call it a chaos, a cauldron of seething excitement. We suppose that it is somewhere in direct contact with somatic processes, and takes over from instinctual needs and gives them mental expression, but we cannot say in what substratum this contact is made. These instincts fill it with energy, but it has no organization and no unified will, only an impulsion to obtain satisfaction for the instinctual needs, in accordance with the pleasure principle. The laws of logic—above all the law of contradiction—do not hold for processes in the id.[43]

And Freud proceeds to reproduce the account of the absence of time and negation which marked the earlier metapsychological papers. If the id is "all that the ego is not," no discourse between them is possible and the whole of mental life becomes unintelligible. Of course, Freud is himself required to deny this extreme position and grant the id and the ego some fundamental identity. But he seems to me wholly unable to account for this connection.

There is a passage in Marx that serves as a very helpful corrective to Freud's hypostatization of the id:

> Production does not only produce man as a *commodity,* the *human commodity,* man in the form of a *commodity;* in conformity with this situation it produced him as a *mentally* and *physically* dehumanized being. . . . Its product is the *self-conscious* and *self-acting* commodity.[44]

It is precisely the self-conscious and self-acting commodity that needs to be understood, that is the conjuncture of self and not-self, of self and otherness in a single being, which remains always a self nevertheless. Freud's account loses this necessary tension and unity and leaves us instead with two realms whose relationship to each other becomes as unfathomable as the unintelligible, demonic character of the id itself. Freud simply juxtaposes a human being (ego) and a negation of humanity (id) within the self. Freud begins with the id as the source of mental life and attempts to develop an understanding of the ego on this foundation. But nothing can grow on the soil of the id. Marx, on the other hand, begins with the human social-individual in the context of social exploitation and derives from this situation the commoditized it-like character of the still active, self-conscious self and the alienated social world in their dialectical connection.

The Etiology of Self-Estrangement

It is critical to distinguish between Freud's profound insight into the existence of the repressed unconscious on the one hand, and his specific metapsychological explanation of the phenomenon on the other. What must be incorporated into a significant social theory of the self is the character of peremptory demand, impersonality, archaic preservation, irrationality, and continuous assault that distinguishes the phenomenological id. But we neither understand nor effectively alter this condition if we do not trace its origin back to the condition of social domination that constitute its cause. An adequate account of self-estrangement is the subject of another work; we must content ourselves with the following brief suggestions toward a satisfactory theory:

1. It is necessary to avoid personalizing the various regions of the self. It is not only that nothing is gained by imagining various selves in the guise of ego-self, id-self, and superego-self contending with each other like antagonistic family members. Even more, once we begin to speak of the superego as an observer and critic of the self, it becomes very difficult to avoid the image of one "person" passing judgment upon another. To add that the superego is made up of the internalized commands of one's parents contributes nothing to our understanding on the level of inquiry in which we are presently engaged. For we are not asking about the contents of the superego's commands but about the structure of its constitution. And the notion of "internalization" is merely a metaphor without explanatory power. Parents are not literally within one's self. But even more important, since the only speaker is the self, the voices that are heard are also the voices that are spoken, and the problem remains how the speaker can discourse with itself in such a way as to fail to recognize itself as its own agent.

2. That aspect of the self which is split off from the central, self-conscious agent—the self which then becomes repressed or

colonialized—is buried in perpetuity in the condition in which it existed at the time of its interment. This is one of Freud's most valuable insights about the repressed unconscious. Paradoxically, however, it is an insight that permits us to dispense with Freud's ontology. For if we consider that the most drastic acts of repression occur in early childhood, before the child is fully formed, we can understand that the content of the repressed unconscious will be constructed out of the most rudimentary remnants of the self—out of those aspects of its existence formed at stages that are relatively primitive compared with the organization of a mature individual. These are characteristics that approximate Freud's reification of the id.

Parts of the self *become* idlike because they are cut off from the continued growth of the conscious agent. They persist in rudimentary form, dated, as it were, at the primitive stage of their segregation. What is really valuable in Freud's insight then is not his view of psychic regions but his understanding of the reification of genetic development, or simply put, of fixation. On the ground of this insight we can eliminate Freud's theory of dual regions of the self, and proceed quite adequately with a single self which has been sedimented along its way, with the result that it continues to reproduce itself according to both the dictates of its present reality and its past level of disorganization. The advantage we derive from this reconceptualization is not merely that it permits us to dispense with an unnecessary ontological realm but rather that it makes it possible to understand how the self can become lost to its own purview and power, and how it can liberate itself from this condition of imposed but self-generated tyranny.

A full Marxist account of the self is perfectly capable of integrating what is valid in the works of Piaget, Mahler, Jacobson, Loevinger, Spitz, etc. At the same time, it is crucial in learning from the work of traditional writers in the field that we carefully scrutinize the tendency toward reification that continuously impregnates much of their theory and systematically attributes to a universal process of development what is in fact strongly influenced by specific social factors. This is particularly true of accounts of the "mature" or "autonomous" self which derive from various forms of ego and object–relation theories. For these accounts reflect much more than their authors realize the specific forms of the atomized, competitive, performance-oriented selfhood that is the particular paradigm of contemporary capitalist society. Apparently innocent terms like "narcissism," "ego-boundaries," and "compentence" bear a great deal of the ideology of bourgeois culture. Therefore, in the very process of incorporating the insights of genetic psychology, it is imperative that we simultaneously hold these theories up to social scrutiny.

3. Although I will not undertake any account of the specific childhood development of the self in this study, it is reasonably safe to say

something quite general which will still prove useful at this stage of our analysis.

a. The critical dialectic at the formative stage of individual development is between language and desire. The child's conceptual–linguistic structure gains maturity in degree as does its capacity to articulate and integrate desire into a total characterological framework. Conceptualization presents desire with its object and structural channels; desire presents thought with the motive of its articulation. The deformation of either affects the other. Both of these processes are obviously aborted by the intervention of repression. The child becomes incapable of conceptualizing itself in the world and, consequently, of formulating the structures of its demands, drives, needs, desires, and wishes—that is, the heirarchy of stages from compelling biophysical requirements like the demand for breath, up to the wish for imaginative integration.

As Freud discovered, the child's self-understanding is disfigured. Some aspect of its own internal text is so censored that it becomes unintelligible to its bearer. This text is, however, the very fabric of the self, so that the content of its understanding and its ability to understand are sacrificed in one blow. And, as desire is always elaborated through judgment, it is simultaneously rendered unintelligible. But the result is not mere negation, the absence of mature understanding; it is rather the continued reproduction of such conceptual categories and primitive structures of desire as have been formed at the time of repression. And this consideration indicates that the rudimentary schemata that form the self will persist in the unconscious and exert their alien power in precisely these ancient, archaic modes. Repressed as primitive, the unconscious self persists as primitive.

Since on the basis of cognitive considerations alone it is plausible to hold that fundamental notions of time, space, causality, object constancy and the larger forms of global comprehension are all achieved in stages, we must speculate that the repressed self will function with only such a set of primitive conceptual structures as have been developed at the time of its self-dissociation. We are consequently in a position to replace Freud's mystified assertions about the peculiar illogic of the Ucs-id with the more plausible consideration that the aberrations of judgment which Freud selected as one of the principle features of the dynamic unconscious do not belong to its topography but to the particular stage of arrested development which is the content of repression. For example, it is no longer necessary to postulate a psychic realm free of temporal judgment. It is far more intelligible to hold that such distortions of the awareness of time as distinguish the unconscious owe their existence to the inchoate forms of temporal comprehension that exist in the child at the moment it undergoes repression. So, we dereify the proposal of a distinct timeless realm (a view impossible to understand and which Freud himself violates on numerous occasions) and replace it with the assertion that the repressed self bears in its internment such a degree of temporal competence or *incompetence* as it had developed us to the point of its dissociation. We can thereby reconceptualize two processes Freud noted without being bound to his reified metapsychology. First, we can understand both the similarities and differences between conscious and unconscious time, and second, we can grasp why desire, articulated through an inchoate temporal structure, will possess so isolated and fragmentary a nature.

b. In a full account of the development of the self it would be important to distinguish between the "normal" and "pathological" conditions that prevail at the time of repression. Since repression is not likely to occur through a single traumatic episode but rather through the steady imposition of portentious and insatiable demands, the child is likely to have suffered the ravages of oppressive authority over the course of a long development. Whatever situation of terror, hatred, vulnerability, or stifling constraint has led to the need for dissociation will become slowly fixed as a permanent ritual in the mind. In short, since repression disrupts the self, the repressed self is usually also a disfigured, or pathological, self.

But accompanying this perverse condition will be the stage of normal development which is "appropriately" inchoate at the time of burial. Memory, for example, which is always problematic in regard to childhood, is particularly open to distortion. This is in part because even its normal operation is highly vulnerable. Schachtel has some particularly cogent comments on the general difficulty of remembering childhood experience:

> The categories (or schemata) of adult memory are not suitable receptacles for early childhood experiences and therefore not fit to preserve these experiences and enable their recall. The functional capacity of the conscious, adult memory is usually limited to those types of experience which the adult consciously is aware of and is capable of having.
>
> It is not merely the repression of a specific content, such as early sexual experience, that accounts for the general childhood amnesia; the biologically, culturally and socially influenced process of memory organization results in the formation of categories (schemata) of memory which are not suitable vehicles to receive and reproduce experiences of the quality and intensity typical of early childhood. The world of modern Western civilization has no use for this type of experience.[45]

Now, the condition to which Schachtel refers might be regarded as normal only in the sense that it is the normal pathology of "modern Western civilization." Nevertheless, it is a condition that is endemic to this culture. It is not a matter of specific content, but, as Schachtel notes, the general mode of cognitive organization:

> The adult is usually not capable of experiencing what the child experiences; more often than not he is not even capable of imagining what the child experiences. It should not be surprising then, that he should be incapable of recalling his own childhood experiences since his whole mode of experiencing has changed.[46]

If we impose on the fragility of normal childhood memory the factors which led to pathologicl denial, we can more easily understand how the alienation of the self—the *thinglike* quality of repressed unconscious—comes into being. *For though it is our experience that is severed from our grasp, it is experience in a form that does not accommodate to the structures of our present life.* It is our self in a form that is alien to our present categories. We therefore have the sense of being lived through as by an alien figure. But like Marx's "self-conscious and self-acting commodity," this figure has some human form, however grotesque, and the form is of us, if not fully ourselves. The id therefore retains its similarities and continuity with our present self as well as its uncanny strangeness.

Only such an interpretation makes it possible to understand how the self can be healed in any act of therapy, however understood. For if the id were as Freud described it—everything the ego is not—its integration into the ego would remain unintelligible. On our account, it is our own exiled self which we welcome back into our current selves. The act of therapeutic reintegration is always an act of redemption in which what was previously undergone and discarded is welcomed into the current order of the living self. But there is reciprocity, too, and the child in one's self which has been abandoned returns only when its previous needs can be currently embraced.

c. Desire, as well as cognition, develops genetically; and, of course, the two are dialectically related. Since comprehension and self-comprehension are not merely *means* to the development of the self, but are *constitutive* of its being, the child's comparative inability to understand its place in the world and converse adequately with itself will certainly affect the coherence of its structure. It's life is fragmentary and limited at best, and under conditions of repression the dissociated self will continue to fester out of sight—which not only robs the self of an aspect of its being but requires, as Freud significantly noted, the application of constant intervention to reproduce the original denial. This is a vital point: Insofar as the act of repression must be continuously recreated, the self must continue to *act* at the level of its original intervention.

At this point the archeological analogy breaks down. Fossil remains simply exist; they do not participate in their continued recreation. But both the act of repression and the tendency of the repressed self to satisfy its original desire appear, like Descartes's universe, to require constant recreation. The continuous repressive effort of the self is carried on *in the present,* so that while the repressed and repressing self is comparatively primitive, the task must be accomplished with current labor. The fetishism of the past is therefore an "accomplishment" of the present self, which thereby mortgages its emerging future to the limited strictures of its original powerlessness.

d. Because the point is so consistently ignored by psychoanalysis, it is important to make explicit the social context of these processes of self-alienation. Nor does the extension of Freud's paradigm to contemporary theories of object-relations, family systems, and network therapy adequately approach a social dimension. One cannot begin with Freud's account and then simply add layers of social contact, for the problem with Freud's paradigm is that it begins at the wrong point and moves in the wrong direction. It views the interpersonal transactions of childhood solely as the agency of the child; others represent merely the object-terminus of an originally prescribed instinctual pattern. Parents receive the child's activity, but they are not codeterminers of its being. And because Freud views society as essentially constituted out of such unilateral childhood interactions and their vicissitudes, he wholly ignores the manner in which the family acts as the *mediation* of larger social–historical processes. Freud lacks any category of social totality. This is not an error that can be corrected by enlarging the scope of inquiry to include mobs, armies, churches, and other institutions. The modality of the explanation remains inverted in Freud's explanation, so that the social order is continually reduced to variations of the individual's perennial struggle with a fixed, repressive order. Nothing can be gained here without inverting the vector of explanation and locating the growth of the child in the context of its socially mediated existence.

Whatever we have previously said about the inchoate, fragmentary development of the self must consequently be translated into a statement of the developmental level of the child's relation to others-in-the-world. Repression is not merely of the self, but of the self in its relationships. With the child's self-immolation the other is simultaneously sacrificed. But everything depends on not being seduced by the image of internalization, which is so pervasive in the psychoanalytic literature. For internalization contains, in distilled form, the entire system of bourgeois confusions which mark off the ideology of psychoanalytic theory.

First, what psychoanalysis conceived of as internalized is rarely viewed in a context more extensive than the biological family. Every larger social pattern is consequently eliminated, with the inevitable result that the historical being of the family is totally mystified. Second, the spatial-biological metaphor is overwhelming. The prevailing paradigm seems to be the incorporation of the mother's body by the child. But a breast is taken *into* the mouth in a rather straightforward sense which only confuses our understanding of how the parents' character is transmitted to the child. Once the spatial image becomes paramount, the notion of introducing objects into an empty box becomes almost unavoidable. And each box is separate from the others. The child is seen as possessing a vacant interior into which is placed the contents of parental influence. In this conceptual procedure the bourgeois view of privacy is reified, and the contemporary capitalist sense of an atomized subject facing an alienated public realm is ontologized.

However, while the distinctiveness of self is a universal feature of personal existence, privacy, as we assume it, is a social creation. What is fixed by nature is the fact that I cannot become directly aware of your experience, nor you of mine. But this in itself tells us little about whether the pattern of our social life will tend to define our selves in a common convergence toward collective values or scatter us beyond each other's reach. There is a necessary dialectic between "internality" and "externality," between the "personal," "private" dimension of the self and its relation to other human beings in the "public" realm. In the collectivity of primitive societies our form of privacy or internality is incomprehensible; and in our form of atomized mass society it is unavoidable.

This leads us to the third defect implicit in the idea of internalization. For the spatial analogy, misleading as it is, merely covers a functional confusion. The self is formed in process—that is, in its movement in and through the world. The child becomes a person in discourse with other persons *at the point of their meeting.* To become a person, however formed or malformed, is, as Mead noted, a matter of reciprocally identifying one's self as the referent of the personal acknowledgment of other persons. This process is, again, dialectical. I come to recognize myself as a person in the process of coming to understand that I am so defined by others. But I can come to define myself in relation to the other's act of definition only by coming to recognize the other as a person. In short, I can come to recognize myself as a particular human being only because I can recognize that *other human beings* have defined me as human. It would make as much sense to call this a process of externalization as internalization. Both terms are inadequate.

The emergence of the self is best defined as a reciprocal, social act of establishing the lived and presented forms of selfhood in the course of human relationships. The neglect of the concept of social reciprocity in Freudian thought is what joins the limitations of form and content—the misleading notion of internalization and the reified content of social interaction. For it is only when our relationships are taken seriously that the specific historical, social aspects of these relationships will be noted.

And although there is often an impressive overture in regard to social factors in some psychoanalytic works, the promise is rarely fulfilled. I take this fact to indicate that the acknowledgment of social reality is both more ritual than real and represents what might be viewed as a form of theoretical splitting, one of a number of political defense mechanisms useful to the protection of the status quo.

e. These considerations lead to practical and theoretical consequences. The privatization of psychoanalytic theory is closely related to the prevailing form of its practice. I will return to this theme more fully in the last chapter, but I wish to note in passing that when we take the social context of repression seriously we have to shift our focus from the dominant paradigm of projection and transference to an emphasis on the reproduction of social relations, in both their normal and pathological forms. Since what the child represses is not some private part of its exclusively personal being, but some form of its relatedness to others, its continued development will be marked by the reproduction of its earlier interpersonal patterns. In other words, it will continue to illicit from others the predominant forms of relatedness that constituted its original development. As Wachtel has noted:

> If one does look closely from a somewhat different perspective, it is usually possible to see how the desires and conflicts which may dominate a person's life can be understood as *following from,* as well as causing the way he or she lives that life. Consider, for example, the patient who seems compulsively to go out of his way to be active, independent, and responsible for others. Often such individuals are found to long unconsciously for dependent gratification, and to fear the extent of their passive yearnings. We need not, however, assume that the conscious attitudes are simply a defense against desires from the past. We may valuably examine how this very pattern of compulsive activity and responsibility *creates* the so-called oral needs: by constantly taking on excessive burdens and simultaneously denying himself almost any opportunity to manifest normal dependence, such a person is kept continually yearning for dependence to an unusual degree (as he also continues to pursue an excessively independent way of life because, in large part, of the frightening strength of these continually created longings).[47]

There is an important implication of this perspective shift for therapeutic practice. In the orthodox formulation, transference is encouraged and clarified by the constancy of the therapist's response, who by the adoption of a neutral stance forces the client into the major responsibility for the patterns that are imposed on the therapeutic transaction. If the analyst were to concretely intervene, so the traditional view maintains, it would be possible to attribute the client's response to the therapist's action, a procedure that would minimize the possibility of using the session to reveal and transcend the past. Wachtel comments:

From an interpersonal perspective, however, the series of increasingly primitive and bizarre reactions in the course of an analysis would appear not as an exposure, through regression, of 'layers of the personality,' but rather as a view of the hierarchy of reactions this person has *to this particular kind of frustration*. One doesn't elude the limits of participant observation, or, so to speak, undo the Heisenberg principle, by being constant. One merely limits one's direct observations about the patient to his way of dealing with one kind of situation only. The analyst is cautioned not to gratify the patient's transference demands, or, in behavioral terms, to reinforce the patient's initial efforts in the situation. Not surprisingly, meeting with little reward for his first efforts, the patient resorts to others lower on his hierarchy of responses for that situation, until he has displayed his most desperately irrational efforts at trying to get some response from the person he has turned to for help.[48]

f. Now, we can extend this insight to what Schatzman has called "trans-personal" defenses.[49] These are operations designed not merely to change my own experience and to disaffiliate it from my consciousness, but to protect myself against the reminder of what I have repressed in myself by eliminating its vestiges in the behavior of others—by a procedure which may require my eliminating in others the thoughts and feelings which would lead them to their distressing behavior.

> Behavior reflects experience; therefore, if one needs or wishes to make oneself even safer, one should prevail upon the others not even to know such events do, ever did, or even could, occur in their minds.[50]

In this manner, defenses are not merely intrapersonal but transpersonal:

> A person (often a parent) orders another person (often a child) to forget thoughts, feelings, or acts that the first person cannot or will not allow in the other ... If the first person's aim is to protect himself from experience of which he fears the other may remind him, if the other experiences too much, the order serves as a transpersonal *defense* ... a transpersonal defense can be an *attack* on another person's experience, against which the other may in turn need to build a defense.[51]

In the course of this chapter we have continually moved outward from the individual as a point of origin. And, once again, the scope of the dialectic of interpersonal defenses has been extended. It is true that one's act of self-repression is often the result of an attempt to defend one's self against the transpersonal defense adopted by another and imposed by an act of interpersonal oppression. But, of course, these transactions are not merely interpersonal, but *institutional*. The procedures adopted by parents are repeated in the remainder of social institutions with important variations around a common theme. Schools, media, work, family, leisure, etc., recapitulate the patterns of subservience and powerlessness, alienation and mystification that have been set down in childhood. The implication of this recurrence is that those who repress the child and force the adoption of its defenses are themselves disfigured through their own social oppression. So that the aspects of the self that are disaffiliated from the individual are so divorced as a result of relationships with others who are themselves unable to bear the revelation of those specific characteristics. Since we only develop in response to the recognition of others, what is unavailable to them cannot be recognized by them, nor therefore elicited from us.

g. The whole course of the previous argument moves toward one basic realization: The defense mechanisms are intrinsically social. Not in Freud's sense of universal compromise formations between instinct and repression, but in the rich and variable sense that the specific historical–social situation determines what is to be defended against, by whom, for what purpose, against which authority, and in what particular manner. As in many other instances we have noted, Freud occasionally acknowledges the fact, but not its general significance:

> The people of Israel had believed themselves to be the favorite child of God, and when the great Father caused misfortune after misfortune to rain down on these people of his, they were never shaken in their belief in his relationship to them or questioned his power or righteousness. Instead, they produced the prophets, who held up their sinfulness before them; and out of their sense of guilt they created the over-strict commandments of their priestly religion. It is remarkable how differently a primitive man behaves. If he has met with a misfortune, he does not throw the blame on himself but on his fetish, which has obviously not done its duty, and he gives it a thrashing instead of punishing himself.[52]

It is this very "remarkable difference" which seems to me the most significant aspect of Freud's account, for it indicates nothing less than a striking disparity between people in regard to the manner in which they constitute their selfhood through their relation to nature. Nor can these differences be viewed simply as a difference in the content of defenses, for clearly, a very different process is ingredient in the manner in which the boundaries of the primitive self are established; differences in boundaries which constitute a difference in the selves which are bound.

The very least that must be acknowledged is that different defenses will predominate in different historical periods and among different social classes, genders, ethnic groups, and occupational divisions. Since, on my argument, the id is constructed out of the dissociated aspects of the self through the mechanisms of defense, the id will be differentially constituted in different social contexts. What is beyond consciousness will be dialectically related to what is within consciousness and even the possibility of reintegration will vary depending on the manner in which the original disaffiliation was carried out. So much seems to me to be implied in the following reflection by Fenichel:

> Perhaps the fact that sexual impulses very often are repressed, whereas aggressive impulses are more often the subject of other defense mechanisms, is due to the circumstance that education frequently handles the subject of sex by simply not mentioning it, whereas the existence of aggressiveness is acknowledged but is designated as bad. . . . The consistency of present-day education, uncertain as to which instinctual claims to permit and which to suppress, resulting in initial permission and in subsequent sudden, unexpected (and therefore frequently more cruel) deprivation, favors the use of defense mechanisms other than repression.[53]

The fact that educational practices have changed as much as they have in twenty-five years gives a certain forcefulness to the passage beyond its original intention. It throws a particularly vivid light on Fenichel's important insight into the selectivity of defense mechanisms. We need to take this point somewhat further, however. The contradiction Fenichel rightly notes between permission and deprivation not only extends to aggressiveness itself—which is decried in rhetoric and admired in practice—but is a particular hallmark of liberal education and the ideological requirements of capitalism. It even suggests that the ego and superego will be differently formed in the varying social circumstances in which one form of defense comes to prevail over another.

Consider the following comments of Fanon's:

> We understand now why the black man cannot take pleasure in his insularity. For him there is only one way out, and it leads into the white world. Whence his constant preoccupation with attracting the attention of the white man, his concern with being powerful like the white man, his determined effort to acquire protective qualities—that is, the proportion of being or having what enters into the composition of an ego.
>
>   Ego-withdrawal as a successful defense mechanism is impossible for the Negro.[54]

Ego-withdrawal is impossible because the black psyche has been permeated by the criteria of the white world. To withdraw is to move away from the ultimate principles of confirmation toward a void in which mere animality is the ultimate terror. "The composition of the ego," its "proportion of being or having," are differently formed. For the heart of the issue is not merely the pragmatic consideration of choosing the convenience of one defense mechanism over another, but of "choosing" one self over another, in accordance with one set of normative principles (or "superego constraints") which define humanity in the world.

If we continue to use Freud's topographical or structural divisions of the psyche, we will have to recognize them as socially demarcated aspects of a single, social-self. Let us return to Fenichel's observation regarding the provisional granting and ultimate withdrawal of selected permissions. The superego of a self formed in this context will bear the imprint of an entirely different ideological structure from that of a self that has been educated to consistent criteria, no matter how oppressively imposed. For ingrained in the self-reflectiveness of the first ambivalent context will be contained not only the implicit structures of class conflict and ideological contradiction of that social order but the self-obfuscating rule that such contradictions are not to be acknowledged, and, in fact, do not exist. In the culture of capitalism the structural discrepancy between reality and ideal—aggressiveness and cooperation—must be located within the individual self, because the ideology of the system is incompatible with a recognition that prevailing capitalist structure denies the explicit value of cooperation and that capitalist exploitation destroys the promise of human dignity. The instrumental mechanization of nature robs us of the capacity to ascribe responsibility to a fetish, while the atomistic competitiveness of the society from which this immense productivity emenates, forces the locus of agency back upon the individualized self; the victim is once again forced into his or her own self-immolation. So we can return to the problem we raised earlier—the unconscious nature of the defense mechanisms. The origin of repression lies in the contradictions of the social order. The mechanisms of defense are individually unconscious, because the actual nature of capitalist oppression must be kept from the oppressed, and because *the isolated individual must bear the burden.*

From a social perspective the traditional psychoanalytic theme of ego vs. drive takes on a new meaning. For the drives, or instincts, that originate in the id are the product of a society that requires their contribution but cannot acknowledge their existence. Hostility and envy are obvious examples. The id does not and cannot develop,[55] because there is no acknowledged social terminus toward which its energy can be directed. Since it is constructed precisely in order to be hidden, there is nothing here to surprise us. But this fact is reified in psychoanalytic theory as in Anna Freud's reference to "the ego's primary antagonism to instinct—its dread of the strength of the instincts," manifested by "the innate hostility between the ego and the instincts, which is indiscriminate, primary and primitive."[56]

The argument is all of one piece when the same author goes on to note:

> All through childhood a maturation process is at work which, in the service of an increasing *knowledge and adaptation* to reality, aims at perfecting (ego) functions and rendering them more and more objective and independent of the emotions until they can become *as accurate and reliable as a mechanical apparatus* [emphasis added].[57]

Of course, this "mechanical apparatus," which sets the measure of realiability, objectivity, "knowledge," and "adaptation," is the mechanical instrumentality of capitalist exploitation, whose pervasive intrusion into the heart of the self is inadvertently acknowledged. What needs to be addressed here is the precise nature of such emotions as require such ego independence. For, since as Rapaport has noted, the most autonomous ego is that of the obsessional, a characterological trait particularly useful in a highly bureaucratized society, we are moved to inquire into the emotional pattern created to sustain an ego of such dissociated isolation.

It is only because the drives and emotions are socially created as socially antagonistic that a "strong" ego must be pitted against them. But the dualism of asocial impulse controlled and channeled by an "objective and reliable mechanical apparatus" is a paradigm of capitalist domination. Freud could never move beyond the view that self and society are intrinsically antagonistic, a position which as late as *Civilization and Its Discontents* was expressed in the opposition between individual happiness and altruism:

> The development of the individual seems to us to be a product of the interaction between two urges, the urge toward happiness, which we usually call "egoistic," and the urge toward union with others in the community, which we call "altruistic."[58]

Of course, since Freud regards altruism as a reaction formation against saidsm it is little wonder that the urge toward "union with others" must be viewed with considerable suspicion.

These reflections permit us to return to an issue to which I previously alluded, the conflicting views of the ego as the highest psychic system on the one hand, and as essentially contentless on the other. But this duality is the expression of an even deeper conflict between two theories of the ego which have divided psychoanalytic writers. According to the view of the ego psychologists, their own contribution to Freud's theory represents the progression he himself would have achieved had time permitted his endeavor. Their own insistence on the "reality ego" simply represents the logical conclusion of Freud's fundamental position. But this view is challenged by a group for whom Jones can be taken as the spokesman, which insists that Freud presented two separate theories which are basically incompatible.

According to the first school, represented here by Hartman, "as early as in the nineties ... Freud speaks of an ego. ... However, the closer elaboration of this part of his work had to be postponed."[59] For Jones, however, "when Freud wrote his important metapsychological essays in the spring of 1915 he felt he had completed his life work."[60] Later theoretical developments produced a wholly new addition to a previously well-completed position. Applebaum sums up the dispute in the following passage:

> The "reality ego" emphasizes the ego's temporizing, compromising function—as a busy mediator between the demands of the reality and of the drives. The "defense ego" is a more active principle, having superordinate goals of its own, before which both reality and the drives must yield. The ego psychologists think of the reality ego as Freud's basic conception throughout his work. The opposing view is that while the reality ego was an integral part of Freud's early model, it was supplanted in his later model by the defense ego.[61]

In Freud's earlier writings the ego and instincts are viewed as antagonistic. It is for that reason that the two basic instincts are those of sexuality and self-preservation. For sexuality represents the demands of the species and self-preservation the resistance of the discrete individual.

> The ego's resistance to instinct was taken for granted, being seen as much like the natural resistance of a host organism to invading organisms. The instincts were assumed to conflict in a very immediate way with pride, self-respect, even "noblemindedness," and, above all, with the demands of objective reality, that is, with the need to act and feel appropriately and properly.[62]

But in his later writings Freud began to implicate the ego in the pathological onslaught of the drives against the self. The notion of an "ego instinct"—and instinct of self-preservation—disappears, and is subsumed under the new dualism of eros and thanatos. And in this later conceptualization, the ego can be viewed as much the representation of self-destructiveness as of the tendency to form larger and more comprehensive social totalities. The ego becomes bound up with the id, for better or worse, though the specific reasons for the transformation of the theory seem more closely linked to despair than to hope.

This debate between defense and reality theories of the ego seems to me to obscure the real issue: that the primary reality which faces the ego is the contradiction between the claims of ideology and the actual structure of social power. This is simply another way of saying that in dealing with the superego Freud remained oblivious to its essential contradictions. It is not possible to choose between the ego's need for adaptation to reality on the one hand, or defense against instinct on the other, because the two are dialectically related. The primary feature of reality to which the ego must adapt is the system of structural contradictions that so elaborates the "instincts" that they must be experienced as destructive of the self. For, as we have noted on several occasions, the imperatives of capitalist culture create drives that cannot be gratified by any available set of social relations; first, because these relations are in fact absent, and second, because they are in principle required to be so absent by the contradictions inherent in capitalism between its actual structures and its rhetorical directives.

In short, the basic reality that faces the individual in capitalist society is the need to defend one's self against socially constructed antagonisms. The "defensive ego" and "reality ego" are revealed as one and the same.

A primary task of the individual's "ego functions" is to reconcile reality and ideology. But each realm is self-contradictory and conflicts with the other. What is deemed by ego-psychologists the "conflict-free" realm of the ego, is the elaboration by the individual of the *pretense* that social reality is conflict-free. The set of skills that reproduce this illusion require the simultaneous capacity to navigate the phenomonological forms of everyday domination under the rubric of bourgeois illusions of freedom and individual autonomy. The fundamental and unheralded competence which all individuals must acquire in an alienated, class-dominated society is the ability to negotiate the requirements of imposed power through the use of such concepts as are constitutive of this realm, while simultaneously categorizing their experience of power through the conceptual structures of justificatory ideology. The fundamental social skill obtained in bourgeois society is the ability to function bilingually, as it were—conversant in two dimensions and in the competence to relate them to each other while keeping their schema bifurcated in consciousness.

So, as Freud rightly noted, the defense mechanisms are central to the self, and so fundamentally constitutive of our nature that it is impossible to imagine what we would be like in a society that did not make such contradictory demands upon us. Freud was, of course, unwilling to grant that a nonrepressive society was conceivable, but we have sufficient reason to find the grounds of his judgment unpersuasive.

In drawing this discussion of Freud's metapsychology to a close I wish to refer in passing to the role of the superego. Two of its features which Freud noted, but never satisfactorily explained, could well serve as the focus of a separate study: (1) the tendency for moderate, liberal parents to raise children with severe superegos, and (2) the relationship between the superego and the id. The second connection is of no surprise from the vantage point of the analysis of this chapter. The id is articulated out of the requirements society imposes on the individual through the mediation of the individual superego. Freud inverts the relationship because his energic model requires him to account for the activity of the superego in terms of the origin of its force. The only source he can locate on his own terms is the id, so that the actual relationship through which the imposition of unattainable superego demands forms an insatiable, peremptory id is mistaken for the need of the id to bind its own excess through the aid of the superego.

This reflection leads immediately to Freud's observation that liberal parents often produce children whose superegos seem to exceed the punitiveness that has been imposed upon them. His explanation, that the child is robbed of an object of its natural hostility and so internalizes its hatred, reflects Freud's persistent tendency to absolve parents of responsibility in the formation of their children. Because Freud understands the term "liberal" in the phrase "liberal parent" in the sense in which the bourgeoisie understands it, that is, ideologically, he is precluded from raising any relevant question in regard to the destructiveness the "liberal" ideal serves to mask. He takes the benign apparance of liberal parents at face value, though in instances like the Schreber case and the case of little Hans, contradictory material is readily available and even indicated by Freud himself.

I will turn to the connection between liberalism and therapy once more in the conclusion of this work. In drawing this chapter to a close we can note the dialectic that arises between the clinical practice and metaphysical theory that Freud elaborated. Though they are different levels of theoretical practice, both participate in a common perspective; they reify the human condition and render social change more difficult.

Summary and
Prospectus

I should like briefly to summarize the previous two chapters and to point the direction I will take in the remainder of this book. My summary will take the form of a rather speculative digression.

Kant invented the phrase "the schematism of the categories" to indicate that the most abstract categories we apply to experience are too formal for use without some intermediary notions. These mediations he called the schemata. I introduce this reflection to raise the question of the relationship between Freud's abstract concepts as developed in the metapsychology (mp) and his view of human experience as exemplified in clinical practice (cp). Although the notion of an intermediary schematism may seem unnecessary, there do appear to be structures that bridge the two aspects of Freud's work with which we have been concerned in the previous chapters. Articulating these notions will help to suggest, however hurriedly, the deeper aspects of Freud's total perspective. But I will not make any attempt here to prioritize one or the other side of this theoretical–practical dyad. I do not know whether Freud adopted his practice in response to previously established metaphysical assumptions, or the reverse. In fact, I suspect that such a dissection is impossible, and that our view of nature, human nature, and political and social processes is too intermixed to admit of such an isolation or weighting of individual factors. Nor do I wish to maintain that these aspects can only coalesce in one prescribed system. Although I believe that certain metaphysical and social perspectives seem, historically, often to be conjoined, I will not argue the logical necessity in this fact. Radical and conservative politics may share common ontological principles and diverse metaphysical foundations may accompany similar political views. It is not vital to the conjecture of this interlude to settle the question definitively.

Nevertheless, in Freud's case, there do seem to be various "convergent categories" which facilitate movement from the mp to the cp and back again. The adaptation of the one seems to ease the task of adapting the other. Consider the notion of "reversal," for example. On the one side, Freud distinguishes ultimate reality from appearance, quantity from quality, unconscious-id from conscious-ego; on the other, he maintains that social civility is the mere façade of a deeper social dimension. Whether we are concerned with the mp or the cp we are involved in a dualism in which the prima facie appearance of reality is shown to be superficial, to turn into or become intelligible upon the basis of another structure originally hidden from sight. Dualism and reversal are convergent categories that bridge the gap between theory and practice.

Or again, the notion of "conflictual forces" serves to underlie both the patterns of mechanical and instinctual energy and of human motives toward self and other, toward pleasure and survival, toward life and death. Or more methodologically, the idea that the *differentiated* derives from the *undifferentiated* or that the *unit* is the proper starting point of explanation—be it neuron, reflex, instinct, idea or individual person—is common to both sides of Freud's analysis.

But it is when we approach the notions of energy and its accumulation, quantification, and discharge that the functions of convergent concepts become particularly striking. Whether it was the quantification of nature as accomplished by Newtonian physics or the quantification of human relations produced by the commodification of capitalist economics, the fact of importance is the convergence of these notions in Freud's hands. Freud's definition of libido as abstract, quantified desire is surely a notion that would have been unintelligible to most other cultures. In following Helmholtz, Brucke and the other mechanists, Freud agreed to apply physics to the mind, but the mind to which he applied this mathematical method had already been prepared in the growing quantification of capitalist exchange. In focusing his early efforts on neurophysiology, Freud located the intersection of physics and psychology and developed precisely that system of general categories that he would apply alternatively in his theoretical and practical efforts. The conservation of energy, the summation of stimulation, the reception and transmission of excitation, were all notions that bridged physics and human nature in a social context in which the amalgamation of the two was already a constant social tendency.

The idea of accumulated, or "dammed" (technology as practical physics), energy continued to be one of Freud's fundamental constructs. In certain circumstances it was converted, as physical energy was converted to heat. At other times it was dissociated and repressed into a region as "itlike" as the fetishized world Marx discovered in the realm of social relations. What is fascinating in Freud's account is the convergence of the unit of psychophysical explanation—the neuron as receptacle— and the view of bourgeois human nature.

The neuron was conceived of as a receptacle that received, accumulated, and discharged different quantities of excitation. It held, withheld, released, and transmitted what had been imposed upon it. In the original "Scientific Project," Freud viewed the excitation as similar to chemical and physical energy, called it "Q" and held it accountable to the laws of physics. Its most important property was its capacity to fill up, or "cathect," the individual neuron.[1] Some stimulation was held to originate outside the organism (exogenous) and the remainder from within the organism itself (endogenous). Freud proceeds in the Project to chart the course of thse energy flows and to consider the "optimal" distribution of energy at the disposal of the nervous system. The conclusion of his lengthy discussion was that the nervous system "requires" a constant reservoir of Q which it may utilize to protect itself from external intrusion, to gratify its needs, and provide flexibility in its manipulative responses. But these are all characteristics that dimly begin to resemble the optimal characteristics of successful market exchange.

Freud postulated the existence of an ego to allow for the adaptation of the organism to the external world. Its primary function was to distinguish mere wish from reality and the primary mechanism at its disposal was the ability to modify the flow of impulse so as to match the disposition of the organism to the condition of external reality. A "strong" ego is seen by Freud as one in which there is an even distribution of Q in the nervous system. This condition is itself facilitated by early situations in which energy is distributed among a large number of diverse neurons. A strong ego is marked by its ability to disperse energy evenly so as to inhibit discharge and lessen the dependency of the organism on its environment.

But the ability to delay response is similary an important virtue in the bourgeois conception of human nature. In fact, the economic foundation of this character disposition is the very real need to accumulate capital, and maintain it in as "mobile" a condition as possible in order to avoid dependency upon those with the power to withold what one needs and must satisfy "exogenously." "Mobile accumulation" of energy/capital is a convergent concept which functions through both domains of the Freudian perspective.

The clearest manifestation of accumulation and loss in personal experience is the Carmen letter I have previously cited:

> The mob gives vent to their impulses, and we deprive ourselves. We do so in order to maintain our integrity. We economize with our health, our capacity for enjoyment, our forces: we save up for something, not knowing ourselves for what. . . . We also feel more deeply and therefore dare not demand much of ourselves. . . . Why don't we fall in love over again every month? Because with every parting something of our heart is torn away. . . . Thus our striving is more concerned with avoiding pain than with creating enjoyment.[2]

The remainder of this letter sets out the distinction between classes on the analogy of the primary to the secondary system: The one is driven to immediate discharge; the other, through "privation," through freedom from "the evils of our social structure," experiences the isolation of its life in the refinement of its denial.

It is in discharge that both gratification and more primitive existence reside. To withold is to maintain integrity and separation. This is commonplace bourgeois reflection. What is striking in the intersection of Freud's mp and cp (social perspective) is the fact that need is not viewed primarily as an absence but as a presence—the presence of stimulation whose excessive intrusion and accumulation in one region of the organism signifies vulnerability and danger. Under such excessive stimulation the organism must rid itself, discharge, and return to homeostasis.

Need may strike us as more intelligibly as an absence than a presence, but (of course, Freud's "machanical" mp foundation does not provide a place for absence, which is only intelligible as an attribute of mind) for Freud it is the sense of being imposed upon, of being violated, of being threatened by overwhelming forces, either beyond us or emanating from our own selves. At rest, the energy of the organism is self-balanced and self-contained. It is pressurized to a state of equilibrium with the environment. In this way it cannot be crushed by overwhelming external forces or threatened by the witholding of external means of support. It is no surprise that Freud applies this convergent concept in his account of men and women, the one seen as full and superior, the other lacking and deficient. The mp and cp are suited to each other, for this pair, "fullness–emptiness," categorizes both sides of the mp/cp polarity and lends each side the credibility of mutual support.

Perhaps the most important schemata contained in Freud's view is the predisposition toward fetishism which derives from the mechanical and instinctual foundation of the system. From the side of either forces or drives, from energy or meaning, what prevails is domination by fixed, controlling, ineradicable factors. In my view, this is the primary political significance of Freud's theoretical and practical project. The emancipatory significance of therapy itself—"Where id was, there shall ego be"—must always be seen in the very restricted context of Freud's conception of the limits of transformation—"A great deal will have been accomplished if we can succeed in transforming neurotic misery into ordinary unhappiness." Humane effort is necessarily constrained by features of the human world which exist on the frontier of physical and chemical constraints and which are therefore beyond any possible transformation.

By contrast, I have maintained that the inhuman force that dominates our lives is the contorted semblance of a human presence. Contradictions in the structure of capitalism, particularly between the actual nature of power and the pretense of liberal ideology, produces the social antagonisms that necessitate individual repression. Nothing in our biological nature imposes conflict and repression. It is always the incompatible social meanings attached to aspects of the body that institute personal suppression and structural anguish. Even the meaning of pain, as Jules Henry so aptly noted, must be socially learned:

> Since the orientations of which I speak are learned and are determined by a culture, it would follow that in some cultures relatively minor physical pain has a tremendous effect on a child, while in others—like that of the Plains Indians, for example—even severe physical stress will be borne without flinching. . . . Vulnerability to the weapon used to force him into line must be cultivated in a child; thus, in a satanic way, we are moved without being aware of it, to make our children vulnerable even as we protect them.[3]

In fact, vulnerability and protection are dialectically related, for only by being able to move the child can we protect it, and only by making it vulnerable, can we move it. By eliciting the growth of the child through expansion, joy, and realization we could avoid this contradiction, but such a pedagogocal transformation would require a wholly different social world in which it might be practiced.

In the previous chapter we moved from an account of individual repression to its larger social context. We now need to reverse the process and begin with the social structure that determines individual repression. For the relationship between the repressed unconscious (our reinterpretation of Freud) and the structural unconscious (Marx) is dialectical. Each determines and defines the other. This is another way of saying that while only individuals can bear the consequence of repression, it is the relations among individuals which determines what in fact is repressed and why. So our starting point once again is the "identity" of the "individual" as an ensemble of social relationships. But we can now advance our argument.

The meaning of the phrase "ensemble of social relations" is equivalent to the phrase "social structure." Neither phrase wears its meaning on its sleeve. A somewhat lengthy explication of these notions will make up a considerable part of the next chapters. I do not regard this work as merely idle academic exegesis—the sort which evokes the comment "interesting" from liberal theoreticians. In Marx's account of the form and content of exchange relations lies a definitive repudiation of bourgeois individualism. Beginning with the general fact of social exchange and the particular exchange of labor power required of each of us, Marx proceeds to show how our individuality is shaped and corrupted by that system of exchange. The notion of "the individual" is incomplete. We are individual producers, consumers, exchangers—members of a class, of a family, of a nation. In short, we are individual members of a capitalist society who are massively constituted out of the structures and contradictions of this society. In examining the formal properties of this system, then, we come to reflect on the meaning of individualism as the social individuals we in fact are. To follow Marx through *Capital* or the *Grundrisse* is to follow capitalism through the wellsprings of our being, and to come face to face with the need for social transformation as the hope of a renewed life.

PART III

Social Structure and Therapeutic Practice

CHAPTER SEVEN

The Marxist Unconscious

Free Dependence

The belief that individual self-realization is to be achieved outside of society is one of the deepest principles of bourgeois ideology.

The bourgeois world view constantly confuses two notions: that individuals differentiate themselves *within* a group, and that individuals differentiate themselves beyond a group. The first claim is true, and even necessary; the latter is an unexamined first premise. Rather than a self-evident truth, however, this proposition would have struck the overwhelming majority of previous human beings as totally incomprehensible. For it is a conviction that arises only in highly atomistic and competitive societies, which not only produce this ideology but systematically mystify its social origins. Since the last several chapters have dealt with the consequences of Freud's application of this individualist presupposition, it is important now to deal with Marx's very different analysis in order to grasp the contrast between these perspectives and the possibility of any conceivable integration.

The category of "the individual" is a universal, anthropological fact that needs to be distinguished from "individualism," a specific product of capitalist social relations. Society is an "ensemble of social relations,"

which obviously obtain among individuals. It is a standing accusation of
bourgeois ideology that Marx either denied the existence of individuals
or dedicated himself to their eradication. In fact he believed the exact
opposite, holding that while individual existence is ineradicable individual *self-realization* can in fact only occur under communism.

> Individual human life and species-life are not different things, even though
> the mode of existence of individual life is necessarily either a more *specific* or
> a more *general* mode of species-life, or that of species-life a *specific* or more
> *general* mode of individual life.
>
> Though man is a unique individual—and it is just his particularity which
> makes him an *individual*, a really individual communal being—he is equally
> the *whole*, the ideal whole, the subjective existence of society as thought and
> experienced.[1]

Like other dialectically related notions, individual life and species
(communal) life can neither be separated from each other nor identified.
Though joined, their mode of existence does not coincide. Individual
life is the mode of "experience" of the social whole, and the social whole
has itself no existence separate from the fact of its being experienced in
the lives of individuals. Each individual is an experiencing nodule or
terminus of the ensemble of relations that constitutes the social system.
This is not to reduce society to the sum of individual experiences. For
what individuals experience is primarily the structure of social relations
in dialectical polarity with the world of nature. But even more significant
is the fact that how this experience is itself structured is also a dialectical
consequence and cause of the particular form of individualism in a historical epoch. In short, the specific conscious experience of individuals
occurs in the context of the totality of structural relationships among
individuals, structural relationships among the aspects of nature, and
the structure of relationships between these distinct but reciprocal realms.
And, of course, there is that part of the human psyche, which plays
no part in Marx's system—the structure of the repressed unconscious.

However, putting the question as I just have harbors real difficulties.
To say that personal experience occurs "in the context" of social structures hardly clarifies the relationship between them. For though what
Marx says about individual life under capitalist domination seems to me
both clear and profound, his discussion of the formal relationship between social "reality" and individual conscious experience is subject to
diverse interpretations. It is necessary to focus on this problem, both
from the side of its content and from the side of its formal relationships.

The relationship between individual experience and social life is in-
tersected by the distinction between appearance and reality. In fact,
since Marx views "individual experience" as constituting appearance
rather than reality, we must deal with both sets of distinctions simultaneously. Consider the following passage:

Vulgar economy actually does no more than interpret, systematize and defend in doctrinaire fashion the conceptions of the agents of bourgeois production who are entrapped in bourgeois production relations. It should not astonish us, then, that vulgar economy feels particularly at home in the estranged outward appearances of economic relations in which these prima facie absurd and perfect contradictions appear and that these relations seem the more self-evident the more their internal relationships are concealed from it, although they are understandable to the popular mind. *But all science would be superfluous if the outward appearance and the essence of things directly coincided* [emphasis added].[2]

Except for the rhetorical reference to the "popular mind," this is paradigmatic Marx. Unfortunately, the popular mind is no more immune from ideological corruption than the vulgar social sciences, and Marx is ordinarily well aware of the fact:

On the *surface* of bourgeois society the wage of the labourer *appears as the* price of labour, a certain quantity of money that is paid for a certain quantity of labour [emphasis added].[3]

In the expression "value of labor," the idea of value is not only completely obliterated, but actually reversed. It is an expression as imaginary as the value of the earth. These *imaginary expressions,* arise, however, from the relations of production themselves. They *are categories for the phenomenal forms of essential relations.* That in their appearance things often represent themselves in inverted form is pretty well known in every science except political science [emphasis added].[4]

The wage-form thus extinguishes every trace of the division of the working-day into necessary labour and surplus-labour, into paid and unpaid labour. All labour appears as paid labour.[5]

Obviously, labor appears to the laborer as wholly paid. Both the capitalist and the laborer are mystified by "imaginary expressions which are the categories for the phenomenal forms of essential relations." Now, these "phenomenal forms," which invert and obliterate the essential relation of capital to labor, are the ubiquitous forms of everyday life. Men and women, capitalists and laborers, businessmen and vulgar economists, all live in the appearance of bourgeois illusions. But if this is so, what precisely are the obliterated "essential relations" to which Marx refers; and even more significantly, what is the connection between the real structures which govern social life and the phenomenal forms within which social life comes to "understand itself" in ordinary consciousness?

As we have noted, all societies are constituted out of individual social relations. Ontologically, neither the individual nor the ensemble of social relations can take priority. The question of which category is fundamental already signifies an alienated consciousness, and arises compellingly under capitalism only because capitalism splits these aspects of existence and sets them against each other as antagonistic spheres. The developing universal powers of human beings come to stand over against these human beings as a set of forces determining their activity and consciousness. Personal subjectivity develops as a pervasive atomism, in which isulated individuals, themselves the product of capitalist social relations, imagine themselves the ultimate solipsistic creators of the world.

> The more deeply we go back into history, the more does the individual, and hence also the producing individual, appear as dependent, as belonging to a greater whole: in a still quite natural way in the family and in the family expanded into the clan; then later into various forms of communal society arising out of the antitheses and fusion of the clans. *Only in the eighteenth century, in "civil society," do the various forms of social connectedness confront the individual as a means towards his private purposes, as external necessity.* But the epoch which produces this standpoint, that of the *isolated individual,* is also precisely that of the hitherto most developed social . . . relations [emphasis added].[6]

The pervasive experience of capitalist society is the sense of isolated individuals confronting external social necessity. It is the basic "phenomenal" illusion and the source of such misadventures as the attempt of the contemporory therapy movement to *cure individuals* in separation or even opposition to society, which is experienced solely as an external irrelevance. As capitalism undergoes historical change the forms of individuality and the forms of external necessity change; from independent producer facing the classical laissez-faire market, to corporatized mass laborer overwhelmed by immense state-bureaucratic apparatus. But the antagonism remains, and it was one of Marx's major contributions to have located and explained its existence.

> The owners of commodities therefore find out, that the same division of labor that turns them into independent private producers, also *frees the social process* of production and the relations of the individual producers to each other within that process, *from all dependence on the will of those producers,* and that the *seeming mutual independence* of the individuals is supplemented by a system of general and *mutual dependence* . . . [emphasis added].[7]

This passage seems to me the key to the structure of capitalist repression. The paradoxes of bourgeois individualism are here stated with exceptional incisiveness: individual, private independence "frees" the social process to exercise its own distinct autonomy as a system of alienated structures independent of individual control; independent producers reproduce the structure of mutual dependence which frees the social process from individual will; the phenomenal forms of free individuality are dialectically related to the structure of real dependence which constitutes the essential relations of the system; the phenomenal form of freedom maintains the structure of domination which makes individual freedom impotent except as a means to the reproduction of domination.

Alienation necessarily involves two aspects: a system of external domination imposed upon individuals independently of their will and comprehension; and these same individuals providing the energy that reproduces the system that subordinates them. It is the act of enforced and voluntary self-destruction that marks off the uniqueness of an alienated system and marks alienation as a "pathological achievement" of which only human beings are capable.

There are two important considerations contained in this peculiar social formation. First, the relation of appearance to reality, of phenomenal forms to underlying essential relations, cannot be one of mere *epiphenomena* to their determining agency. For the illusions of bourgeois individuality and freedom can only be sustained by granting some genuine possibility of personal movement to the participants. And this, in a double sense: first, because if the individual agents cannot participate in the semblance of individual autonomy the illusion of freedom will clearly collapse; and second, because the system of capitalist domination can only proceed through the voluntary compliance, however materially compelled, of its participants. This means that the essential structure of capitalist domination can only be sustained through the active engagement of the "phenomenally" formed consciousness of the individuals who constitute the system. The essence of the system, its structure of exploitation, is dependent upon the realm of appearance.

If the exploited classes clearly understood the nature of their exploitation they might better effect the collapse of the system which oppresses them; in any case, domination would have to proceed differently. So the essential structure of surplus accumulation depends for its reproduction upon the continual mystification of those from whom this surplus value is extracted. They must be made to believe, for example, that all their labor is paid labor. In this sense, then, appearance is necessary to the structure of essential relations, or, more graphically, *appearances are themselves necessary.*

> Hence, we may understand the decisive importance of the transformation of value and price of labour-power into the form of wages, or into the value and price of labour itself. This phenomenal form, which makes the actual relation invisible, and, indeed, shows the direct opposite of that relation, *forms the basis of all the juridical notions of both labourer and capitalist, of all the mystifications of the capitalist mode of production, of all its illusions as to liberty, of all the apologetic shifts of the vulgar economists* [emphasis added].[8]

This is to credit the "phenomenal" form with considerable, even indispensable, power. It is only through "phenomenological consciousness" that the "essential relations" can be reproduced. Workers must act out of their inverted consciousness, and the capitalist must be driven by the externally imposed, but subjectively motivated, compulsion to amass wealth.

I am belaboring this point because, as we shall shortly note, there is a strong tendency in Marxist thought to treat the illusory, ideological consciousness of individuals as *merely* superficial forms of an underlying reality. This error is of inestimable significance, for in severing the connection between underlying structure and lived experience the dialectical tension that constitutes social alienation becomes unintelligible, and the possibility of overcoming the estrangement of social life is further removed from realization. No matter how "deep" the structures of capitalist exploitation or how esoteric the transformations of surplus value, they can only be sustained and reproduced by what ordinary human beings do in the common, banal functioning of their ordinary existence.

The most profound and difficult problem facing Marxist social theory has gone largely unanswered: how the illusory and phenomenal consciousness of men and women in capitalist societies reproduce the essential relations of exploitation which in turn regenerate the opaque awareness of common life. Consequently, Marxist theory has tended to divide between those on the one hand who discuss economic structure independent of the vagaries of mere culture and those on the other for whom cultural forms are independent of the aridity of economic analysis. It is not my purpose here to discuss the dramatic personnel in each camp. The point at issue is the split itself. For though Marx raised the issue in a profound way, his distinction between "phenomenal form" and "essential relations" remained unmediated in his own explication. The distinction remains crucial, however, and Marx himself provides critical clues to its resolution.

This brings us to a second consideration: the fundamental dialectic of "seeming independence" masking "mutual dependence" must mean that

> private interest is itself already a socially determined interest, which can be achieved only within the conditions laid down by society and with the means provided by society.[9]

It is not merely that the "private" is already structured as "social," but that the distinct nature of "private interest" is critically formed by the particular character of antagonistic social relations which constitute it. What Marx provides in the *Grundrisse* is a highly trenchant account of the fundamental *social nature of private interest as it is formed under capitalist interdependence.* Marx's analysis succeeds in establishing the existence of a "social unconscious" which makes luminously clear the total futility of such attempts at individual transformation as distinguish much of contemporary culture. But Marx's analysis also contains a vital lacunae which can only be filled with Freudian insights. The analysis of this issue seems to me to deserve serious consideration and will make up the subject of the remainder of this chapter.

The capitalist marketplace produces individuals who are simultaneously wholly dependent upon each other and either indifferent or antagonistic to each other's interests. This antagonistic atomism masquerades in the guise of autonomy, self-realization, and personal freedom. The more profound the sense of social powerlessness the more luxurious the growth of "personal" hyperbole. The other is simultaneously a means and an obstruction to my ends. Each of us simultaneously chooses and is compelled to be free, so that for the prescribed pathology of powerlessness the remedy of continuously more seclusive independence is constantly prescribed. The proposed cure is simply the dialectical underside of the illness.

Because "individualism" is constructed out of social powerlessness rather than autonomy, attempts at individual remedy are unable to reach their proposed ends. Each new venture seems both accidental and quickly converted into a new oppressive necessity. For "chance is only one pole of an interrelation, the other pole of which is called necessity."[10]

> Men make their history themselves, but not as yet with a collective will according to a collective plan or even in a definite, delimited given society. Their aspirations clash, and for that very reason all such societies are governed by *necessity,* which is complemented by, and appears under the forms of *accident.*[11]

But again, it is not quite adequate to assign necessity to reality and chance or accident to appearance. Because the necessity which "governs" proceeds through the will of individuals, who thereby register in one consciousness both the reality of necessity, experienced as *resignation,* and of accident, experienced phenomenally as *superfluousness.* It is more accurate to say that necessity is experienced under the phenomenal form of accident, a paradox which is only intelligible when lived through as compulsion (necessity) which renders one's deepest aspirations and dreams futile (accidental).

But the reality of capitalism appears to derive from the choices of individuals. So we are driven to conceptualize our helplessness as a personal failing. We thereby gain the appearance of individual responsibility both for the necessity we in fact cannot master and for the accidental character of our response to this domination. But the contradiction cannot be stayed in this manner and constantly intrudes itself through the inverse rise and fall of its polarities: the more power we grant to external necessity the more helpless we feel, but the greater our release from responsibility; while the more we take responsibility, the less we are overwhelmed by our powerlessness in the face of necessity, at the expense of the self-lacerating accusation of personal guilt and failure. We can only claim sufficient power to be considered responsible if we are willing to accept responsibility for our powerlessness.

The uniqueness of capitalist individualism lies in the conjuncture of increasing social dependence, extreme isolation, and hysterical denial of both. Capitalism is not organized to culture our original vulnerability toward empathy, compassion, or more generalized forms of social love. The mutual imposition of actual dependence and the pretense of independence produces exaggerated forms of helplessness, guilt, and violence. Our dependence (judged by the ideology of autonomy) produces a sense of weakness and hatred toward ourselves for our inability to stand emotionally unsupported. The denial of dependence leads on the other hand to fantasies of individual power which are not only delusional but which engender guilt for denying the legitimacy of passive resignation. The rage we experience for either "losing" or "winning" renders us more vulnerable still, and motivates a need to keep this wretched failure from the eyes of the world. Of course this general process is differentiated among class, ethnic group, and gender. Women, for example, are trained to feel guilt in independence more than men, for whom the opposite is true.

But the contradiction in consciousness between chance and necessity is also experienced as the contradiction between what is humanly constituted and what is "naturally" determined. And this is precisely what "the fetishism of consciousness" means—that our own conscious existence is self-conceived under natural categories, as a fact of nature. We have noted how pervasive was Freud's tendency to turn social relations into natural occurrences.

> But it is an insipid notion to conceive of this merely *objective bond* as a spontaneous, natural attribute inherent in individuals and inseparable from their nature (in antithesis to their conscious knowing and willing). This bond is their product. It is a historic product. It belongs to a specific phase of their development. The alien and independent character in which it presently exists vis-à-vis individuals proves only that the latter are still engaged in the creation of the conditions of their social life, and that they have not yet begun, on the basis of these conditions, to live it.[12]

And we have also noted how similar the Freudian instinctual structure is to the external necessity Marx ascribes to the essential relations of capitalism; and this is the very ground for our pursuit of the Marxist unconscious.

Now, the dependence of individuals upon each other only acts as a tyranny because, rather than being willed, it is imposed. Our reciprocal reliance upon each other's production and consumption is not under our collective control. Furthermore, its "operations" are antagonistic to our explicit human intentions and experienced as such. That is why capitalist consciousness is so permeated by despair, resignation, and guilt. If the phenomenal forms of ideological consciousness were wholly isolated from the "underlying" essential relationships of which Marx spoke, we would be insulated against the existence and awareness of our ubiquitous vulnerability. But, in fact, the mutual dependence that constitutes the deep structure of our social reality cannot help but penetrate our lived experience. Marx made this point quite clear when he noted that "the owners of commodities therefore find out . . . that the *seeming mutual independence* of the individuals is supplemented by a system of general and mutual *dependence*." That is why theories that split essence from phenomena and reality from appearance serve only to disfigure experience and are fated to speak past our own sense of our human malaise. But neither is this to put dependence and independence on the same level, nor to regard them as equally valid presentations of the social world.

Reciprocal dependence is the ultimate and inexpungable fact of capitalist structure. Its real dialectical counterpart is atomism; its ideological façade—individualism. It cannot be emphasized too strongly, however, that ideology is not illusion but the distorted presentation of reality. The experience of atomistic isolation and personal helplessness does not disappear; it is simply misunderstood under a set of mystified categories. But the term "simply" is not meant disparagingly. Conceptions *and* misconceptions govern our actual movement in the world. It is only because we act through *some* understanding of our actual dependence that we keep our conception of autonomy within practical limits; that is, within the limits of the expectations of others. And this implies that we function with two conceptual systems, one embodied in lived experience and another conceptually articulated as an explicit ideology. This issue has been addressed by Gramsci, and I only allude to the point here to avoid the apparent contradiction of postulating a form of consciousness that is in contradiction to its own theoretical articulation.[13]

Marx views the potential history of human evolution as moving from the stage of personal dependence, to "personal independence founded on *objective* dependence" to a system of "free individuality, based on the universal development of individuals and on their subordination of their communal, social productivity as their social wealth."[14] It is only from the vantage point of this unrealized ideal that our own situation becomes intelligible. And it is from this perspective, too, that we can begin to comprehend the uniqueness of capitalist development. For individuals in "underdeveloped societies," where relations of material productivity and exchange are limited

> although their relations appear to be more personal, enter into connection with one another only as individuals imprisoned with a certain definition, as

feudal lord and vassal, landlord and serf, etc., or as members of a caste etc. or as members of an estate etc.

But under a developed system of material exchange

the ties of personal dependence, of distinctions of blood, education, etc. are in fact exploded, ripped up (at least, personal ties all appear as *personal* relations); and individuals *seem* independent (this is an independence which is at bottom merely an illusion, and it is more correctly called indifference), free to collide with one another and to engage in exchange within this freedom; but they appear thus only for someone who abstracts from the *conditions, the conditions of existence* within which these individuals enter into contract (and these conditions, in turn, are independent of the individuals and, although created by society, appear as if they were *natural conditions,* not controllable by individuals). The definedness of individuals, which in the former case appears as a personal restriction of the individual by another, appears in the latter case as developed into an objective restriction of the individual by relations independent of him and sufficient unto themselves. (Since the single individual cannot strip away his personal definition, but may very well overcome and master external relations, his freedom *seems* to be greater in case 2. A closer examination of these external relations, these conditions, shows, however, that it is impossible for the individuals of a class etc. to overcome them *en masse* without destroying them. A particular individual may by chance get on top of these relations, but the mass of those under their rule cannot, since their mere existence expresses subordination, the necessary subordination of the mass of individuals.) These external relations are very far from being an abolition of "relations of dependence"; they are rather the dissolution of these relations into a general form; they are merely the elaboration and emergence of the general *foundation* of the relations of personal dependence. . . . These *objective* dependency relations also appear, in antithesis to those of *personal* dependence (the objective dependency relation is nothing more than social relations which have become independent and now enter into opposition to the seemingly independent individuals; i.e., the reciprocal relations of production separated from and autonomous of individuals) in such a way that individuals are now ruled by *abstractions,* whereas earlier they depended on one another.[15]

I have quoted this passage at considerable length because I believe that the illusion of liberal autonomy has never been more cogently stated. I am reminded of Freud's contention that the organism discriminates the inner from the outer world on the basis of its ability to avoid the distress of the latter by direct action, while the former persists as continual source of demand.[16] This point represents an ironic inversion, for the imperiousness of internal instinct is, as we maintained in the previous chapter, a direct result of those ubiquitous external forces that constitute what Marx here refers to as the general form of objective personal dependency. As Marx notes, since the anonymity of external domination appears to set us loose from personal restriction, we labor under the illusion of readily transforming the external world. However, we are merely brought face to face with the "general *foundation* of the relations of personal dependence."

We are left with a structural dichotomy which is endemic to capitalist culture: on the one side a system of abstract, objective, general, external impositions that subordinate the individual to their anonymous determination; and on the other, seemingly independent individuals marked by isolation, indifference, and a "freedom" which is, in fact, the absence of personal relationships. It is no wonder that such conditions breed a desperate need for personal relatedness and, even more, for definitions of the self as something more than a random, instrumental cipher. Nor is it surprising that an industry should arise whose quintessential commodity is intimacy, growth, and personal relatedness, offered to its adherents without mention of any necessity to comprehend external conditions of restraint, let alone destroy them.

Nevertheless the bourgeois fantasy of freedom as the absence of restraint has long since lost its charm. The fetters of external, anonymous domination are more clearly recognized to permeate, with increasing subtlety and power, the most private and intimate attempts at flight. The social and individual productivity that was the primary achievement of bourgeois freedom has long since exhausted its fruitfulness. Every system of production creates both the structure of value and the appropriate characterology to sustain and reproduce its particular condition. So it feels free in its own constraints. But when it becomes clear that its accomplishment is exhausted, or that its ever existent contradictions are now too blatant to ignore, its apparent freedom comes to be felt as desperation, despair, and constraint. Then, as Marx insists,

> this kind of individual freedom is therefore at the same time the most complete abolition of individual freedom, and the most complete subjugation of individuality under social conditions which assume the form of objective powers, even of *overpowering objects* [emphasis added].[17]

It is not sufficient to leave the analysis at this level, however. For the dialectic between external compulsion and personal emptiness has not been adequately articulated. Why could we not just as appropriately speak of personal compulsion and external chance and accident? In fact, we already have, and not without reason. To better understand the relationship between internal and external tyranny it will be helpful to follow Marx through an analysis that seems at first sight esoteric, but will prove itself, finally, highly germane.

As is so often the case, this particular account or digression occurs in the context of a lengthy and highly abstract discussion of capital, in which Marx begins by noting that the formal–political structure of capitalist exchange is rooted in a presupposition of equality. For

> in so far as the commodity or labour is conceived of only as exchange value, and the relation in which the various commodities are brought into connection with one another is conceived as the exchange of these exchange values with one another, as their equation, then the individuals, the subjects between whom this process goes on, are simply and only conceived of as exchangers. As far as the formal character is concerned, there is absolutely no distinction between them . . . as subjects of exchange, their relation is therefore that of *equality*.[18]

Here, the equality of individuals is derived from the equality inherent in their social functions—as the exhangers of abstract value. This is contradictory to the ideology of liberalism, of course, which makes of equality an inalienable right independent of mere material circumstances. It does, nevertheless, join our individual persons and our deepest normative sense of ourselves with an external structure clearly larger than our own conscious intentions. The pure form of this relation contains three distinct moments: the subjects of the relationship, the exchangers; the object of exchange, exchange value equivalents; and the act of exchange itself. Marx placed *the content* of the exchange not only outside his discussion, but "entirely outside economics"[19] (a move which seems to me an important error in his analysis, to which we shall return later in this chapter).

Now, the "equivalents are the objectification of one subject for another" and, as such, "are equals, at the same time also indifferent to each other." Since Marx is currently deriving the characteristics of persons from their exchange functions, it will follow that individuals too are equal and indifferent. The real needs of individuals, which Marx had located outside of economics proper, actually ensure the equality of exchange. For it is only because these needs are distinct and complementary that any act of exchange is required at all. As Marx notes, "Only the differences between their needs and between their production gives rise to exchange"[20]—which suggests that the economic structure must reproduce these distinctions as a precondition to its continued existence. However, whether we regard the structure of need as natural and therefore, outside of economics, or socially and economically constituted, and therefore of its essence, Marx does correctly note that divergent needs place the subjects of exchange not merely in a relation of indifference to each other but into a relationship of

> need of one another; so that individual B, as objectified in the commodity, is a need of individual A, and vice versa; so that they stand . . . also in a social relation to one another. This is not all. The fact that this need on the part of one can be satisfied by the product of the other, and vice versa, and that the one is capable of producing the object of the need of the other, and that each confronts the other as owner of the object of the other's need, this proves that each of them reaches beyond his own particular need, etc., as a *human*

being, and that they relate to one another as human beings; that their common species-being is acknowledged by all.[21]

We have proceeded in this argument then from formal equality to material need and dependence. Thus far, the second stage does not cancel the first. We are equal in our dependency and in the fact that we "confront each other as the reciprocal owners of the objects of each other's needs." Despite the high level of abstraction of this account, it remains the foundation of the specific mediations of the remainder of social life. So far, however, the exposition has a rather rosy air: a small Eden of equality and human acknowledgement. But the tone begins to change.

For we have to note more specifically the way in which individuals serve each other.

> Each serves the other in order to serve himself; each makes use of the other, reciprocally, as his means. Now both things are *contained in the consciousness of the two individuals;* (1) that each arrives at his end only in so far as he serves the other as means; (2) that each becomes means for the other (being for another) only as end in himself (being for self); (3) that the reciprocity in which each is at the same time means and end, and attains his end only in so far as he becomes a means and becomes a means only in so far as he posits himself as end, that each thus posits himself as being for another, in so far as he is being for self, and the other as being for him, in so far as he is being for himself—that this reciprocity is a necessary fact, presupposed as natural precondition of exchange, but that, as such, it is irrelevant to each of the two subjects in exchange, and that this reciprocity interests him only in so far as it satisfies his interest to the exclusion of, without reference to the other [emphasis added].[22]

I do not believe it is possible to improve on Marx's statement of the reciprocity of the simultaneous casting of self and other as means and ends. I wish to call attention to one point that is particularly relevant for what is to come: that these complex relations are not merely ascribed to the structure, but *to the consciousness of the individuals in exchange.* In fact, the two notions are reciprocal. According to Marx, the structural configuration he is here articulating is, however implicitly, "contained in the consciousness" of the individuals. Each recognizes himself and the other through this conceptual framework and acts toward the other and his or her own self through the mediation of this same conceptual structure. Furthermore, while this reciprocity is "presupposed" in consciousness as the condition of exchange, it is "irrelevant" to each of the subjects who cares ultimately only for his or her own interest. In short, *consciousness is divided between its general presupposition and its explicit interest:*

> That is, the common interest which appears as the motive of the act as a whole is recognized as a fact by both sides; but, as such, it is not the motive,

but rather proceeds, as it were, *behind the back* of these self-reflected particular interests, *behind the back* of one individual's interest in opposition to that of the other [emphasis added].[23]

Now, what precisely is the "common interest" which appears to be but is not the motive of the agents and instead proceeds behind their backs? And what does Marx mean when he notes that the common interest "appears" as the motive of the act as a whole; is this appearance an *illusion* or a *manifestation* of the actual situation?

It is impossible to follow this passage without noting that for Marx the term "common interest" means something contrary to "communal interest." This is true of Marx in the German ideology:

> Just because individuals seek only their particular interest, which for them does not coincide with their communal interest (in fact the general is the illusory form of communal life) the latter will be imposed on them as an interest "alien" to them, and independent of them, as in its turn a particular peculiar "general interest."[24]

And later in the *Grundrisse:* "The general interest is precisely the generality of self-seeking interest."[25] The "common interest which appears as the motive of the act as a whole" is the structural presupposition of the act of self-interested exchange. Each agent recognizes the reciprocity of means–ends which makes up the precondition of individual self-interest and gratification. And this condition is, of course, "presupposed as a natural condition of exchange." Reciprocal use of the other and myself as simultaneously means and ends is the "motive of the act as a whole" but not my specific interest, which is indifferent and antagonistic to the interest of the other. So, a structure obtains among the agents which is their fundamental conceptual framework, the implicitly conscious, unarticulated premise of their collectively antagonistic action.

Two crucial notions are contained in this aspect of Marx's analysis: first, that individual self-interest and social competitiveness depend upon a general structure which gives meaning to the individual acts of self-aggrandizement and which must be implicitly understood and acknowledged by the actors. Capitalism is a *system* which must be sustained in order that competition can occur within it. Just as a sport, no matter how dominated in practice by individual motives of achievement, must reproduce its common rules, so the system of capitalist exchange requires a dual reproduction of its rules, or social framework, and of the individual motives of success the system defines and makes possible.

Second, since there is dependency as well as discrepancy between the needs of the system and the needs of the individuals within it, the agents can only achieve their intended consequences by reinforcing the system; even to the extent that it negates their individual efforts and turns their actions against their intentions. The system captures the consequences of action and employs them for its own systemic purpose. Athletes are motivated to defeat their opponents; but only actions falling within the rules can contribute to their success as defined within the game. And the rules of capitalism structure the meaning of individual acts so that even the motive of acceptable protest is given its meaning by the way its consequences are defined by the prevailing structure of power. So a strike may reduce overextended inventories and improve the competitive position of the firm. For a strike is an acceptable move, even if its private motive is the defeat of the capitalist. In short, the manner in which private interest is structurally defined makes possible its inclusion within the system whose action can thereby be captured and used against its primary personal intention.

This structure of exchange is the formal basis of the juridical conceptions of equality and freedom that permeate the system of bourgeois transactions. Although reciprocity—however instrumental—is the motive of the act as a whole, it is a motive that acts "behind the back of the individual." It is still the individual that is posited as the "exclusive and dominant (determinant) subject."

> With that, then, the complete freedom of the individual is posited: voluntary transaction; no force on either side; positing of the self as means, or as serving, only as means, in order to posit the self as end in itself, as dominant and primary.[26]

Therefore, when we consider the formal equality of subjects in exchange, the primary value of their transaction is freedom. So freedom and equality, originating in exchange, become the idealized expression of this exchange relation as manifested in "juridical, political, social relations; they are merely this basis to a higher power."[27]

Now, *still within the formal mode of exchange,* a certain compulsion must be acknowledged. But this is

> on one side, itself only the other's indifference to my need as such, to my natural individuality, hence his equality with me and his freedom, which are at the same time the precondition of my own; on the other side, if I am determined, forced, by my needs, it is only my own nature, this totality of needs and drives, which exerts a force upon me; it is nothing alien (or, my *interest* posited in a general, reflected form).[28]

However, *Marx introduces a consideration at this point which inverts the whole meaning of the preceding analysis:*

> If this way of conceiving the matter is not advanced *in its historical context,* but is instead raised as a refutation of the more developed economic relations in which individuals relate to one another no longer merely as exchangers or as buyers and sellers, but in specific relations, no longer all of the same character; then it is the same as if it were asserted that there is no difference, to say

nothing of antithesis and contradiction, between natural bodies, because all of them occupy three dimensions [emphasis added].[29]

In other words, Marx's preceding analysis of individual freedom and equality took place at a level of abstraction which precluded specific historical developments and the actual concrete relations of agents in the marketplace. This most abstract level of capitalism is equivalent to the *ideology* of capitalist exchange. In reality, this appearance exists as its negation, as actual dependence and subordination.

However, in the Depths

> In present bourgeois society as a whole, this positing of prices and the circulation etc. appears as the surface process, beneath which, however, in the depths, entirely different processes go on, in which this apparent individual equality and liberty disappear. It is forgotten, on one side, that the *presupposition* of exchange value, as the objective basis of the whole of the system of production already in itself implies compulsion over the individual, since his immediate product is not a product for him, but only *becomes* such in the social process, and since it *must* take on this general but nevertheless external form; and that the individual has an existence only as a producer of exchange value . . . that he is therefore entirely determined by society, that this further presupposes a division of labour etc., in which the individual is already posited in relations other than that of mere *exchanger*. That therefore this presupposition by no means arises either out of the individual's will or out of the immediate nature of the individual, but that it is, rather, *historical,* and posits the individual as already *determined* by society. . . . What is overlooked, finally, is that already these simple forms of exchange value and of money latently contain the opposition between labor and capital.[30]

The essential terms here are "determined," "external form," and, most significantly, "as the surface process, beneath which, however, in the depths, entirely different processes go on." What is hereby indicated is not that the previous formal discussion is annulled but that, in the Hegelian sense, it is transcended, incorporated into the next level of development. Therefore, the mode of the previous analysis must be recast so that the reciprocal positing of individuals as means and ends, the discrimination between general motive and self-interest, the dialectic between equality and indifference, and participation of indviduals in their subordination to their own needs—that this whole system is now comprehended as compulsion over the individual, determination by society, and as a system wholly beyond individual control. This alienated modality extends also to a striking passage in which Marx, on the ground of a lofty speculation regarding the possibilities of human development under socialism, looks down upon the corruption of capitalist prehistory:

> In fact, however, when the limited bourgeois form is stripped away, what is wealth other than the universality of individual needs, capacities, pleasures, productive forces . . . the full development of human mastery . . . the active working out of . . . creative potentialities . . . the development of all human powers as such the end in itself. . . . In bourgeois economics—and in the epoch of production to which it corresponds—this complete working-out of the human content appears as a complete *emptying-out*, this universal *objectification as total alienation,* and the tearing-down of all limited, one-sided aims as sacrifice of the human end-in-itself to an entirely external end [emphasis added].[31]

"Behind one's back" and "in the depths" this fateful contradiction reasserts itself: on the one side the emptied-out individual, and on the other the objective alienation of "overpower objects."

We have now reached a critical point in Marx's argument, and I should like to focus its primary relevance for our discussion. Marx's analysis of formal exchange relations on the one hand, and their inversion in the depths of society, on the other, indicate how the actions of individuals are captured and turned against their will; how, in other words, consequences are severed from intentions and appropriated by the capitalist class.

The first instance of the discrepancy occurs on the level of formal exchange relations, where "the common interest which appears as the motive of the act as a whole is . . . not the motive, but rather proceeds . . . *behind the back* . . . of one individual's interest in opposition to that of the other." I understand this claim to mean that individual interests are constituted by the structure of the system that defines them and that this structure is reproduced in the course of pursuing individual ends. But the second discrepancy takes us past the formal exchange relationship "which appears as *the surface process, beneath which, however, in the depths entirely different processes go on, in which this apparent individual equality and liberty disappear.*"

Now the fact that individuals' private actions dialectically constitute the social structure of dependence manifests itself concretely as the "complete emptying out" of these individuals under the domination of "total alienation." The abstract, formal discrepancy between intention and consequence reveals itself concretely as the dominance of external compulsion over the socially atomized individual. We have thereby reached that aspect of Marx's analysis that is the counterpart to the Freudian unconscious, for both can be described analogously as operating behind one's back, in the depths, through the dominance of overpowering objects. Nor is this convergence an artificial imposition; rather, it represents the agreement noted in the first chapter, that individual life is the manifestation of powerful forces that cannot be adequately represented in consciousness.

This development in the argument requires that we return to the original question of the relationship between essential structures and phenomenological forms. How, precisely, do these processes, which operate behind our backs and in our depths, reveal and obscure themselves through the presented categories of lived experience? What is the relationship between structure and experience? In the writings of Maurice Godelier there is an analysis which through its insight and error can be used to advance our understanding. The basic issue is what constitutes a social structure.

> What both structuralists and Marxists reject are the empiricist definitions of what constitutes a social structure. For Radcliffe-Brown and Nadel, a social structure is an aspect of *reality* itself; it is order, the ordering of the *visible* relations between men, an ordering that explains the logic of the complementariness of these visible relations.
>
> For Marx . . . a structure is *not* a reality that is *directly* visible, and so directly observable, but a level of reality that exists *beyond* the visible relations between men, and the functioning of which constitutes the underlying logic of the system, the subjacent order by which the apparent order is to be explained.[32]

Godelier seems to me correct in arguing as he does against the empiricist account of structure. Structure, which is defined as "visible relations," is irrelevant to the primary features of contemporary social life, alienation, and ideological mystification. There is some distinction between what occurs behind one's back and before one's eyes that is inexpungable. But Godelier seems to me fundamentally mistaken in the view he himself espouses and attributes to Marx—that structure exists *beyond* visible relations, or, as Godelier puts it alternatively, "that what is visible is a *reality* concealing *another*, deeper reality, which is hidden and the discovery of which is the very purpose of scientific cognition."[33]

Once reality is placed totally beyond and out of view of lived experience it becomes impossible to locate structure, to understand how it manifests itself in experience, why experience bears the deep structural imprint, or how structure is reproduced. Such a perspective leads Godelier inevitably to the implausible claim that "capacities are therefore the objective properties of the structures, which *do not depend on the individual members of the society* and of which the individual is, for the most part, unconscious" (emphasis added).[34] The objectionable aspect of this account is not that individuals are unconscious of various objective properties of social structures but that the structure is held to exist independently of its individual members. Such a dichotomization between structure and individual, and between reality and appearance, leads to a reification of social structure which has remarkable similarities to the

Hegelian "geist" that Marx ridculed for its extraordinary power to act independently of its human manifestations.[35] Nor do I accept the "charitable" interpretation of Godelier which might claim that he does not intend to divorce structure from individuals but only from specific individuals. For the further conclusions Godelier proceeds to draw are, we shall see, incompatible with this moderate reading.

I certainly have no quarrel with the notion that individuals systematically misconstrue their social existence nor with the contention that the deep structures of the social world exist beneath the awareness of ordinary consciousness and exert a compelling influence upon everyday practice and consciousness. What I believe is fundamentally mistaken in Godelier's account is the separation of structure from lived, individual conscious existence. A structure that does not "depend on the individual members of the society" is simply not a social structure. It may be the Platonic form of a social structure, the reified "spirit" of a social structure, or the logical essence of a social structure. But society, as an "ensemble of social relations," is at least the ensemble of individuals who constitute these social relations. The structuralist account continually obliterates the fact that Marx's theory of ideology insists not only upon the inversion of reality by appearance, but, simultaneously, upon its reflection.

Even the idea of inversion does not argue in behalf of independent structures. Godelier cites on his behalf the following passage from Marx:

> The final pattern of economic relations as *seen* on the surface in their real existence and consequently in the conceptions by which the bearers and agents of these relations seek to understand them, is very much different from, and indeed quite the *reverse, of their inner but concealed essential patterns and the conception corresponding to it.*[36]

The fact that there are *inner,* essential relations *concealed* to the agents of these relations, cannot justify a claim to the *independence* of these patterns from the agents. Godelier illegitimately equates the meaning of these terms. The Freudian unconscious is an obvious alternative. In fact, the notion of reversal undermines Godelier's case completely, because only human beings are capable of reversal.[37] Only human beings are capable of error or illusion, which obviously have no existence independent of human mentality. Search as one will, it is impossible to locate "appearances," "illusions," "reversals," or "mystifications" of any sort independent of mind. Both "seeing" and "concealing" are human achievements.

Godelier's confusion on this point leads to the reductio ad absurdum of his position:

> The fetishizing of commodities is not the effect of the alienation of consciousness but the effect *in* and *for* consciousness of the disguising of social

relations *in* and *behind* their appearances. Now these appearances are the *necessary* point of departure of the representations of their economic relations that individuals *spontaneously* form for themselves. Such images thus constitute a more or less coherent body of illusory beliefs concerning the social reality within which these individuals live, and serve them as means of *acting* within and upon this social reality.[38]

Consequently, it is not man who deceives *himself* over reality, it is reality which is deceiving *him,* by inevitably appearing in a form which conceals and presents itself the wrong way up to the spontaneous consciousness of people living in the commercial world.[39]

Now, since the fetishism of commodities, and, I presume, the fetishism of consciousness as a whole, has its foundation not *in* consciousness, but "outside it, in the objective reality of social relations,"[40] all we need do to change these social relations is to locate their objective reality and overturn it. But were to look! Where is this realm which lies behind and outside of consciousness? In the unconscious of individuals? But Godelier does not claim that man unconsciously deceives himself. Again, he makes the extreme claim that reality deceives man. Perhaps, but we are given no direction as to how this realm is to be located or conceived. The whole conception is fundamentally unintelligible.

Godelier's difficulty stems from a dualism of reality and appearance, disguis*ing* social relations and disguis*ed* consciousness. But what is this underlying social reality, stripped of consciousness, which has the power *to disguise itself in the consciousness of human beings?* The heart of the matter is this: Shorn of consciousness, the world is devoid of human beings, and without a human population we can attach no sense to the "underlying social reality." Nor can we understand how reality deceives us, nor how appearances, which are "spontaneously" formed, come to constitute a "more or less coherent body of illusory beliefs," nor, even more starkly, how these illusions can serve us "as means of *acting* within and upon this social reality." The initial division is entirely too stark, too dichotomized, for any dialectic between these realms to become intelligible.

Thus far I have not argued whether Godelier is correct in claiming Marx as an advocate of this theory of social structures. As I will shortly contend, it is not possible to find a consistent, developed theory in Marx. But it is suggestive that Marx is cited by Godelier to prove that a commodity is "complex and obscure," for the reason that "social labour does not *appear* as such."[41] And the following passage from Marx is offered in evidence:

The existence of the things qua commodities, and the value relation between the products of labour which stamps them as commodities, have absolutely no connection with their physical properties and with the material relations arising therefrom. There it is a definite social relation between men, that assumes, in their eyes, the fantastic form of a relation between things.[42]

My own understanding is that this passage ought to be taken to contradict the entire thrust of Godelier's argument, because, for Marx, the fetishism of commodities which rests on the "social relations between men," is a resultant of human labor, which Marx conceives as follows:

> Labor is . . . a process . . . in which man of his own accord starts, regulates, and controls the material re-actions between himself and Nature. . . . We presuppose labor in a form that stamps it as *exclusively human.* . . . But what distinguishes the worst architect from the best of bees is this, that the architect raises his structure *in imagination* before he erects it in reality. . . . He not only effects a change of form in the material on which he works, but he also *realizes a purpose* of his own that gives the law to his modus operandi, and to which he must subordinate his will.[43]

It is the structure *of* labor, not the structure *behind it,* that is crucial in Marx's analysis of the fetishism of commodities and of his entire account of the reality of exploitation and surplus value: labor stamped as conscious, intentional, and purposeful.

Unfortunately, Marx is not always so clear. These are numerous statements supporting either a theory of structure as independent of human activity on the one hand, or a theory of structure as embodied human activity on the other. Marx often writes in the following mode:

> Money in its final, completed character now appears in all directions as a contradiction, a contradiction which *dissolves itself,* drives toward its own dissolution [emphasis added].[44]

> Capital as such creates a specific surplus value because it cannot create an infinite one all at once; but *it is the constant movement to create* more of the same [emphasis added].[45]

> The more developed capital already is . . . the more terribly must it develop the productive force *in order to realize itself* in only smaller proportions [emphasis added].[46]

> We perceive, at first sight, the deficiencies of the elementary form of value: it is a mere germ, *which must undergo a series of metamorphoses* before it can ripen into the Price-form [emphasis added].[47]

Over and over Marx appears to attribute agency to concepts and structures, and to lay himself open to precisely that form of acrid sarcasm he employed against the reifications of the Hegelian dialectic. Furthermore, in a less technical vein, Marx himself, in the first preface to *Capital,* insists that

> here individuals are dealt with only in so far as they are the personifications of economic categories, embodiments of particular class-relations and class-interests. My stand-point, from which the evolution of the economic formation of society is viewed as a process of natural history, can less than any other make the individual responsible for relations whose creature he socially remains.[48]

And, as we noted in the first chapter of this work, Marx approvingly cites a Russian reviewer who paraphrases Marx's position in the following terms:

> Marx treats the social movement as a process of natural history, governed by laws not only *independent of human will, consciousness and intelligence,* but rather, on the contrary, determining that will, consciousness and intelligence . . . a critical inquiry whose subject matter . . . can, less than anything else, have for its basis any form of, or any result of, consciousness [emphasis added].[49]

One could argue the point of these passages but their prima facie meaning is clear. However, there is another modality in Marx's presentation:

> It is plain that commodities cannot go to market and make exchanges of their own account. We must, therefore, have recourse to the guardians, who are also their owners. Commodities are things, and therefore without power of resistance against man. If they are wanting in docility he can use force; in other words, he can take possession of them. In order that these objects may enter into relation with each other as commodities, *their guardians must place themselves in relation to one another, as persons whose will resides in those objects* [emphasis added].[50]

In Ricardo's works the analysis is already so far advanced that

> *the independent material form of wealth disappears* and wealth is shown to be simply the activity of men. Everything which is not the result of human activity, of labour, is nature and, as such, is not social wealth. The phantom of the world of goods fades away and it is seen to be simply a continually disappearing and continually reproduced objectivisation of human labour. All solid material wealth is only transitory materialisation of social labour, crystallization of the production process whose measure is time, the measure of movement itself.[51]

When we consider bourgeois society in the long view and as a whole, then the final result of the process of social production always appears as the society itself, i.e. the human being itself in its social relations. Everything that has a fixed form, such as the product, etc., appears as merely a moment, a vanishing moment, in this movement . . . *and its only subjects are the individuals, but individuals in mutual relationships, which they equally reproduce and produce anew.* The constant process of their own movement, in which they renew themselves even as they renew the world of wealth *they create* [emphasis added].[52]

And as if in direct reply to the passages we previously cited as evidence for independent structures, Marx writes in the *Grundrisse:*

> It will be necessary later, before this question is dropped, *to correct the idealist manner of its presentation, which makes it seem as if it were merely a matter of conceptual determinations and of the dialectic of these concepts.* Above all in the case

of the phrase: product (or activity) becomes commodity; commodity, exchange value; exchange value, money [emphasis added].[53]

Of course, it is Marx's second perspective that is most congenial to the argument I am here presenting. I believe that his "idealist manner" of presentation was a shorthand, which, as he noted, had finally to be translated into the set of embodied meanings by which human beings carried the system of "conceptual determinations" with them through the social world. But it is less important to discover what Marx meant than to indicate what he should have meant. Since the interpretation of structure as independent of human activity seems clearly inadequate, we are either thrown back upon the vulgar empiricist account of structure as manifest behavior, or we are required to illucidate some third position. And such a position is available. It is suggested by our earlier analysis of the discrepancy between intention and practice, and by Marx's reference to the replacement of "fixed forms" by "individuals in mutual relationships."

Consciousness and Structure

The first premise of a viable position is the indissoluble unity of consciousness and world structure. It is not merely that consciousness is directed toward objects; it is simultaneously constituted by the system of social relations in which these objects are reproduced. The view which must by emphatically rejected is the dualism of external objects of consciousness on the one hand, and pure, private, self-contained acts of conscious illumination on the other. We are not only conscious of the world, but in, through, and with the world. Therefore, if we divide human activity into motivation, intention, purpose, and meaning on the one side, and the structure of objective relations on the other, we are merely engaging in a heuristic device that we understand to be a moment of analysis later to be integrated.

Structure and consciousness are dialectically related, both logically and historically. The term "structure" is equivocal, however, and its meaning varies with its context—with the material of which it is the structure. The structures that are crucial to our analysis are material, formal, and sociopsychological. The manner in which they are both imposed and created makes up the genesis and sense of their present relevance. A material structure is a causal relationship that exists independently of our consciousness and will. It may obtain in the external world described by physics and chemistry, or in the biological nature of the body. Though we can utilize such processes for our own purposes, the laws in question are independent of our choice.

But just as there are fixed material relationships, and structures of the material world, so there are sociopsychological relations which de-limit the circumstances of human social existence. For in this realm, too, laws obtain that cannot be voluntarily vanquished. If, for example, we treat children with cruelty rather than kindness, consequences will emerge and later impose themselves just as surely and adamantly as any of the facts that make up the realm of physics. The causal lines may be more difficult to trace, but that is another matter. It is true that we have the power to intervene so as to modify previous influences, but, of course, each later intervention produces its own consequences which stand obdurately against our mere wish. Our freedom in regard to our own sociopsychological existence consists in part in our ability to choose our original determinations within a range of considerable latitude; but we are then bound to struggle with the effects of our freedom. What Engels described in regard to naturalistic ecology obtains in the entire realm of human existence:

> Let us not flatter ourselves overmuch on account of our human conquest over nature. For each such conquest takes its revenge on us. Each of them, it is true, has in the first place the consequences on which we counted, but in the second and third places it has quite different, unforeseen effects which only too often cancel out the first. The people who, in Mesopotamia, Greece, Asia Minor, and elsewhere, destroyed the forests to obtain cultivable land, never dreamed that they were laying the basis for the present devastated condition of these countries, by removing along with the forests the collect-ing centers and reservoirs of moisture.
>
> But if it has already required the labor of thousands of years for us to learn to some extent to calculate the more remote natural consequences of our actions aiming at production, it has been still more difficult in regard to the more remote social consequences of these actions.[54]

An economic system includes aspects of material and sociopsycholo-gical structures. An example of such a complex of structures is the fact that human beings *can* work past the point of reproducing their subsis-tence. The fact is not a creation of human will but an externally consti-tuted reality which contains elements of physiology, ecology, and socio-psychology. But it is not a necessary fact, for it is quite conceivable that human beings might have been so constituted that all of their labor was necessary for their mere survival. Whether such a condition ever ob-tained is beside the point. It is a logical possibility. But the sheer facts of the world are different. Human inventiveness has, therefore, the power to provide for material reproduction and for surplus, beyond. This fact, too, is not a human invention, though what use is made of it is, whatever the constraints, a matter of human decision. So exploitation becomes a possibility because of imposed biological and psychological factors. And the manner in which human beings exercise their freedom, which is also originally imposed rather than created, obviously transforms the original physiological determinants that first gave rise to the possibility of human determination. All of this occurs within reciprocal limits, of course, for nature has its obduracy to which human inventiveness must eventually succomb. A people which obstinately imposes its arbitrary will on recalcitrant nature will perish in the process.

Some of the relationships in the world are neither material nor sociopsychological, but formal—necessary in virtue of their formal structure alone. It has been argued by some (conventionalists) that these necessary connections are true by the simple fact of human definition, and by others (realists), that these relationships are logically necessary characteristics of any structure of being. My own view is that once the basic terms of mathematics and logic are defined, the consequences of this original choice are no longer arbitrary. To deny this position is to fall into self-contradiction or irrelevance. Either conventionalism argues for its own position on the basis of compelling reasons, and so contradicts the thesis that good reasons are so by mere choice, or it simply declares itself true by fiat, in which case no other person is compelled to accept it.

A socioeconomic system contains material, sociopsychological and formal relationships. Like any human construction it involves an initial determination that is neither imposed by logical necessity nor totally arbitrary. It may be judged more or less appropriate to its circumstances by criteria of survival and maximum human fulfillment. Since all social decisions are ultimately mediated through the determinate structures of the world, the more we lose control over our fundamental social choices, the more the fixed, imposed properties of the world come to dominate us. This is, in part, what Marx meant by the fetishism of our social relations. Our inability to collectively construct our social relations makes us subject to the fact that these relations are determined by the exercising of class power. But our *compliance* in the decisions of others is necessary for the continued reproduction of the capitalist system, which is why we experience our subordination as alienation rather than sheer natural imposition. As our attitude toward the world becomes passive, we come to view its structures as wholly necessary. We thereby relinquish our power to select out of the range of possible determinations those that would most fully liberate us as human beings. The hypothetical laws of the natural and sociopsychological world, laws that state which consequences would follow from particular premises, appear as categorical determinations—universal, unalterable processes beyond any human contrivance.

When human purpose is not fully realized, that is, when the system of social relations is inadvertently rather than intentionally produced, the material and sociopsychological structures through which this abortive action manifests itself gains power over our human nature. Social relations become thinglike, and resemble merely natural laws, because they are equally imposed and seemingly unalterable. The external and social structures that might carry our intentions, carry us instead in the wake of their facticity.

It is important to note that social structure, as such, is neither good nor bad. A collectively chosen social system will also contain and impose necessary patterns of power, experience, and consciousness upon its members. But the greater the understanding and power of the social agents, and the more democratically they can exercise their capacity to control nature and themselves, the more likely they are to construct a system that meets the various dimensions of their social existence, from individual self-reflection to collective action. For under such an arrangement these dimensions are capable of sustaining each other, and the antagonisms that rend capitalist society along class, sexual, and ethnic divisions imposed upon the social division of labor, lose much of their destructiveness. It is not that all disagreement, friction, and conflict of interest will cease; but such motives are likely to diminish and be transformed as the arsenal of economic weaponry which elicits these responses is dismantled.

Under capitalism, divisions between the powerful and the powerless, manifested in an antagonism between individual interest and the structure of social power, always prove invidious. Consider the case of an individual capitalist who attempts to minimize the wages paid his own workers but suffers the consequences of a general decline in purchasing power when his own practice becomes common policy. There appears to be some contradiction in the logic of the individual situation. For what is reasonable for the capitalist as a single employer is illogical for him as a member of a system. And yet the imperatives of that system appear to dictate both its particular and its global prerequisites.

For the critical point about the social system is that it depends on a conceptual framework to organize the relationship among formal, sociopsychological, and material determinations. It can thus harbor contradictions between its general meaning or syntax and the specific intentions of its agents. But since it is also a system of class power, one group can use this potential disparity for its actual advantage. This situation seems precisely what Marx intended when he distinguished between "the common interest which appears as the motive of the act as a whole ... but, as such ... is not the motive" and the "self-reflected particular interests" of one individual "in opposition to that of the other." The common interest is the structural framework of the system as a whole and of the particular "logic" of the individuals who constitute it. On the surface, this is a framework of freedom, of formally equal subjects of exchange. On the surface, the structure of the economy appears to be a democratically elaborated formal arrangement, created by its individual members and subject to their transformation. It appears, in other words, as a conventional structure justified by its beneficial consequences. "In the depths," however, external compulsion dominates the system. The social world thereby becomes for its subjects an imposed necessity, a system more closely resembling the properties of the natural world than of a genuine human community. On its formal, ideological surface, capitalism appears to have the character of a human invention serving the common interest. In fact, it contains the natural necessity of material relationships because

> men make their history themselves, but not as yet with a collective will according to a collective plan . . . *and for that very reason all such societies are governed by necessity* [emphasis added].[55]

Social structures become independent of the will of their members in a twofold manner: (1) They proceed through actually independent causal relations which (2) are given their meaning through the estranged determinations of an alienated society. The logical structure of a socioeconomic system thereby is shown to depend on the level of alienation or freedom that obtains within it.

Motives and structural presuppositions are inseparable. That is why Marx emphasized the fact that "the common interest which appears as the motive of the act as a whole is *recognized as a fact* by both sides." The act by which individuals reproduce their own individual interests is simultaneously the act by which they reproduce the system as a whole. Of course, they do not act directly on behalf of the system, but they cannot act without reproducing its logic. For their individual acts are defined by that system and only intelligible within it. Like the elements of a language, which have no significance in themselves but derive their meaning from their place in a larger configuration, the individual competitive acts of distinct capitalists appropriate the larger logic while they are explicitly directed to particular ends. In other words, the particular motives of individuals within the capitalist system are motives as defined by that system, while the system itself requires for its reproduction the general awareness and particular interests of its individual members. The logic of the concepts and the logic of human practice are two aspects of the same activity. However abstractly and idealistically Marx may speak of the categories of capitalism, and however much he may seem to derive these concepts merely from each other in the style of Hegel, it is important to keep in mind the human existence which grounds conceptual categories in the actual practice of human beings. However much value is described "as a mere germ, which must undergo a series of metamorphoses before it can ripen into the Price-form," it is crucial to

insist on what Marx was apparently well aware of, but neglected to explicate systematically:

> What, first of all, practically concerns producers when they make an ex-
> change, is the question, how much of some other product they get for their
> own? in what proportions the products are exchangeable? When these pro-
> portions have, *by custom*, attained a certain stability they appear to result from
> the nature of the products [emphasis added].[56]

However much value is determined by labor time, unless this structure
comes to be embodied in the practice of human beings, it will not determine the nature of exchange.

Since I have so much emphasized my disagreement with Godelier's
contention that social "structures do not depend on the individual members of society," I want to be certain that I am not taken to assert that
social structures are what their individual members understand them to
be. There is a fundamental and ineradicable distinction in capitalist society between the structured system of individual beliefs and the actual
fundamental social structures. The *structural unconscious,* the determinate social compulsion Marx uncovered, does, tragically, act behind the
backs of individuals and in their depths. But it is out of individual
human activity that it comes into being and exercises power over its
creators. The whole issue is contained in the phrase of Marx's Russian
reviewer, that Marx treats social structure as "governed by laws not only
independent of human will, consciousness and intelligence, but rather,
on the contrary, determining that will, consciousness and intelligence."

If this phrase is taken literally to indicate that the structure does not
depend on the individual members of society, it is misconceived, for the
reasons I have offered. But it can be understood to mean that while the
structures are wholly dependent upon human will, consciousness, and
intelligence, they do not coincide with the self-understanding of that
will, consciousness, and intelligence possessed by the members of society.
Two facts are true: A social structure that does not depend on human
intention is a contradiction in terms; but the actual prevailing social
structures do not coincide with human intentions as the subjects of those
intentions understand them. Marx himself is often careless in his exposition: "These quantities (values) vary continually, independently of the
will, foresight and action of the producers."[57] Independently of the
action—no; but independently of the intended action—yes.

In this chapter I have been concerned to develop the rudiments of an
account, based on Marx's views of social structure, that would explain
how the conscious intentions of human agents come to be so embodied
in the world as to defeat their will and understanding. The next stage of
analysis would consist of a detailed account of the specific institutions
through which human action is structurally formed. Such a presentation

is the subject of another work, though we can say something general about the functioning of all institutions.

Their most important characteristic is that they channel human action in accordance with previously constituted relations of *power* and *meaning*. Every significant institution serves the same structure of power—the domination of the productive process by the class with predominant control over its property and forms of accumulation. But this purpose is served in a multitude of ways, and the structural conflicts Marx noted manifest themselves not only within single institutions but among their diverse functions. Schools must form attitudes of subordination, the acceptance of anonymous authority, the division of means from ends, and the inculcation of specific skills. Mass advertising is concerned to further fantasies of social escape, consumptive gratification and the release of inhibition. Even the media play very different roles: Newspapers articulate the ideology of the political process which makes the semblance of democracy credible and efficient. Television and film provide cultural paradigms of success, appropriate character, and collective delusion. An institution like the family bears the imprint of these various tendencies, which are not easily reconciled, as they in fact must attempt to reconcile each other. Education, for example, must distribute enough literacy to make a contemporary industrial system possible, but not in such a way that reason becomes a technique commonly employed to dissect and challenge the system of power. The conduit of social structure is the institution, which articulates individual existence through a system of variegated roles.

It is therefore very important to avoid the kind of approach to the issue taken by Michael Schneider in *Neurosis and Civilization*. Much of this book is illuminating and profound. But Schneider has a tendency to derive the characteristics of individual life *directly* from the most abstract features of the capitalist system. Basing himself on Marx's distinction between concrete use value and abstract exchange value, Schneider argues

> our main thesis . . . that the structure of social instincts and needs becomes, with the historical development of the structure of commodity and money, just as *abstract* as the latter.[58]

In his most careful statement, Schneider maintains that

> we are aware, of course, that the clinical phenomenon of "repression" is not simply identical with the political–economic phenomenon of "abstraction" of use-values and of the usable needs and satisfactions related thereto. However, it can be shown that a necessary connection exists between the degree of abstraction which (capitalist) commodity society has reached in the course of its history and its degree of social instinctual repression.[59]

There are two difficulties with this statement, however: First, it is highly improbable that any measure of degrees of historical repression can be articulated because society simultaneously elicits and denies the needs of its members. Even if such a standard were available, it is extremely unlikely that primitive societies based on use value are uniformly less repressive than contemporary capitalism.

Second, Schneider does not heed his own careful noting of the distinction between repression and abstraction and welds them together throughout the remainder of his analysis. First, he asserts that "exchange-value consciousness thus is indifferent, even blind to the sensuous-concrete quality and diversity of the use-value"[60] and, after favorably citing the following statement of Haug's:

> A training in self-mastery to the point of indifference, as the preparation of sensuality adequate to the exchange principle, is the prerequisite for the execution of social relationships which reverberate from the exchange society into individual life.[61]

Schneider proceeds to the claim that "'abstract man,' who is the personification of 'abstract human labor,' has just as abstract a relationship to his own sensuality as to the sensuality of use-value" and is therefore the "materialistic foundation of that psychic 'process of abstraction' which Freud described through the concept of 'repression.'"[62]

Now, Marx undoubtedly made a fundamental and significant contribution to our understanding in the powerful manner in which he urged the distinction between use and exchange value. The fact that capitalists are concerned to accumulate abstract value (profit) and are ultimately indifferent to the specific manner in which their profit is amassed can hardly be overemphasized. It is finally quite irrelevant to the capitalist whether his profit derives from the sale of automobiles, patent rights, medical services, or books critical of corporate capitalism. Nor is it possible to understand the alienation of contemporary life without focusing on the central fact of capitalist production—that the capitalist cares nothing for the particular nature and needs of the laborer, and is only interested in the laborer's abstract capacity to produce more value for the capitalist than is required for his own reproduction. To the capitalist it is quite certainly a matter of indifference what specifically the concrete nature of the work force, the consumer, or the population at large amounts to. But capitalism does not function only in the long run, or at the level of ultimate purpose, and for capitalism to reproduce itself as a daily occurrence it is absolutely vital that the capitalist grasp, master, and elicit the specific system of needs and material and psychological gratifications upon which the entire capitalist enterprise depends. The ultimate purpose of exchanging use values may well be the accumulation of abstract value, that is, profit, but unless the material process which elaborates use value remains within capitalist control, the process of abstract exchange will simply cease to exist.

The second and more significant difficulty with Schneider's emphasis on abstraction is that it tends to separate the self into two distinct realms: the ego, as the "rational" calculator of abstract, exchange value and the id as repository of abstracted–repressed use value. Something in this account is certainly correct and there is an important measure of the truth in R. Reiche's characterization of the contemporary psychoanalytic understanding of positive ego functions as

> grouped around control, domination, decision, limitation, comprehensiveness, overview, subordination, watchfulness: all negative associations go in the direction of dissolution, inability to draw a limit, letting oneself go. . . . The category of the ego only unlocks its secret meaning when regarded in the context of a social formation that is based on competition; it is bound to the commodity-selling, market-oriented bourgeois who must defeat his opponent but by *emotionally neutral means,* that is, without directly killing him [emphasis added] [63]

An observation that Schneider crystallizes with the comment:

> The other half of psychic activity, the "passions," "sensuousness," and the "instinctual nature" of man is shunted off into the incalculable (and therefore rebellious) psychological remnant of the private sphere, that is, into the underground of the "personality," into the "id."[64]

But the problem with this dualism is, first, that it leads Schneider to the view that "immediate sensuous needs" can neither be destroyed not inhibited,[65] that is, that they are simply *given;* and even more significantly, to the strange misconception that conscious life is devoid of concrete need, desire, passion, and character, and that under the domination of capitalist exchange, we have somehow become abstract beings. The original structural dualism between essential relations and phenomenal forms is replicated as a new dichotomy between concrete passion operating in the depths and abstract calculation exhaustively characterizing consciousness. However, the unconscious contains its own abstractions, and our lived experience is massively, obviously, and irreducibly passionate, needful, sensuous, and wholly concrete.

Marx noted:

> Money is therefore not only *an* object, but is *the* object of greed. . . . Greed as such, as a particular form of the drive, i.e. as distinct from the craving for a particular kind of wealth, e.g. for clothes, weapons, jewels, women, wine etc., is possible only when general wealth, wealth as such, has become individualized in a particular thing, i.e. as soon as money is posited in its third quality (representing a general social result). Money is therefore not only the object but also the fountainhead of greed.[66]

What is crucial in this passage is the account of greed as "a particular form of the drive." Schneider moves from *a passion for abstraction to abstract passion*. The latter phrase is a contradiction in terms. There are no needs, desires, images, feelings, or longings that are not concretely this particular need, desire, etc., rather than that. They are of course influenced and permeated by abstract considerations, but this can hardly remove them from the immediate world of concrete existence. The bourgeois may wish to defeat his opponent without killing him, but his means are anything but "emotionally neutral." They are motivated by very definite anticipations of power, prestige, authority, dominance, and popularity and produce very definite emotional experiences in those who are affected by this action.

I noted earlier that when Marx placed the *content* of exchange "entirely outside economics" he was engaged in a serious mistake. It was an error that stems from a strong tendency in Marx's analysis to overlook the fundamental significance of use value for an understanding of society. Of course, Marx recognized that nothing will be exchanged unless it is in some way "useful" to its purchaser. But he seems to assume that since all societies produce use value while only capitalism is defined by the production of exchange value, it is in the process of exchange and its foundation in abstract value and labor that the uniqueness of capitalism lies.

Formally, the assumption is correct. Materially, however, what Marx articulates so profoundly in the introduction to the *Grundrisse*—that production and consumption, use and exchange, are dialectically related—tends to disappear from the detailed development of his argument. Marx's opposition to subjective–bourgeois theories of value led him finally to overemphasize the "objective" constitution, the independent existence, the quantifiable measurability of value. Through this tendency Marx was again led to minimize one of his own important economic insights—that the value of labor power itself is ultimately defined in terms of socially necessary labor power required for its *subsistence,* a notion that can only be understood historically, politically, socially, and subjectively.

Therefore, while Marx does not deny the continued existence of use value as the presupposition of exchange value, he does not incorporate a history or social critique of use, need, or human nature in his explicit analysis of capitalist development. And this emphasis, rooted in a concern for scientific objectivity, leads Marx, against his own profound insight in the *Philosophic Manuscripts* and introduction to the *Grundrisse,* to take the concreteness of practical subjectivity, for granted.

> It is the necessry pre-requisite of a commodity to be a use-value, but it is immaterial to the use-value whether it is a commodity or not. Use-value in this indifference to the nature of its economic destination, i.e. use-value as such lies outside the sphere of investigation of political economy. It falls

within the sphere of the latter only in so far as it forms its own economic destination. It forms the material basis which directly underlies a definite economic relation called exchange value.[67]

The dialectic of production–consumption implies that use is the material *product* as well as the "material basis" of a definite "economic relation," and that, finally, no dualism between content and form, use and exchange, is possible. Nor is this merely an issue of abstract dialectics. For contemporary capitalism is marked precisely by the fact that natural use value ceases to exist, and that every need of the individual is mediated by commodities. It is very misleading, then, when Schneider, building on Marx's ambivalence, interprets capitalism as the repression of use value. It is one thing to be told that capitalism is indifferent to any particular use value, or, more accurately, that it is sustained precisely by the rapid succession of one use value by another. It is a very different matter to be told that capitalism is indifferent to use value as such. The first contention is suggestive; the second, mystifying. The frenzied, manipulative, profit-oriented replacement of previous commodities and needs by new instances is a very concrete structure which results in a very concrete consequence—exhaustion, anxiety, shallowness, despair, impotence, and fear of commitment. These experiences are not abstractions, but very concrete moments of social anguish.

However abstract the structure of economic development may be in the understanding, or even in the practices of capitalist replacement, it is a structure sustained by concrete activity. It is a structure that functions through human experience, not beyond it. If we note that contemporary sexuality is marked by a tendency toward the hoarding and substitution of sexual partners, it will not explain much to identify these features with the deep structures of capitalist production and exchange. For what occurs in the sexual lives of individuals is mediated by particular social experiences, and is the result of (a) the use of sexuality as a narcotic to assuage strong feelings of anxiety, (b) a socially determinate consumptive compulsion to accumulate experiences as well as tangible commodities, (c) a deeply maintained achievement orientation which is transformed in the capacity–need to produce erotic experiences in another, and (d) the recognition of sexuality as a still occasionally uncommoditized experience, which, in its "useless" intimacy, transcends the predominant forms of capitalist instrumentality. The tendency to abstract from the uniqueness of other individuals is caused by a very definite historical structure.

Marx is closer to the truth when he notes:

Indifference toward a specific kind of labour presupposes a very developed totality of real kinds of labour, of which no single one is any longer dominant. As a rule, the most general abstractions arise only in the midst of the richest possible concrete development[68]

But this fact, as it operates under the capitalist compulsion to commoditize all experience, alters the very nature of use value as a category. As a commentator on the writings of the French critic Baudrillard has noted:

> Marx asserts in *Capital* that use values, unlike exchange values, are "incomparable" and their irreducible particularity makes it impossible to treat them in a homogeneous fashion. Baudrillard's point is that this is simply inconsistent. For there to be exchange value it is already necessary that *utility* become the principle of reality for the object as product. Exchange presupposes that the objects are already *rationalized as useful.*[69]

The Structurally Repressed Unconscious

The underlying social structures of which Marx wrote must be understood to be concrete constituents in the lives of men and women. These structures are the relations men and women sustain and reproduce in regard to nature and the system of their own interdependence. I have noted, briefly, *how in general* these relations become independent of their own creators and stand over and against them as unintelligible and malignant forces. As I previously suggested, it is one of the primary tasks of Marxist social analysis to elaborate this process of estrangement in its detail. It is a task that cannot be completed, however, without incorporating the conclusions reached in the preceding chapter. For in our previous critique of Freudian metapsychology we developed a conception of the repressed unconscious which must now be drawn into our understanding of the structural or Marxist unconscious. Social structures are sustained not merely by the rules of the social system, however estranged and autonomous, but by the tendencies, hidden to the agents themselves, which reproduce the deepest aspects of character necessary to the continued maintenance of the social system.

The structural unconscious is the estranged system of human powers that constitutes both the patterns of capitalist power and bourgeois ideology. The repressed unconscious is the repository of the irreconcilable conflicts between this capitalist reality and bourgeois appearance. We have simply explicated the meaning of a basic contention of the previous chapter: "An aspect of mental life *becomes a defense* to the extent that the inclination it is employed to structure is defined as socially prohibitory. And an originally amorphous inclination *becomes a determinate, unconscious motive, or drive,* to the extent that it is defined as censorable, and so forced away from the self's consciousness and into the literally alien province of the id-unconscious." The repressed unconscious and the structural unconscious are merely mirror images of each other. What is socially elicited and socially denied constitutes the visible structure of social life, the invisible meaning of social relations, and the structured, substantive energy of unconscious reproductions of social life. Since social structures are constituted out of (but are not exhausted by) human relationships, every feature of the social structure will have a counterpart in human character, conscious or unconscious. No characteristic of capitalist life, none of the features of its institutions—corporations, media, bureaucracies, schools, unions, culture—is finally intelligible until its objective structure can be translated into the interpersonal relations of its members. Marx was correct when he wrote that "society does not consist of individuals, but expresses the sum of interrelations, the relations within which these individuals stand."[70] What he could not incorporate into his understanding of these relations was, to the detriment of his theory, the role of the repressed unconscious.

It is crucial to realize that I am not here synthesizing the Marxist and Freudian notions of the unconscious. Such an attempt is futile because of the basic contradictions between the theories, which I have previously discussed. Efforts in this direction, by writers like Reich and Marcuse, for example, have produced brilliant insights unmoored to any theoretical foundation. Freud's metapsychology, and particularly his instinct theory, cannot be integrated into a Marxist perspective. Few writers deeply exposed to the literature and practice of psychoanalysis have ever emerged from it unscathed. Either, as in the case of Reich, some form of the instinct theory has been surreptitiously retained, or, as in the case of Fromm, instinct has been abandoned for a theoretical melange consisting of part Marxism and various other exotic ingredients, including an ahistorical existentialism. What I have argued for in this work is a synthesis of the Marxist–structural unconscious and the repressed unconscious, *itself understood as constituted out of the social conflict endemic to capitalism* between simultaneous and contradictory encitement and denial of antagonistic social dispositions.

The repressed unconscious as understood in this essay is inherently social. We are not burdened with the task of integrating a universal, asocial, biopsychical theory of instincts into a social theory of socioeconomic self-reproduction. Nor is our basic paradigm individual instinct versus social constraint. The fundamental contradictions of individual–social life arise out of irrationality of social structures. That these contradictions are embedded in individuals is obvious and does not support the notion that the contradiction is between the individual and society. Contradictions, sustained by individuals in their relationships, define individuals who reciprocally reproduce the antagonisms that reproduce their nature.

Every "permanent" structure of society is rooted in a comparably "permanent" disposition in individuals. This is not to be taken as theory of isomorphism; that is, the features do not mirror each other literally.

An apparent respect for authority may be grounded in fear; an emphasis on continual excitement—"fun morality"—may derive from a terror of boredom; and gregariousness may stem from both its sheer, compelled unavoidability as well as any personal interest in its continuance. Nor can all of these personal dispositions be explicitly or even implicitly conscious. For there are crucial modes of social life in which the antagonism between what is actually required and what must be believed is so massive that only unconscious denial will make the process bearable. The ubiquitous, overarching contradiction in capitalism between apparent independence and actual dependence, embodied in the formative institutions of family, school, work, and cultural imagination, are too excruciating to be continually recognized and consciously confronted.

Of course there is truth in the claim that the roots of our vulnerability lie in the universal biopsychological helplessness of childhood rather than in any social structure. But nothing which is merely given as a biopsychological fact can determine its own meaning. The vulnerability of childhood might be as much a joyful source of later sensitivity, spontaneity, empathy, and the capacity for "surrender," as a basis for the fear of personal intimacy and human commitment. Only the prevailing social order will determine which of the possible outcomes is realized in later social life. The way in which an original dependency is continuously reproduced and alleviated serves to establish the parameters of human "development" and the purposes and forms of social institutions. The social necessity, under capitalism, for mindless obedience to media self-definition, bureaucratic estrangement of means and ends, state domination and mystification, and corporate brutality and deceit must be rooted in character in a process begun at birth.

Marxist theory has suffered from an egregious split between structure and consciousness, objectivity and subjectivity. At the source of this dichotomy is the old distinction between base and superstructure; so it is not surprising to find that more structural analyses tend to be grouped around economic analysis and the functions of the state (Sweezy, Braverman, Althusser, and Poulantzas), while the phenomenological humanists have been concerned with culture, philosophy, the family, and psychology (Sartre, Lukacs, Gramaci, and Marcuse). However, capitalism is as much a structure of estranged human intentions as culture is the elaboration of material processes. The whole disposition of Marx's writings lends itself to this dualism. For Marx sometimes writes from the position of the scientist who explains the rise and fall of capitalism, and at other times from the perspective of the revolutionary who is dedicated to its overthrow.[71] In the first mode, Marx provides an objective analysis of the laws of capitalism, understood as a process of natural occurrences. In the second mode he understands that the laws of capitalism are the formulations of fetishized social relations that are intrinsically inverted and dehumanizing and must be transcended through revolution.

The laws of capitalism are objective so long as mystified men and women reproduce them through alienated labor. Therefore their objectivity has no counterpart in the remainder of the world; for the stars move in their orbits through processes no intervention can alter.

> These formulae, which bear stamped upon them in unmistakable letters, that they belong to a state of society, in which the process of production has the mastery over man, instead of being controlled by him, such formulae appear to the bourgeois intellect to be as much a self-evident necessity imposed by nature as productive labour itself.[72]

There is a solution within the Marxist perspective to the apparent dichotomy between structure and consciousness. It was not sufficiently elaborated by Marx, however. We have few guidelines, then, in dealing with the revolutionary cultivation of consciousness understood as a structurally objective process. And we have even less guidance in dealing with the issue of the unconscious and the possibility of revolutionary "therapy." I wish to make suggestions about such a possibility in the next and concluding chapter of this work.

CHAPTER EIGHT

Conclusion: The Politics of Therapy

Appearance and Reality

We have seen that there is a tendency in Marxist theory to fall into reified and abstract forms of structuralism. A valid emphasis on the system of alienated relations acting behind the backs of individuals comes to be replaced by a doctrine that structures exist and act *independently of* individuals. Not only is this view unintelligible but its political consequences are likely to be regressive. To hold that we do not deceive ourselves but that reality deceives us implies that we are absolved from struggling through the ambivalent vicissitudes and of our own lived experience. Since the structure of alienation is considered to be separate from us, a structure of real forces which we merely bear or represent in the world, it is these structures and not ourselves that become the object of theoretical praxis. We must discover the real character of this reified system and then oppose it. Is it idle fear that suggests that this perspective encourages the growth of an intellectual elite skilled in the comprehension and demystification of the real world, a cadre of theorists charged with the revelation of reality. But Marx spoke not only of structures "behind our backs"; he spoke also of underlying realities "in the depths" of our beings.

256

Structures do not act; only human beings act. That human activity under capitalism is incompletely human, that it is the semblance of purpose, freedom, and self-determination, dominated by the reality of needful compulsion, is the heart of Marx's contention. "Semblance," however, is a very dangerous term. What it means in the dialectical tradition to which Marx was committed is the adumbration of a more complete and perfect conclusion, not a thoroughly disfigured appearance ontologically divided from its essence. So, under capitalism we do in fact act with some intention, purpose, and power. But it is always less than we propose and ultimately displaced. That is, our intentions do not reach the ends we have translucently prefigured.

If, however, we were to misconceive ourselves as wholly acted upon rather than acting, not only would we render ourselves unable to comprehend the activity of our imminent reflection, but we would sever ourselves from any grasp of our own agency sufficient to make a transition to a higher stage of our lives a viable and intelligible potentiality. To so misconceive ourselves is to reify our alienation by having absorbed the mere facticity to which we have reduced the world into the very conception of ourselves. Fortunately, even such an act of self-mutilation is an *act,* and thereby defeats the possibility of its own fetishism.

However abstract and esoteric the structures of socioeconomic reality, or how buried and archaic the peremptory forces of the id, they are human constructs. To maintain that these forces are not voluntarily chosen but imposed is only to note the problem. It is the point at which a meaningful analysis must begin. Of course these curtailments are not chosen out of knowledge and power. But a process of social estrangement is simply one side of the dialectic of individual self-estrangement. To insist on the role we human beings play in the expanding reproduction of our own alienation is not to collapse into bourgeois voluntarism, however, if that is the fear behind the flight into structure. For we do not understand what bourgeois culture understands by the notion of the individual as agent, just as we do not accept what Freud contended was the nature of the repressed unconscious. We know that we who reproduce the estrangement of the world and our selves are individuals who have been birthed through the filaments of social domination. We cannot help but create ourselves with materials bequeathed us from the past. However, every appropriation of the world and of others is simultaneously the appropriation of ourselves. The world can be massively pressed upon us, but to be *im*pressed requires our participation, however unconscious and compelled. Duress and even necessity are real, but they do not bypass agency. To be necessitated means that the only course of action available in the world is wholly unsatisfactory to our human aspirations. Even this most pathological situation does not eliminate agency, but merely indicates the severe contraction of the *in*human condition in which it is required.

> Production does not only produce man as a *commodity*, the *human commodity*, man in the form of a commodity; in conformity with this situation it produces him as a *mentally* and *physically* dehumanized being. . . . Its product is the *self-conscious* and *self-acting* commodity.[1]

In the phrase "*self-conscious* and *self-acting* commodity," the whole of the problem of alienation is compressed. How we can be both human and thinglike is precisely what we need to make intelligible, and the arguments I have made on behalf of the conceptions of the repressed and structural unconscious, understood as estranged human activities, are efforts in this direction. Marx was speaking of the formal structure of capitalism when he wrote:

> If I am determined, forced, by my needs, it is only *my own nature*, this totality of needs and drives, which exerts a force upon me; it is *nothing alien* (or, my interest posited in a general, reflected form). But it is, after all, precisely in this way that *I exercise compulsion* over the other and drive him into the exchange system [emphasis added].[2]

But it is simultaneously true that: "Man is no longer in a condition of external tension with the external substance of private property; *he has himself become the tension-ridden being of private property*" (emphasis added).[3]

Capitalist social structures are relationships *among individuals*, separated from their understanding and control. Compared with reified forms of structuralism which misconstrue this point, Freud's contribution becomes all the more attractive. For in the Freudian perspective every social phenomenon originates in the unconscious dynamic of its individual members. This is Freud's strength and weakness. On the one hand, he does not fall prey to attributing independent existence to compelling structural forces. For he regards such forces as the sum of individual drives and his powerful nominalism thus spares him the confusions of structural reification. But this is precisely Freud's weakness; he lacks an understanding of social relations and therefore of the social nature of "individual" existence. Consequently, his efforts at the demystification of personal experience always reproduce some critical aspect of that demystification, for he never escapes taking the consequence of capitalist individualism for its cause. The framework through which he reveals the reality of the human condition is limited by the inhumanity of the capitalist condition which is then mistaken for the human condition itself. So, while Freud eschews any assertion of the significance of social structure, he reproduces this very structure in his uncritical acceptance of the deepest aspects of the capitalist world view.

We noted in the first chapter of this work that Marx and Freud shared a profound mistrust of the common sense self-understanding of everyday life. Both regarded conscious experience as the illusory representation of an underlying and distant reality. On the basis of our previous discussion we must also underscore the critical differences between their accounts of the distinction between appearance and reality. The differences reduce to two: Freud's individual vs. Marx's social understanding of reality; and Freud's anthropological vs. Marx's revolutionary understanding of the transcendence of appearance. Of course, the two are linked.

Let us return to Marx's phrase—"the phenomenal forms of essential relations." For Marx, these relations, properly understood, are the estranged powers of individual–social life. They are the logical–motivational properties of the system of capitalism separated from their agents and standing over against them as powers beyond control or comprehension. Since human beings are the active concatenation of their social relations, and, consequently, of the logical structure of these relations, social structure and individual motivation are converse mirror images. Marx focused on structure and left the issue of motivation largely untouched, but this represents an absence in his work rather than a positive error. However if structure and motivation are truly dialectical concepts, it must be the case that in avoiding the issue of motivation Marx simultaneously avoided some aspect of social structure too. And we have already noted that his analysis lacks any real account of the *embodiment* of logical structures in the lives of individual men and women. Without a theory of motivation and its alienation we cannot grasp the active character of logical structures. Therefore treating human persons as the congeries of their relations will always appear to reduce them to those relations understood as an abstract pattern of merely conceptual determinations. In short, until the gap between real structure and phenomenal appearance, between essential relations and human motivation, between intention and consequence, is mediated, Marxism is left without a coherent theory of social alienation and its positive transcendence. Now, such efforts have of course been made, and every account which makes the institutions of daily life—family, media, schools, play, culture—intelligible in terms of the determinations of capital reproduction, and *simultaneously, makes the movements of capital intelligible in terms of the transformations of everyday life,* further completes the elaboration of a Marxist theory. Marxism is therefore an incomplete theory in practice, but not in theory.

Psychoanalytic theory is, however, fundamentally mistaken in its view of the relationship between appearance and reality; its project cannot be completed.

Before justifying this claim it is necessary to remove two sources of resistance. First, it seems difficult still for many to believe that Freud, who so often penetrated the surface of bourgeois pretension, could himself fall prey to its deeper fetishism. I have already presented arguments that such was the case both in regard to Freud's metapsychology and his clinical practice and I have nothing new to add to those considerations. I will shortly attempt to indicate how this semblance of demystification was achieved.

But there is a second source of resistance to the notion that Freud's "uncovering" of reality was itself infected by a critical blindness. Freud's theory and practice are reflections of the alienation of capitalist life and, consequently, are consonant with its structure. Like every system of ideology, psychoanalytic doctrine both distorts and reflects the reality it purports to disclose. Freud's misconceptions are the misconceptions that resonate through the structures of bourgeois culture. The mystification in which psychoanalytic theory participates is therefore more difficult to detect because its theory and practice are organized to treat a social pathology produced through capitalist exploitation with a cure that embodies the basic assumptions of the system ultimately responsible for the original disorder. There is consequently a certain correspondence between the alienation of capitalist society, which produces the human anguish that requires therapeutic "relief," on the one hand, and the practice of psychoanalytic therapy—*itself alienated in that its presuppositions do not transcend the social order that has produced the original pathology*—which is the source of "cure," on the other.

Psychoanalytic assumptions regarding human nature and its pathology are credible because they remain thoroughly isomorphic with the structures of the capitalist world. This is a powerful and disturbing fact which helps to explain why even those therapists and theorists who have substantial disagreements with Freudian conceptions tend to succumb to its perspective. For we have all been formed in the world to which Freud speaks and which speaks through him, and so this world, which is of us, speaks familarly to us through his theory and practice. In comparison with the weight of the world as it is, and as we have been deeply constituted by it as egoistic, privatized, consumatory, and vulnerable, the visionary outlines of Marx's conceptions seem pallid and powerless, merely utopian conceptions which lack the force to dislodge us from the mass of the bourgeois gravitational field. So, while the vision of a new being resonates to something undeniable in our condition, it requires a willed defiance of the inertia of our formed being to remain loyal to its eschatology. It is only too easy to find Freud credible, however; his pessimism is the entropy of our alienation.

We can now turn to Freud's analysis of the relationship between psychic reality and appearance and represent the Freudian conception by a diagram composed of vertical and horizontal lines intersecting at right angles (Figure 1). Above the horizontal is the realm of conscious ego, or appearance, and below, separated by the process of repressive

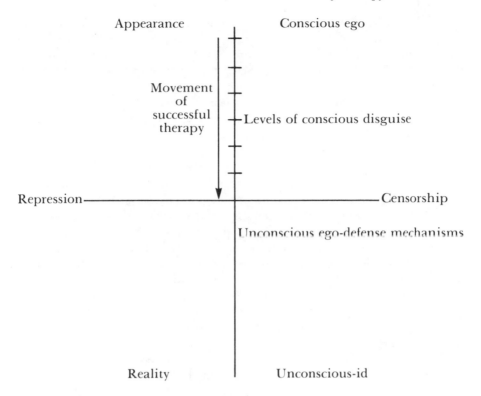

Figure 1

censorship, is the reality of the unconscious-id. With the help of this simple aid it is possible to note both the contribution and simultaneous limitation of Freud's theory.

Freud noted that as successful therapy proceeds, conscious experience becomes more transparent. The individual is progressively better able to draw the aspects of conscious experience and unconscious dynamics together. As awareness of unconscious forces deepens, symptoms gradually lessen their hold, the power of these forces diminishes and the self grows in and through its capacity to abandon defenses and reknit the sundered fabric of its life. If Dora's consciousness was permeated with the effect of her denial of forbidden unconscious sexual longings, a successful recognition and real acceptance of these inclinations could be expected to transform not only her presenting symptoms but the pervasive character of her lived awareness. Every successful step in therapy would have brought Dora so much closer to her unconscious dynamics and would simultaneously have altered the manifestation of that dynamic in her consciousness experience. Still within the realm of individual experience, her awareness would have increased in lucidity.

A post-Freudian, Marxism must include this analytic insight and extend the Marxist definition of ideology. For there are two distinct levels of mystification, ideology and false consciousness: (1) the masking of underlying essential social structures through the phenomenal forms of individual life; and (2) the further distortion of that individual phenomenal realm through the mechanisms of defense. Marx used the terms "ideology" and "fetishism" in various contexts to refer to the first transformation. He was unaware of the second and, obviously, lacked any appropriate vocabulary.

For example, the fact that the deeply conflictural structures of capitalism manifest themselves in personal accusation and self-blame is an instance of ideological mystification—the masking of essential relations through individualized ideology. But, whereas Marx distinguished between "essential relations" and "phenomenal forms," Freud established that individual conscious experience is itself the result of disguised defenses against these phenomenal forms. Marx's position is too simple. He knew that we do not understand the fundamental structures of our social world but he assumed that the phenomenal world was transparent in its own phenomenology. He did not realize what Freud so well knew—that individual conscious experience is the result of transformations of individual experience ("phenomenal experience") beneath the level of consciousness. Freud discovered that there were degrees of mystification within the pysche of the individual. The fact that personal hatred, self-contempt, and guilt are themselves repressed and replaced by the conscious experience of love and self-sacrifice represents the work of false consciousness. Freud discovered this second process, which was a profound contribution to our understanding of mystification.

On the other hand, Freud believed that such a discovery exhausted the ground of mystification, and this was a profound error. The therapeutic movement which uncovers the unconscious dynamics behind false consciousness remains bound to the categories of the capitalist phenomenal world, because unconscious forces are themselves the transformation of reified social structures. This contention would, of course, have been vehemently rejected by Freud, who viewed his own contribution as the revelation of psychic reality in its essence. When Freud uncovered the repressed unconscious—the realm of instinct, primal memory, dissociated experience, and fantasy—he understood himself to have revealed *the ultimate reality of individual life*. The truth of the claim lies in the fact that conscious experience disguises a deeper domain of unconscious forces. Marx had no sense of such a domain, which cannot be located in the Marxist dichotomy of structural social reality and conscious, phenomenal form. But even as a successful therapy proceeds to disclose the various levels of impulse and defense that rest upon each other down to the primary needs and vicissitudes of the individual, it proceeds from the level of superficial bourgeois civility to the depth of irrational, individual bourgeois compulsion. That this "deeper" level is also constructed out of the contradictions of capitalist relations is beyond psychoanalytic understanding. But conversely, the traditional Marxist account never distinguished among *levels of reality within the realm of phenomenal forms,* for it mistakenly identified "phenomenal" with "conscious," a common misconception which it took Freud's discovery to destroy.

When Freud reached the ultimate level of theoretical understanding or therapeutic disclosure, he believed he had traced reality to its root. In fact, he had passed from one stratum of individual psychic existence to another, albeit more profound, dimension. The structural logic of the social world, the system of compulsory and constrictive "domination" which defines the possibility and meaning of human action in capitalism, remained beyond his theoretical awareness. We have already noted in discussing the case of Dora that Freud often registered social facts whose *meaning* he could not integrate into this formal theory. In pursuing individual consciousness to its unconscious lair, Freud could not leave the terrain of the individual. As Marx lacked a theory of the individual unconscious, Freud lacked a theory of the social construction of the individual unconscious. So he was left with no alternative to the reification of bourgeois individualism whose consequences in the unconscious he mistakenly took for the original causes of social life.

The social distinction between appearance and reality is actually threefold, for it requires mediation. Between the social, structural unconscious and individual, phenomenal experience is the realm of the individual repressed unconscious. Marx moved mistakenly from structure to consciousness; his theory lacked critical mediations. Freud moved from individual consciousness to the individual unconscious; his theory lacked a critical foundation.

From Practice to Theory

It is possible to illuminate this procedure by viewing it in a somewhat different light. Let us turn from Freud's theoretical conception to the actual practice of therapy. But now, instead of considering therapeutic practice as the consequence of applying psychoanalytic theory, as one would consider engineering the result of applying physics to practical tasks in the world, let us perform a minor Copernican inversion and begin with the practice of therapy in the world of capitalist social reality. The primary consideration here is the fact that the therapist has no power over any aspect of social reality larger than the voluntary, individual, contractual relationship with his own client. The only "cure" the therapist can effect is one that falls within the parameters of this bourgeois condition. For whereas in other cultures the healer cures through public ceremonies which involve the active participation of the group—usually through the intermediary of powerful incitement, both emotional and physical, to the accompaniment of music and dance, for the purpose of direct catharsis and transformation—therapy in the modern world fits the liberal paradigm of individual transformation, contractually structured, through speech rather than action, for the sake of individual, voluntary self-transformation.

If we follow this "inversion" a step further we soon realize that as much as the cure for a malady follows an understanding of the cause, the cause can only be understood in terms of possible cure. What the therapist cannot alter through his intervention is pragmatically irrelevant as a practical cause of the given pathology. The cause of the psychopathology, then, is only what the individual therapist has the power, personally, to effect. *It is "effective intervention" that retrospectively determines what shall count as a "meaningful" cause of an ailment.* But Freud is only empowered to reach the individual client intrapsychically. He has no power, nor even any conception of the power, to reach any larger social configuration. His activity is confined to such practice as can be stipulated through an individual social contract.

The individualism that permeates the world of Freud's relationship to his client also permeates the basic structures of Freud's theoretical grasp of his relationship to his client. Freud selects out of the entire universe of possible causal determinants only such factors as are susceptible of individual alteration through individual intervention. The larger social causes drop out of sight. So the "social structure" of individual therapy under capitalism determines the possible form of theoretical understanding of the nature of individual pathology.

I would like to explore this issue further by utilizing a concept Levi-Strauss introduced in *Structural Anthropology* during a discussion of shamanism. He describes the ritual employed by the shaman in dealing with a difficult childbirth. "Treatment" is effected through incantations and recitations of "sham battles." Levi-Strauss asks "how specific psychological representations are invoked to combat equally specific physiological disturbances." He answers that the incantation and song serve to unite the mother's physiological reactions—the childbirth, with mythic categories—the mythic struggle over the woman's soul. The myth forms the experience and just so makes it accessible to consciousness.

The same myth forms the social practice of the group:

> The cure will consist of rendering thinkable a situation given first in emotional terms; and to make the mind accept pains the body refuses to tolerate. It is of no importance that the mythology of the shaman does not correspond

to objective reality; the woman in birth believes it and *she is a member of a society that believes it* [emphasis added].⁴

The use of the mythic narrative introduces a "complicated itinerary that is a true mythical anatomy corresponding less to the real structure of the genital organs than to a kind of emotional geography."⁵ But how exactly does the myth form experience and transform a physiological response?

> The relation between microbes and sickness is external to the patient's mind, it is a cause and effect relation; whereas the relation between monsters and sickness is interior to the conscious or unconscious mind itself; it is a relation of symbol to thing symbolized, or . . . of signifier to signified. The shaman furnishes a *language* to the sick person, in which otherwise inexpressible states can be immediately expressed. And it is this passage to verbal expression (which permits, simultaneously, living through in an intelligible 'and ordered form an actual experience which would otherwise be chaotic and ineffable) which induces the release of the physiological process, that is, the reorganization, in a favorable direction, of the sequence of events to which the patient is subjected.⁶

Now the relation of this process to psychoanalysis is obviously called into question and Levi-Strauss makes the following interesting observation:

> When a transference is established, the patient puts words into the mouth of the psychoanalyst by attributing to him alleged feelings and intentions; in the incantations, on the contrary, the shaman speaks for his patient. He questions her and puts into her mouth answers that correspond to the interpretations of her condition that she must come to see through (se penetrer).⁷

I have utilized Levi-Strauss's example to note the similarities and dissimilarities between "primitive" cures and psychoanalysis. The mixture of the two is rather complicated: For on the one hand, psychoanalysis utilizes scientific explanation to frame the process of cure (though it does not present this explanation in the course of the cure) while the shaman uses the myth of demons; analysis is not employed to produce physiological alterations, though working through hysterical symptoms is an obvious exception; the analyst does not literally speak for the patient, though interpretation could be understood as a form of such speech. Of course, it may be said that the primary difference is the fact that the shaman employs myth while the analyst relies on scientifically verifiable explanation. But it is not the truth claim of the myth or explanation as such that I want to note. It is the isomorphism between the symbolic structure of the cure and the social practice of the group that is crucial. The practice of society in which the shaman functions is permeated by the same conceptual structure that is used in the course of the treatment of the pains of childbirth. The myth is socially embedded. But the same situation can be ascribed to the society in which psychoanalysis flourishes.

For while we do not regard ourselves as sharing a common myth, we do in fact function collectively on the basis of a mythology of our own. We share the mythology of privatization; the view that our own demons reside wholly in our individual psyches, that they have no external existence beyond the individual lives in which they bury themselves and continue to live an isolated, underground existence. If primitives are guilty of an error we would categorize as anthropomorphic projection, then we, in turn, are guilty of fetishized individualization. Primitives may ontologize their shared myths, but we desocialize our common oppression. We refract this dehumanization through the prism of capitalist individuation and so experience as private failure and anguish what has real existence beyond each in the collective exploitation of us all. How shall we compare ourselves to the woman whom Levi-Strauss noted as a member of a society that believes its common myth of demons? It cannot be said that we collectively believe the symbolic structure of psychoanalysis. But we do believe collectively in the deepest core of analytic practice—the attribution of pathology and pain to individual forces, technologically conceptualized, arising out of the personal lives of the separate members of society.

The fact is that both "primitives" and "moderns" believe through collective myths. But for the primitive the content of the collective myth is collective, while for us, the content of the collective myth is instrumentally privatized. Everyone tends to believe that he or she is the source of the irrationality and suffering that are pervasive features of our individual lives. This is not the ultimate reality of our world, but it is isomorphic with the atomization which capitalist society imposes upon us as the specific character of its social domination. If we do not suffer the mythology of the primitive, we do suffer the ideology of fetishized individual consciousness, which is the highest form of collective illusion available in a society which through technical domination has reduced nature and human nature to a system of instrumental means to the acquisition to profit and the defense against its incursion.

Therapeutic cures, following the inspiration of psychoanalysis, take place inside the office, inside the therapeutic relationship, inside the psyche. The "outside" is irrelevant or a real hindrance to cure. The form of capitalist relations is the private ownership of commodities and property including one's self, its success and failure. Freudian theory is isomorphic with this private attribution, which, as Marx noted, is rooted in market exchange and forms the judicial foundation and pervasive category of the entire social experience.

If we picture the relation of individual and society through the diagram in Figure 2, we can see that Freud wholly discarded the first

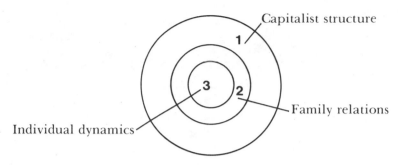

Capitalist structure

1

3 2

Family relations

Individual dynamics

Figure 2

realm—capitalist structure—registered the second—family relations—but interpreted their function in the light of his understanding of the third realm—individual psychodynamics. It is not merely Freud's theory but his therapeutic practice which embodies this individualized vision.

Psychoanalysis dissolves the illusions of individual, conscious experience through a practice that rests on a theory of reified individualism. But this Freudian misunderstanding of the relationship of appearance and reality combines with Freud's specific understanding of demystification to reinforce his conservative stance. Freud's theory is archeological and understands demystification as the uncovering of material already in existence. Of course the cured patient stands in a new relationship to this material, which is simultaneously himself or herself, and in this very important sense therapy creates, and does not merely reproduce, experience. But the creation involves a new relationship to one's previous and persisting primitive existence. And since the state of this existence as well as the tools used to uncover it are formed in the self-understanding of bourgeois practice, the discovery can only reproduce these same bourgeois categories. In other words, the unconscious—which is constructed in capitalist society—is liberated through a technique that is isomorphic with capitalist society. The result cannot be anything other than *capitalist liberation; that is, not liberation from capitalism but liberation from the most dysfunctional disturbances of capitalist society for the sake of its normal pathology.*

Psychoanalysis, and all other systems of therapy that are basically in accord with its individualistic paradigm, is of necessity a conservative social force. The previous analysis makes it possible to understand theoretically as well as impressionalistically why this is so.

It is, I think, a common experience in therapy that clients emerge with approximately the same political dispositions with which they entered. I do not deny the claim of various therapists that particular pathologies of character, when eliminated, also signal a shift in political attitude. Certain dispositions toward sadism, subordination, passivity, and hatred may well be eliminated through successful therapy and mark a change in political orientation. But these symptoms are impediments to the smooth functioning of capitalist domination, which "best" governs through impersonal, bureaucratic technique rather than personal violence or masochism. The therapist who eliminates the varieties of psychopathology that flourish under capitalism simply leaves the client open to the pervasive "normalcy" of capitalist alienation and its fetishism of consciousness. Just as the capitalist system flourishes on the basis of legal equality and representative democracy, so it flourishes equally with a character structure whose sharp, abrasive peculiarities have been worn smooth in the constant pedagogy of homogenous subordination.

The theoretical question to be put to the practice of therapy is this: Does the demystification of false consciousness within the phenomenal realm lead by necessity or general tendency to a demystification of the ideology which masks the essential relations of capitalist exploitation? I believe that the answer is negative for the two reasons previously stated: that the categories of therapy are individualistic and so reproduce the individual structures of capitalist domination, and that the mode of emancipation is archeological, so that the freedom from oppression which is achieved remains limited to freedom from one's own archaic past, not from one's present social configuration. It is even possible to understand why "successful" therapy often produces a cure that seems to replace past rebelliousness, however inchoate, with a contentment that makes further political movement more difficult. For there can be no doubt that the experience of therapeutic transformation is a powerful, positive, and compelling occurrence. To free one's self from past, personal tyrannies, whether this process is deemed politically emancipatory or not, is to experience a profound transformation and the lifting of a cruel and punishing burden. Nobody who has enjoyed such an experience is likely to be unimpressed by its significance, and the sense that emerges from such transcendence often produces the conviction that one has at last achieved full liberation. Those who ridicule therapy in the name of political demands will never convince individuals whose only and every transformation has occurred within parameters of individual therapeutic change.

However, when I am freed from my own repressed unconscious, from my individual neurosis—to the extent that such transformation is possible under the conditions of capitalism—I am still subject to all the overwhelming power and seductiveness of capitalist ideology. It is true that one's understanding is "deepened" through successful therapy, but the term is ambivalent. For having penetrated the surface of bourgeois self-deception does not bring one any closer to the fundamental social structures that have made this self-deception necessary. The "successful" client has, therefore, simultaneously moved beneath the façade of bourgeois false consciousness, and more wholly into the self-mystification of bourgeois ideology.

Liberal analysts seem systematically unwilling or unable to acknowledge this fact. Though many of them would oppose the asocial perspective embedded in this fasionable banality of Roszak—"Alienation . . . is primarily psychic, not sociological. It is not a propriety distinction that exists *between* men . . . but rather a disease that is rooted *inside* all men. The true students of alienation, therefore, are not social scientists, but the psychiatrists."[8]—they do, however, tend to justify their practice in the light of his contention that "revolution which will free us from alienation must be primarily therapeutic in character."[9] Orthodox therapy, that is the sort of therapy practiced by the overwhelming majority of contemporary therapists, is counterrevolutionary. It may clarify and endorse the sentiments toward revolution that already exist latently in the lives of its clients, and it may also increase the power of those already explicitly committed to radical social emancipation. These are certainly progressive transformations and valuable therapeutic byproducts. But they do not constitute the essence of therapeutic practice, for their occurrence is fortuitous and depends on the previous dispositions in their clients which precede, both logically and historically, the influence of therapy itself.

The reason that therapy is conservative is not that a revolutionary client would destroy the society from which the therapist derives privilege, or even less that such a client would undermine the specific status the therapist enjoys. The issue is rather that the categories that define therapeutic practice are bound to the social structure in which they are practiced. Just as the Greeks defined the function of politics as the production of virtuous individuals through their participation in a well-ordered polis, so our society defines the function of therapy, conversely, as the "empowering" of individuals to minimize or overcome individual pain through the techniques of individual transformation. Therapy cannot replace revolution, though, as we shall note, it can participate fruitfully in the slow, patient, laborious development of such a revolutionary practice.

As we observed in the first chapter, while Freud's model of demystification of appearance is archeological, Marx's conception is revolutionary. The society that would nurture luminous consciousness is still to be created. For society does not throw off its mystical, fetishized façade until it has been replaced, through the willed activity of its members, by a form of social life which they collectively order for their well-being and humane gratification. However, there is certainly the appearance of either a vicious circle or infinite regress in this argument; for how can we know how to change our lives if adequate knowledge occurs only after a successful revolution. Of course, the reply experience as well as theory provides is that such transformation is a matter of degree. The fetishism of consciousness gives way slowly and unevenly. Theoretical comprehension of the necessity of exploitation under capitalism and, consequently, of the necessity of a radical rupture to destroy such de-humanization—absolutely essential conditions for successful revolu-tion—gives way to lived conviction in the practice of gradually acquiring social power. In the process, elements of alienation and liberation are likely to be conjoined in peculiar configurations. For the fetishism of consciousness is something like those optical illusions reproduced in psychology textbooks—parallel lines which only appear to converge—which do not yield to the theoretical understanding of their effect. No matter how much one understands of the nature of optics, the physiology of the brain, the tendency toward gestalt the mind imposes on raw perceptual data, the truth is that one continues to be visually deceived. The expectation of throwing off the ideology of social life is not so de-limited, however, for its foundation is the social practice it dialectically reproduces. Eventually, Marx is an empiricist and maintains that one can only come to believe in the power of selftransformation through the activity of transforming ourselves in the world. So a therapy which is to free us from the dead weight of capitalist domination will have to be ingredient in a movement which is engaged in the practice of destroying that alien power and replacing it with a social world which its agents can recognize and embrace as their social creation.

Freud's conception of therapy was bound to be ambivalent in its social practice. For its loyalties were rooted in a model of cathexis and opposed countercathexis which could not abandon either side of the perennial contradiction between individual instinct and social repres-sion. Therefore it is no surprise to learn that Freud has been read from both poles of the opposition. Some have particularly noted the "ethic of honesty,"[10] and the liberation of instinct; the absence of doctrinal *Wel-tanschauung*, the curative power of contentless method—of pure "liberal" negative freedom devoid of value judgment, or the equation of all beliefs in so far as their "validity" is concerned; the sanction for the violence of war as a counter to the dead growth of hypocritical culture; the envy of the lower, laboring classes with their ease of instinctual gratification which permits avoidance of the exhausting domination of civilized re-pression; the unmasking of morality understood as a pathological reac-tion formation to the demands of libidinal desire. But Freud is equally the advocate of renunciation; the "secular spiritual guide"; the moralist dedicated to rational self-mastery; the demystifier of infantile illusions of erotic happiness; the opponent, in manner and doctrine, of barbarism and the archtypical defender of the necessity of repression; the perfect representative of the "cultured" bourgeoisie's burden of cultural re-finement. Of course, Freud is to be located in both perspectives:

> Psychoanalysis has never said a word in favour of unfettering instincts that would injure our community.[11]

> To believe that psychoanalysis seeks a cure for neurotic disorders by giving a free reign to sexuality is a serious misunderstanding which can only be jus-tified by ignorance. The making conscious of repressed sexual desires in analysis makes it possible, on the contrary, to obtain a mastery over them which the previous repression had been unable to achieve.[12]

> Certain instinctual impulses, with whose suppressions society has gone too far, should be permitted a greater amount of satisfaction; in the case of certain others the inefficient method of suppressing them by means of re-pression should be replaced by a beter and securer procedure.[13]

Freud stands for a more humane and efficient suppression of the instincts. The two notions are intimately linked and raise the question of the nature of the system on whose behalf this more prudential com-promise is to be exercised. The ideal of rational self-mastery is formed within the parameters of capitalist society and its claim to legitimacy is rarely questioned.[14] In so defining the goal of therapy as rational "sup-pression" rather than unconscious "repression" Freud, inadvertently but quite perfectly, fits the requirements of capitalist domination. For the uniqueness of capitalist exploitation lies neither in the fact that individu-als are dominated by the interests of ruling class—this condition is histor-ically common; nor in the fact that the oppressed are deputized as their own oppressors—for this is also commonplace. Capitalism is unique in promoting the illusion of equality between oppressor and oppressed, a conviction which is a conerstone of its cultural hegemony.

Since liberal ideology insists on the equal value of all individuals it is required to contend that such disparities of power as exist have been freely chosen by all the participants in the social contract. The rationali-zation for inequality in the political realm is the theory of freely chosen "representative" government, while the underlying disparity of eco-nomic power is held to derive from the better use some have made of their initially equal opportunities. Those who are "exploited" or "gov-erned" are induced to believe that they have willingly concurred in the constitution of their society because it supports their own self-interest, rationally considered. It is obvious that "conscious suppression" is the appropriate mode of psychological self-control which corresponds to economic and political illusions of freedom, and that psychotherapy is the perfect internal technology for encouraging and administering this conviction.

Schatzman's perforation of Freud's account of Schreber brings the issue clearly to light. What is unique in the father's discipline of his son is neither its harshness nor its pedagogical foundation. We approach the heart of Schreber's distinct domination when we note that it is not enough that the young Schreber do something or refrain from doing it; he must also do it for the right reason. But this does not differentiate Schreber's pedagogy from that of various Christian sects that were equally harsh, doctrinal, and concerned with internal control. It is the thoroughness of Schreber's discipline combined with the insistence that the son's acts follow freely from his own will that marks its distinctiness.

> Now, the ways and means of developing and consolidating moral will power and character do not need to be sought.... The most generally necessary condition for the attainment of this goal is the *unconditional obedience* of the child.[15]

And on the very same page of Schreber's pedagogic manual:

> If the child had been led in the first stage of development [before one year old] along the path toward habituation to unconscious obedience, so now [after one] it is timely and indispensable for the attainment of the noble aim of upbringing, that this habit should be *gradually raised to an act of free will*, that obedience is conscious. The child should be *trained . . . to noble independence and full strength of his own will* [emphasis added].[16]

It is the conjunction of "unconditional obedience" and "noble independence" that sets this particular instance of parental power aside from other historical modes. We are witness to the developing paradigm of liberal authority, a system in which subordinates must be seen, and must see themselves, as freely choosing their subordination—understood as self-determination. The Schreber case illustrates a point Marx made with great insistence in regard to economic ideology—that the mystification produced by capitalist culture is more difficult to detect than any others that have previously existed.

It is also interesting to observe that the senior Schreber is concerned with the stages of the child's life and the critical mode of intervention "appropriate" to each phase of development. Freud elaborated just such intuitive reflections, as he was to provide the developed technique (internal technology) for the comprehension and control of subjective, psychological nature. The more capitalism required the total fetishism of humanity, a necessity produced by the manner in which capitalism split the public and private realms and made the latter the arena of privatized selfhood and commoditized consumption, the more it required some apparatus to organize the internal realm and "cure" its most obvious pathologies. Psychoanalytic theory provided the cornerstone for this construction.

But it now becomes crucial to ask on those behalf the technique was to be employed. Of course, the liberal self-understanding of the new practice was to hold it neutral, and regard it as a device designed simply to enlarge the client's alternatives and thereby enhance the possibility of self-determination. We have already noted that neither Freudian theory nor its practice can possibly be regarded as a neutral construction. The very notion of enlarging choice is itself a choice of one particular goal over various possible alternatives. The freedom that the Christian craved, for instance, was no such enlargement, but precisely the contraction of choice to the point of total and unwavering commitment to God.

We have noted, too, that Freud's deepest conception of human existence and of the service of therapy was contrapuntal: a view of contradictions which required compromise between instinct and repression and between the opposing instincts themselves. Rational "suppression" of desire provided both (a) individual mastery and a moderate expectation of the avoidance of suffering and (b) communal security. In the case of therapy, then, as in Schreber's adumbration of the liberal paradigm, individual will, freed of its external, unconscious domination, freely chooses a reasonable form of subordination to authority. The fact that Freud supported parental, particularly patriarchal authority in particular therapeutic encounters[17] follows from his deeper view of the necessity of "legitimately" constituted political rule, i.e., of not "injuring our community." It is provocative to consider the following passage on transference-love and to generalize it to the basic relationship between the therapist and client:

> And yet the analyst is absolutely debarred from giving way. However highly he may prize love, he must prize even more highly the opportunity to help his patient over a decisive moment in her life. She has to give up a *gratification which lies to hand but is not sanctioned by the world she lives in,* in *favour of a distant and perhaps altogether doubtful one,* which is, however, *socially and psychologically unimpeachable.* To achieve this mastery of herself she *has to be taken through* the primordial era of her mental development and in this way reach that greater freedom within the mind which distinguishes conscious mental activity—in the systematic sense—from unconscious [emphasis added].[18]

Giving up an immediate, socially unsanctioned gratification for a doubtful, future gratification is essential to Freud's view of the nature and task of human existence. What is, perhaps, even more significant about this passage is the role afforded to society in determining appropriate criteria of acceptable gratification, and the role afforded the therapist in representing and facilitating this larger social function. To say that the "patient" has to be taken from her primordial unconscious to freedom of conscious activity means that the therapist must not only accompany her on this journey but, even more, motivate the passage and interpret the significance of the transformation. For as in the case of the shaman to whom Levi-Strauss referred, it is not rational explanation that affects the cure but identification with a figure who represents the mastery of the skill that is both socially sanctioned and definitive of the nature and purpose of individual life.

As we noted in our previous discussion of Dora, the analyst is charged to enhance the client's freedom without insisting on a particular content, to act, in other words, as a "secular spiritual guide" of process rather than substance. For the transference put "the analyst in the place of" the client's father or mother. So reconstituted, the new superego can "correct" the mistakes of the parents and ally itself with the subject's autonomy. The liberal conception of freedom as choice among "alternatives" and the dilemma of liberal pedagogy—influence for the sake of self-determination—are both implicit in Freud's observation:

> The eventual *independence* of the patient is our ultimate object when we use *suggestion* to bring him to carry out a mental operation that will necessarily result in a lasting improvement in his mental condition [emphasis added].[19]

What is naïvely "suggested" in Freud's account is that the suggestion which encourages independence does not contribute to the formation of its structure and the nature of its outcome.

Identification with "prevailing" figures is a mode of enhancing the domination of prevailing power. But it is, of course, simultaneously a mode of increasing the freedom of the client as that freedom is defined within the parameters of society as presently constituted. That is why successful, orthodox therapy cannot affect political change. For the Freudian ideal of freeing the individual from the crippling domination of the past for the sake of a new capacity to determine one's own nature simply ignores the enormous, pervasive influence of social domination and ideology in determining both the form and content of current choice. While in the foundation of capitalist society momentous decisions are made by corporate–bureaucratic institutions of inordinate, irresponsible, and insulated power, the self-pretense of bourgeois ideology misconceives itself in the illusion of choice and a multitude of reasonable alternatives. The more we are freed from past terrors and archaic fantasies, the more we become susceptible to the subordination which obtains beneath the façade of liberal "self-determination." The growing dominance of the "rational" ego permits the increased intrusion of irrational social reality. For it is the ego that transmits the social world, and analysis is enjoined not to advise, but merely to act as mirror to the client's presentation. The more the "Freudian unconscious" recedes, the more the structural unconscious advances.

Of all healing modalities, psychoanalysis is in fact the least able to justify itself as a guide to the "secular spiritually perplexed." For its definition of morality as reaction formation leaves it peculiarly devoid of any foundation for the direction of purpose and ideal. We come back to the point we left suspended at the end of Chapter 6—the conflicting analytic theories of the ego as either contentless or as the highest psychic function. The mediating, "reality" ego has no demands of its own; it merely compromises the demands of reality and the drives. The "defense" ego has goals of its own to which reality and the drives must yield. Yet, we note once again how these perspectives converge. For strengthening the reality ego strengthens its ability to integrate the drives, which have been socially constituted, with social reality, the social constitutor. And strengthening the defense ego facilitates the same purpose. The rational, "conflict-free" reality ego can be viewed as autonomous only to the extent that the powers it serves are systematically exempt from critical scrutiny. The ego devoid of its own content is filled with the alien matter of surrounding destructiveness. The ascent from the primordial unconscious to free consciousness would suggest a journey of growing emancipation if only one could conceive the desirable power to be exercised through this difficult attainment. But nothing beckons except the vacuity of more "efficient methods of suppression."

The social conservatism of analytically modelled therapy has nothing to do with the decency and little to do with the political perspective of the therapist.[20] It is the form of the therapeutic mode that determines its political function. And the form remains verbal, archeological, self-reflective, ironic, contemplative, and, above all, privatized. The fact that the analyst with whom the client identifies is likely to be male, affluent, liberal, tolerant, and socially respectable is not irrelevant to the content of transference and cure. But it is not the crucial factor. Were the analyst *personally* revolutionary it would matter very little. Not merely because the analyst is enjoined from introducing political judgment into the therapy but for the more fundamental reason that at the present moment no appropriate social context exists for the introduction of such reflection or inducement. The recreation of the self which is the ideal of revolutionary "therapy" would appear possible only in the context of a significant revolutionary movement.[21]

Collective Transference

In linking emancipatory therapy to a viable socialist political movement I do not intend to merely repeat the old Marxist liturgy, fixated at the stage of "dominant base and superficial superstructure." I agree with Gramsci that cultural change must precede a successful revolution rather than follow as a reflex. But there is all the difference between the completion of a revolutionary movement and its inception. A therapy that hopes to liberate men and women from past tyrannies does not require the completion of a successful political movement, but it does require a movement in progress. There are two fundamental aspects of this consideration: First, the experience of alienation, which lies at the heart of the formation of selfhood under capitalism, is a social fact that can only be destroyed and replaced by another social fact—a mass, collective, democratic, political movement whose aim is the equalization of humane power. The sense of reification that pervades our lives is not the result of media indoctrination; it is a real, obdurate, socially constituted presence. The long, slow, downward entropic pull of social anomie and unreason reverberates through our archaic past and our present reality. It is what Freud, in his *Carmen* letter, noted as bourgeois exhaustion, and what the current "growth movement," like Canute at the edge of the wild sea, vainly imploring, frantically demanding, laughingly "enhances" itself to deny. The "sensitivity," "aliveness," "communication," and "fulfillment" which are the slogans of this new "failure of nerve" are poignant fantasies in an age of "mechanical reproduction." And yet, these are voids that speak legitimately out of horror with the present and from an unremitting desire for a new being. Just as the multitude of religions that sprang up with the fall of Rome not only spoke to a displaced human hope, but nurtured the fleeting instances of classless, nonexploitative love, so, too, the new therapy movement responds to the pulse of aspiring humanity where it finds it. No ideology can flourish on mere promise; some response to present anguish and gratification of desire are also requisite.

But the incipient budding of this submerged humanity is reminiscent of desert flowers—their presence specks an otherwise barren landscape which they are incapable, ever, of making full with their bloom. The existence and feeling of alienation can only be broken through the act of freedom. The conviction of agency, wholeness, and graceful power cannot be sustained in the unbiquitious presence of social subordination. It is only through a movement of growing democratic change that the sense of personal despair can be challenged, distanced, and dissolved. Even the very fragile instances of the new left and the woman's movement point in this direction. Coming to believe that our powerlessness is social requires the *lived* conviction that our power is social. It is power than vanquishes powerlessness and the sense of despair. Socialism is the collective, practical, engaged recognition of this fact. However much such a movement is rightly motivated by responsibility for the world's oppressed and the hatred for injustice, its daily life can only be sustained by the love of friends and unseen comrades, and the love for one's self as a member of this new constituency.

As significant change in traditional analysis is understood to depend upon personal identification with the therapist[22] so, I am suggesting by analogy, social transformation depends upon our identification with an emerging, collective social subject. Of course, we do not pass from being individual to social, because our "individuality" is itself a social fact. But it is possible to conceive of moving from a situation in which the social order is so imposed upon us as to define us as insular antagonists to another in which we seize control of our social nature and direct it for our chosen purposes. The dialectic of need and object suggests that a new selfhood requires a new object. But as self and other are reciprocally determined, the emergence of selfhood as subject requires that this object be as fully subject as ourselves. Mead noted that the development of self-consciousness required our being made the referent of other selves. In imitating the other's recognition of me as self, I am initiated into self-consciousness. But Mead did not sufficiently stress the converse of his basic insight—that I must recognize that those who recognize me as human are themselves human. If my self-conscious humanity depends on my being so located by another, then I must recognize in the other a being with the capacity to identify me as human. My selfhood lives in the reciprocal recognition of myself and the other as self. But the fuller, more sensitive, more favorable and concerned the recognition I receive, the more I can grasp myself as valuable in an alliance with other significant human beings. That is why collective engagement in political democracy is a prerequisite for the development of a genuinely constituted personal existence. Mead's insight into the reciprocity of selfhood needs to be realized through political transformation.

We can also link this point to our previous critique of the concept of internalization. For the term now takes on its appropriate dual meaning under capitalism; as the introduction of the identity of the parent into the being of the child; and as the mode through which the public and private realms are separated from each other in accordance with the needs of capitalist fragmentation. As an "ideal type" we can speculate that to internalize the father is to identify the child with the parent as socially competitive and "separate" so that the child is simultaneously constructed as identical and different from the parent—since the parent's identity is itself marked by its isolation from others. Traditionally, the father transmits the public realm as atomistic; the child becomes *identical as distinct*. The internalization of the mother brings to the child the identity of nurturance, merging, and release in the context of a nuclear family, so that such mutuality as is possible is itself framed in isolation from the area of public activity and is again marked by its internal isolation.

The term "internalization" is derived from the public/private dualism of capitalist existence. "Identification" is the more appropriate term to distinguish the conditions of personal existence under socialism. It is the absence of such a collective selfhood that throws the theory of the Frankfurt school and of writers like Lasch back into the paradox of extolling the authority of the bourgeois father as the necessary defense against the intrusion of capitalist society. The dominance of father, it is maintained, can only be vanquished through the internalization of the father's power.[23] But the father for whom this theory nostaligically longs as the defense against capitalist encroachment was, in fact, the necessary mediation of capitalist domination at the moment of its earlier market stage. The insulating father of Lasch and Adorno provided that set of motives and skills required by capitalism before its atomism fully succumbed to corporate administration. The contrast, therefore, is not between previous personal autonomy and present mass domination, but between two stages of domination, each of which was functionally required by the particular stage of capitalist accumulation. It is not the case that character was once based on identification with the father but is now dominated by mass culture instead. What is true is that the father through whom one's identity is partially constituted has changed from the individual of handicrafts, small market competition, individualized work, and characterological hoarding to the father of massive corporate–bureaucratic domination. And children suffer a crisis of identity not because they are devoid of "internal representations," or split between good and bad "objects" but because the old mode of social control and the new are both oppressive and repressive, and, to exacerbate the difficulty, are in contradiction.

Capitalism, at the stage of comparative scarcity and the priority of material accumulation, required the control of individual life through the subordination of gratification to restraint.[24] Energy was both retained and released in the service of work discipline, hygienic leisure, and the needs of family reproduction. But the present epoch tends to reverse the priority and place restraint in the service of gratification; for the first time in history production becomes equally dependent upon consumption. From a temporary respite from the rigors of labor, consumptive gratification becomes a prime object of capitalist accumulation, social construction, and individual self-definition. Even the modes of time begin to change; the older conception of temporal order as linear, instrumental, causal, and expedient begins to give way to the immediate, ecstatic, discontinuous mode of continually dissolving and reappearing moments. But the specter of total abandonment of the self to release and pleasure, which is often raised as the logical outcome of this development, is not a possibility. First, because capitalism requires for its social motive that desire overreach available satisfaction. Second, because the structure of class domination ensures that poverty remain as persistent as wealth, particularly at this moment of world historical change. Third, because gratification depends logically on the reporduction of the desire whose release is experienced as gratifying. And finally, because consumption continues to depend upon production, which is itself bound to an order of discipline.

What is occurring at the present moment, as in the relationship between contemporary adolescents and their parents, for example, is the conflictual struggle over the priority of these modes. The past appears as an archaic and punitive irrelevance to the young, while the present beckons as an attractively seductive but portentious vacuum to those who were formed in the previous stage of discipline. But the gratifications that are so compelling to adolescence are surreptitiously experienced as exhausting, an awareness which the absence of alternatives forces out of explicit attention. The difficulty is magnified by the fact that the obsolescence of replaceable experience threatens to dissolve the self, which is therefore drawn back into an old order which is without authority. For the creation of a new society in which needs are nurtured as a fulfillment of the self remains a task.

In such an order one can envision not only a transformation of self and society but of the lived meaning of time. For now, the analytic paradigm of the past determining the future is given its power through the fact that the establishment of character in childhood is reinforced by the remaining social institutions in which the person is formed. The past dominates because it is the past that is serviceable to the demands of the present. If one conceives of radically transforming the future, the past changes, too. Not the sheer facticity of the past, which is as real and independent as the external world, but the *meaning* of the past, which is always constructed in terms of prospects for the future that presently obtain. The more the future is opened, the more the past changes from an overpowering determination to a conditional influence. The past possesses predominant power so long as we are powerless to change our present subordination. And, circularly, the psychoanalytic view of the self as constituted by the internalization of the past reifies the stagnation of the present through the conception of its inalterability.

The lived sense of powerlessness reflects and reifies real powerlessness.[25] Its actuality derives from capitalist atomism and the estrangement of public from personal existence. Its mystification derives from the fetishism of belief which invests facts with the power of inevitability. Its destruction requires the making of a contrary reality. "The call to abandon their illusions about their condition is a *call to abandon a condition which requires illusion.*"[26] In a time of such fragmented individuality, however, even one's fantasies tend to be private and personal. "The neurosis takes, in our time, the place of the cloister."[27] The pervasive subjectification of social life is, of course, dialectically related to the growth of therapy. The rootless isolation of individual life under capitalism was the basic fact that called forth therapy as a cure and which the therapeutic mode of privatization reciprocally encouraged as a social pathology. But there is a potentially emancipatory side to this development, which represents the second link between therapy and political development. For it is not only the case that social change is crucial to the development of a viable, progressive therapy; it is equally true that therapeutic awareness can play a very important role in the development of an emancipatory politics.

The reason for this positive side of the dialectic is not hard to state. Therapeutic awareness, by which I mean not merely distinct therapeutic practice but the generalized understanding of the relationship between conscious experience and the dynamic unconscious, is even in its present mystified form, conversant with the manifestations of capitalist estrangement. It is one of the striking facts about the practice of therapy that the smooth, comfortable façade of everyday life so quickly and wholly collapses to reveal another reality beneath the surface. Therapists may bring to their work a largely privatized misconception of the causes and possible cures of this anguish, but its sheer presence is difficult to ignore. The articulation of such dispersed and repressed suffering is a potentially critical tool in the development of a movement for critical social change. Therapeutic awareness is a lever that can dislodge the complacency that masks defeated hope. It makes possible an entry into the lives of men and women under capitalism which, if properly interpreted and acted upon, can enhance the awareness of new possibilities of personal–social existence. For behind every defeat of the self in repression is some strangled longing. A movement that understands the need for sensitivity to this underside of existence can both articulate the aborted desire and point politically to an appropriate social context for its realization.

In fact, these are two sides of the same prospect. For as we previously noted the theoretical dialectic of need and object, we have now to draw the practical conclusion that individuals can recognize and accept their lack of fulfillment to the extent that their nascent desire has at least the possibility of realization in practice.

For just as the repressed unconscious originates in the denial of desire already formed, so the structural unconscious, while predicated upon repression, also depends for its reproduction on the fact that the personal longings that arise under capitalism have no adequate object within the capitalist structure: That is, the systematic absence of comprehension arises from the absence of that which needs to be comprehended. Just as capitalism produces technical skills and powers it cannot direct toward a humane end, so it continually elicits aspirations that are yet without an appropriate terminus for their movement. The chaos of present desire arises not only from the fact that desire as formed within capitalism is fragmentary, dislocated, and contradictory, but from the more positive fact that new movements which are generated out of capitalism but which transcend its logic are as yet without proper ends or constituted goals of action.

For such ends are themselves dependent on a structure of social relations yet to be realized. The slow, piecemeal, local development of institutions that counter the demands of capitalist reproduction—new collectivities of culture, economics, politics, and social reproduction—are not immediately important because they threaten to overthrow capitalist power. Their vital and irreplaceable role lies in the fact that they are the arenas in which new desire, new longing, and new hope are permitted articulation and satisfaction—to an extent corresponding with their political limits. Of course, these modest rebellions must coalesce and constitute themselves as sufficiently powerful to challenge and over-throw the existing structure of capitalist domination. For not only are these countermovements too limited to remake very much of the social world; they are in constant danger of being destroyed both by the exhaustion of their own energy in the continual counter to a persistent and seemingly permanent tyranny and by their literal destruction at the hands of the state.

Certainly this is a period of despair. Yet as such, it is the *opposite* of acceptance. The contradictions in capitalist social life are inseparable from the erosion of conviction and its replacement by fearful disquiet. But as capitalism creates its own anguish, it also creates the forms of sensitivity that are potentially necessary for its transcendence. It is in this sense that mankind only takes up such problems as it can solve. Only that is termed as a "problem" the resolution of which is at least adumbrated as lying within human reconstruction. At first, the knowledge of sheer failure is stronger than any awareness of alternatives. One knows that something is wrong, and even vaguely how it is wrong, before one knows how to set it right. The realization of this latter form of knowledge depends upon practical inventions, political reconstruction, in short, on a movement toward the reconstruction of social life.

Let me offer an example from some recent and still vivid personal experience. For the past several years I have supervised community therapists and employment counselors who were themselves ministering to the unemployed. That experience forced me into more direct contact with the pain, humiliation, and depression that ravage the unemployed. But of course, that is what we would expect in a society in which well-being, dignity, and even identity are predicated upon the ability to locate one's self in the social hierarchy of prestigious work and consumption. What I was unprepared for, in fact, though it is theoretically well known,[28] is the magnification of this original distress produced by the belief of the unemployed that their "failure" is due to their personal incompetence, stupidity, or lack of will. It has been noted that while we have the term "paranoia" to indicate delusional belief in the malicious conspiracy of others, we have no term to locate an inability recognize the existence of either structural evil or actual conspiracies where they in fact exist. There is no surprise in this, of course, since such lack of awareness is ingredient in the structure of capitalist ideology and thereby defines the normal form of pathology that is endemic to the system.

It is true that some individuals are less competent, intelligent, and motivated than others, and that these conditions are somehow related to the incidence of their unemployment. But these characteristics are not personal inventions; they are themselves produced by the division of labor, class, sex, and racial identity as these categories are structured in capitalist society. Furthermore, even the maldistribution of such personal dispositions is not a relevant account of unemployment, as witnessed by the fact that unemployment rates vary in accordance with features of social life that clearly cannot be attributed to the rise and fall of personal character traits. So, during the Second World War unemployment all but vanished. The basic reason was that jobs were available at wage rates which made them acceptable. But the availability of work depends upon macroeconomic factors—monopoly profit maximization, investment potentialities, currency fluctuation, international competition, the search for cheap labor and foreign markets, etc., which have little to do with personality characteristics. These are changes that emenate from the bowels of the capitalist system; not from the vicissitudes of instincts, but from the transmogrifications of capitalist accumulation.

However, those who suffer most the results of capitalist irrationality take its pathology upon themselves. They deny, stigmatize, berate, and punish themselves for what they believe to have been their "fault." If only they had worked harder, stayed in school longer, been more accommodating to their superiors, showed more dedication and zeal—"this would not have happened." Even those with considerable sophistication and awareness of the economic realities of social life—unemployed aerospace engineers, for example—are as subject to self-scorn as those with little such understanding; at times, they seem even more self-punitive. Perhaps, on second thought, this is not so surprising either, for those who have advanced furthest have had to accept more of the structure of capitalist reality as the price of the journey, and they have, up until the moment of their fall, been most sustained by common beliefs in the rewards of hard work and diligent corporate loyalty.

These men and women do not see anything of themselves in the laws of the social world which disposses them. It is all well and good to accept necessity when it is your ally, but when it is systematically destroying your hope and life its effect is bewilderment, self-hatred, and despair. Over and over, the paradigmatic form of late capitalist freedom asserts itself: Accept the evil of this social world and its predominant power over my life and accommodate to the fact of my helplessness; or ascribe real choice and opportunity to this society and accept personal responsibility for my failure. The growing tendency in liberalism is the provision of the freedom to decide upon which horn of the dilemma one chooses to be impaled. The grotesque comic litany of the contemporary therapy movement—that one is individually responsible for one's own life—is largely a counterphobic reaction to the growing awareness of this contradiction, to the vacuity of available freedom. It is an incantation that serves both as an artificial stimulus against depression and a narcotic against the failure of disguise.

Now, the reflections I am presenting here were often more or less agreed to by the counselors and therapists with whom I worked. I was therefore all the more surprised to realize that "social health workers" were as subject to the pathologies of self-blame as their designated clients. For as the unemployed take the failures of capitalism upon themselves, their "mentors" are similarly forced to assume the burden of personal failure which afflicts their "cases." The lack of steady improvement in clients is taken as a sign of the failure of the counselor or the therapist to change or cure what needs to be altered. For as the unemployed cannot change their lives, so those who minister to the unemployed cannot change the objective conditions that render unemployment necessary. Therefore, since they also accept the conviction of personal responsibility, they are forced to personalize their own failure to affect the lives of those they are charged to help. So, they often believe, if only they were more competent, sensitive, or dedicated they would be able to slice through the personal failure and sufferings of their clients and provide some relief, or conversely, and simultaneously, they come to blame the victims for their failures, and attribute the cause of their misery to a willful stubbornness or self-indulgent unwillingness to work. So the blame is laid to some combination of the corruption of the welfare state, oral character structure or defiance, and a personal choice to use these conditions for personal gain. "If 100 million other people have managed, why can't you find a job?" However, this is less a question than an accusation.

It is not difficult to understand why so little discussion goes on among health workers in public institutions. Each is afraid to reveal his or her incompetence and afraid to discover the miraculous success being enjoyed by colleagues. The social caretakers can therefore be seen to be suffering from the same pathology of self-blame that affects their clients. For in fact, both groups are afflicted by a similar social powerlessness and despair. Therapists are, however, more identified with the values of the system and more practiced and skillful in dissociation and rationalization. These are characteristics that make it difficult for them to understand that their situation requires common cause with those whom they are dedicated to support. The exhaustion and despondency that afflicts all varieties of social worker is testimony to the recognized impossibility of carrying out a task that is structurally contradictory. One cannot rehabilitate lives in a social structure that is directed to their dehumanization. The irrationalities of work and worklessness cannot be solved in a capitalist society. Both conditions are oppressive and create their own failures and illness. The way out of the dilemma is only possible through a defeat of the system which makes it necessary.[29]

This is not the place to argue the fundamental irrationality of work and its rewards under capitalism. Most workers have some understanding of the loss of their lives in work and a vague awareness that this depletion of their selves permeates the remainder of their existence. The ideological apparatus which guards capitalist domination is not a perfectly structured tool. It is fashioned out of too massive a set of contradictions to stand unsuspected, unchallenged, and wholly comprehended. It can hardly be otherwise in a system whose highest ideal—the dignity of the individual—can only be realized (in both senses of the term) through the possession of economic power, which is necessarily withheld from the greatest majority of the population.

The structure of economic power renders individuals powerless, whether in work or worklessness. There simply is no solution within capitalism to these massive sufferings that individuals undergo through their involvement in capitalist institutions. Not all the counterculture (the counter of a nonculture remains a nonculture), religious transcendence, or individual enlightenment through physical and therapeutic means will reclaim the social world and the loss of such selfhood which needs nurturing there. The stimulation and marketing of private eschatology provides a new cottage industry in a period of high unemployment, but it is a cure that only exacerbates the illness.[30] For personal growth, intimacy, love, and spontaneity as popularly pursued are, at best, increasingly fragile outposts. Therapists, who so well know the fetishism of shoes and gloves, seem unwilling to explore the ultimate fetishism of partial social relations and individual isolation. In a society that separates public production from private consumption, there is considerable poignancy in the efforts of individuals to reverse this estrangement by claiming the right to the production of their very selves.

> This notion of oneself as a kind of continuing career-something to work at, work on, "make an effort" for and subject to an hour a day of emotional Nautilus training all in the interest not of attaining grace but improving one's "relationships"—is fairly recent in the world.[31]

The self has always been the ultimate career under capitalism, but in earlier stages the impression held that one achieved one's ambitions and definition through the mastery of the world. But the prospect of such development has dimmed and the self is forced more into the exhausting role of simultaneously producing and consuming its own identity.

For all the recent writing on narcissism (so privatized in its own conception), nothing can match Buber's insight into the pathology of this reversal:

> The kingdom of the lame-winged Eros is a world of mirrors and mirrorings.
> The Eros of dialogue has the simplicity of fullness; the Eros of monologue is manifold. Many years I have wandered through the land of men, and have not yet reached an end of studying the varieties of the "erotic man" (as the vassal of the broken-winged one at times describes himself). There a lover stamps around and is in love only with his passion. There one is wearing his differentiated feelings like medal-ribbons. There one is enjoying the adventures of his own fascinating effect. There one is gazing enraptured at the spectacle of his own supposed surrender. There one is collecting excitement. There one is displaying his "power." There one is preening himself with borrowed vitality. There one is delighting to exist simultaneously as himself and as an idol very unlike himself. There one is warming himself at the blaze of what has fallen to his lot. There one is experimenting. And so on and on—all the manifold monologists with their mirrors, in the apartment of the most intimate dialogue![32]

The forms of dialogue or monologue are the forms of the social world. Therapeutic awareness—the recognition of the unconscious dynamics behind lived experience—is an essential ingredient in the world of advanced capitalism. Like capitalist production, it both supports the system of its origin and points beyond itself. No matter how fully one excavates the repressed unconscious, the external world of exploitation, fragmentation, and purposelessness continues to reproduce itself. The capitalist system can produce pathology more quickly and profoundly than any exercise in therapy can ameliorate, let alone cure it. Just as the slogans of liberal ideology—dignity, freedom, and equality—are the cutting edge of a radical critique and rebellion against the perversity of actual power, so the self-proclaimed ideal of therapy—the empowering of clients to choose their own lives—must be seen not merely for the absurdity it represents in the current capitalist order but for the ideal hope and responsibility it imposes to change the world. The whole spectrum of human engineering from social work through institutional treatment to private therapy is charged, in its obligation to further the health of its clients-patients, with the radical transformation of society. Nor is there a more fruitful point of political intervention, for here suffering is the presented symptom and pointing to the social conditions of its origin is the only ultimate remedy.

Capitalism encourages the development of needs it cannot satisfy—not only for the formal values of justice and equality but for the substantive ends of love, creation, grace, and recognition. These alternatives are not merely conceptual possibilities; they are potentialities adumbrated in the persistent lived sense all of us vaguely know, of a life far richer and more humane than our own. The material motivations of capitalism have always been presented as a means to ultimately spiritual ends— liberty, equality, and fraternity in their diverse forms. And as the materiality of capitalist production has expanded, the horizon of personal gratification has intensified. The present therapy movement stands looking back at the capitalist world with desire for a new life, and forward toward ends that are barely articulated. So the past continues to exercise its power even in those tendencies that would oppose it.

There is, of course, no historical surprise in the fact that the early stages of developing movements are burdened with the form of the past. So, to revert to my previous example, the current solution to unemployment is an incoherent compound of welfare reform, empty advocacy of full employment, denigration of the unemployed and general apathy. These are the alternatives which are *object*ified within the structure of capitalism—that is, objective institutions provide the context for these actions and sentiments. But what begins to emerge slowly, haltingly behind the form of capitalist wage labor is the possibility of *expanding* the realm of *unemployment* as *employment* is defined with capitalism. For employment, wage labor for pecuniary advantage, is a capitalist need. It is neither universal nor beneficial. Beyond it is the human capacity for creative self-realization, a potential need that cannot be given an object for its articulation within capitalism for the simple reason that capitalism has no other procedure for distributing social wealth than individual ownership of property or work.

In the short run, work and the structure of needs in which it is embodied will continue to dominate policy. But both the exhausting debasement of capitalist labor and the increasingly punitive structure of capitalism distribution can be forced to a crisis. For the growth of capitalist technology intensifies the dehumanization of the work process and more thoroughly undermines the system of values upon which it depends. There is an implicit social pedagogy, always in operation, which can be seized upon for the purpose of confronting and destroying this social order. What the majority knows but does not sufficiently know that it knows is that life under capitalism is truncated and grievous. The self-consciousness of this realization is blocked to a considerable extent by the structural and institutional production of false consciousness. A political movement that has absorbed and transcended the insight of therapeutic consciousness can articulate radical needs for radical objects—for structures and relations whose compelling necessity is a counter to such mystification as is generated by prevailing power.

In this society most men and women still lead lives of quiet desperation. If Thoreau's insight needs to be recast it is only because it implies that one knows perfectly well, but has chosen not to speak. This is rather an age of muted desperation, where the voice of rebellion speaks obliquely, often in grotesque cries and pleadings. It is when the perimeter dissolves that the center will not hold. The loss of social cohesion is the loss of the self. On the one side society confronts us as an external and malignant fact; or what is the same thing, others present themselves primarily in their otherness. Conversely, we live individually at a distance from the world of human nurturing and from ourselves; we are so free of everything but ourselves that we are emptied out. Each side of this toxic polarity splits again: The world appears as an alien constriction or irrelevant and we seem to ourselves bound by our own oppressive nature or wholly open to our willed remaking. Nothing desirable is possible; nothing possible is desirable. The society in which we have been formed engenders aspirations it must defeat, longings almost inarticulate, hopes it must leave festering. It is not possible to say whether we will succeed in creating a world adequate to ourselves. But it is possible to say that this society will not succeed in gratifying the needs it has itself brought into existence. However strangled in its self-reflection, the desire for a world of communal recognition is ineradicable. Despair toward future change cannot be viewed as a logical deduction from the "facts"; it is, rather, compliance in apathy, a self-exacerbating will to will-lesness. The seclusive interiorization of the self, flooded by its own subjectivity, may yet provide the soil for growth in the world. But the cunning of history is a human achievement. And while the hand that inflicts the would may well be the hand that heals it, it must wield a different instrument and, in the line of its motion, embody a new social gesture.

Notes

Introduction

1. Karl Marx, *Capital* (New York: Modern Library, 1906), p. 809.
2. The phrase is in Engels's "Socialism, Utopian and Scientific," in Lewis S. Feuer, ed., *Marx and Engels: Basic Writings on Politics and Philosophy* (Garden City, N.Y.: Anchor Books, 1959), p. 109.
3. Paul Baran, "Crisis of Marxism," *Monthly Review*, October 1958, p. 233.
4. Ibid.
5. Ibid.
6. Alvin W. Gouldner, *The Coming Crisis of Western Sociology* (New York: Basic Books, 1970), p. 52.
7. Adam Smith, *The Wealth of Nations* (New York: Modern Library, 1937), p. 423.
8. David Ricardo, *Principles of Political Economy and Taxation* (New York: Everyman's Library, 1926), p. 383.
9. Max Weber, *The Protestant Ethic and the Spirit of Capitalism* (New York: Scribner's, 1958), pp. 181–82.
10. Marx, *Capital*, pp. 22–23.
11. Ibid., p. 837.
12. Ibid., p. 15.
13. Marx, *The Holy Family* (Moscow: Foreign Languages Publishing House, 1956), pp. 52–53.

14. Engels to Starkenburg, London, January 25, 1894, in Feuer, *Marx and Engels: Basic Writings,* p. 109.
15. Engels, "Socialism, Utopian and Scientific," in Feuer, *Marx and Engels: Basic Writings,* p. 109.
16. Wilhelm Reich, *Sex-Pol Essays 1929–1934,* ed. Lee Baxandall (New York: Vintage Books, 1972), p. 284.
17. Karl Korsch, *Marxism and Philosophy* (London: New Left Books, 1970), pp. 9–10.
18. Sigmund Freud, *An Outline of Psychoanalysis* (New York: W. W. Norton, 1970), pp. 9–10.
19. Ibid., p. 121
20. Reich, *Invasion of Compulsory Sex Morality* (New York: Farrar, Strauss & Giroux, 1971), p. 164.
21. Reich, *Character Analysis* (New York: Farrar, Straus & Giroux, 1949), pp. xxii–xxiii.
22. Reich, *The Sexual Revolution* (New York: Farrar, Straus & Giroux, 1970), p. 72.
23. Ibid., p. 79.
24. Reich, *The Function of the Orgasm* (New York: Farrar, Straus & Giroux, 1970), p. 208.

1. Convergence

1. This translation is cited in Ricoeur, who provides some background and cites information relevant to the text. See Paul Ricoeur, *Freud and Philosophy* (New Haven: Yale University Press, 1970), p. 71.
2. Ibid., p. 72.
3. Sigmund Freud, *New Introductory Lectures on Psychoanalysis* (New York: W. W. Norton, 1933), p. 237 (hereafter, *NIL*).
4. Ibid., p. 219.
5. T. B. Bottomore and Maximilien Rubel, eds., *Karl Marx, Selected Writings in Sociology and Philosophy* (New York: McGraw-Hill, 1964), p. 14.
6. Ibid., p. 15.
7. Karl Marx, *Early Writings,* translated and edited by T. B. Bottomore (New York: McGraw-Hill, 1964), p. 164 (hereafter, *EW*).
8. Ludwig Feurbach, *The Essence of Christianity* (New York: Harper Torchbooks, 1957), p. 23.
9. See Freud, *Civilization and Its Discontents* (New York: W. W. Norton, 1962), section 3 (hereafter, *CD*).
10. Karl Marx and Friedrich Engels, *On Religion* (Moscow: Foreign Languages Publishing House, 1955), pp. 147–48. The selection is from *Anti-Dühring.*
11. Freud, *The Future of an Illusion* (New York: Doubleday paperback edition), pp. 27–27 (hereafter, *FI*).
12. Freud, *CD,* p. 21.
13. Marx and Engels, *On Religion,* pp. 334–36.
14. Freud, *FI,* p. 89.

15. Marx, *EW*, pp. 43–44.
16. Freud, *FI*, pp. 84, 96–97.
17. Engels, "Ludwig Feuerbach and the End of Classical German Philosophy," in *Selected Works*, 2 vols. (Moscow: Foreign Languages Publishing House, 1962), 2:391 (hereafter, *SW*).
18. Freud, *CD*, pp. 12–13.
19. Reich, *Function*, p. 20.
20. Cited in Michael Schneider, *Neurosis and Civilization* (New York: Seabury Press, 1975), pp. 25–26.
21. Engels, in Feuer, *Marx and Engels: Basic Writings*, p. 72.
22. See Richard Lichtman, "Marx's Theory of Ideology," in *Socialist Revolution* 23 (1975):45–76.
23. Engels, *SW*, 3:391.
24. Marx, *Capital*, p. 195.
25. Ibid., pp. 588–92.
20. Norman Geras, "Feilshilsm in Marx's Capital, New Left Review 65 (January–February 1971):69–85. See Lichtman, "Marx's Theory."
27. Philip Rieff, *Freud: The Mind of the Moralist* (New York: Viking Press, 1959), p. 80.
28. Freud, *Wit and Its Relation to the Unconscious*, in *The Basic Writings of Sigmund Freud* (New York: Modern Library, 1965), p. 707.
29. Freud, *CD*, pp. 56–59. I have altered the translation slightly in accordance with the translation provided by Joan Rivière in the Anchor edition.
30. Otto Fenichel, *The Psychoanalytical Theory of the Neuroses* (New York: W. W. Norton, 1965), p. 151.
31. Freud, *Collected Papers*, translation supervised by Joan Rivière, 5 vols. (New York: Basic Books, 1959), 5:182 (hereafter, *CP*).
32. Ibid., p. 185.
33. Ibid.
34. Freud, *The Standard Edition of the Complete Works of Sigmund Freud*, translated under the supervision of James Strachey, 24 vols. (London: Hogarth Press, 1973), 7:58–59 (hereafter, *SE*).
35. Marx, in Feuer, *Marx and Engels: Basic Writings*, pp. 254–56.
36. Freud, *SE*, 20:97.
37. Freud, *SE*, 19:48.
38. Marx, *Capital*, pp. 636–37.
39. Freud, *CD*, 75–76.
40. Erich Fromm, *Beyond the Chains of Illusion* (New York: Simon & Schuster, 1962), p. 52.
41. Marx, *Capital*, p. 188.
42. Marx, *The 18th Brumaire of Louis Bonaparte* (New York: New World, International Publishers, 1967), p. 15.
43. Ralph R. Greenson, *The Technique and Practice of Psychoanalysis* (New York: International Universities Press, 1972), p. 177.
44. Freud, *CP*, 5:359.
45. Freud, *The Origin and Development of Psychoanalysis*, in John Rickman, ed., *A General Selection from the Works of Sigmund Freud* (Garden City, N.Y.: Doubleday, 1957), p. 7 (hereafter, *GS*).

46. In Greenson, *Technique and Practice,* p. 182. This phrase is actually used to refer to transference but is equally applicable to neurosis in general.
47. Marx, in Feuer, *Marx and Engels: Basic Writings,* p. 44.
48. Freud, *SE,* 13:90.
49. Freud, *FI,* 77–78.
50. Marx, *18th Brumaire,* p. 17.
51. Marx, *Capital,* pp. 588–91.
52. Engels, in Feuer, *Marx and Engels: Basic Writings,* pp. 4, 104–109.
53. Freud, *A General Introduction to Psychoanalysis* (New York: Garden City Publishing Co., 1953), p. 242 (hereafter, *GIP*).
54. Ibid., p. 248.
55. Ibid., p. 249.
56. Ibid.
57. Freud, *SE,* 7:252.
58. Ibid., 11:225.
59. Ibid., 17:161.
60. Freud, *GIP,* p. 392.
61. Rieff, *Freud,* pp. 10–11.
62. Freud, *SE,* 19:133.
63. Freud, *NIL,* p. 392.
64. Jurgen Habermas, *Knowledge and Human Interests* (Boston: Beacon Press, 1971), pp. 235–36.
65. Cited in Shlomo Avineri, *The Social and Political Thought of Karl Marx* (Cambridge: Cambridge University Press, 1968), p. 185.
66. Freud, *CD,* p. 42.
67. Ibid., p. 87.
68. Freud, *NIL,* p. 204.
69. Ibid., p. 58.
70. Freud, *FI,* pp. 6–7.
71. Freud, *NIL,* pp. 244–45.
72. Freud, *SE,* 5:316.
73. Freud, *OP,* p. 43.
74. Freud, *NIL,* p. 107.
75. In Rickman, p. 215.
76. Freud, *NIL,* pp. 103–104.
77. In Rickman, *GS,* p. 160.
78. Lloyd D. Easton and Kurt H. Guddart, eds., *Writings of the Young Marx on Philosophy and Society* (Garden City, N.Y.: Doubleday Anchor Books, 1967), pp. 457–58 (hereafter, *WYM*).
79. Marx, *A Contribution to the Critique of Political Economy* (Chicago: Charles H. Kerr, 1904), p. 268.
80. In Feuer, *Marx and Engels: Basic Writings,* p. 29.
81. Ibid., p. 23.
82. Marx, *EW,* p. 163.
83. In Feuer, *Marx and Engels: Basic Writings,* p. 22.
84. Marx *WYM,* p. 420.
85. Marx, *EW,* p. 127.
86. Ibid., 164–65.

87. Marx, *Pre-Capitalist Economic Formations,* introduction by Eric J. Hobsbawm (New York: International Publishers, 1965), pp. 84–85. This small work is a selection from the *Grundrisse.* In the edition published by Penguin Books, 1973, translated with a foreword by Martin Nicolaus, the passage appears on p. 488.

2. Antagonism

1. Sigmund Freud, *The Standard Edition of the Complete Works of Sigmund Freud,* translated under the supervision of James Strachey, 24 vols. (London: Hogarth Press, 1973), 5:63 (hereafter, *SE*).
2. Freud, *SE,* 14:177.
3. Freud, *An Outline of Psychoanalysis* (New York: W. W. Norton, 1949), p. 105 (hereafter, *OP*).
4. G. W. F. Hegel, *The Logic,* translated by William Wallace from *The Encyclopedia of the Philosophical Sciences* (London: Oxford University Press, 1965), p. 239.
5. See my essay "Marx's Theory of Ideology," *Socialist Revolution* 23 (1975):45–76.
6. Karl Marx, *Capital* (New York: Modern Library, 1906), p. 83.
7. Ibid., p. 87.
8. Lenin, *Collected Works* (Moscow: Foreign Languages Publishing House, 1963), 38:134.
9. Freud develops this point very beautifully in *Civilization and Its Discontents,* section 1. Also see *Moses and Monotheism* (New York: Vintage Books, 1955), pp. 120ff.
10. Marx, *Capital,* p. 92.
11. Marx, *Grundrisse: Introduction to the Critique of Political Economy,* translated with a foreword by Martin Nicolaus (Baltimore: Penguin Books, 1973), p. 265.
12. Freud, *New Introductory Lectures on Psychoanalysis* (New York: W. W. Norton, 1933), p. 265 (hereafter, *NIL*).
13. Freud, *SE,* 18:73.
14. Freud, *Civilization and Its Discontents* (New York: W. W. Norton, 1962), p. 42 (hereafter, *CD*).
15. Freud, *NIL,* p. 203.
16. *Marx and Engels: Basic Writings on Politics and Philosophy,* edited by Lewis S. Feuer (Garden City, N.Y.: Anchor Books, 1959), p. 22.
17. See Paul Ricoeur, *Freud and Philosophy* (New Haven: Yale University Press, 1970), p. 69, passim, and also Daniel Yankelovich and William Barrett, *Ego and Instinct* (New York: Random House, 1970), p. 44, passim.
18. Ernest Jones, *The Life and Works of Sigmund Freud,* 3 vols. (New York: Basic Books, 1957), 1:29.
19. Sigfried Bernfeld, "Freud's Earliest Theories and the School of Helmholtz," *Psychoanalytic Quarterly,* p. 348.
20. Freud, *OP,* p. 14.
21. Ibid., p. 19.

22. John Rickman, *A General Selection from the Works of Sigmund Freud* (Garden City, N.Y.: Anchor Books, 1957), p. 214 (hereafter, *GS*).
23. Freud, *NIL,* p. 104.
24. Quoted in Michael Schneider, *Neurosis and Civilization* (New York: Seabury Press, 1975), p. 16.
25. Freud, *Collected Papers,* authorized translation by Joan Rivière, 5 vols. (New York: Basic Books, 1959), 2:376 (hereafter, *CP*).
26. Marx, *Grundrisse,* p. 105.
27. Ibid., p. 458.
28. Friedrich Engels, *The Dialectics of Nature* (New York: International Publishers, 1940), p. 187.
29. Marx, *Grundrisse,* p. 162.
30. Ibid., p. 99.
31. Marx and Engels, *The German Ideology* (London: Lawrence and Wishart, 1965), p. 50.
32. Marx, *Capital,* pp. 23–24.
33. Marx, *Grundrisse,* p. 85.
34. Freud, *CP,* 5:343.
35. Philip Rieff, *Freud: The Mind of the Moralist* (New York: Viking Press, 1959), p. 193.
36. Ibid., p. 194.
37. Ibid., p. 189.
38. Freud, *Moses and Monotheism,* pp. 139–40; see also *SE,* 18:78.
39. Rieff, *Freud,* pp. 240, 252.
40. Freud, *CP,* 5:197.
41. Freud, *SE,* 18:79.
42. Freud, *Moses and Monotheism,* p. 127.
43. Ibid., p. 128.
44. Ibid., p. 165.
45. Ibid., p. 169.
46. Freud, *OP,* 123–24.
47. Feuer, *Marx and Engels: Basic Writings,* p. 22.
48. Some of the better brief accounts of Freud's theory are: Edward Bibring, "The Development and Problems of the Theory of the Instincts," *International Journal of Psychoanalysis* 22, 1941, pp. 102–131; Erich Fromm, *Beyond the Chains of Illusion* (New York: Simon & Schuster, 1962); Helen Lynd, *On Shame and the Search for Identity* (New York: Science Editions, 1965), chap. 3; Freud, *OP;* Freud, *NIL,* chaps. 3 and 4; Freud, *Instincts and Their Vicissitudes;* Freud, "Three Essays on Sexuality"; Bernard Apfelbaum, "On Ego Psychology," *International Journal of Psychoanalysis* 47, 1966, pp. 451–475; the introduction by Robert Holt to the *Abstracts of the Standard Edition of the Complete Psychological Works of Sigmund Freud* (New York: Jason Aronson, 1974).
49. Freud, *SE,* 7:217.
50. Freud, *SE,* 14:213.
51. Freud, *SE,* 7:168; also Bibring, "Development and Problems."
52. Bibring, "Development and Problems."
53. Freud, *NIL,* p. 104.
54. Rickman, *GS,* p. 215.

55. Freud, *NIL*, pp. 107–108.
56. See Freud, *Beyond the Pleasure Principle*, in Rickman, *GS*, pp. 72, 141, 142, 166; Freud, *SE*, vol. 14, section 5; Freud, *CP*, 2:225, 5:135; Freud, *NIL*, p. 105.
57. Freud, *SE*, 7:218; Freud, *NIL*, pp. 133–34; Freud, *OP*, p. 23; Freud, *CP*, 4:42, 81; Freud, *A General Introduction to Psychoanalysis* (New York: Garden City Publishing Co., 1953), p. 360.
58. Freud, *CP*, 4:42.
59. *Beyond the Pleasure Principle* and *Civilization and Its Discontents*.
60. Freud, *OP*, pp. 16–17.
61. Freud, *CP*, 5:149.
62. Freud, *NIL*, p. 134.
63. Freud, *CP.*, 4:69.
64. Ibid., p. 64.
65. Ibid., p. 66.
66. Ibid., p. 66.
67. Ibid.
68. J. Laplanche and J.-B. Pontalis, *The Language of Psycho-Analysis* (New York: W. W. Norton, 1973), p. 22.
69. Freud, *CP*, 4:70.
70. Ibid.
71. Freud, "Three Essays on Sexuality," in *The Basic Writings of Sigmund Freud* (New York: Modern Library, 1965), p. 564n.
72. Otto Fenichel, *The Psychoanalytic Theory of Neurosis* (New York: W. W. Norton, 1945), p. 153.
73. Ibid., p. 13.

3. Marx's View of Human Nature

1. *Critique of the Gotha Programme* and the section of the Economic-Philosophic Manuscripts entitled "Private Property and Communism," which begins with Marx's notice: "The supersession of self-estrangement follows the same course as self-estrangement."
2. Lionel Trilling, *Beyond Culture* (New York: Viking Press, 1955), p. 113.
3. A. H. Maslow, *Toward a Psychology of Being* (Princeton, N.J.: Van Nostrand, 1968), p. 160.
4. Erich Fromm, *Man for Himself* (New York: Rinehart, 1947), pp. 19–20.
5. Karl Marx, *Grundrisse: Introduction to the Critique of Political Economy*, translated with a foreword by Martin Nicolaus (Baltimore: Penguin Books, 1973), p. 265.
6. Marx, *Early Writings*, translated and edited by T. B. Bottomore (New York: McGraw-Hill, 1964), p. 43 (hereafter, *EW*).
7. Ibid., p. 158.
8. Marx, *Grundrisse*, p. 85.
9. Marx, *EW*, p. 158.
10. Sigmund Freud, *Civilization and Its Discontents* (New York: W. W. Norton, 1962), pp. 19–50 (hereafter, *CD*).

11. Wilhelm Reich, *Sex-Pol Essays 1929–1934,* edited by Lee Baxendal (New York: Vintage Books, 1972), p. 71.
12. Ibid., p. 56.
13. Freud, *A General Introduction to Psychoanalysis* (New York: Garden City Publishing Co., 1953), p. 302 (hereafter, *GIP*).
14. Daniel Yankelovich and William Barrett, *Ego and Instinct* (New York: Random House, 1970), p. 62.
15. Marx, *Grundrisse,* p. 85.
16. Marx, *Capital* (New York: Modern Library, 1906), p. 668n.
17. Marx, *The Poverty of Philosophy* (New York: International Publishers, 1963), p. 147 (hereafter, *PPh*).
18. Friedrich Engels, *The Dialectics of Nature* (New York: International Publishers, 1940), p. 74.
19. Marx, *Capital,* pp. 197–98.
20. Engels, *Dialectics of Nature,* p. 161.
21. Ibid., p. 286.
22. Marx, *Capital,* 198.
23. Marx, *EW,* p. 127.
24. See the valuable discussion in Bertell Ollman, *Alienation: Marx's Conception of Man in Capitalist Society* (London: Cambridge University Press), pt. 2.
25. Marx, *EW,* p. 207–208.
26. Ibid., p. 208.
27. M. Merleau-Ponty, *Sense and Nonsense* (Evanston, Ill.: Northwestern University Press, 1964), pp. 52–53.
28. R. Kwant, "Merleau-Ponty and Phenomenology," in J. Kockelmans, ed., *Phenomenology* (Garden City, N.Y.: Doubleday Anchor Books, 1967), p. 387.
29. Fritz Perls, *Gestalt Therapy Verbatim* (New York: Bantam Books, 1971), p. 23.
30. Freud, "The Origin and Development of Psychoanalysis," in John Rickman, ed., *A General Selection from the Works of Sigmund Freud* (Garden City, N.Y.: Doubleday, 1957), p. 30.
31. Marx, *EW,* p. 127.
32. Ibid., p. 126.
33. Ibid., p. 127.
34. Ibid., p. 128.
35. Marx, *Grundrisse,* p. 88.
36. Marx, *EW,* p. 161.
37. Ibid., pp. 161–65.
38. Freud, *CD,* p. 51.
39. Freud, *Collected Papers,* translation supervised by Joan Rivière, 5 vols. (New York: Basic Books, 1959), 1:75 (hereafter *CP*).
40. Freud, *CD,* p. 50.
41. Freud, *CP,* II: 33; see also pp. 45–47, 55, 57.
42. Marx, *EW,* p. 168.
43. Freud, *CP,* II:42.
44. Philip Slater, *The Pursuit of Loneliness* (Boston: Beacon Press, 1970), p. 86.
45. Marx, *EW,* p. 125.
46. Freud, *CD,* p. 27n.

47. Freud, cited in Ernest Jones, *The Life and Work of Sigmund Freud,* 3 vols. (New York: Science Editions, 1965), 3:464.
48. Ibid., 1:190–91.
49. Freud, *CP,* 5:297.
50. Marx, *EW,* p. 160.
51. Ibid., p. 164.
52. Marx, in Lloyd D. Easton and Kurt H. Guddat, eds., *Writings of the Young Marx on Philosophy and Society* (Garden City, N.Y.: Doubleday Anchor Press, 1967), pp. 421, 420, 461.
53. Marx, *PPh,* p. 42.
54. J. S. Mill, *On Liberty* (New York: Modern Library), p. 197.
55. Herbert Marcuse, *One-Dimensional Man* (New York: Beacon Press, 1969), p. 1.
56. Marx, *EW,* p. 28n.
57. Marx, *Capital,* 3:805–806.
58. Ibid., p. 159.
59. Marx, *PPH,* p. 159.
60. Marx, *Grundrisse,* pp. 91–92.
61. Ibid., p. 92.
62. Ibid.
63. Freud, *The Standard Edition of the Complete Works of Sigmund Freud,* translated under the supervision of James Strachey, 24 vols. (London: Hogarth Press, 1973), 7:147–48 (hereafter, *SE*).
64. Freud, in Rickman, *General Selection,* p. 74.
65. Marx, *Grundrisse,* p. 222.
66. It is not always recognized how deeply intrapsychic a theory of conflict Freud held. Long before the development of his late theory with its internal strife between Eros and Thanatos, Freud had written: "It is during this period of total or only partial latency that are built up the mental forces which are later to impede the course of the sexual instinct and, like dams, restrict its flow — disgust, feelings of shame and the claims of aesthetic and moral ideals. One gets the impression from civilized children that the construction of these dams is a product of education, and no doubt education has much to do with it. But in reality this development is organically determined and fixed by heredity, and it can occasionally occur without any help from education" (*SE,* 7:197).
67. Marx, *EW,* p. 162.
68. Marx and Engels, *The German Ideology* (London: Lawrence and Wishart, 1965), p. 50 (hereafter, *GI*).
69. Ibid., p. 83.
70. Marx, *Grundrisse,* p. 494.
71. Freud, *CD,* p. 43.
72. Cited in Martin Jay, *The Dialectical Imagination* (Boston: Little, Brown, 1973), p. 103.
73. Marx and Engels, *GI,* p. 93.
74. Marx, *Grundrisse,* p. 162.
75. Marx and Engels, *GI,* p. 83.

76. Marx, *Grundrisse,* p. 188.
77. Marx, Third Thesis on Feuerbach, *Theses on Feuerbach.*
78. Marx, *EW,* pp. 160, 161.
79. Freud, in Rickman, *General Selection,* p. 218.
80. Otto Fenichel, *The Psychoanalytic Theory of Neurosis* (New York: W. W. Norton, 1945), p. 84.
81. Marx, *EW,* p. 161.

4. The Demystification of Freudian Theory

1. Cited in Michael Schneider, *Neurosis and Civilization* (New York: Seabury Press, 1975), p. 57.
2. Philip Rieff, *The Triumph of the Therapeutic* (New York: Harper Torchbooks, 1966), p. 143.
3. Karl Marx, *The Poverty of Philosophy* (New York: International Publishers, 1963), pp. 111–112.
4. Russell Jacoby, *Social Amnesia* (Boston: Beacon Press, 1973), p. 120.
5. Theodore W. Adorno, cited in ibid., pp. 27–28.
6. Ibid., p. 73.
7. Ibid., pp. 73–74.
8. Ibid., p. 74.
9. Ibid., p. 26.
10. Ibid.
11. Ibid., p. 78.
12. Sigmund Freud, *New Introductory Lectures on Psychoanalysis* (New York: W. W. Norton, 1933), p. 245.
13. Adorno, cited in Jacoby, *Social Amnesia,* p. 74.
14. Cited in ibid., p. 104.
15. Cited in ibid., p. 87.
16. Cited in ibid., pp. 90–91.
17. Ibid., p. 25.
18. Ibid., p. 13.
19. Ibid., p. 26.
20. Ibid.
21. Ibid., p. 27.
22. Ibid., p. 26.
23. Ibid.
24. Ibid., p. 48.
25. Ibid.
26. Ibid., p. 121.
27. Ibid.
28. Ibid., p. 122.
29. Daniel Yankelovich and William Barrett, *Ego and Instinct* (New York: Random House, 1970), p. 269.
30. H. J. Home, "The Concept of the Mind," *International Journal of Psychoanalysis* 47 (1966):44 (hereafter, *IJPA*).

31. George Klein, *Psychoanalytic Theory* (New York: International Universities Press, 1976), pp. 42–43.

32. Ibid., p. 47.

33. Robert Holt, "The Past and Future of Ego Psychology," *Psychoanalytic Quarterly* 44, no. 4 (1975):567 (hereafter, *PQ*).

34. Ibid., p. 573.

35. See Morton M. Gill, "Metapsychology Is Not Psychology," *Psychological Issues* 9, no. 4, monograph 36 (1976): 75–83 (hereafter, *PI*); and Philip Rieff, *Freud: The Mind of the Moralist* (New York: Viking Press, 1959), chap. 1.

36. Freud, *The Standard Edition of the Complete Works of Sigmund Freud*, translated under the supervision of James Strachey, 24 vols. (London: Hogarth Press, 1973), 14:181 (hereafter, *SE*).

37. See also the paper by David Rapaport and Morton M. Gill, "The Points of View and Assumptions of Metapsychology," *IJPA* 40 (1959): 153–62.

38. Freud, *SE*, 16–17:67.

39. Jacob A. Arlow, *PQ*, 44, no. 4 (1975):511.

40. Ibid., p. 516.

41. Robert S. Wallerstein, "Psychoanalysis as a Science: Its Present Status and Its Future Tasks," *PI* 9, no, 4, monograph 36 (1976):220.

42. Ibid.

43. C. I. Lewis, *Mind and the World Order* (New York: Dover Press, 1956), p. 37.

44. Ibid., p. 38.

45. See the discussion on metapsychology in *IJPA* 50 (1970): 245–49.

46. Rapaport and Gill, "Points of View."

47. The paraphrase is by Ernest R. Hilgard in "The Scientific Status of Psychoanalysis," in S. G. M. Lee and Martin Herbert, eds., *Freud and Psychology* (Penguin: New York, 1970), pp. 29–44.

48. Emanuel Peterfreund, "The Need for a New General Theoretical Frame of Reference for Psychoanalysis," *PQ* 44, no. 4 (1975): 535–49. There is also a useful bibliography at the end of this essay.

49. Benjamin B. Rubenstein, "Explanation and More Description: A Metascientific Examination of Certain Aspects of the Psychoanalytic Theory of Motivation," *Psychological Issues* 5, nos. 2–3 (1967): 18–75.

50. See primarily Roy Schaefer, *A New Action Language for Psychoanalysis* (New Haven: Yale University Press, 1978). It can be argued either that this book is a rejection of metapsychology or a new metapsychology designed to replace Freud's mechanistic system.

51. Klein, *Psychanalytic Theory*.

52. Ibid., p. 11.

53. Ibid., p. 26.

54. Ibid., p. 27.

55. Ibid., p. 30.

56. Ibid., p. 31.

57. Ibid., p. 30.

58. Ibid.

59. Ibid., p. 56.

60. Ibid., p. 57.

61. Ibid., p. 241.

62. Ibid., p. 242.
63. Ibid., p. 251.
64. Ibid.
65. Ibid., p. 253.
66. Ibid., p. 28.
67. Ibid., p. 261.
68. Ibid., p. 262.
69. Ibid., p. 266.
70. Robert Merton, *Social Theory and Social Structure* (New York: The Free Press, 1968 ed.), pp. 250–51.
71. Karl Marx, *Capital* (New York: Modern Library, 1906), p. 87.

5. Clinical Practice: The Case of Dora

1. Sigmund Freud, "Fragment of an Analysis of a Case of Hysteria," in *Collected Papers,* authorized translation by Alix and James Strachey, 5 vols. (New York: Basic Books, 1959), 3:14 (hereafter, *CP*).
2. See Philip Rieff, *Freud: The Mind of the Moralist* (New York: Viking Press, 1959), pp. 302–306.
3. Freud, *CP*, 3:19-20.
4. Ibid., p. 25.
5. Freud, *The Standard Edition of the Works of Sigmund Freud,* translated under the supervision of James Strachey, 24 vols. (London: Hogarth Press, 1973), 22:14.
6. Ibid., p. 9.
7. Jürgen Habermas, *Knowledge and Human Interest,* (Boston: Beacon Press, 1968), pp. 227–28.
8. Freud, *CP*, 3:26.
9. Ibid.
10. Ibid., pp. 26–27.
11. Ibid., p. 27.
12. Ibid., p. 28.
13. Ibid., p. 27.
14. Ibid., p. 31.
15. Ibid., p. 33.
16. Ibid., pp. 32–33.
17. Ibid., p. 37.
18. Ibid., p. 38.
19. See the valuable discussion in Dieter Wyss, *Psychoanalytic Schools From the Beginning to the Present* (New York: Jason Aronson, 1973), pp. 450–68.
20. Freud, *CP*, 3:40–41.
21. Ibid., p. 41.
22. Ibid.
23. Ibid.
24. Ibid., p. 44.
25. Ibid., p. 131.

26. Ibid., p. 46.
27. Ibid., pp. 74–75.
28. Ibid., p. 76.
29. Ibid., p. 128.
30. Ibid., p. 43.
31. Ibid., pp. 44–45.
32. Ibid., p. 47.
33. Ibid., p. 48.
34. Ibid., p. 49.
35. Ibid., p. 50.
36. Karl Marx, "The 18th Brumaire of Louis Bonaparte," in *Karl Marx and Frederick Engels, Selected Works,* vol. 1 (Moscow: Foreign Languages Publishing House, 1962), p. 275.
37. Freud, *CP,* 3:51.
38. Ibid.
39. Ibid.
40. Ibid., p. 53.
41. Ibid.
42. Ibid., p. 54n.
43. Ibid., p. 54.
44. Ibid., pp. 55–56.
45. See the insightful discussion by Barbara Ehrenreich and Deirdre English, *Complaints and Disorders: The Sexual Politics of Sickness,* Glass Mountain Pamphlet No. 2 (Old Westbury, N.Y.: The Feminist Press, 1973), pp. 11–44. For an extended discussion, see, by the same authors, *For Her Own Good,* (New York: Doubleday [Anchor Books], 1978.
46. Ibid., pp. 11–12.
47. Ibid., Mary Putnam Jacobi, cited on p. 19.
48. Ibid., p. 48.
49. Morton Schatzman, *Soul Murder* (New York: Random House, 1973), pp. 105–106.
50. Freud, *CP,* 3:69.
51. Freud, *SE,* 2:47.
52. See also Freud, "The Interpretation of Dreams," in *The Basic Writings of Sigmund Freud* (New York: Modern Library, 1938), p. 304, and *A General Introduction to Psychoanalysis,* English translation by Joan Rivière (New York: Garden City Publishing Co., 1943), p. 308.
53. Freud, *CP,* 2:97.
54. Ibid., p. 93.
55. Freud, *CP,* 4:207.
56. Ibid., p. 209.
57. Ibid., p. 211.
58. Freud, *Civilization and Its Discontents* (New York: W. W. Norton, 1962), p. 61.
59. Freud, *CP,* 3:57.
60. Ibid.
61. Ibid., p. 58 and also p. 136. Freud notes that *one* of the meanings of a symptom is sexual, but typically, that is the only meaning he deals with.
62. Ibid., p. 59.

63. Ibid.
64. Ibid., p. 62.
65. Freud, *CP*, 2:84.
66. Marx cited by Lawrence Krader, *The Ethnological Notebooks of Karl Marx* (New York: Van Gorscum and Co., 1972), p. 61.
67. Freud, *CP*, 3:62.
68. Ibid., p. 63.
69. Ibid., p. 64.
70. Ibid.
71. Freud, *SE*, 23:194.
72. Freud, *CP*, 3:99.
73. Ibid., see pp. 70–72. Here, in interpreting Dora's response, Freud makes use of a contention we will analyze in the next chapter—namely, that there is no "No" in the unconscious, and that expressed denial is the indication of an actual wish which has been repressed. As Freud puts it: "'No' signifies the desired 'Yes.'" However, there are times when Freud takes negation at face value. Furthermore, we are left with the question of why negation cannot exist in the unconscious when hatreted and destructiveness are present there.
74. Ibid., p. 92.
75. See Mark Poster, *Critical Theory of the Family* (New York: Seabury Press, 1976).
76. Freud, *CP*, 3:162.
77. Ibid., p. 61.
78. Ibid., p. 285.
79. Ibid., pp. 132–33.
80. Ibid., p. 141.
81. Ibid.
82. Ibid., p. 142.
83. Freud, *SE*, 18:175.
84. Freud, *CP*, 3:143.

6. The Sociology of Metapsychology

1. Sigmund Freud, *The Standard Edition of the Complete Works of Sigmund Freud*, translated under the supervision of James Strachey, 24 vols. (London: Hogarth Press, 1973), 7:168 (hereafter, *SE*).
2. Ibid., 14:123.
3. Freud, *New Introductory Lectures on Psychoanalysis* (New York: W. W. Norton, 1933), p. 33.
4. Freud, *Collected Papers*, translated under the supervision of Joan Rivière, 5 vols. (New York: Basic Books, 1959), 5:108 (hereafter, *CP*).
5. Charles Brenner, *An Elementary Textbook of Psychoanalysis* (New York: International Universities Press, 1955), p. 28.
6. Freud, *CP*, 4:101.
7. Freud, *SE*, 1:307–308.
8. Ibid., p. 308.

9. Freud, *SE*, 7:168.
10. Freud, *CP*, 2:255–56.
11. Freud, *SE*, 19:25.
12. Freud, *SE*, 20:97.
13. Freud, *CP*, 4:14.
14. Ibid.
15. Ibid., p. 18.
16. Ibid., p. 27.
17. Ibid., p. 101.
18. Ibid., p. 119.
19. Ibid., p. 122.
20. Ibid., p. 134.
21. Ibid., p. 184.
22. Frank Cioffi, "Freud and the Idea of a Pseudo-Science," in Robert Berger and Frank Cioffi, eds., *Explanation in the Behavioral Sciences*, (London: Cambridge University Press, 1970), p. 493
23. Merton M. Gill, "Topography and Systems in Psychoanalytic Theory," *Psychological Issues* 3, no. 2, (1967), p. 29. I have relied heavily on this essay, which I found to be one of the most comprehensive and suggestive of the various accounts of the structure of Freud's theory.
24. Ibid., p. 34.
25. Freud, *SE*, 14:190–91.
26. The translation here is by Rapaport, quoted in Gill, "Topography and Systems," p. 38.
27. Marx, *Early Writings*, translated and edited by T. B. Bottomore (New York: McGraw-Hill, 1963), pp. 120–134 (hereafter, *EW*).
28. Ibid., p. 53.
29. Ibid., p. 148.
30. Freud, *SE*, 14:228.
31. Gill, "Topography and Systems," p. 81.
32. Freud, *SE*, 14:192–93.
33. Freud, *Outline of Psychoanalysis* (New York: W. W. Norton, 1970), pp. 42–43 (hereafter, *OP*).
34. Gill, "Topography and Systems," p. 47.
35. Ibid., pp. 140–41. See also pp. 69, 101, 105.
36. Freud, *SE*, 14:16.
37. Freud, *SE*, 19:17.
38. Freud, *SE*, 18:9; 18:131; 12:67; 18:19.
39. Freud, *SE*, 14:195.
40. Freud, *OP*, p. 43.
41. Jürgen Habermas, *Knowledge and Human Interest* (Boston: Beacon Press, 1971), p. 223.
42. Ibid., p. 345, note 31.
43. Freud, *New Introductory Lectures, on Psychoanalysis* (New York: W. W. Norton, 1933), pp. 103–104.
44. Marx, *EW*, p. 138.
45. Ernest G. Schachtel, *Metamorphosis* (New York: Basic Books, 1959), p. 284.
46. Ibid., p. 285.

47. Paul Wachtel, *Psychoanalysis and Behavior Therapy* (New York: Basic Books, 1973), p. 43.
48. Ibid., pp. 69–70.
49. Morton Schatzman, *Soul Murder* (New York: Random House, 1973), pp. 134–37.
50. Ibid., p. 135.
51. Ibid., pp. 136–37.
52. Freud, *SE,* 21:127.
53. Otto Fenichel, *The Psychoanalytic Theory of Neurosis* (New York: W. W. Norton, 1945), pp. 149–50.
54. Franz Fanon, *Black Skin, White Masks* (New York: Grove Press, 1967), p. 51.
55. Bernard Apfelbaum, "On Ego Psychology: A Critique of the Structural Approach to Psychoanalytic Theory," *International Journal of Psychoanalysis* 47, pt. 4 (1966). I found this essay particularly useful.
56. Anna Freud, *The Ego and the Mechanisms of Defense* (London: Hogarth Press, 1937), p. 172.
57. Anna Freud, "Indications For Child Analysis," *Psychoanalytic Study of the Child* 1 (1945):144.
58. Freud, *SE,* 21:140.
59. Heinz Hartman, "Comments on the Psychoanalytic Theory of the Ego," in *Essays in Ego Psychology* (New York: International Universities Press, 1964), p. 113.
60. Ernest Jones, *The Life and Works of Sigmund Freud,* 3 vols. (New York: Basic Books, 1957), p. 265.
61. Apfelbaum, "On Ego Psychology," p. 463.
62. Ibid.

Summary and Prospectus

1. See Raymond Fancher, *Psychoanalytic Psychology: The Development of Freud's Thought* (New York: W. W. Norton, 1973), chap. 3. Fancher's account is particularly useful for noting the continuity of Freud's thought from the original *Project* through the later developments in Freud's metapsychology.
2. Ernest Jones, *The Life and Works of Sigmund Freud,* 3 vols. (New York: Basic Books, 1953), 190–91.
3. Jules Henry, *Pathways to Madness* (New York: Random House, 1965), p. 113.

7. The Marxian Unconscious

1. Karl Marx, *Early Writings,* translated and edited by T. B. Bottomore (New York: McGraw-Hill, 1964), p. 158.
2. Karl Marx, *Capital,* vol. 3 (Moscow: Foreign Languages Publishing House, 1956), p. 797.
3. Karl Marx, *Capital,* vol. 1 (New York: Modern Library, 1906), p. 568.
4. Ibid., p. 588.
5. Ibid., p. 591.

6. Karl Marx, *Grundrisse: Introduction to the Critique of Political Economy* translated with a foreword by Martin Nicolaus (Baltimore: Penguin Books, 1973), p. 84 (hereafter, *GR*).
7. Marx, *Capital,* vol. 1, p. 121.
8. Ibid., pp. 591–92.
9. Marx, *GR,* p. 156.
10. Karl Marx and Friedrich Engels, *Selected Works,* 2 vols. (Moscow: Foreign Languages Publishing House, 1962), 2:323.
11. Marx and Engels, *Correspondence* (New York: International Publishers, 1942), p. 505, Engels to Starkenberg 1/25/1894.
12. Marx, *GR,* p. 162.
13. See Antoni Gramsci, *Selections from the Prison Notebooks* (New York: International Publishers, 1971), particularly the section, "The Study of Philosophy," pp. 323–77. Gramsci employs a distinction between "lived" conceptualizations and explicit conceptualization which he unfortunately never makes clear. This is not the same distinction employed by Marx between the conceptual structure of the entire system and the self-understanding of the individual act. However, Gramsci's distinction seems to me to have real potential merit and is the only instance of this necessary distinction that has been at all worked out in Marxist theory.
14. Marx, *GR,* p. 158.
15. Ibid., pp. 163–64. Marx here resumes an analysis begun in *The German Ideology.*
16. Sigmund Freud, *Collected Papers,* authorized translation by Joan Rivière, 5 vols. (New York: Basic Books, 1959), 4:62.
17. Marx, *GR,* p. 652.
18. Ibid., p. 241.
19. Ibid.
20. Ibid.
21. Ibid., pp. 242–43.
22. Ibid., pp. 243–44.
23. Ibid., p. 244.
24. Marx and Engels, *The German Ideology* (London: Lawrence and Wishart, 1965), p. 45.
25. Marx, *GR,* p. 245.
26. Ibid., p. 244.
27. Ibid., p. 245.
28. Ibid.
29. Ibid., p. 247.
30. Ibid., pp. 247–48.
31. Ibid., p. 488.
32. Maurice Godelier, *Rationality and Irrationality in Economics* (New York: Monthly Review Press, 1972), p. xviii.
33. Ibid, p. xxiv.
34. Maurice Godelier, "Systems, Structure and Contradiction in Das Kapital," in Michael Lane, ed., *Structuralism* (New York: Basic Books, 1970), p. 347. While I was revising this chapter I came across a more recent essay by Godelier, "The Problem of Determination," *New Left Review* 112 (Nov.–Dec.

1978):84–96, which seems to me superior to his older analysis in recognizing more adequately the role of ideas in the formation of the social world. There is still the tendency, however, to treat ideas as something between "man and material activity," as though either could exist independently of the process of being constituted conceptually.

35. Marx and Engels, *The Holy Family* (Moscow: Foreign Languages Publishing House, 1965), chap. 6 and chap. 5, section 2.
36. Marx, *Capital,* vol. 3, p. 205.
37. See Richard Lichtman, "Marx's Theory of Ideology," *Socialist Revolution* (1975):45–76.
38. Godelier, *Rationality and Irrationality*, p. xxv.
39. Maurice Godelier, *Perspectives in Marxist Anthropology* (New York: Cambridge University Press, 1977), p. 170.
40. Ibid.
41. Godelier, *Rationality and Irrationality,* p. xxiv.
42. Marx, *Capital,* vol. 1, p. 83.
43. Ibid., pp. 197–98.
44. Marx, *GR,* p. 233.
45. Ibid., p. 234.
46. Ibid., p. 340.
47. Marx, *Capital,* vol. 1, p. 71.
48. Ibid., p. 15.
49. Ibid., p. 23.
50. Ibid., p. 96.
51. Marx, *Theories of Surplus Value* (Moscow: Foreign Languages Publishing House, 1962), vol. 3, p. 429.
52. Marx, *GR,* p. 712.
53. Ibid., p. 151.
54. Engels, *The Dialectics of Nature* (New York: International Publishers, 1940), pp. 291–92.
55. Marx and Engels, *Correspondence* p. 518.
56. Marx, *Capital,* vol. 1, p. 86.
57. Ibid.
58. Michael Schneider, *Neurosis and Civilization* (New York: Seabury Press, 1975), p. 122.
59. Ibid., p. 123.
60. Ibid., pp. 126–27.
61. Cited in Schneider, *Neurosis and Civilization,* p. 127.
62. Ibid.
63. Cited in ibid.
64. Ibid., p. 142.
65. Ibid., p. 146.
66. Marx, *GR,* p. 122.
67. Marx, *A Contribution to the Critique of Political Economy* (Chicago: Charles H. Kerr and Company, 1904), pp. 20–21.
68. Marx, *GR,* p. 104.
69. Robert D'Amico, "Desire and Commodity Form," *Telos,* Spring 1978, p. 104.
70. Marx, *GR,* p. 265.

71. The literature on this subject is vast, but see Lucio Colletti, "Marxism: Science or Revolution," in *From Rousseau to Lenin* (New York: Monthly Review Press, 1972), and "The Theory of the Crash," in Bartlett Grahl and Paul Piccone, eds., *Towards a New Marxism: Proceedings of the First Telos Conference* (St. Louis: Telos Press, 1973).

72. Marx, *Capitol,* vol. 1, p. 93.

8. Conclusion: The Politics of Therapy

1. Karl Marx, *Early Writings*, translated and edited by T. B. Bottomore (New York: McGraw-Hill, 1964), p. 138 (hereafter, *EW*).

 2. Karl Marx, *Grundrisse: Introduction to the Critique of Political Economy*, translated with a foreword by Martin Nicolaus (Baltimore: Penguin Books, 1973), p. 245.

 3. Marx, *EW,* p. 148.

 4. I am relying on the account by Robert D'Amico, "Desire and Commodity Form," *Telos* 35 (Spring 1978): 89–91. The translation is also by D'Amico.

 5. Ibid.

 6. Ibid.

 7. Ibid.

 8. Cited in Russell Jacoby, *Social Amnesia* (Boston: Beacon Press, 1973), p. 9.

 9. Ibid.

10. Philip Rieff, *Freud: The Mind of the Moralist* (New York: Viking Press, 1959), chap. 9.

11. Sigmund Freud, *Collected Papers,* authorized translation by Joan Rivière, 5 vols. (New York: Basic Books, 1959), 5:170.

12. Ibid., p. 128.

13. Ibid., p. 171.

14. An interesting exception is *The Future of An Illusion,* probably the most optimistic and "Liberal" of Freud's works. But even here, contempt of the masses is strongly represented.

15. Cited in Morton Schatzman, *Soul Murder* (New York: Random House, 1973), p. 23.

16. Ibid.

17. Besides Dora and Schreber, note the references in Schatzman to the case of "Little Hans," pp. 123–29 and the additional citations on p. 124; the reference to Oedipus on pp. 112–27 is also instructive.

18. Freud, *Collected Papers,* 2:390.

19. Ibid., pp. 319–20.

20. Nor does it seem to me to have much to do with the particular "school" or form of therapy—Psychoanalytic, Gestalt, Behaviorist, "individual," "family," or "network." From the few empirical studies I am aware of I think it would be safe to conjecture that while there are political differences among these positions, they are the differences between liberals and conservatives, at most.

21. The mixed results of the Italian "Democratic Psychiatry Movement" seems to me bear out this contention. What has been accomplished in the move-

ment depends upon the fact that the city in question, i.e., Bologna, is controlled by the Communist Party, which can, therefore, integrate mental institutions into municipal policies. But as the country is capitalist, the experiment is strictly limited.

22. See, for example, Ralph R. Greenson, *The Technique and Practice of Psychoanalysis* (New York: International Humanities Press, 1967), pp. 190–224.

23. See the excellent articles by Jessica Benjamin: "Adorno's Social Psychology," *Telos* 32 (Summer 1977):42–64, and "Authority and the Family Revisited: Or, A World Without Fathers?" *New German Critique* 13 (Winter 1978):35–58.

24. See Martha Wolfenstein, "Fun Morality: An Analysis of Recent Childtraining Literature," in Margaret Mead and Martha Wolfenstein, eds., *Childhood in Contemporary Cultures* (Chicago: University of Chicago Press, 1955), pp. 168–78.

25. See, for example, the important article by Michael Lerner, "Surplus Powerlessness," *Social Policy,* January–February 1979, pp. 1–10.

26. Marx, *EW*, p. 44.

27. Freud, *The Origin and Development of Psychoanalysis*, in John Rickman, ed., *A General Selection from The Works of Sigmund Freud* (Garden City, N.Y.: Doubleday, 1957), p. 31.

28. For two important studies which focus this discussion see Eliot Liebow, *Tally's Corner* (Boston: Little, Brown, 1967) and Richard Sennett and Jonathan Cobb, *The Hidden Injuries of Class* (New York: Vintage Books, 1973).

29. See Joseph Eyer's review of Harvey Brenner's "Unemployment and Mental Illness" in the *International Journal of Health Sciences* 6, no. 1 (1977):139–68.

30. See Philip Slater, *The Pursuit of Loneliness,* (Boston: Beacon Press, 1970).

31. Joan Didion, *New York Review of Books,* August 16, 1979.

32. Martin Buber, *Dialogue Between Man and Man* (London: Routledge and Kegan Paul, 1947), pp. 29–30.

Bibliography

APFELBAUM, BERNARD. "On Ego Psychology." *International Journal of Psychoanalysis* 47, pt. 4 (1966).

ARLOW, JACOB A. "The Structural Hypothesis-Theoretical Considerations." *Psychoanalytic Quarterly* 44, no. 4 (1975).

AVINERI, SHLOMO. *The Social and Political Thought of Karl Marx.* Cambridge: Cambridge University Press, 1968.

BARAN, PAUL. "Crisis of Marxism." *Monthly Review,* October 1958.

BENJAMIN, JESSICA. "Adorno's Social Psychology." *Telos* 32 (Summer 1977).

———. "Authority and the Family Revisited: Or, A World Without Fathers?" *New German Critique* 13 (Winter 1978).

BERNFELD, SIGFRIED. "Freud's Earliest Theories and the School of Helmholtz." *Psychoanalytic Quarterly* 13 (1944).

BRENNER, CHARLES. *An Elementary Textbook of Psychoanalysis.* New York: International Universities Press, 1955.

BUBER, MARTIN. *Dialogue Between Man and Man.* London: Routledge & Kegan Paul, 1947.

CIOFFI, FRANK. "Freud and the Idea of a Pseudo-Science." In *Explanation in the Behavioral Sciences,* edited by Robert Berger and Frank Cioffi. Cambridge: Cambridge University Press, 1970.

COLLETTI, LUCIO. *From Rousseau to Lenin.* New York: Monthly Review Press, 1972.

————. "The Theory of the Crash." In *Towards a New Marxism: Proceedings of the First Telos Conference,* edited by Bartlett Grahl and Paul Piccone. St. Louis: Telos Press, 1973.

D'AMICO, ROBERT. "Desire and Commodity Form." *Telos* 35 (Spring 1978).

DIDION, JOAN. Letter from Manhattan. *New York Review of Books,* August 16, 1979.

ENGELS, FRIEDRICH. *The Dialectics of Nature.* New York: International Publishers, 1940.

————. *Selected Works.* 2 vols. Moscow: Foreign Languages Publishing House, 1962.

ENGLISH, DIERDRE, and EHRENREICH, BARBARA. *Complaints and Disorders: The Sexual Politics of Sickness.* Glass Mountain Pamphlet no. 2. Old Westbury, New York: The Feminist Press, 1973.

EYER, JOSEPH. Review of "Mental Illness and the Economy." *International Journal of Health Sciences* 6, no. 1 (1977).

FANCHER, RAYMOND. *Psychoanalytic Psychology: The Development of Freud's Thought.* New York: Norton, 1973.

FANON, FRANZ. *Black Skin, White Master.* New York: Grove Press, 1967.

FENICHEL, OTTO. *The Psychoanalytic Theory of Neurosis.* New York: Norton, 1945.

FREUD, ANNA. *The Ego and the Mechanisms of Defense.* New York: International Universities Press, 1966.

————. "Indications for Child Analysis." *Psychoanalytic Study of the Child* 1 (1945).

FREUD, SIGMUND. *The Basic Writings of Sigmund Freud.* New York: Modern Library, 1965.

————. *Civilization and Its Discontents.* New York: Norton, 1962.

————. *Collected Papers.* 5 vols. Translated under the supervision of Joan Rivière. New York: Basic Books, 1959.

————. *The Future of an Illusion.* Garden City, N.Y.: Doubleday paperback edition, 1953.

————. *A General Introduction to Psychoanalysis.* New York: Garden City Publishing Co., 1953.

————. *A General Selection from the Works of Sigmund Freud.* Edited by John Rickman. New York: Doubleday, 1957.

————. *Moses and Monotheism.* New York: Vintage, 1955.

————. *New Introductory Lectures on Psychoanalysis.* New York: Norton, 1933.

————. *An Outline of Psychoanalysis.* New York: Norton, 1970.

———— *The Standard Edition of the Complete Works of Sigmund Freud.* 24 vols. Translated under the supervision of James Strachey. London: Hogarth Press, 1973.

FROMM, ERICH. *Beyond the Chains of Illusion.* New York: Simon & Schuster, 1962.

————. *Man for Himself.* New York: Rinehart, 1947.

GERAS, NORMAN. "Fetishism in Marx's *Capital.*" *New Left Review* 64 (January–February 1971).

GILL, MORTON. "Topography and Systems in Psychoanalytic Theory." *Psychological Issues* 3, no. 2, monograph 10 (1967).

GILL, MORTON, and RAPAPORT, DAVID. "The Point of View and Assumptions of Metapsychology." *International Journal of Psychoanalysis* 40 (1959).

GODELIER, MAURICE. *Perspectives in Marxist Anthropology.* New York: Cambridge University Press, 1977.

———. *Rationality and Irrationality in Economics.* New York: Monthly Review Press, 1972.

———. "Systems, Structures and Contradiction in *Das Kapital.*" In *Structuralism,* edited by Michael Lane. New York: Basic Books, 1970.

GRAMSCI, ANTONI. *Selections from the Prison Notebooks.* New York: International Publishers, 1971.

GREENSON, RALPH R. *The Technique and Practice of Psychoanalysis.* New York: International Universities Press, 1972.

GOUDLER, ALVIN W. *The Coming Crisis of Western Sociology.* New York: Basic Books, 1970.

HABERMAS, JÜRGEN. *Knowledge and Human Interest.* Boston: Beacon Press, 1971.

HARTMANN, HEINZ. "Comments on the Psychoanalytic Theory of the Ego." In *Essays on Ego Psychology.* New York. International Universities Press, 1965.

HEGEL, FRIEDRICH. "The Logic." Translated by William Wallace from *The Encyclopedia of the Philosophical Sciences.* London: Oxford University Press, 1965.

HENRY, JULES. *Pathways to Madness.* New York: Random House, 1965.

HILGARD, ERNEST R. "The Scientific Status of Psychoanalysis." In *Freud and Psychology,* edited by S. G. M. Lee and Martin Herbert. Baltimore: Penguin Books, 1970.

HOLT, ROBERT. "The Past and Future of Ego Psychology." *Psychoanalytic Quarterly* 14, no. 4 (1975).

HOME, H. J. "The Concept of Mind." *International Journal of Psychoanalysis* 47 (1966).

JACOBY, RUSSELL. *Social Amnesia.* New York: Beacon Press, 1975.

JAY, MARTIN. *The Dialectical Imagination.* Boston: Little, Brown, 1973.

JONES, ERNEST. *The Life and Works of Sigmund Freud.* New York: Basic Books, 1957.

KLEIN, GEORGE. *Psychoanalytic Theory.* New York: International Universities Press, 1976.

KORSCH, KARL. *Marxism and Philosophy.* London: New Left Books, 1970.

KWANT, R. "Merleau-Ponty and Phenomenology." In *Phenomenology,* edited by J. Kockelmans. Garden City, N.Y.: Doubleday Anchor Books, 1967.

LAPLANCHE, J., and PONTALIS, J. B. *The Language of Psycho-Analysis.* New York: Norton, 1974.

LERNER, MICHAEL. "Surplus Powerlessness." *Social Policy,* January–February 1979.

LENIN, V. I. *Collected Works,* Moscow: Foreign Languages Publishing House, 1963.

LEWIS, C. J. *Mind and the World Order.* New York: Dover Press, 1956.

LICHTMAN, RICHARD. "Marx's Theory of Ideology." *Socialist Revolution* 23 (1975).

LIEBOW, ELLIOT. *Tally's Corner.* Boston: Little, Brown, 1967.

MARX, KARL. *Capital,* vol. 1. New York: Modern Library, 1906.

———. *Capital,* vol. 3. Moscow: Foreign Languages Publishing House, 1956.

———. *Contribution to the Critique of Political Economy.* Chicago: Charles Kerr and Co., 1904.

_____. *Early Writings.* Translated and edited by T. B. Bottomore. New York: McGraw-Hill, 1964.

_____. *The 18th Brumaire of Louis Bonaparte.* New York: New World International Publishers, 1967.

_____. *The Ethnological Notebooks.* Edited by Lawrence Krader. The Hague: Van Gossum and Company, 1972.

_____. *Grundrisse: Introduction to the Critique of Political Economy.* Translated with a foreword by Martin Nicolaus. Baltimore: Penguin Books, 1973.

_____. *Karl Marx: Selected Writings in Sociology and Philosophy.* Edited by T. B. Bottomore and Maximilien Rubel. New York: McGraw-Hill, 1964.

_____. *The Poverty of Philosophy.* New York: International Publishers, 1963.

_____. *Pre-Capitalist Economic Formations.* Introduction by E. J. Hobsbawm. New York: International Publishers, 1965.

_____. *Theories of Surplus Value.* Moscow: Foreign Languages Publishing House, 1963.

_____. *Writings of the Young Marx on Philosophy and Society.* Edited by Lloyd D. Easton and Kurt H. Guddart. Garden City, N.Y.: Doubleday Anchor Books, 1967.

_____. and ENGELS, FRIEDRICH. *Basic Writings on Politics and Philosophy.* Edited by Lewis Feurer. Garden City, N.Y.: Doubleday Anchor Books, 1959.

_____. *Correspondence.* New York: International Publishers, 1942.

_____. *The German Ideology.* London: Lawrence and Wishart, 1965.

_____. *The Holy Family.* Moscow: Foreign Languages Publishing House, 1956.

_____. *On Religion.* Moscow: Foreign Languages Publishing House, 1955.

MASLOW, A. H. *Toward a Psychology of Being.* Princeton, N.J.: Van Nostrand, 1968.

MERLEAU-PONTY, M. *Sense and Nonsense.* Evanston, Ill.: Northwestern University Press, 1964.

MERTON, ROBERT. *Social Theory and Social Structure.* New York: The Free Press, 1968.

MILL, JOHN STUART. *On Liberty.* New York: Modern Library, 1961.

PERLS, FRITZ. *Gestalt Therapy Verbatim.* New York: Bantam Books, 1971.

PETERFREUND, EMANUEL. "The Need for a New General Theoretical Frame of Reference for Psychoanalysis." *Psychoanalytic Quarterly* 44 (1975).

POSTER, MARK. *A Critical Theory of the Family.* New York: Seabury Press, 1978.

REICH, WILHELM. *Character Analysis.* New York: Farrar, Straus & Giroux, 1949.

_____. *The Function of the Orgasm.* New York: Farrar, Straus & Giroux, 1970.

_____. *Invasion of Compulsory Sex Morality.* New York: Farrar, Straus & Giroux, 1971.

_____. *Sex-Pol Essays, 1929–34.* Edited by Lee Boxendall. New York: Vintage Books, 1972.

_____. *The Sexual Revolution.* New York: Farrar, Straus & Giroux, 1970.

RICARDO, DAVID. *Principles of Political Economy and Taxation.* New York: Everyman's Library, 1926.

RICOEUR, PAUL. *Freud and Philosophy.* New Haven: Yale University Press, 1970.

REIFF, PHILIP. *Freud: The Mind of the Moralist.* New York: Viking Press, 1959.

_____. *The Triumph of the Therapeutic.* New York: Harper Torchbooks, 1966.

RUBENSTEIN, BENJAMIN B. "Explanation and More Description: A Metascientific Examination of Certain Aspects of the Psychoanalytic Theory of Motivation." *Psychological Issues* 5, nos 2-3 (1967).

SCHACTEL, ERNEST G. *Metamorphosis.* New York: Basic Books, 1959.

SCHAEFER, ROY. *A New Language for Psychoanalysis.* New Haven: Yale University Press, 1976.

SCHATZMAN, MORTON. *Soul Murder.* New York: Random House, 1973.

SCHNEIDER, MICHAEL. *Neurosis and Civilization.* New York: Seabury Press, 1975.

SENNETT, RICHARD, and COBB, JONATHAN. *The Hidden Injuries of Class.* New York: Vintage Press, 1972.

SLATER, PHILIP. *The Pursuit of Loneliness.* Boston: Beacon Press, 1970.

SMITH, ADAM. *The Wealth of Nations.* New York: Modern Library, 1937, p. 423.

TRILLING, LIONEL. *Beyond Culture.* New York: Viking Press, 1955.

WACHTEL, PAUL L. *Psychoanalysis and Behavior Therapy.* New York: Basic Books, 1973.

WALLERSTEIN, ROBERT S. "Psychoanalysis as a Science: Its Present Status and Its Future Tasks." *Psychological Issues* 9, no. 4, monograph 36: (1976).

WEBER, MAX. *The Protestant Ethic and the Spirit of Capitalism.* New York: Scribners, 1958.

WOLFENSTEIN, MARTHA. "Fun Morality": An Analysis of Recent American Childtraining Literature. In *Childhood in Contemporary Cultures,* edited by Margaret Mead and Martha Wolfenstein. Chicago: University of Chicago Press, 1955.

WYSS, DIETER. *Psychoanalytic Schools.* New York: Jason Aronson, 1973.

YANKELOVICH, DANIEL, and BARRETT, WILLIAM. *Ego and Instinct.* New York: Random House, 1970.

Index